A-Z LEEDS

REFERENCE

Motorway	**M1**	Airport	✈
A Road	**A62**	Car Park (selected)	**P**
B Road	**B6126**	Church or Chapel	†
Dual Carriageway		Cycleway (selected)	🚲
One-way Street		Fire Station	■
Traffic flow on A Roads is also indicated by a heavy line on the driver's left.		Hospital	**H**
Road Under Construction		House Numbers (A & B Roads only)	13 / 8
Opening dates are correct at the time of publication.		Information Centre	**i**
Proposed Road		National Grid Reference	⁴30
Restricted Access		Park and Ride	King Lane **P+R**
Pedestrianized Road		Police Station	▲
Leeds City Centre Loop		Post Office	★
Junction Numbers are shown on large Scale Pages only	①	Toilet	▽
Track / Footpath		Viewpoint	�*
Residential Walkway		Educational Establishment	▨
Railway	Station / Level Crossing / Tunnel	Hospital or Healthcare Building	▨
Built-up Area	MILL RD.	Industrial Building	▢
		Leisure or Recreational Facility	▨
Local Authority Boundary		Place of Interest	▨
Post Town Boundary		Public Building	▨
Postcode Boundary (within Post Town)		Shopping Centre or Market	▨
Map Continuation	**31** / Large Scale City Centre **4**	Other Selected Buildings	▢

SCALE

Large Scale Pages 4-5 1:5,740

| 0 | ⅛ | ¼ Mile |
| 0 | 100 | 200 | 300 Metres |

11 inches (27.94cm) to 1 Mile 17.4cm to 1km

Map Pages 6-53 1:11,480

| 0 | ¼ | ½ Mile |
| 0 | 250 | 500 | 750 Metres |

5.5 inches (13.97cm) to 1 Mile 8.7cm to 1km

EDITION 6 2020

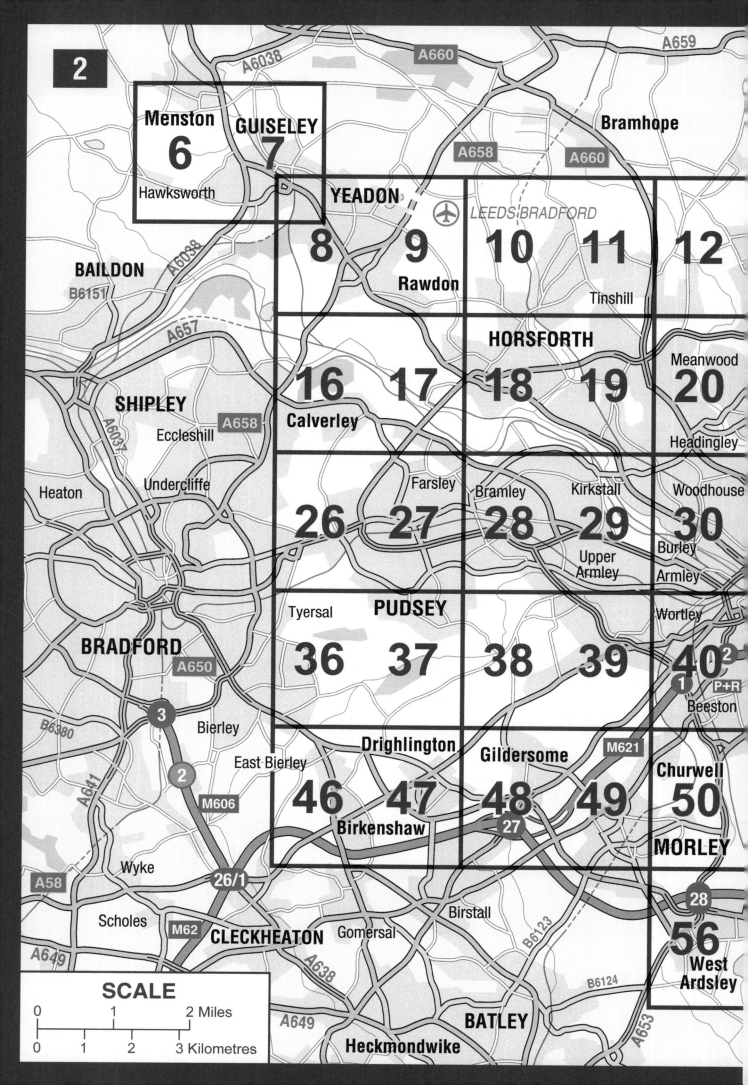

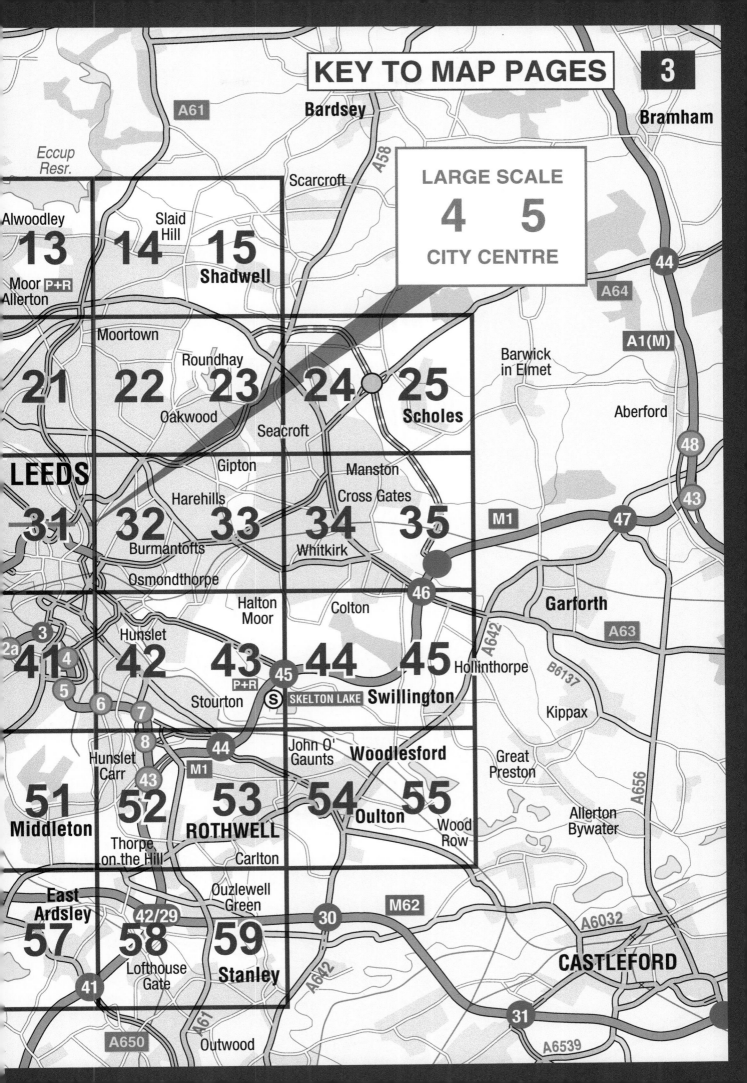

KEY TO MAP PAGES

3

Bardsey

Bramham

A61

Eccup Resr.

Scarcroft

A58

LARGE SCALE

4 **5**

CITY CENTRE

Alwoodley

Slaid Hill

13 **14** **15** Shadwell

Moor **P+R** Allerton

A64

A1(M)

Moortown

Roundhay

Barwick in Elmet

Aberford

21 **22** **23** **24** **25** Scholes

Oakwood

Seacroft

48

LEEDS

Gipton

Manston

Cross Gates

43

Harehills

M1

47

31 **32** **33** **34** **35**

Burmantofts

Whitkirk

Osmondthorpe

46

Garforth

A63

Halton Moor

Colton

A642

3

Hunslet

44 **45** Hollinthorpe

B6137

2a

41 **42** **43** **44** **45**

4

P+R

45

S SKELTON LAKE Swillington

Kippax

5

Stourton

6

7

8

44

John O' Gaunts

Woodlesford

Great Preston

A656

Hunslet Carr

M1

43

Allerton Bywater

51 **52** **53** **54** **55**

Middleton

Oulton

Wood Row

ROTHWELL

Thorpe on the Hill

Carlton

Ouzlewell Green

M62

East Ardsley

42/29

30

A6032

57 **58** **59**

Lofthouse Gate

Stanley

CASTLEFORD

41

A642

31

A650

Outwood

A6539

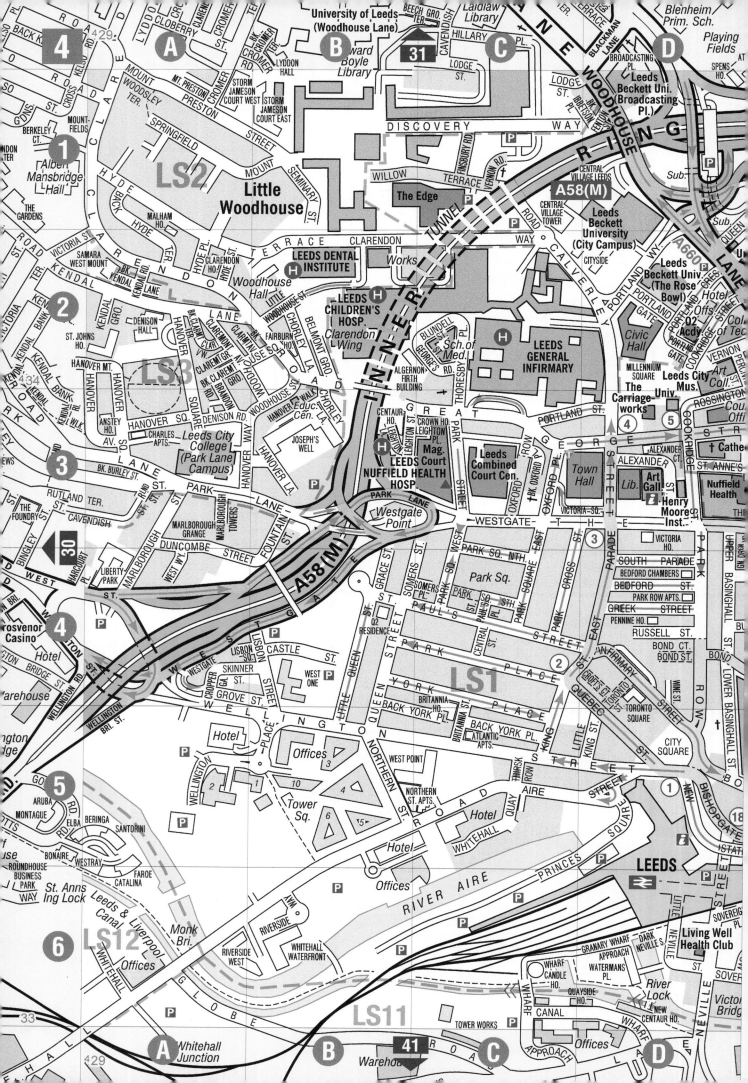

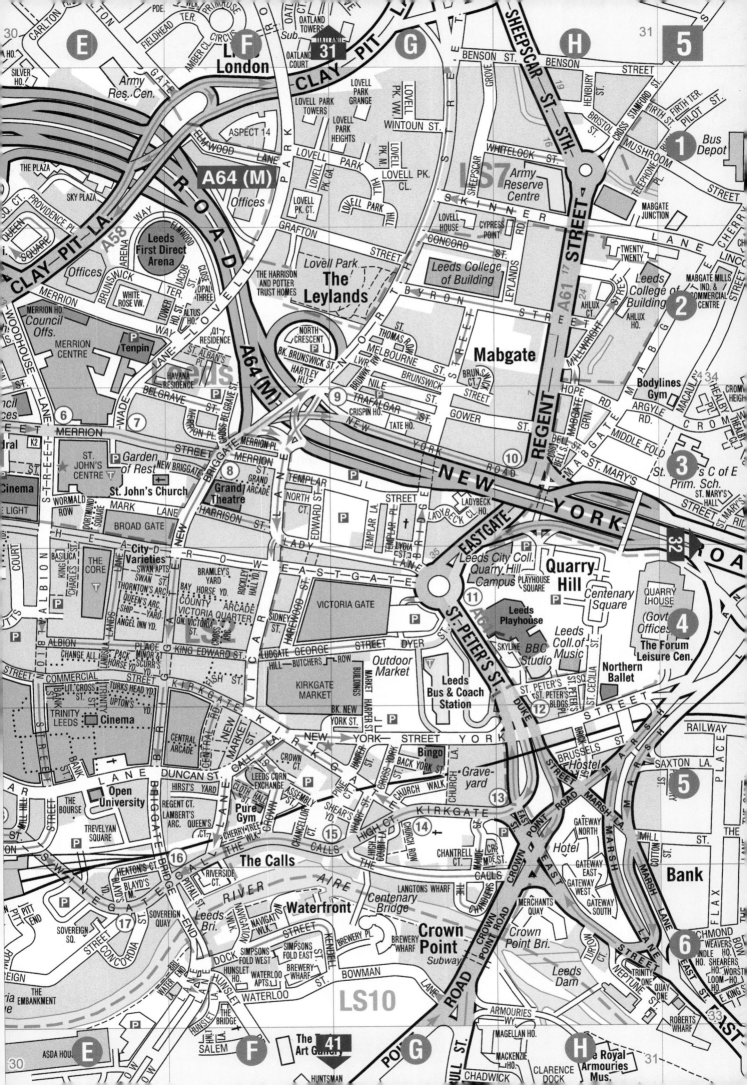

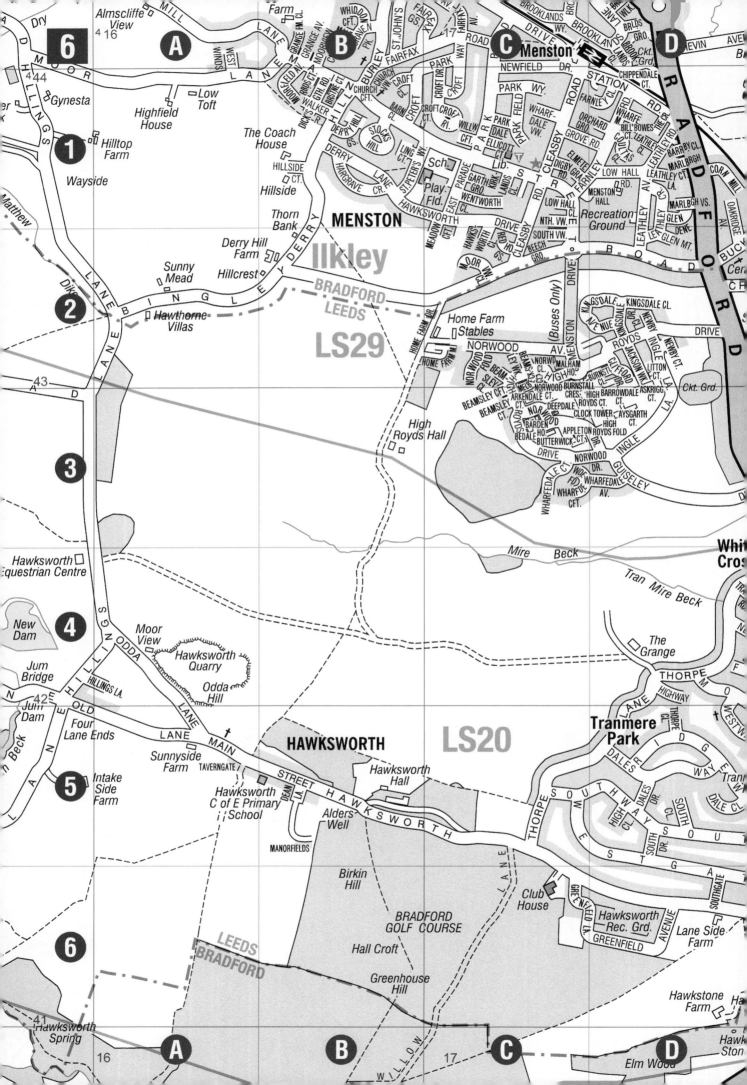

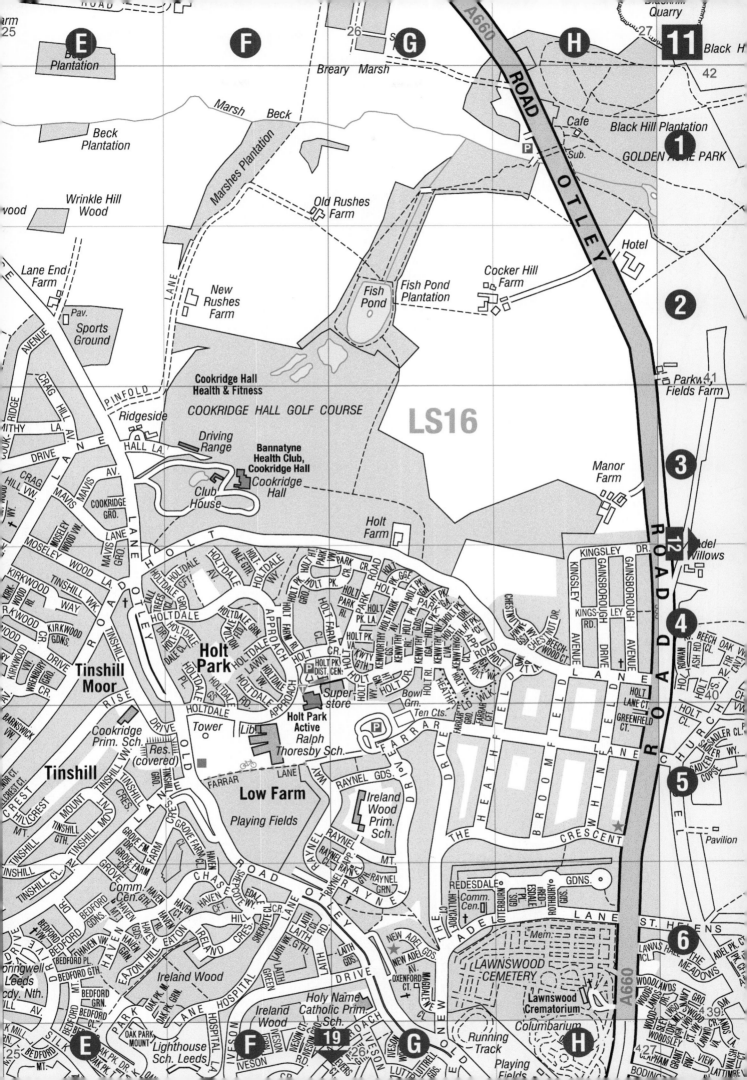

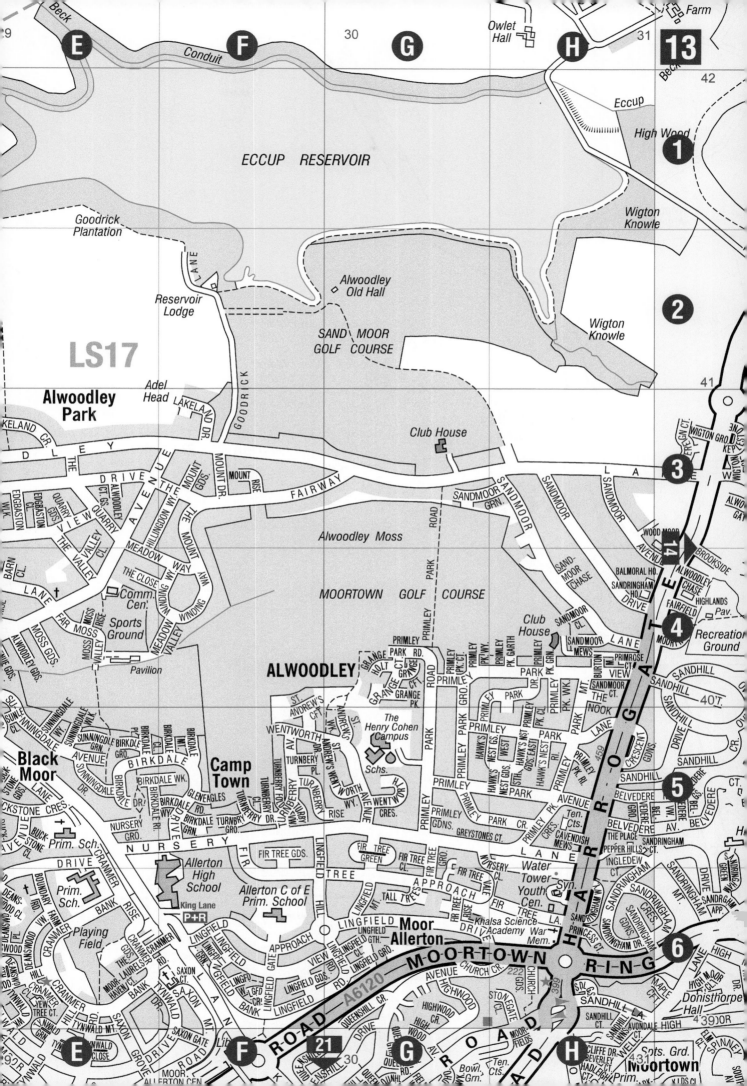

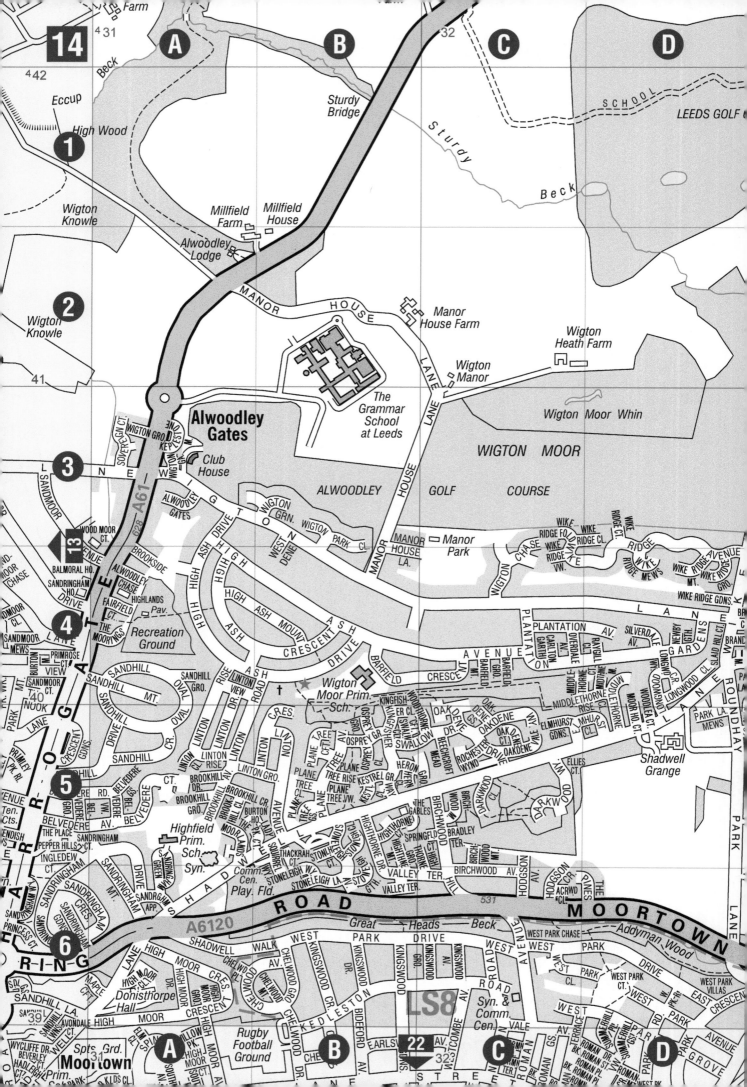

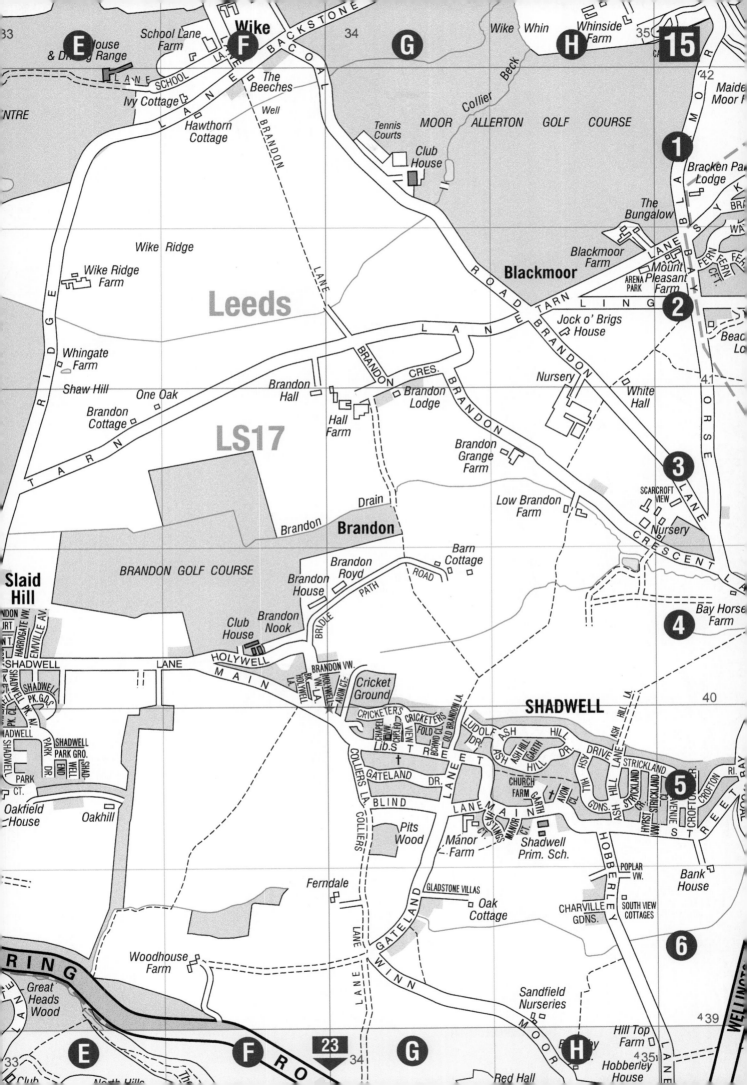

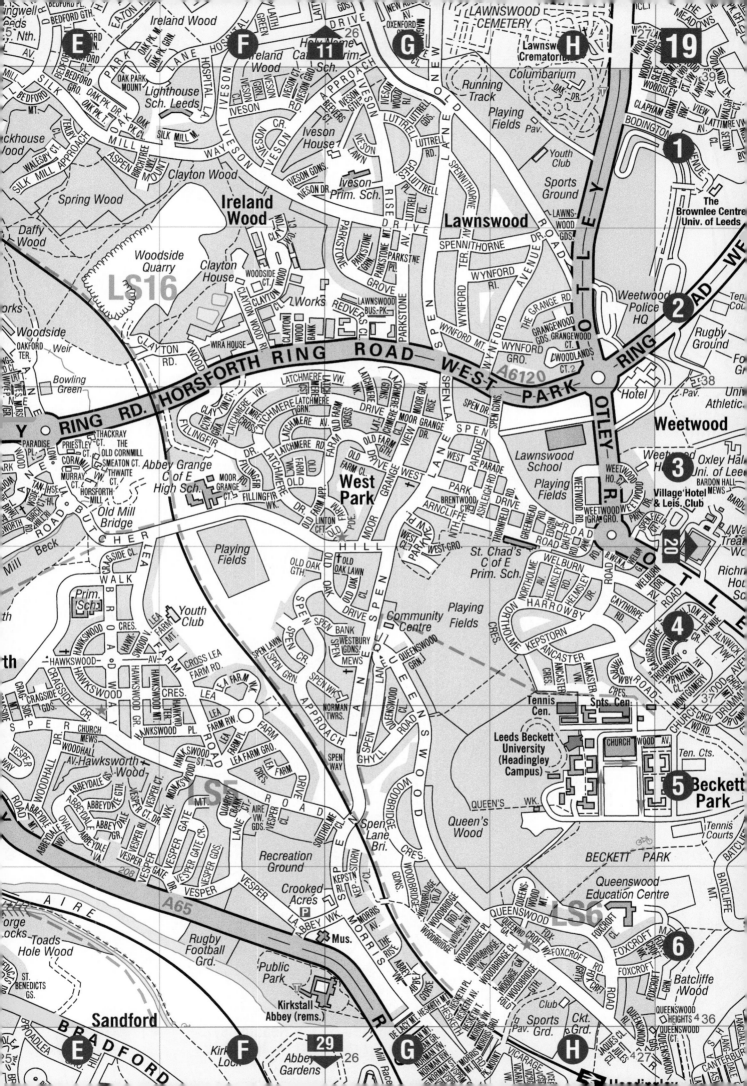

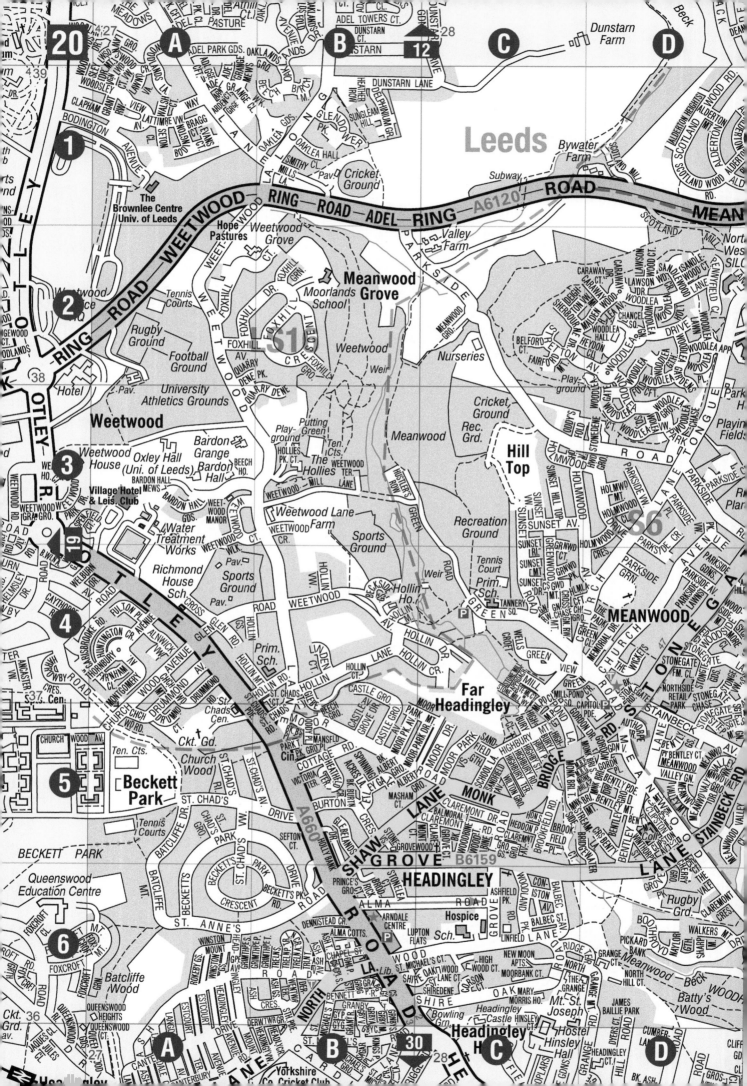

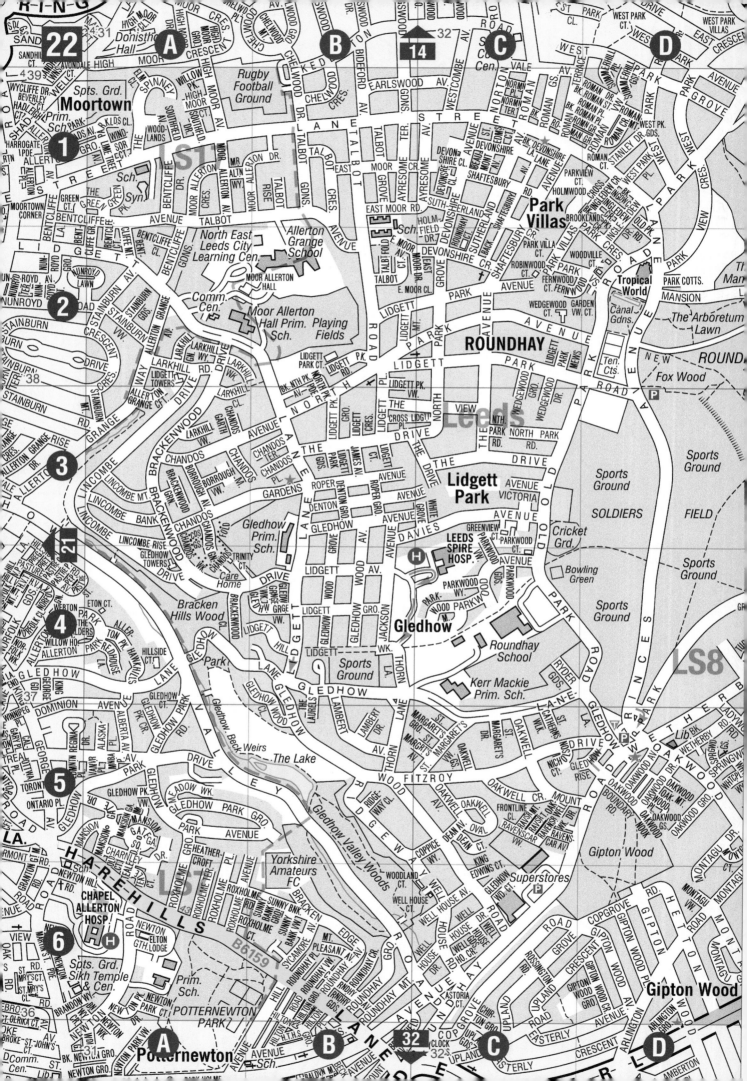

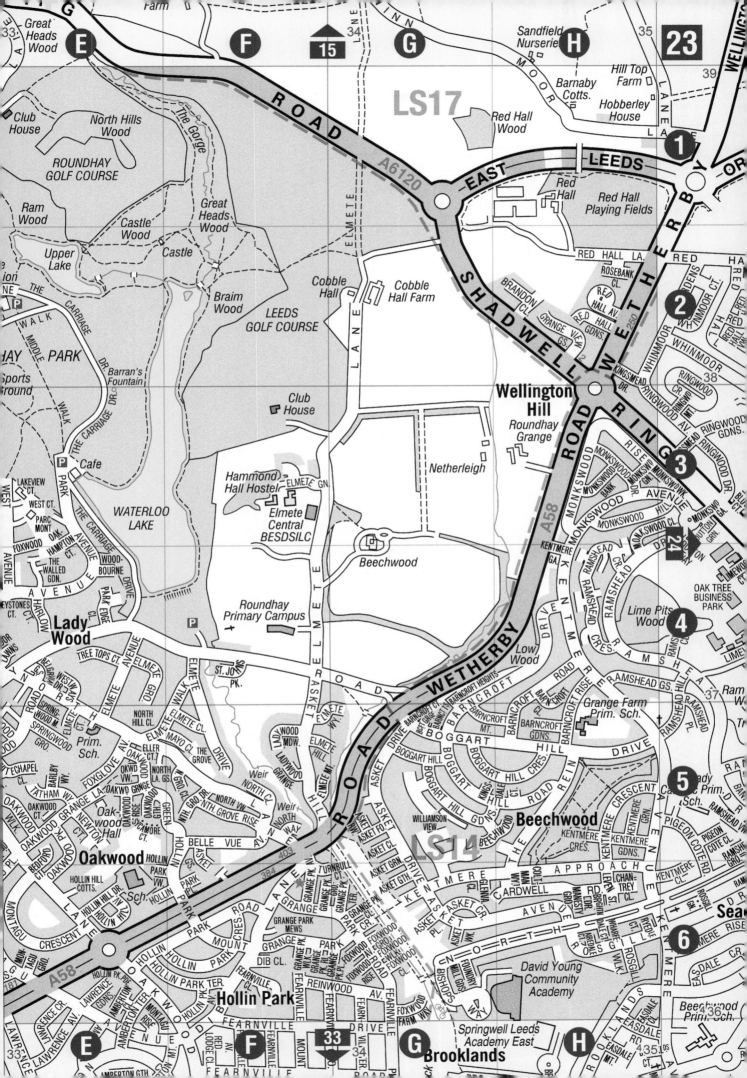

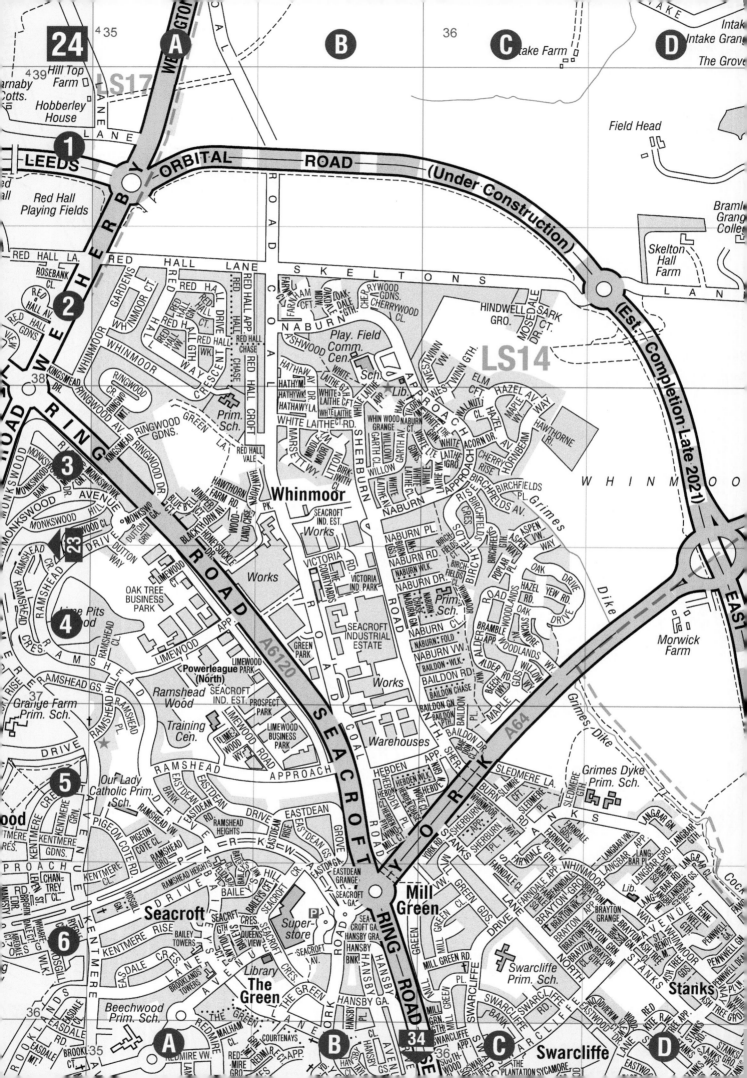

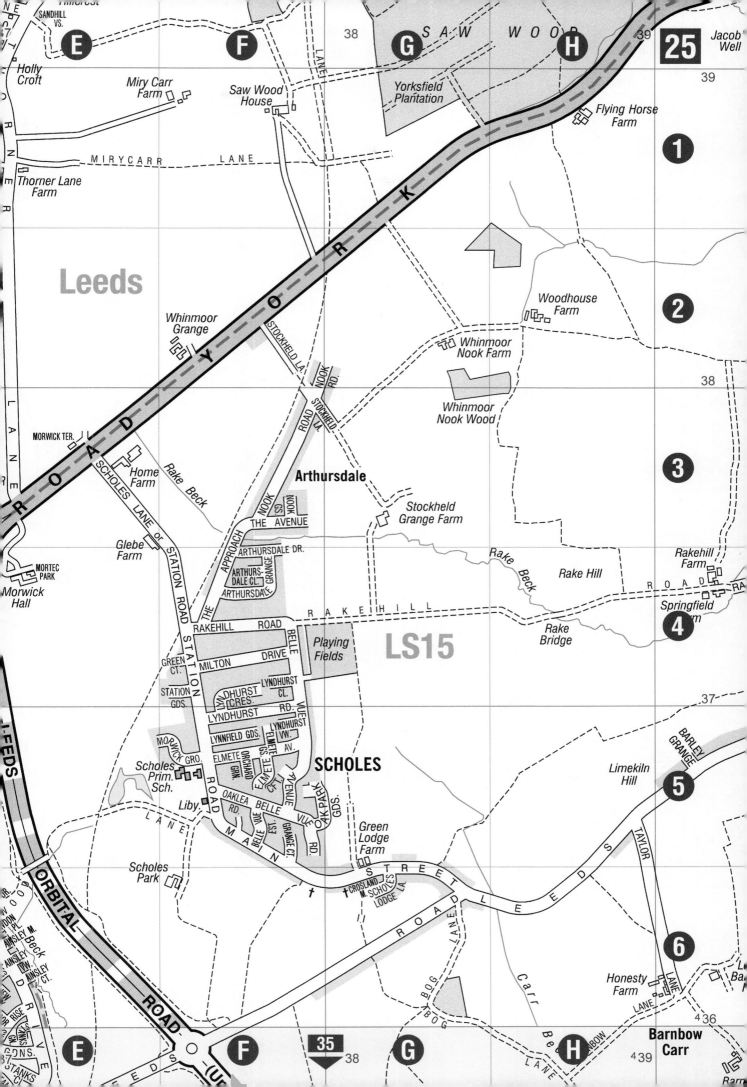

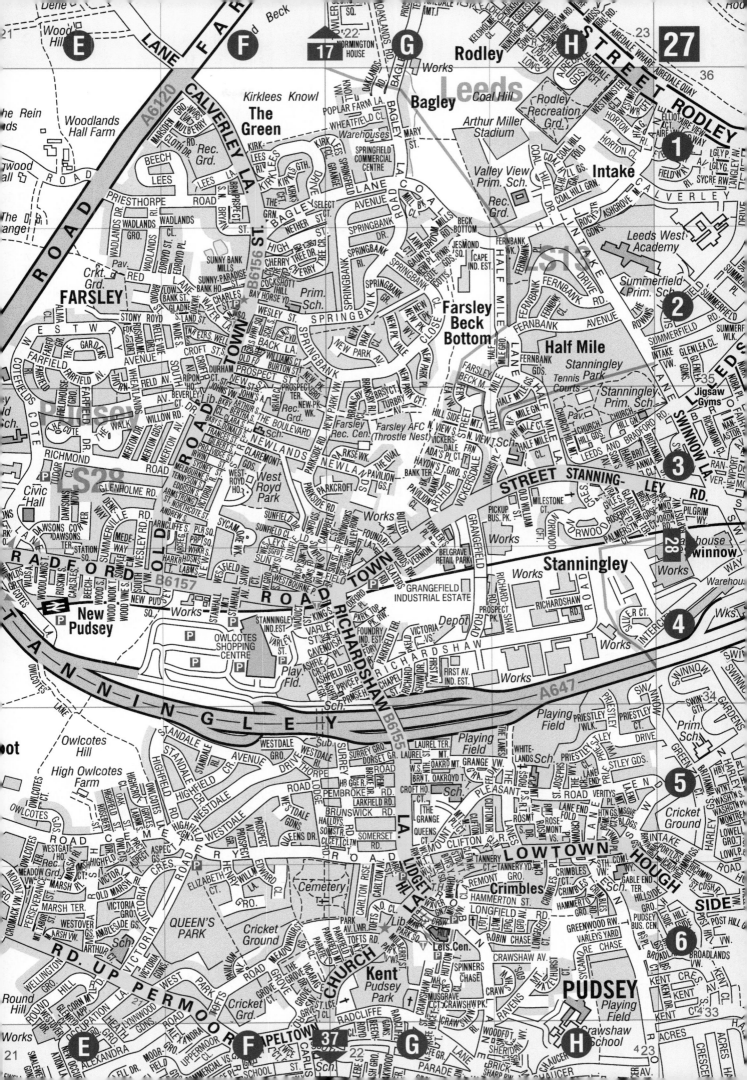

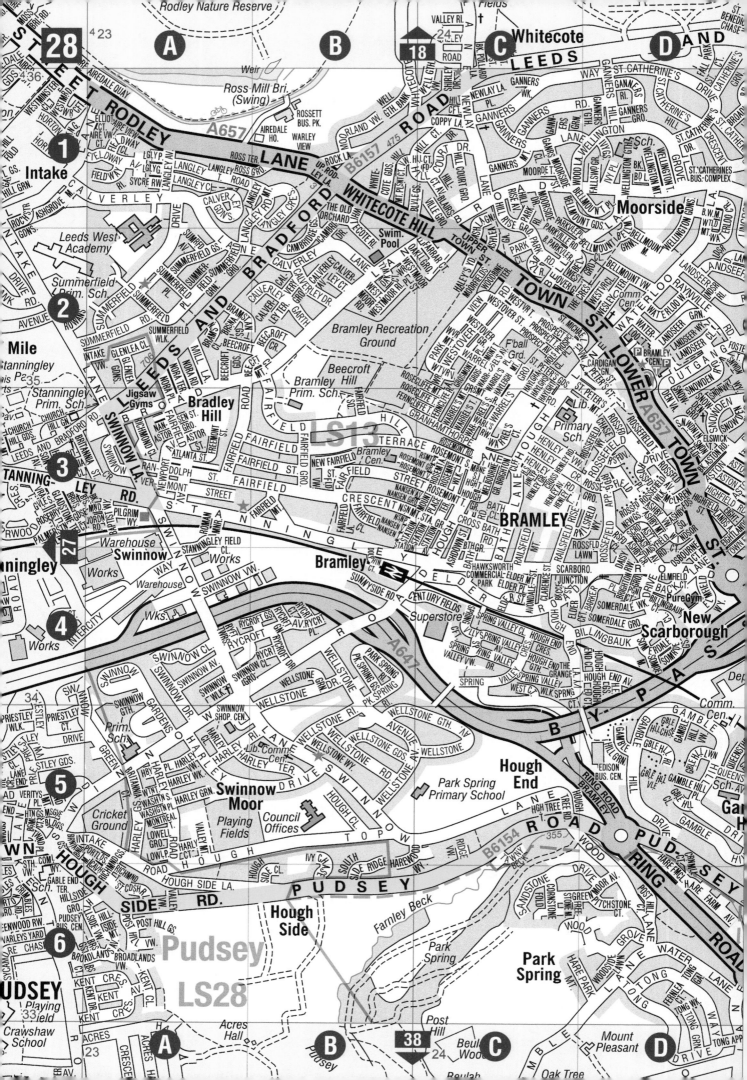

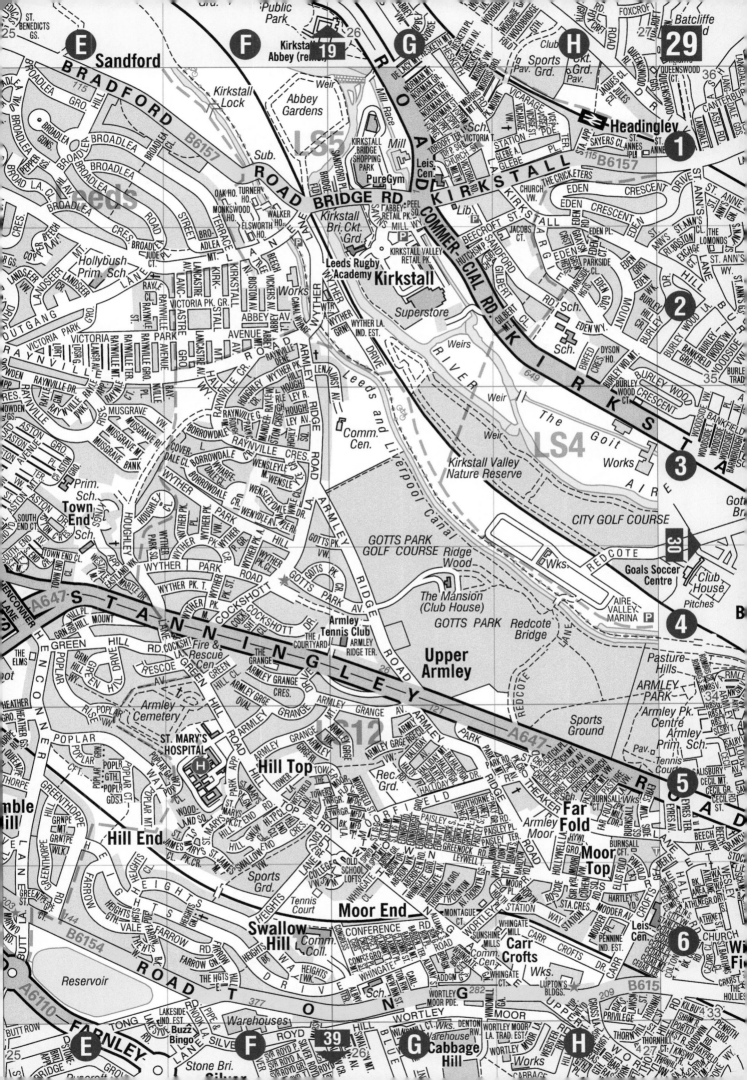

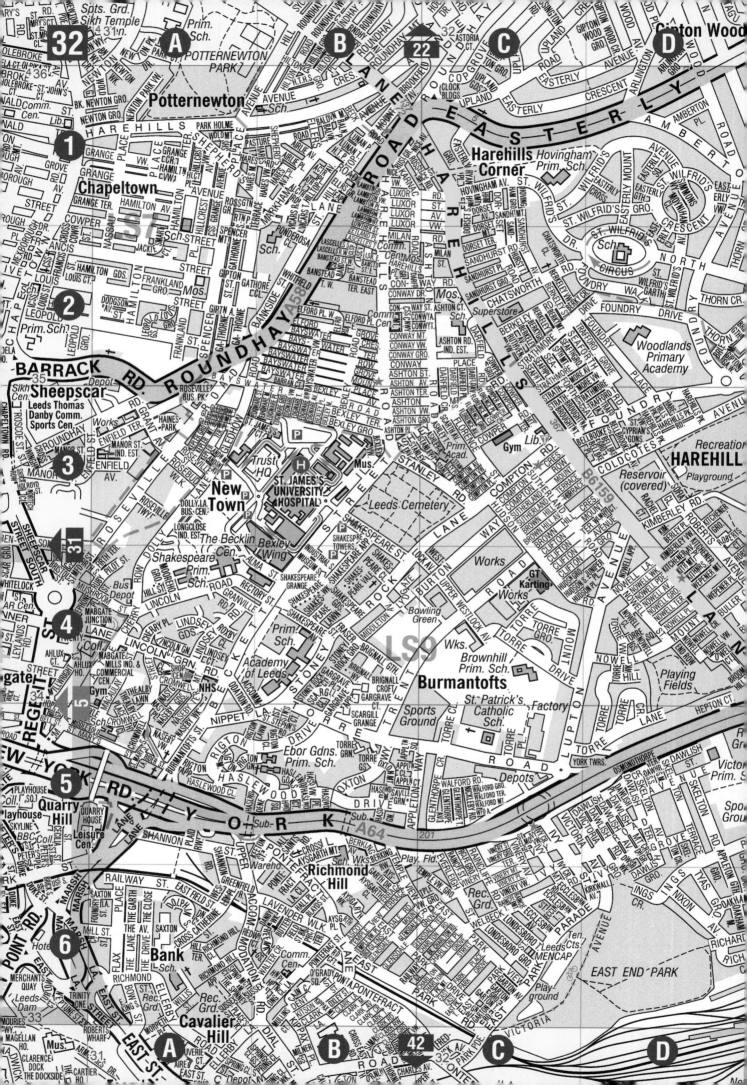

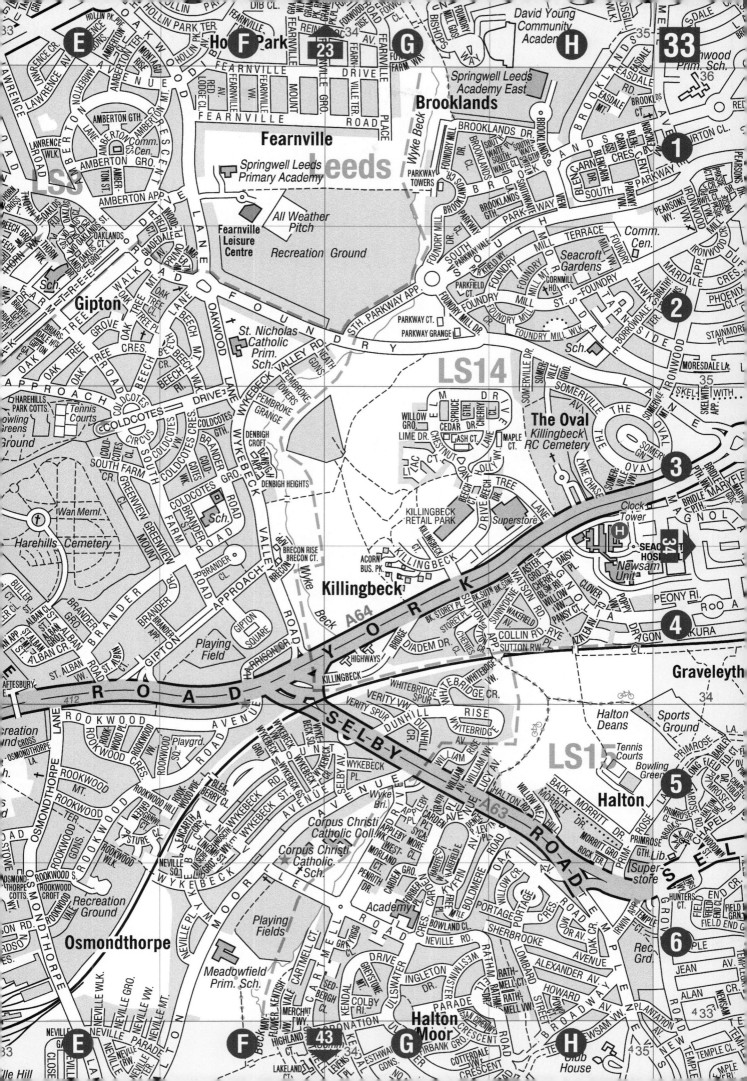

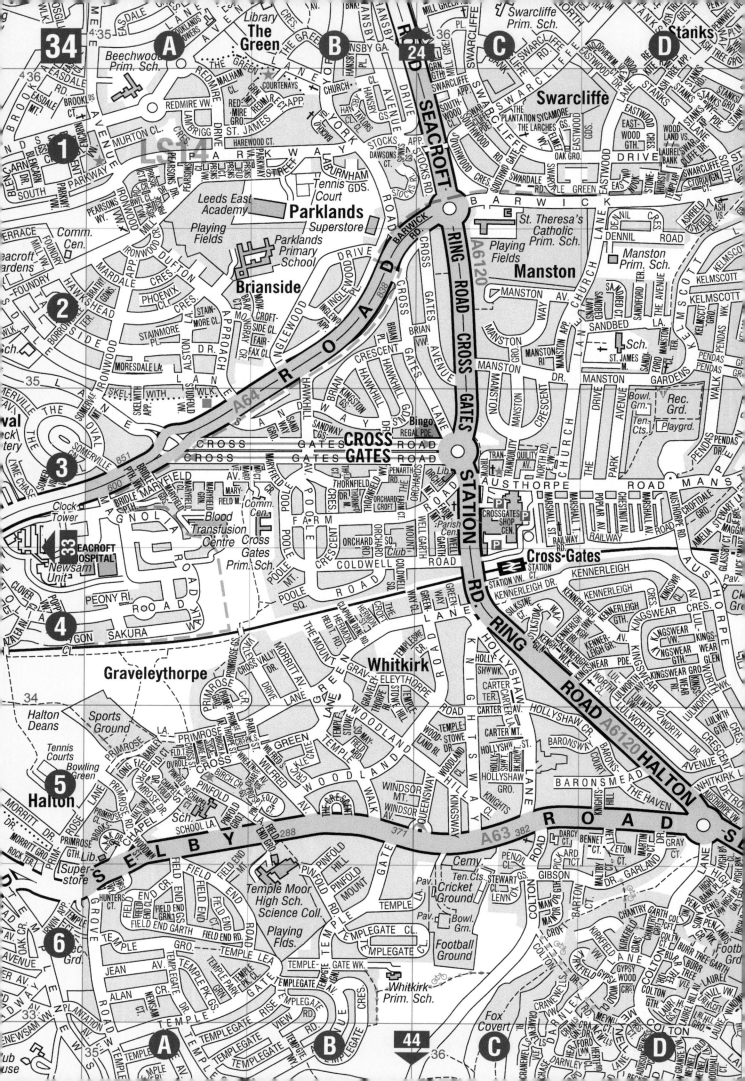

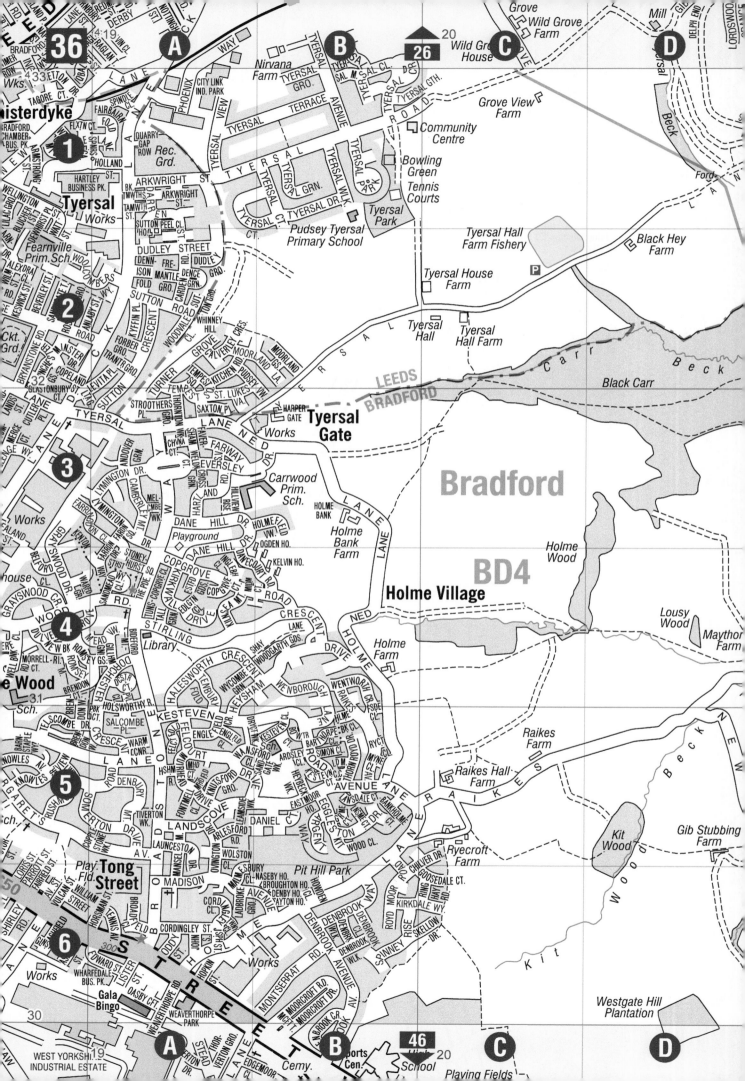

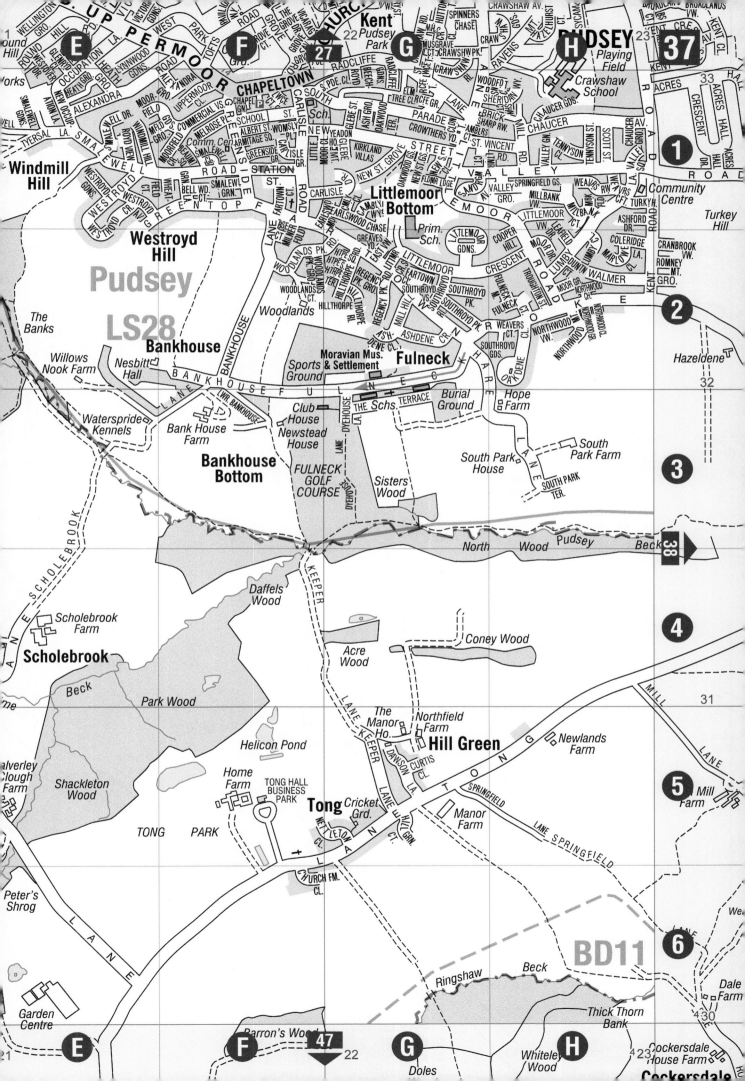

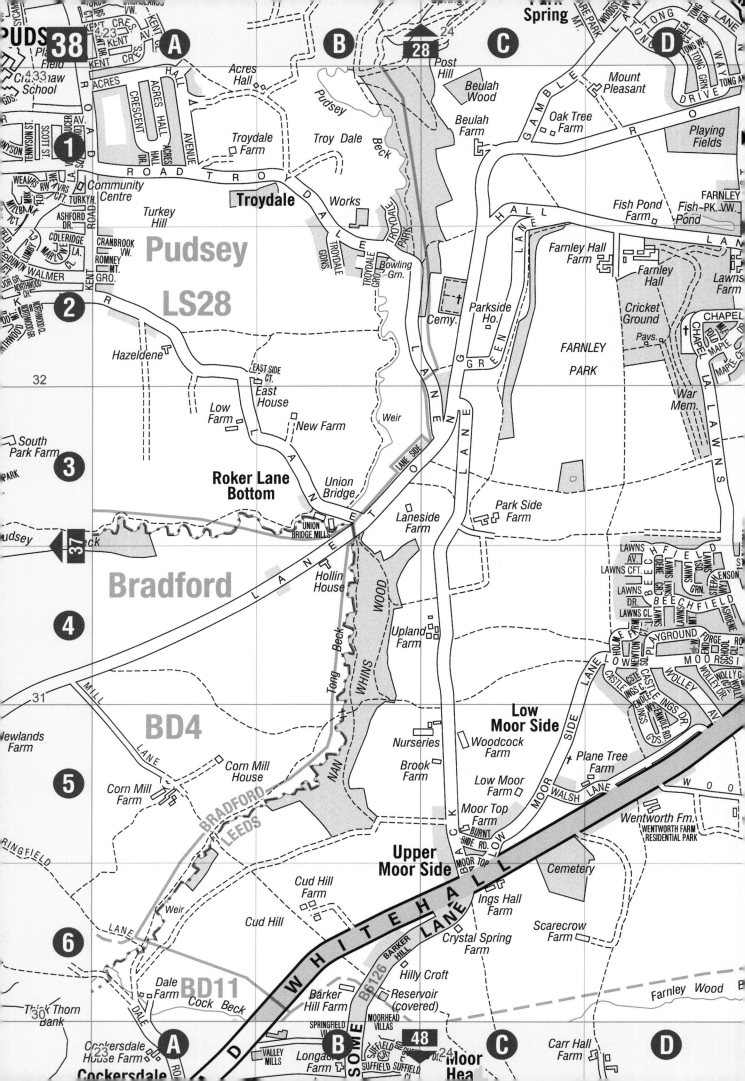

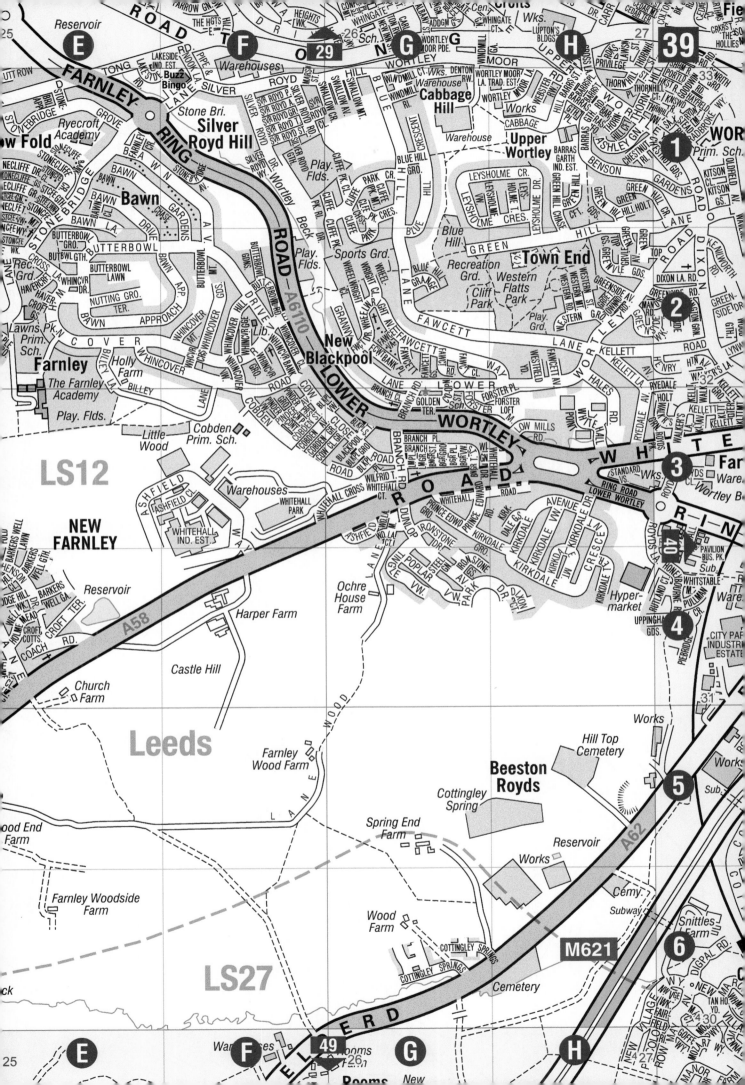

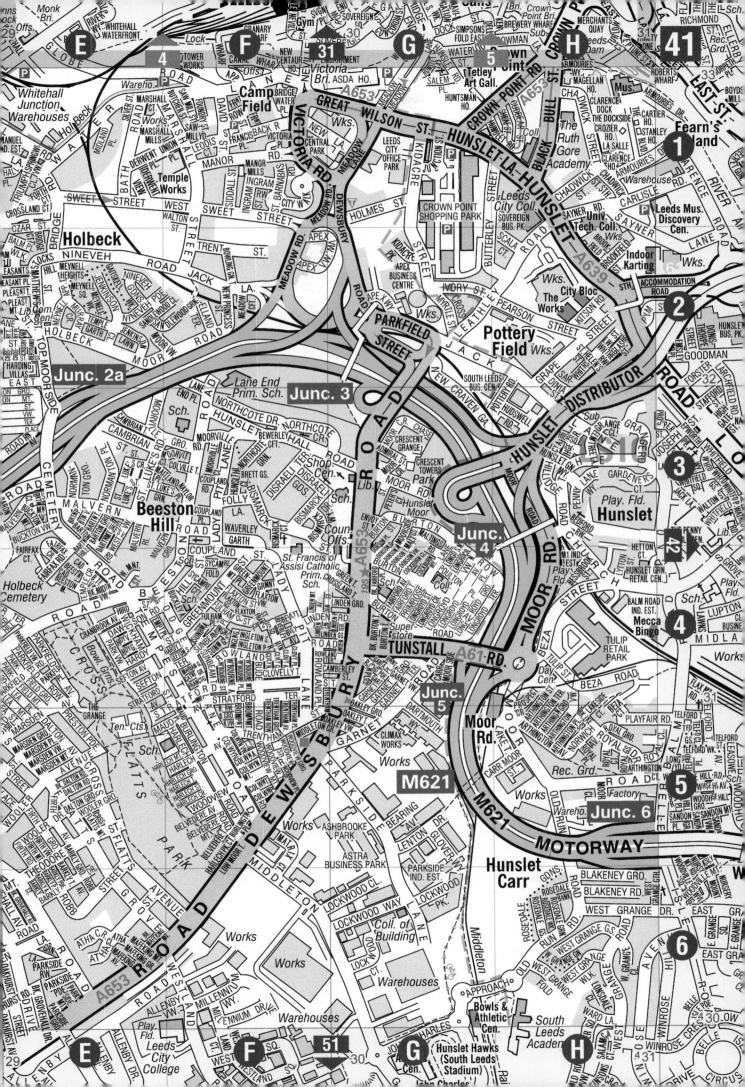

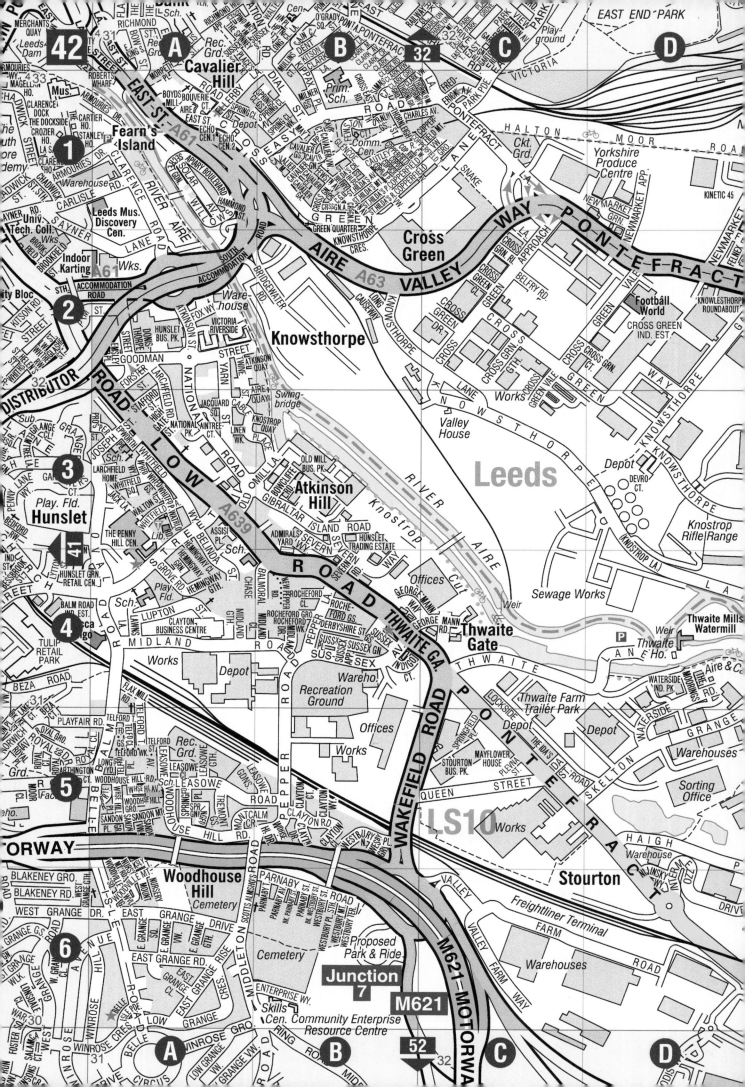

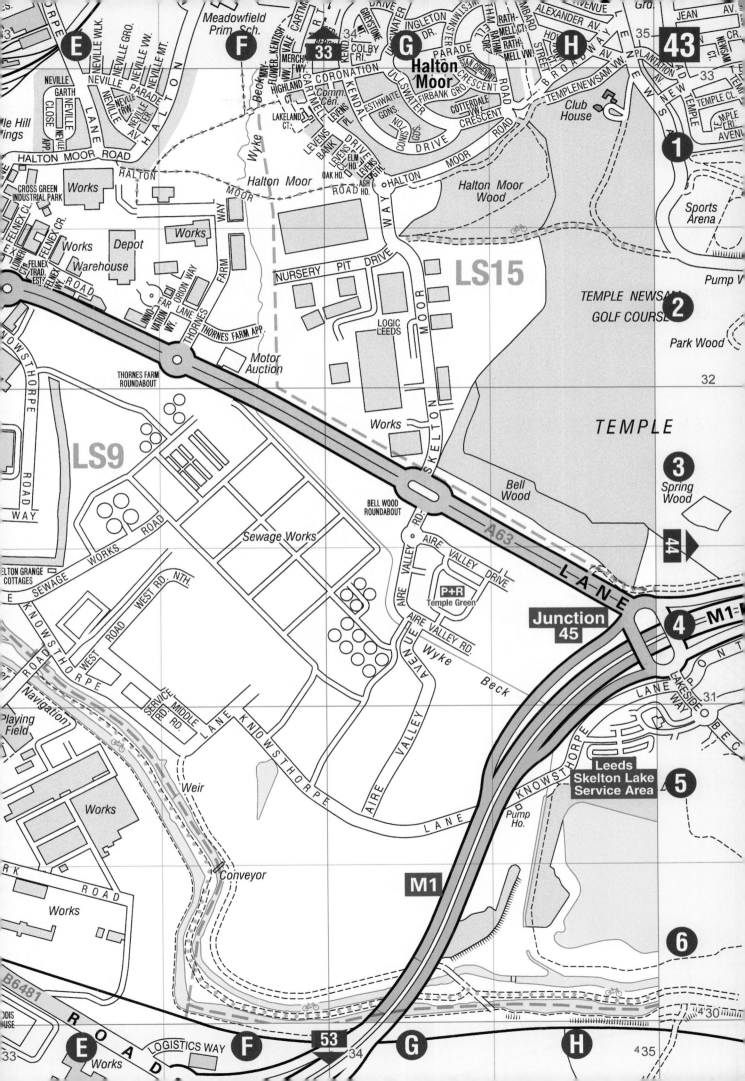

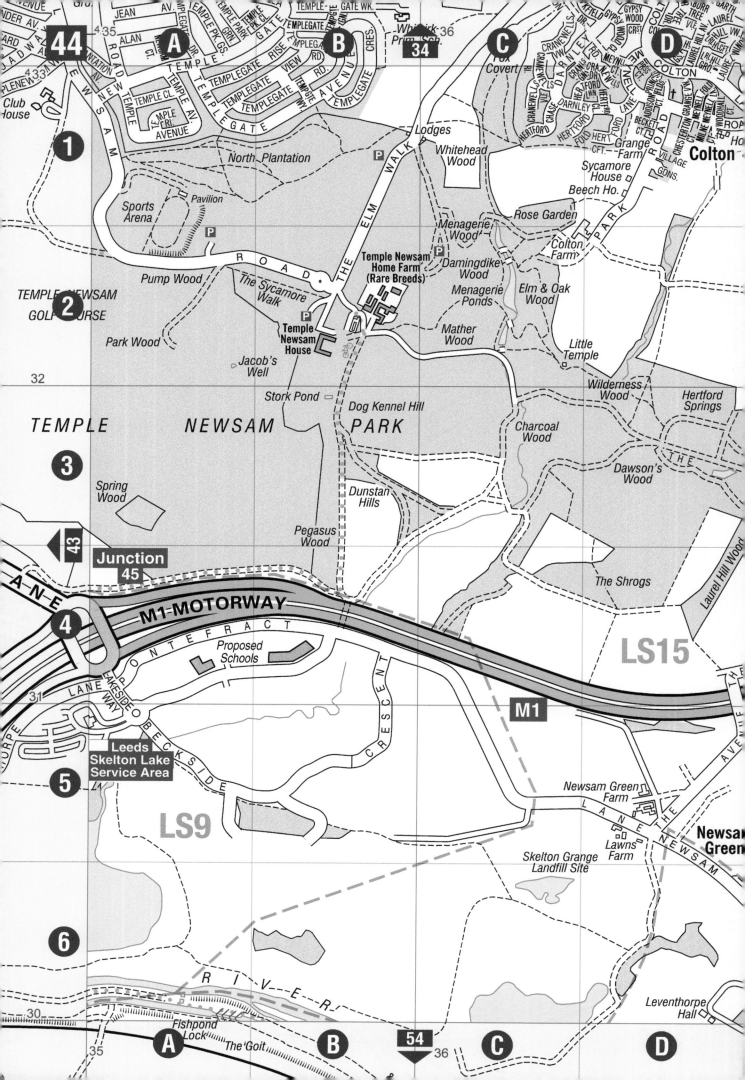

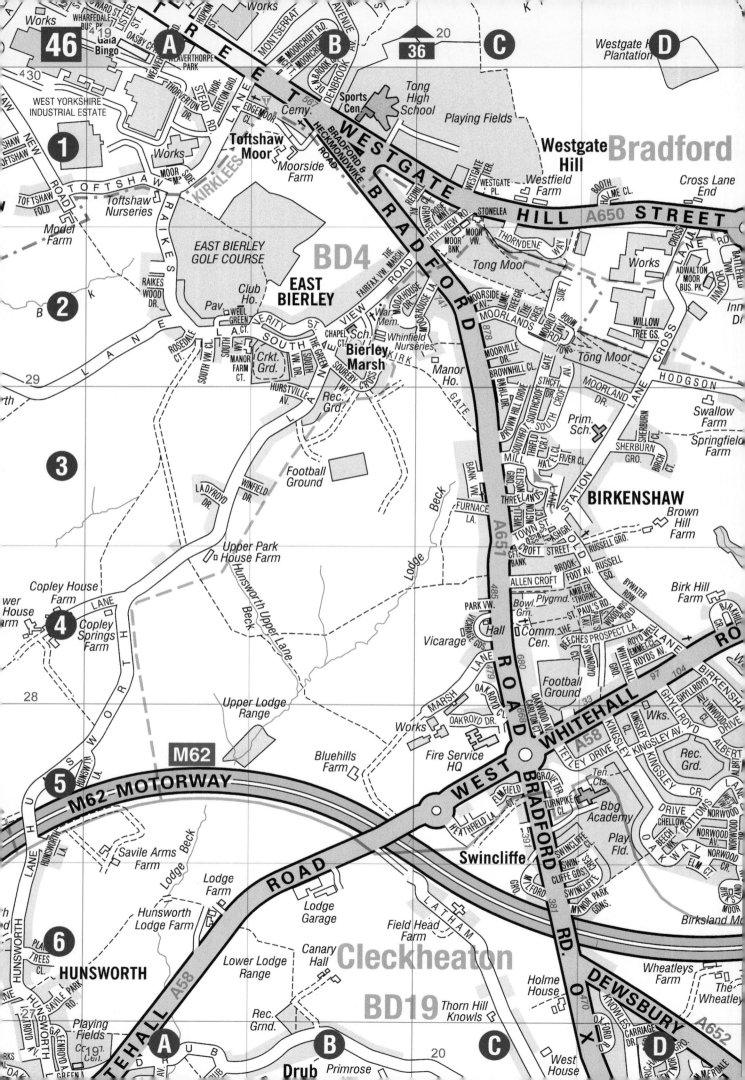

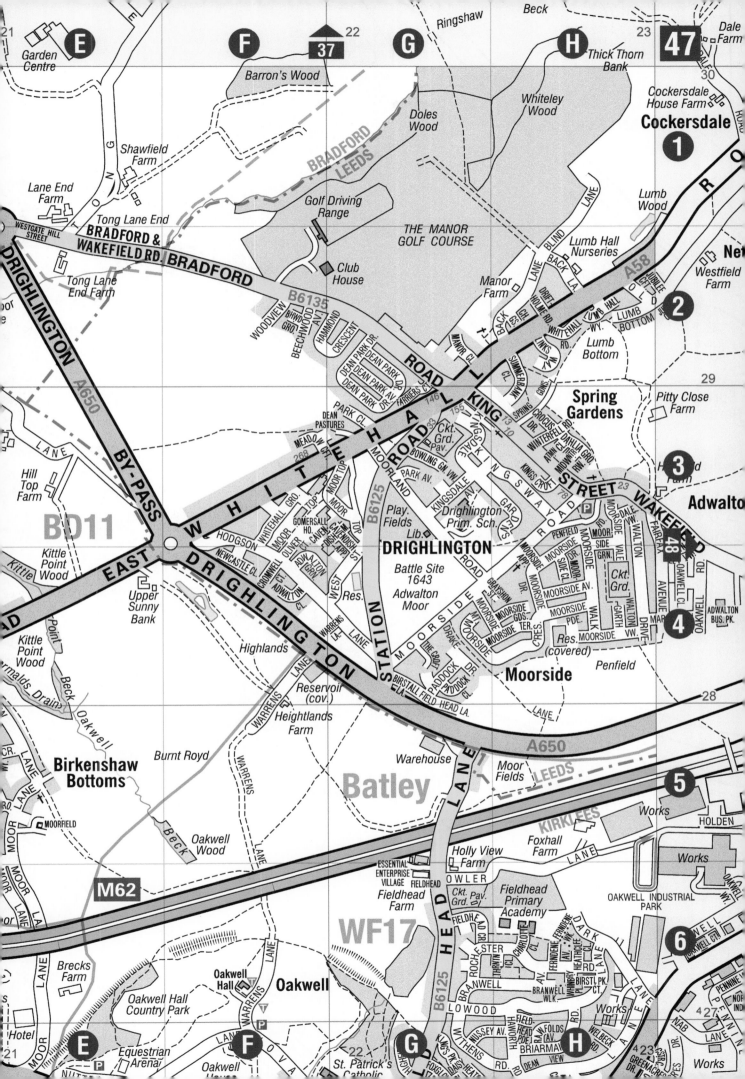

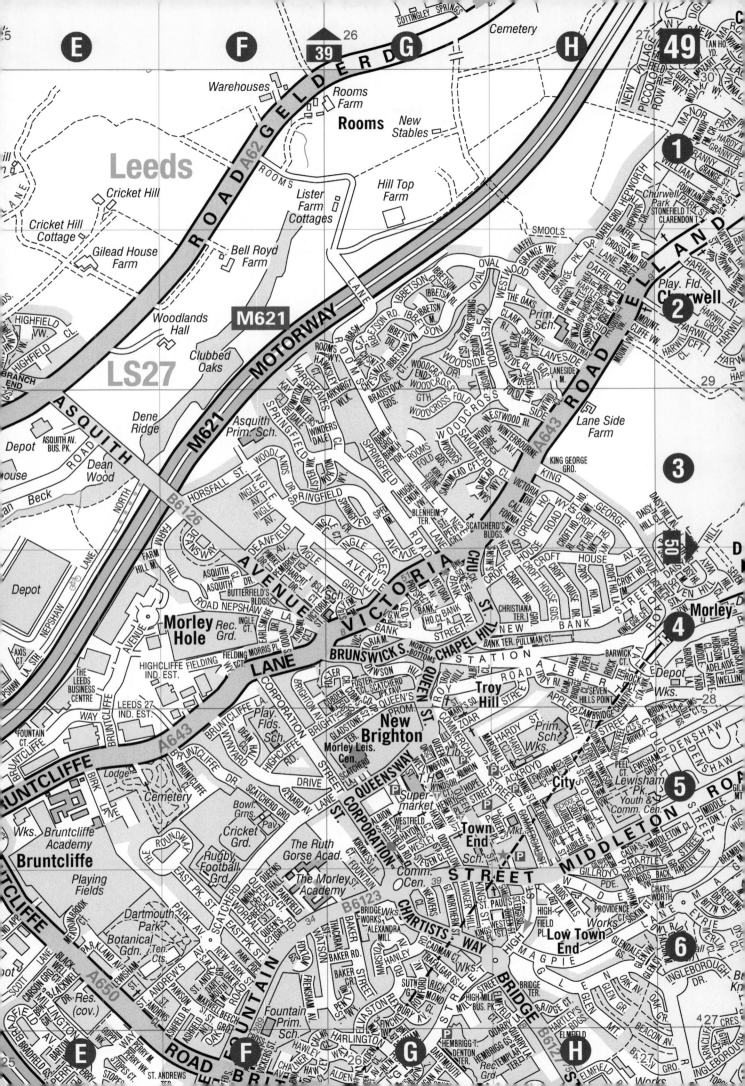

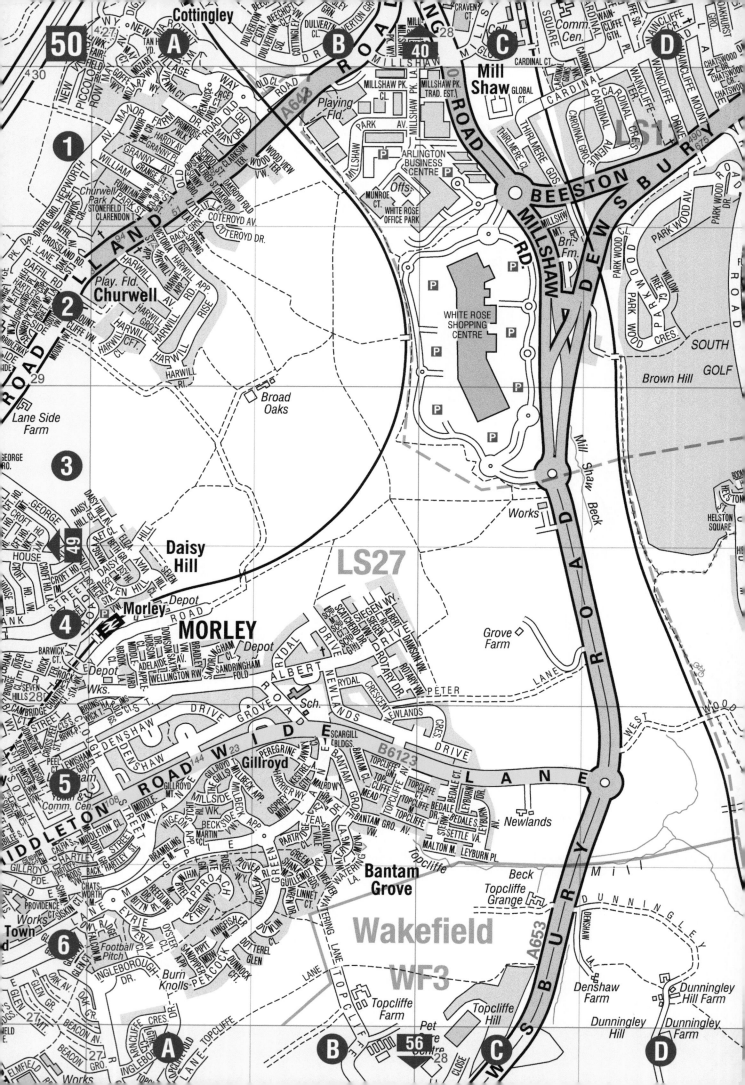

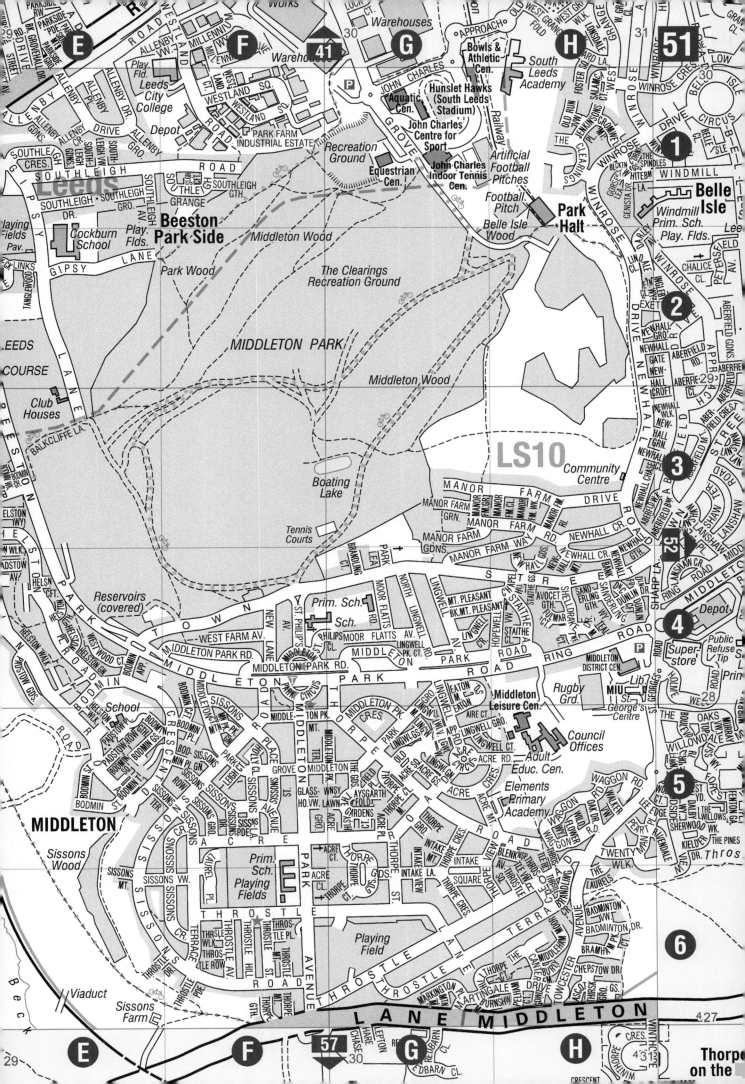

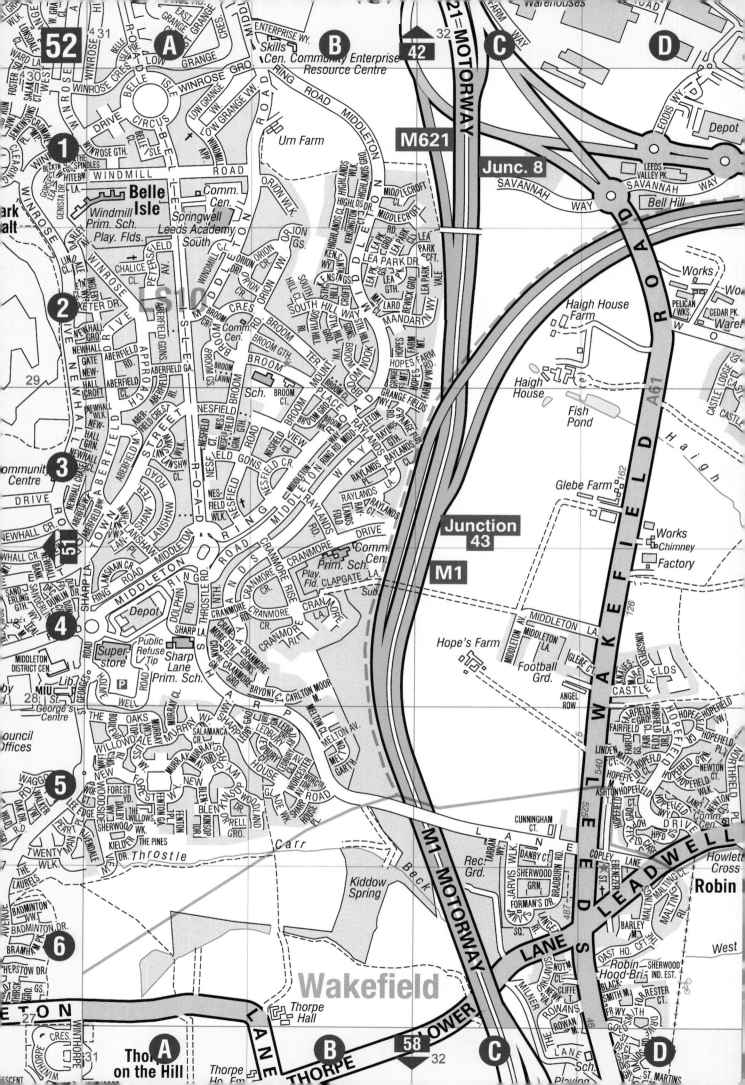

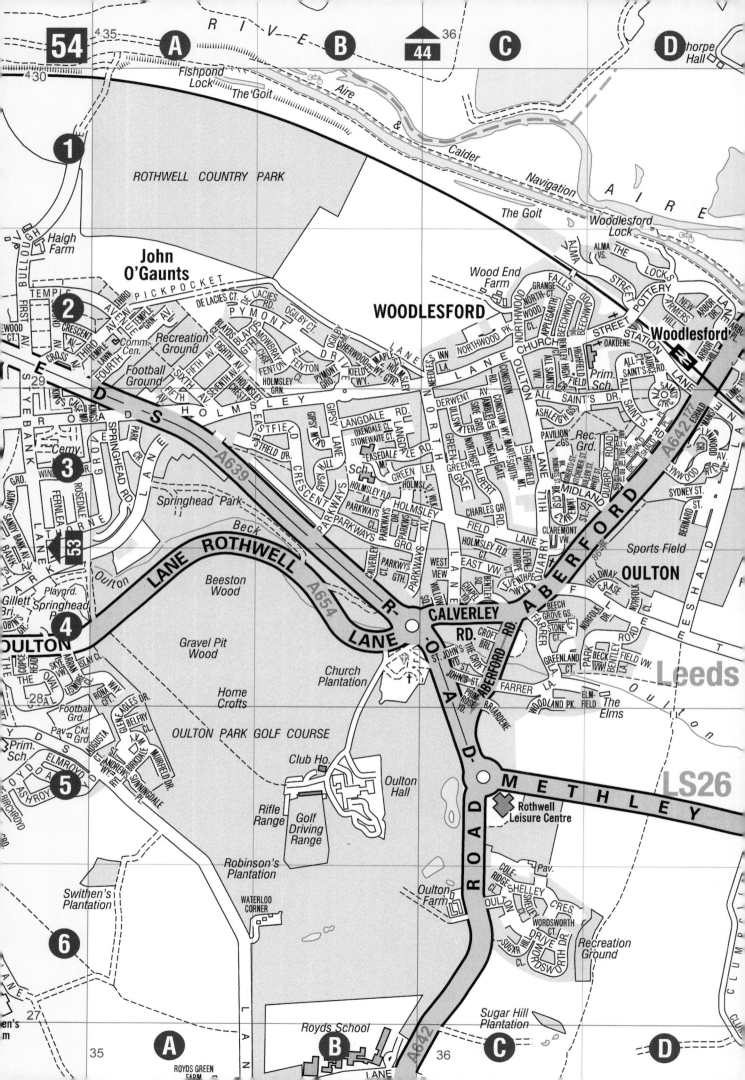

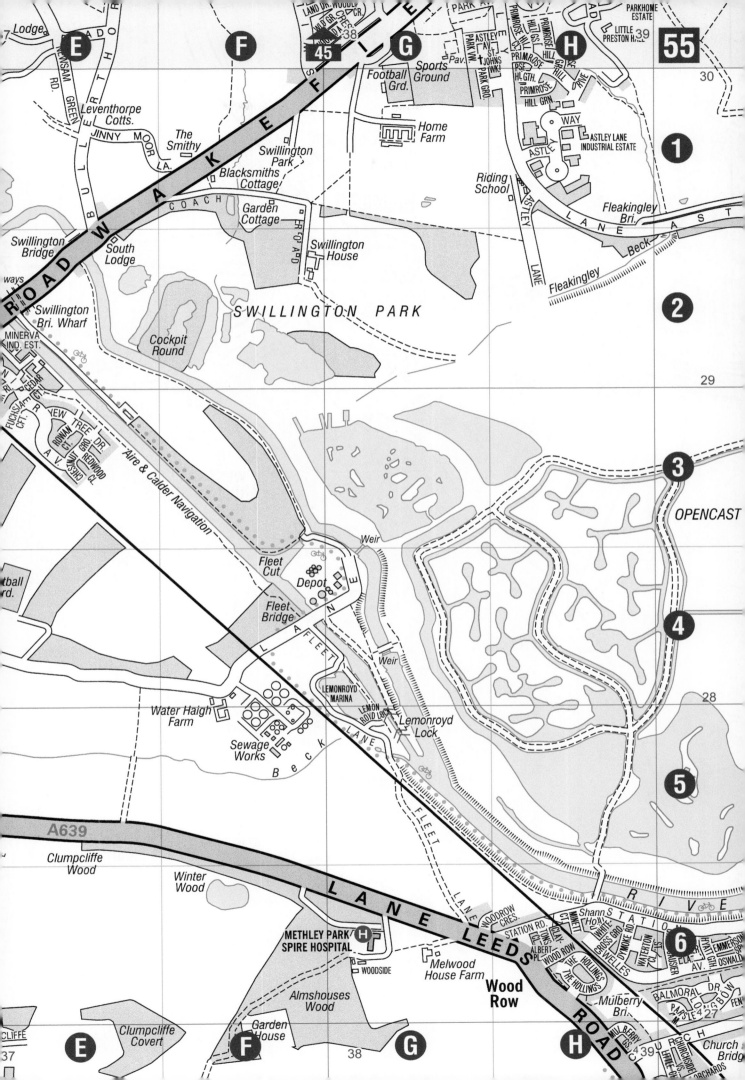

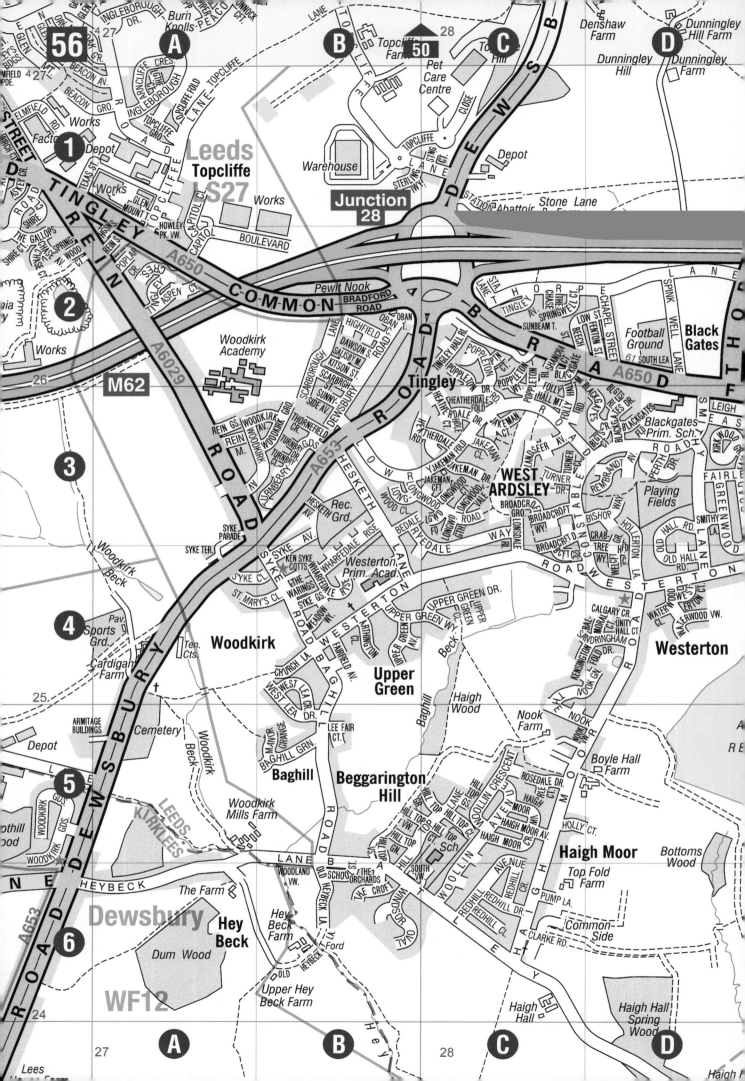

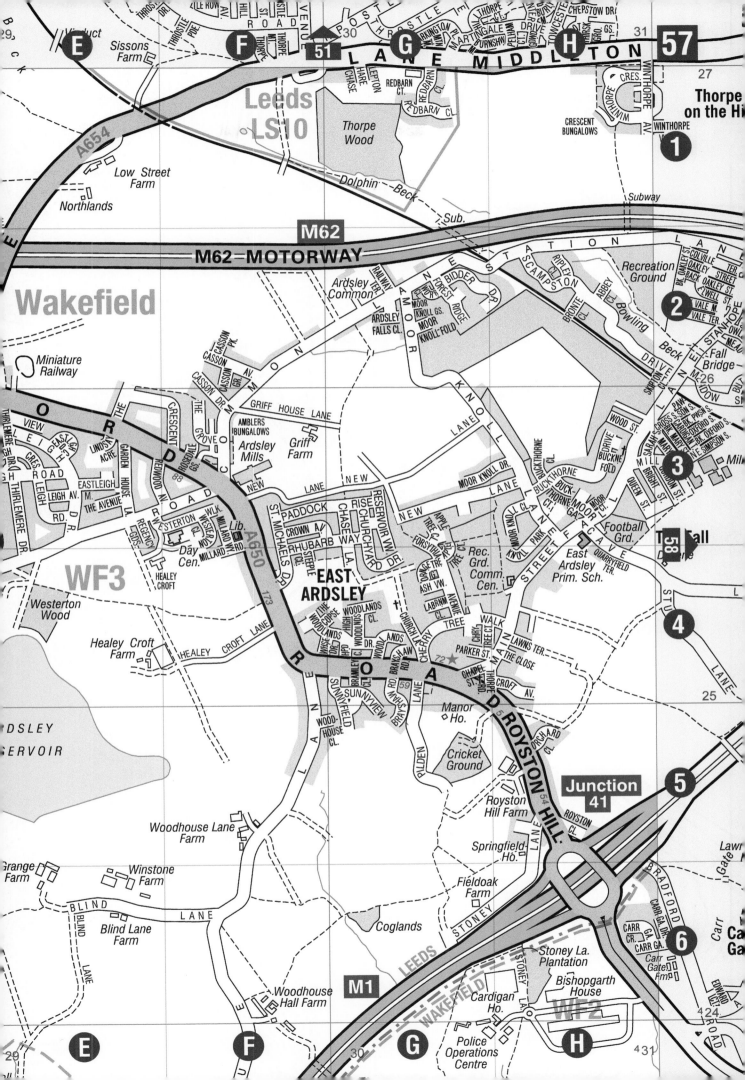

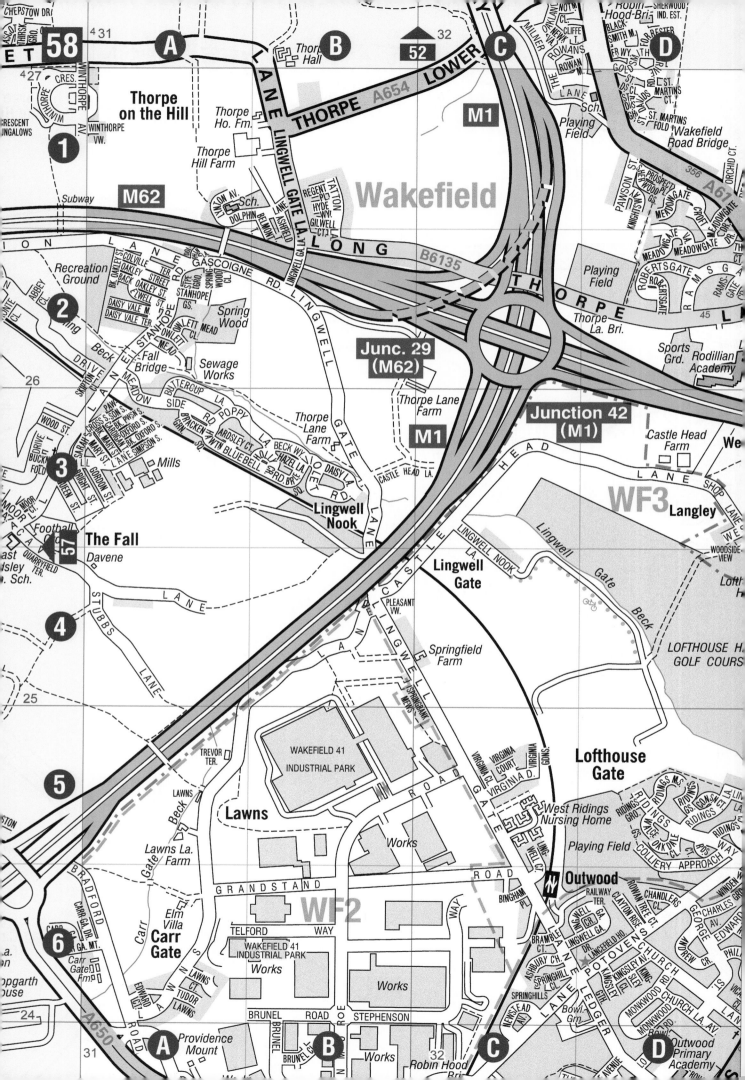

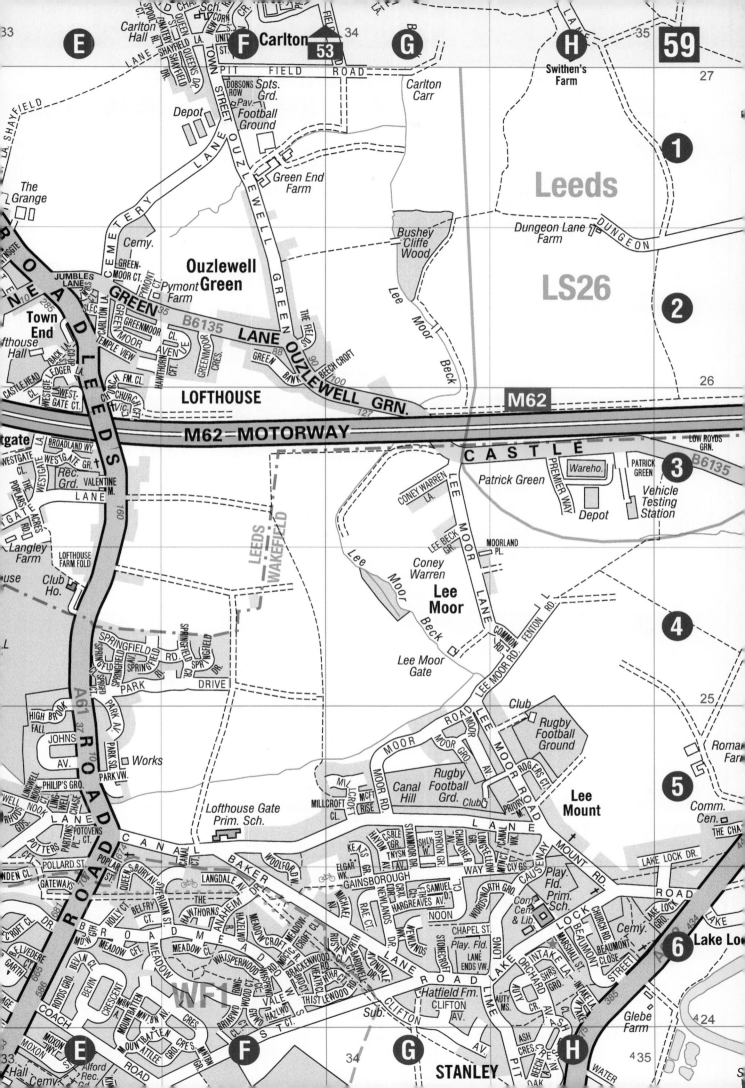

INDEX

Including Streets, Places & Areas, Hospitals etc., Industrial Estates, Junction Names,
Selected Flats & Walkways, Stations and Selected Places of Interest.

HOW TO USE THIS INDEX

1. Each street name is followed by its Postcode District, then by its Locality abbreviation(s) and then by its map reference;
   e.g. **Abbey Rd.** LS5: Leeds..........5D **18** is in the LS5 Postcode District and the Leeds Locality and is to be found in square 5D on page **18**.
   The page number is shown in bold type.

2. A strict alphabetical order is followed in which Av., Rd., St., etc. (though abbreviated) are read in full and as part of the street name;
   e.g. **Ashroyd** appears after **Ash Rd.** but before **Ash Ter.**

3. Streets and a selection of flats and walkways that cannot be shown on the mapping, appear in the index with the thoroughfare to which they are connected shown in brackets;
   e.g. **Abbey Gth.** LS19: Yead..........3D **8** *(off Well Hill)*

4. Addresses that are in more than one part are referred to as not continuous.

5. Places and areas are shown in the index in BLUE TYPE and the map reference is to the actual map square in which the town centre or area is located and
   not to the place name shown on the map; e.g. ALWOODLEY..........5G 13

6. An example of a selected place of interest is Abbey House Mus...........6G 19

7. Examples of stations are:
   Apperley Bridge Station (Rail)..........2A 16;   Elland Road Park & Ride..........4B 40;   Leeds Bus & Coach Station..........4G 5 (5H 31)

8. Junction Names are shown in the index in **BOLD CAPITAL TYPE**; e.g. **BELL WOOD RDBT**..........3G 43

9. An example of a Hospital, Hospice or selected Healthcare facility is CHAPEL ALLERTON HOSPITAL..........6A 22

10. Map references for entries that appear on large scale pages **4** & **5** are shown first, with small scale map references shown in brackets;
    e.g. **Ahlux Ct.** LS2: Leeds..........2H **5** (4H **31**)

GENERAL ABBREVIATIONS

All. : Alley	**Cotts.** : Cottages	**Ho's.** : Houses	**Prom.** : Promenade
App. : Approach	**Ct.** : Court	**Ind.** : Industrial	**Res.** : Residential
Arc. : Arcade	**Cres.** : Crescent	**Info.** : Information	**Ri.** : Rise
Av. : Avenue	**Cft.** : Croft	**Junc.** : Junction	**Rd.** : Road
Bk. : Back	**Dr.** : Drive	**La.** : Lane	**Rdbt.** : Roundabout
Blvd. : Boulevard	**E.** : East	**Lit.** : Little	**Shop.** : Shopping
Bri. : Bridge	**Ent.** : Enterprise	**Lwr.** : Lower	**Sth.** : South
Bldg. : Building	**Est.** : Estate	**Mnr.** : Manor	**Sq.** : Square
Bldgs. : Buildings	**Fld.** : Field	**Mans.** : Mansions	**St.** : Street
Bungs. : Bungalows	**Flds.** : Fields	**Mkt.** : Market	**Ter.** : Terrace
Bus. : Business	**Gdn.** : Garden	**Mdw.** : Meadow	**Twr.** : Tower
Cvn. : Caravan	**Gdns.** : Gardens	**M.** : Mews	**Trad.** : Trading
Cen. : Centre	**Gth.** : Garth	**Mt.** : Mount	**Up.** : Upper
Chu. : Church	**Ga.** : Gate	**Mus.** : Museum	**Va.** : Vale
Circ. : Circle	**Gt.** : Great	**Nth.** : North	**Vw.** : View
Cir. : Circus	**Grn.** : Green	**Pde.** : Parade	**Vs.** : Villas
Cl. : Close	**Gro.** : Grove	**Pk.** : Park	**Wlk.** : Walk
Comn. : Common	**Hgts.** : Heights	**Pas.** : Passage	**W.** : West
Cnr. : Corner	**Ho.** : House	**Pl.** : Place	**Yd.** : Yard

LOCALITY ABBREVIATIONS

Baildon: LS20 .... Bail	**East Ardsley**: WF3,WF12 ....E Ard	**Lofthouse**: WF3 .... Loft	**Stanningley**: LS28.................... Stan
Bardsey: LS14,LS17 ....Bard	**East Bierley**: BD4 ....E Bier	**Menston**: LS20,LS29 .... Men	**Swillington**: LS9,LS15,LS26 ..... Swil
Barwick in Elmet: LS15 ....B Elm	**Eccup**: LS16 .... Ecc	**Methley**: LS26...................... Meth	**Swillington Common**: LS15 .....Swil C
Batley: WF17 .... Bat	**Esholt**: BD17 .... Esh	**Morley**: LS27,WF12 ....Morl	**Thorner**: LS14,LS15 .... T'ner
Birkenshaw: BD11 ....B'haw	**Farsley**: LS13,LS28 ....Fars	**New Farnley**: BD11,LS12 ......N Far	**Thorpe on the Hill**: WF3 ....Thpe H
Birstall: WF17 .... Birs	**Garforth**: LS15,LS25,LS26......Gar	**Otley**: LS21 ....Otl	**Tingley**: WF3 .... Ting
Bradford: BD2-3,BD4,BD10.......B'ford	**Gildersome**: LS12,LS27.......... Gil	**Oulton**: LS26 ....Oult	**West Ardsley**: WF3.............. W Ard
Bramhope: LS16,LS19 ....B'hpe	**Gomersal**: BD19...................Gom	**Outwood**: WF1 ....Outw	**Wike**: LS17 .... Wike
Burley in Wharfedale: LS29 ....Burl W	**Guiseley**: LS20,LS29............Guis	**Pudsey**: BD4,LS12,LS13,LS28 ...... Pud	**Woodlesford**: LS26................. W'frd
Calverley: BD10,LS28............... Cal	**Hawksworth**: LS20 ....Hawk	**Rawdon**: LS18,LS19 .... Raw	**Wrenthorpe**: WF2 .... Wren
Carlton: WF3 ....Car	**Horsforth**: LS18-19 ....Hors	**Robin Hood**: WF3 ....Rob H	**Yeadon**: BD10,LS18,LS19,LS20 .....Yead
Carr Gate: WF2 ....Carr G	**Hunsworth**: BD19 .... Hun	**Rothwell**: LS26,WF3 ....Rothw	
Churwell: LS27 ....Chur	**Kirkhamgate**: WF2,WF3.......... Kirk	**Scarcroft**: LS14,LS17 ....S'cft	
Cleckheaton: BD19 ....Cleck	**Leeds**:	**Scholes**: LS15..................... Scho	
Dewsbury: WF12-17 ....Dew	LS1-9,LS1012,LS13,LS14,LS15,LS16	**Shadwell**: LS17.................... Shad	
Drighlington: BD11,LS27 ....Drig	LS17,LS18,LS25,LS26,LS27,LS28 .... Leeds	**Stanley**: WF3 .... Stly	

A

Abbey Av. LS5: Leeds 2F **29**	**Abbey Rd.** LS5: Leeds 5D **18**	**Aberfield Mt.** LS10: Leeds............3A **52**
Abbey Cl. WF3: E Ard................... 2H **57**	**Abbey St.** LS3: Leeds 5D **30**	**Aberfield Ri.** LS10: Leeds............3A **52**
Abbey Ct. LS18: Hors....................5B **18**	**Abbey Ter.** LS5: Leeds 2F **29**	**Aberfield Rd.** LS10: Leeds 2A **52**
Abbeydale Gdns. LS5: Leeds 5E **19**	**Abbey Vw.** LS5: Leeds 6G **19**	**Aberfield Wlk.** LS10: Leeds 3H **51**
Abbeydale Gth. LS5: Leeds 5E **19**	**Abbey Wlk.** LS5: Leeds 6F **19**	**Aberford Rd.** LS26: Oult 4C **54**
Abbeydale Gro. LS5: Leeds 5E **19**	**Abbots M.** LS4: Leeds 3B **30**	**Aberford Rd.** LS26: W'frd 4C **54**
Abbeydale Mt. LS5: Leeds 5E **19**	**Abbott Ct.** LS12: Leeds 5B **30**	**Abraham Hill** LS26: Rothw 4H **53**
Abbeydale Oval LS5: Leeds 5E **19**	**Abbott Rd.** LS12: Leeds 6B **30**	**Acacia Pk. Cres.** BD10: B'ford.....1B **16**
Abbeydale Va. LS5: Leeds 5E **19**	**Abbott Vw.** LS12: Leeds 5B **30**	**Acacia Pk. Dr.** BD10: B'ford.........1B **16**
Abbeydale Way LS5: Leeds 5E **19**	**Aberdeen Dr.** LS12: Leeds 6G **29**	**Acacia Pk. Ter.** BD10: B'ford.........1C **16**
Abbey Gth. LS19: Yead 3D **8**	**Aberdeen Gro.** LS12: Leeds 5G **29**	**Accommodation Rd.**
.... *(off Well Hill)*	**Aberdeen Rd.** LS12: Leeds 6G **29**	LS9: Leeds 4A **32**
Abbey Gorse LS5: Leeds 6G **19**	**Aberdeen Wlk.** LS12: Leeds 6G **29**	**Ackroyd St.** LS27: Morl 5H **49**
Abbey House Mus...........................6G **19**	**Aberfield Bank** LS10: Leeds........3A **52**	**Ackworth Av.** LS19: Yead 3E **9**
Abbey Mt. LS5: Leeds 2F **29**	**Aberfield Cl.** LS10: Leeds 2A **52**	**Ackworth Cres.** LS19: Yead 3E **9**
Abbey Retail Pk. Kirkstall 1G **29**	**Aberfield Crest** LS10: Leeds 3A **52**	**Ackworth Dr.** LS19: Yead 3E **9**
	Aberfield Dr. LS10: Leeds 3A **52**	**Acorn Bus. Pk.** LS14: Leeds 4G **33**
	Aberfield Gdns. LS10: Leeds 2A **52**	**Acorn Dr.** LS14: Leeds 3C **24**
	Aberfield Ga. LS10: Leeds 2A **52**	**Acre Cir.** LS10: Leeds 5G **51**

Acre Cl. LS10: Leeds 6F **51**		
Acre Ct. LS10: Leeds 5G **51**		
Acre Cres. LS10: Leeds 5G **51**		
Acre Gdns. LS10: Leeds 5G **51**		
Acre Gro. LS10: Leeds 5G **51**		
Acre Mt. LS10: Leeds 5G **51**		
Acre Pl. LS10: Leeds 5G **51**		
Acre Rd. LS10: Leeds 5F **51**		
Acres, The LS17: Leeds...............4D **12**		
.... *(off The Avenue)*		
Acres Hall Av. LS28: Pud.............1A **38**		
Acres Hall Cres. LS28: Pud.........1A **38**		
Acres Hall Dr. LS28: Pud 1A **38**		
Acres Rd. WF3: Loft....................3E **59**		
Acrewood Cl. LS17: Leeds 6C **14**		
Ada Glassby Ct. LS15: Leeds 4D **34**		
Adams Gro. LS15: Leeds 1E **35**		
Adam's Wlk. LS6: Leeds 3D **30**		
Ada's Pl. LS28: Stan 3G **27**		

Addingham Gdns. – Arden Grange

Addingham Gdns. LS12: Leeds 6G **29**
Addison Av. BD3: B'ford 4A **26**
Addison Ct. LS15: Leeds 1D **44**
ADEL 6B 12
Adelaide Av. LS27: Morl 4A **50**
ADEL EAST MOOR 6C 12
Adel Gth. LS16: Leeds 4B **12**
Adel Grange Cl. LS16: Leeds 1A **20**
Adel Grange Cft. LS16: Leeds 1A **20**
Adel Grange M. LS16: Leeds 1A **20**
(not continuous)
Adel Grn. LS16: Leeds 5B **12**
Adel La. LS16: Leeds 5A **12**
Adel Mead LS16: Leeds 5B **12**
Adel Mill LS16: Leeds 3A **12**
ADEL MILL 3B 12
Adel Pk. Cl. LS16: Leeds 6A **12**
Adel Pk. Ct. LS16: Leeds 6A **12**
Adel Pk. Cft. LS16: Leeds 6A **12**
Adel Pk. Dr. LS16: Leeds 6A **12**
Adel Pk. Gdns. LS16: Leeds 6A **12**
Adel Pasture LS16: Leeds 6A **12**
Adel Towers Cl. LS16: Leeds 6B **12**
Adel Towers Ct. LS16: Leeds 6B **12**
Adel Va. LS16: Leeds 5B **12**
Adel Wood Cl. LS16: Leeds 6B **12**
Adel Wood Dr. LS16: Leeds 6B **12**
Adel Wood Gdns. LS16: Leeds 6B **12**
Adel Wood Gro. LS16: Leeds 6B **12**
Adel Wood Pl. LS16: Leeds 6B **12**
Adel Wood Rd. LS16: Leeds 6B **12**
Admiral St. LS11: Leeds 3G **41**
Admirals Yd. LS10: Leeds 3B **42**
ADWALTON 3A 48
Adwalton Bus. Pk. BD11: Drig 4A **48**
Adwalton Cl. BD11: Drig 4F **47**
Adwalton Grn. BD11: Drig 4F **47**
Adwalton Moor Battle Site 4G 47
Adwalton Moor Bus. Pk.
BD11: B'haw 2D **46**
Adwick Pl. LS4: Leeds 3A **30**
Ahlux Ct. LS2: Leeds 2H **5** (4H **31**)
Ahlux Ho. LS2: Leeds 2H **5** (4H **31**)
Ainsley Ct. LS14: Leeds 6E **25**
Ainsley M. LS14: Leeds 6E **25**
Ainsley Vw. LS14: Leeds 6E **25**
Aintree Ct. LS10: Leeds 3A **42**
Airdale Ter. LS13: Leeds 6H **17**
(off Airedale Cft.)
Aire LS9: Leeds 1A **42**
Aireborough Leisure Cen. 5G 7
Aire Ct. LS10: Leeds 5G **51**
Airedale Cliff LS13: Leeds 6C **18**
Airedale Ct. LS14: Leeds 6H **23**
Airedale Cft. LS13: Leeds 6H **17**
Airedale Dr. LS18: Hors 3H **17**
Airedale Gdns. LS13: Leeds 1H **27**
Airedale Gro. LS18: Hors 3H **17**
Airedale Gro. LS26: W'frd 3D **54**
Airedale Ho. LS13: Leeds 1B **28**
Airedale Mt. LS13: Leeds 6G **17**
Airedale Quay LS13: Leeds 1A **28**
Airedale Rd. LS26: W'frd 3D **54**
Airedale Ter. LS26: W'frd 3D **54**
Airedale Ter. LS27: Morl 5H **49**
(off Gillroyd Pde.)
Airedale Vw. LS13: Leeds 6H **17**
(off Town St.)
Airedale Vw. LS19: Raw 6F **9**
Airedale Vw. LS26: W'frd 3D **54**
Airedale Wharf LS13: Leeds 6H **17**
Aire Gro. LS19: Yead 3E **9**
Aire Pl. LS3: Leeds 4C **30**
Aire Quay LS10: Leeds 2B **42**
Aire St. LS1: Leeds 5C **4** (6F **31**)
Aire Valley Av. LS9: Leeds 5G **43**
Aire Valley Dr. LS9: Leeds 3G **43**
Aire Valley Marina LS4: Leeds 4H **29**
Aire Valley Rd. LS9: Leeds 4G **43**
Aire Valley Way LS9: Leeds 2B **42**
Aire Vw. LS19: Yead 3E **9**
Aire Vw. Ct. LS13: Leeds 1A **28**
Aire Vw. Gdns. LS5: Leeds 5F **19**
Aire Vw. Ter. LS13: Leeds 1A **28**
Airlie Av. LS8: Leeds 1B **32**
Airlie Pl. LS8: Leeds 1B **32**
Airport W. LS19: Yead 1G **9**
Alan Cres. LS15: Leeds 6A **34**
Alaska Pl. LS7: Leeds 5A **22**
Albany Rd. LS26: Rothw 3F **53**
Albany St. LS12: Leeds 6G **29**
Albany Ter. LS12: Leeds 6G **29**
Alberta Av. LS7: Leeds 5A **22**
Albert Cl. LS27: Morl 4G **49**
Albert Cres. BD11: B'haw 5D **46**
Albert Dr. LS27: Morl 4B **50**
Albert Gro. LS6: Leeds 5B **20**
Albert Mansbridge Hall 4D **30**
Albert Mt. LS18: Hors 3D **18**
(off Broadgate La.)
Albert Pl. BD3: B'ford 5A **26**
Albert Pl. LS18: Hors 2C **18**
Albert Pl. LS26: Meth 6H **55**
Albert Ri. LS27: Morl 4B **50**
Albert Rd. LS26: Oult 3C **54**
Albert Rd. LS27: Morl 4H **49**
Albert Sq. LS19: Yead 2E **9**
Albert St. LS28: Pud 1F **37**
Albert Ter. LS19: Yead 2E **9**
(off Rockfield Ter.)
Albert Way BD11: B'haw 5D **46**
Albion Av. LS12: Leeds 6B **30**
Albion Pk. LS12: Leeds 5C **30**
Albion Pl. LS1: Leeds 4E **5** (5G **31**)
Albion Pl. LS20: Guis 4G **7**
Albion St. LS27: Morl
Corporation St. 5G **49**
Albion St. LS27: Morl
Windsor Ct. 5G **49**
Albion St. LS1: Leeds 4E **5** (5G **31**)
Albion St. LS2: Leeds 3E **5** (5G **31**)
Albion St. WF3: Car 6F **53**
Albion Way LS12: Leeds 5C **30**
Alcester Pl. LS8: Leeds 1B **32**
Alcester Rd. LS8: Leeds 1B **32**
Alcester Ter. LS8: Leeds 1B **32**
Alden Av. LS27: Morl 6G **49**
Alden Cl. LS27: Morl 6G **49**
Alder Dr. LS28: Pud 5C **26**
Alder Gth. LS28: Pud 5D **26**
Alder Hill Av. LS6: Leeds 4E **21**
Alder Hill Cotts. LS6: Leeds 4D **20**
Alder Hill Gro. LS7: Leeds 4E **21**
Alder Rd. LS14: Leeds 4C **24**
Alders, The LS7: Leeds 4H **21**
Aldersgate LS12: Leeds 6A **30**
(off Wesley Rd.)
Aldersyde Rd. LS20: Guis 5F **7**
Aldersyde Way LS20: Guis 5F **7**
Alderton Bank LS17: Leeds 1D **20**
Alderton Cres. LS17: Leeds 1D **20**
Alderton Hgts. LS17: Leeds 1D **20**
Alderton Mt. LS17: Leeds 1D **20**
Alderton Pl. LS17: Leeds 1D **20**
Alderton Ri. LS17: Leeds 1E **21**
Alexander Av. LS15: Leeds 6H **33**
Alexander Ct.
LS1: Leeds 3D **4** (5F **31**)
Alexander St.
LS1: Leeds 3D **4** (5F **31**)
Alexandra Cl. BD4: B'ford 2A **36**
Alexandra Gro. LS28: Pud 1F **37**
Alexandra Gro. LS6: Leeds 3C **30**
Alexandra Mill LS27: Morl 6G **49**
Alexandra Rd. LS18: Hors 2C **18**
Alexandra Rd. LS28: Pud 1E **37**
Alexandra Rd. LS6: Leeds 3C **30**
Alexandra Ter. LS19: Yead 2E **9**
(not continuous)
Alfred St. LS27: Chur 1A **50**
Algernon Firth Bldg.
LS1: Leeds 2B **4** (4F **31**)
Alice Smart Cl. LS15: Leeds 4D **34**
Allenby Cres. LS11: Leeds 1E **51**
Allenby Dr. LS11: Leeds 1E **51**
Allenby Gdns. LS11: Leeds 1E **51**
Allenby Gro. LS11: Leeds 1E **51**
Allenby Pl. LS11: Leeds 1E **51**
Allenby Rd. LS11: Leeds 1E **51**
Allenby Vw. LS11: Leeds 6F **41**
Allen Cft. BD11: B'haw 4C **46**
Allerton Av. LS17: Leeds 1H **21**
Allerton Ct. LS17: Leeds 1H **21**
(off Allerton Gro.)
Allerton Cft. LS7: Leeds 6A **22**
(off Harehills La.)
Allerton Grange Av.
LS17: Leeds 2A **22**
Allerton Grange Cl.
LS17: Leeds 3G **21**
Allerton Grange Cres.
LS17: Leeds 3H **21**
Allerton Grange Cft. LS8: Leeds 3A **22**
Allerton Grange Dr.
LS17: Leeds 3H **21**
Allerton Grange Gdns.
LS17: Leeds 3H **21**
Allerton Grange Ri.
LS17: Leeds 3G **21**
Allerton Grange Va.
LS17: Leeds 3H **21**
Allerton Grange Wlk.
LS17: Leeds 3H **21**
Allerton Grange Way
LS17: Leeds 3H **21**
Allerton Grange Way
LS8: Leeds 3A **22**
Allerton Gro. LS17: Leeds 1H **21**
Allerton Hall LS7: Leeds 4G **21**
Allerton Hill LS7: Leeds 4G **21**
Allerton M. LS17: Leeds 2H **21**
Allerton Pk. LS7: Leeds 4H **21**
Allerton Pl. LS17: Leeds 1H **21**
Allerton St. LS4: Leeds 3B **30**
Allerton Ter. LS4: Leeds 3B **30**
Alliance St. LS12: Leeds 6G **29**
Allinson St. LS12: Leeds 1C **40**
All Saints Av. LS9: Leeds 5B **32**
(off Aysgarth Mt.)
All Saint's Circ. LS26: W'frd 3D **54**
All Saint's Dr. LS26: W'frd 3C **54**
All Saint's Rd. LS26: W'frd 2D **54**
All Saints Rd. LS9: Leeds 5B **32**
All Saints Ter. LS9: Leeds 5B **32**
(off Aysgarth Mt.)
All Saint's Vw. LS26: W'frd 2C **54**
Alma Cl. LS28: Fars 2E **27**
Alma Cotts. LS6: Leeds 6B **20**
Alma Rd. LS6: Leeds 6B **20**
Alma St. LS19: Yead 2E **9**
Alma St. LS26: W'frd 2C **54**
Alma St. LS9: Leeds 4B **32**
Alma Ter. LS26: Rothw 3F **53**
Alma Vs. LS26: W'frd 2D **54**
Alnwick Vw. LS16: Leeds 4A **20**
Alpine Ter. LS26: Rothw 3G **53**
Alston La. LS14: Leeds 2A **34**
Altus Ho. LS2: Leeds 4G **31**
Alva Cl. LS20: Guis 3F **7**
Alva Ct. LS20: Guis 3F **7**
ALWOODLEY 5G 13
Alwoodley Chase LS17: Leeds 4A **14**
Alwoodley Ct. LS17: Leeds 4D **12**
Alwoodley Ct. Gdns.
LS17: Leeds 3E **13**
Alwoodley Gdns. LS17: Leeds 4E **13**
Alwoodley Gates LS17: Leeds 3A **14**
ALWOODLEY GATES 3A 14
Alwoodley Golf Course 3A 14
Alwoodley La. LS17: Leeds 3D **12**
ALWOODLEY PK. 3E 13
Amber Cl. LS7: Leeds 1F **5** (3G **31**)
Amberley Gdns. LS12: Leeds 1A **40**
Amberley Rd. LS12: Leeds 1A **40**
Amberley St. LS12: Leeds 1A **40**
Amberton App. LS8: Leeds 1E **33**
Amberton Cl. LS8: Leeds 6E **23**
Amberton Cres. LS8: Leeds 1E **33**
Amberton Gdns. LS8: Leeds 1E **33**
Amberton Gth. LS8: Leeds 1E **33**
Amberton Gro. LS8: Leeds 1E **33**
Amberton La. LS8: Leeds 1E **33**
Amberton M. LS8: Leeds 2F **33**
Amberton Mt. LS8: Leeds 1E **33**
Amberton Pl. LS8: Leeds 1D **32**
Amberton Rd. LS8: Leeds 1D **32**
Amberton Rd. LS9: Leeds 2E **33**
Amberton St. LS8: Leeds 1E **33**
Amberton Ter. LS8: Leeds 1E **33**
Amblers Bldgs. LS28: Pud 1G **37**
(off Amblers Ct.)
Amblers Bungs. WF3: E Ard 3F **57**
Amblers Ct. LS28: Pud 1G **37**
Amblerthorne BD11: B'haw 4D **46**
Ambleside Gdns. LS28: Pud 6E **27**
Ambleside Gro. LS26: W'frd 3C **54**
Amelia Stewart La.
LS15: Leeds 3D **34**
Amspool Ct. WF3: Car 6E **53**
Anaheim Dr. WF1: Outw 6F **59**
Ancaster Cres. LS16: Leeds 4H **19**
Ancaster Rd. LS16: Leeds 4H **19**
Ancaster Vw. LS16: Leeds 4H **19**
Anderson Av. LS8: Leeds 3A **32**
Anderson Mt. LS8: Leeds 3A **32**
Andover Grn. BD4: B'ford 3A **36**
Andrew Cres. WF1: Outw 6D **58**
Andrew Ho. LS28: Fars 2F **27**
(off Water La.)
Andrews Mnr. LS19: Yead 2D **8**
(off Haworth La.)
Andrew Sq. LS28: Fars 2F **27**
Andrew St. LS28: Fars 3F **27**
Angel Ct. LS3: Leeds 4D **30**
Angel Inn Yd.
LS1: Leeds 4E **5** (5G **31**)
(off Briggate)
Angel Row LS26: Rothw 4C **52**
Anlaby St. BD4: B'ford 2A **36**
Annie St. LS27: Morl 5H **49**
Anstey Ho. LS3: Leeds 3A **4** (5E **31**)
(off Hanover Av.)
Antler Complex LS27: Morl 5D **48**
Apex Bus. Cen. LS11: Leeds 2G **41**
Apex Vw. LS11: Leeds 2F **41**
Apex Way LS11: Leeds 2G **41**
Apiary Blvd. LS9: Leeds 1A **42**
APPERLEY BRIDGE 3A 16
Apperley Bridge Station (Rail) 2A 16
Apperley Gdns. BD10: B'ford 3A **16**
Apperley La. BD10: B'ford 3A **16**
Apperley La. BD10: Yead 3A **16**
Apperley La. LS19: Raw 1B **16**
Apperley La. LS19: Yead 1B **16**
Appleby Pl. LS15: Leeds 5G **33**
Appleby Wlk. LS15: Leeds 5G **33**
Appleby Way LS27: Morl 4H **49**
Applegarth LS26: W'frd 2C **54**
Appleton Cl. LS9: Leeds 5B **32**
Appleton Ct. LS29: Men 3C **6**
Appleton Ct. LS9: Leeds 5B **32**
Appleton Gro. LS9: Leeds 5D **32**
Appleton Sq. LS9: Leeds 5B **32**
Appleton Way LS9: Leeds 5B **32**
Apple Tree Cl. WF3: E Ard 3G **57**
Apple Tree Ct. WF3: E Ard 4G **57**
Appleyard La. LS27: Morl 4A **50**
Approach, The LS15: Scho 4F **25**
Aragon Ct. LS7: Leeds 4E **21**
Arbor Dr. LS26: W'frd 2D **54**
Arbor Hill LS26: W'frd 2D **54**
Arbor Pl. LS26: W'frd 2D **54**
Archery Pl. LS2: Leeds 3F **31**
Archery Rd. LS2: Leeds 3F **31**
Archery St. LS2: Leeds 3F **31**
Archery Ter. LS2: Leeds 3F **31**
Arden Ct. LS16: Leeds 1A **20**
Arden Grange LS16: Leeds 1A **20**

A-Z Leeds 61

Ardsley Cl. – Aviary Row

Ardsley Cl. BD4: B'ford.................5B **36**
Ardsley Ct. WF3: E Ard.................3A **58**
Ardsley Falls Cl. WF3: E Ard........ 2G **57**
Arena Pk. LS17: Leeds................ 2H **15**
Arena Way LS2: Leeds...... 2E **5** (4G **31**)
Argent Way BD4: B'ford..............5B **36**
Argie Av. LS4: Leeds.................... 2H **29**
Argie Gdns. LS4: Leeds................3A **30**
Argie Rd. LS4: Leeds....................3A **30**
Argie Ter. LS4: Leeds....................3A **30**
Argyle Rd. LS9: Leeds.......3H **5** (5H **31**)
Argyll Cl. LS18: Hors....................5B **10**
Arkendale Ct. LS29: Men..............3C **6**
Arksey Pl. LS12: Leeds.................5A **30**
Arksey Ter. LS12: Leeds................5A **30**
Arkwright St. BD4: B'ford.............1A **36**
Arkwright Wlk. LS27: Morl.......... 3G **49**
Arlesford Rd. BD4: B'ford..............5A **36**
Arley Gro. LS12: Leeds..................5A **30**
Arley Pl. LS12: Leeds....................5A **30**
Arley St. LS12: Leeds....................4A **30**
Arley Ter. LS12: Leeds...................5A **30**
Arlington Bus. Cen. LS11: Leeds..............................1B **50**
Arlington Gro. LS8: Leeds........... 6D **22**
Arlington Rd. LS8: Leeds............. 1D **32**
Armitage Bldgs. WF12: Dew........5A **56**
Armitage Ct. LS28: Pud................1F **37**
.................................*(off Armitage Sq.)*
Armitage Sq. LS28: Pud...............1F **37**
Armitage St. LS26: Rothw........... 5G **53**
ARMLEY...5B 30
Armley Ct. LS12: Leeds.................5B **30**
Armley Grange Av. LS12: Leeds...4F **29**
Armley Grange Cres. LS12: Leeds...............................4F **29**
Armley Grange Dr. LS12: Leeds...5F **29**
Armley Grange Mt. LS12: Leeds..5F **29**
Armley Grange Oval LS12: Leeds...............................4F **29**
Armley Grange Ri. LS12: Leeds...5F **29**
Armley Grange Vw. LS12: Leeds.............................. 5G **29**
Armley Grange Wlk. LS12: Leeds...............................5F **29**
Armley Gro. Pl. LS12: Leeds.........6B **30**
Armley Ho. LS14: Leeds............. 5G **23**
.................................*(off Kingsdale Ct.)*
Armley Leisure Cen.....................6H 29
Armley Lodge Rd. LS12: Leeds....4A **30**
Armley Mills Leeds Industrial Mus.........................4B 30
Armley Pk. Ct. LS12: Leeds..........5A **30**
....*(off Cecil Rd.)*
Armley Pk. Rd. LS12: Leeds........4A **30**
Armley Ridge Cl. LS12: Leeds..... 5G **29**
Armley Ridge Rd. LS12: Leeds.....2F **29**
.................................(not continuous)
Armley Ridge Ter. LS12: Leeds... 4G **29**
Armley Rd. LS12: Leeds..............5A **30**
.................................(not continuous)
Armley Tennis Club.....................4G 29
Armouries Dr. LS10: Leeds.......... 1H **41**
Armouries Way LS10: Leeds.....................6H **5** (6H **31**)
Armstrong St. BD4: B'ford............1A **36**
Armstrong St. LS28: Fars.............3F **27**
Arncliffe Cres. LS27: Morl............1A **56**
Arncliffe Gth. LS28: Stan...............3F **27**
Arncliffe Grange LS17: Leeds..... 1H **21**
Arncliffe Rd. LS16: Leeds............ 3G **19**
Arncliffe St. LS28: Stan................3F **27**
Arndale Cen. Headingley..............6B **20**
Arran Dr. LS18: Hors.....................5B **10**
Arran Way LS26: Rothw.............. 4H **53**
Arthington Av. LS10: Leeds......... 5H **41**
Arthington Cl. WF3: W Ard...........4B **56**
Arthington Ct. LS10: Leeds......... 5H **41**
Arthington Gro. LS10: Leeds....... 5H **41**
Arthington Pl. LS10: Leeds......... 5H **41**
Arthington St. LS10: Leeds......... 5H **41**
Arthington Ter. LS10: Leeds........ 5H **41**
Arthington Vw. LS10: Leeds........ 5H **41**
Arthur Ct. LS28: Pud....................6E **27**
ARTHURSDALE.............................3F 25
Arthursdale Cl. LS15: Scho..........4F **25**
Arthursdale Dr. LS15: Scho..........4F **25**
Arthursdale Grange LS15: Scho..4F **25**
Arthur St. LS28: Fars....................3F **27**
Arthur St. LS28: Stan.................. 3G **27**
Arthur Ter. LS28: Fars..................3F **27**
......................................*(off Arthur St.)*
Artist St. LS12: Leeds.................. 6D **30**
Aruba LS12: Leeds...........5A **4** (6D **30**)
......................................*(off Gotts Rd.)*
Arundel St. LS28: Pud................. 6G **27**
Arundel Ter. LS15: Leeds.............3C **34**
..............................*(off Tranquility Av.)*
Ascot Gdns. LS10: Leeds............ 6H **51**
Ascot Ter. LS9: Leeds..................6B **32**
Asda Ho. LS11: Leeds.......6E **5** (1G **41**)
Ash Av. LS6: Leeds......................6B **20**
Ashbourne Av. LS15: Leeds.........4F **35**
Ashbourne Ct. LS15: Leeds..........4F **35**
Ashbrooke Pk. LS11: Leeds.........5F **41**
Ashbury Chase WF1: Outw..........6C **58**
Ashby Av. LS13: Leeds................ 3D **28**
Ashby Cres. LS13: Leeds............ 4D **28**
Ashby Mt. LS13: Leeds................ 3D **28**
Ashby Sq. LS13: Leeds................ 3D **28**
Ashby Ter. LS13: Leeds............... 3D **28**
Ashby Vw. LS13: Leeds............... 3D **28**
Ash Cl. LS27: Gil........................ 3D **48**
Ash Ct. LS14: Leeds................... 3G **33**
Ash Cres. LS6: Leeds...................6A **20**
Ash Cres. WF3: Stly..................... 6H **59**
Ashdene LS12: N Far.................. 4D **38**
Ashdene Cl. LS28: Pud................ 2G **37**
Ashdene Cres. LS28: Pud............ 2G **37**
Ashdown St. LS13: Leeds............4C **28**
Ashfield BD4: B'ford.....................6A **36**
Ashfield LS12: N Far.................... 3G **39**
Ashfield Av. LS27: Morl................6F **49**
Ashfield Cl. LS12: N Far...............3F **39**
Ashfield Cl. LS15: Leeds............. 1D **34**
Ashfield Cres. LS28: Stan............4F **27**
Ashfield Gro. LS28: Stan............. 4G **27**
Ashfield Pk. LS6: Leeds...............6C **20**
Ashfield Rd. LS27: Morl................6F **49**
Ashfield Rd. LS28: Stan................4F **27**
Ashfield Ter. LS15: Leeds........... 1D **34**
Ashfield Ter. WF3: Thpe H............1B **58**
Ashfield Way LS12: N Far............3E **39**
Ashford Dr. LS28: Pud................. 1H **37**
Ash Gdns. LS6: Leeds..................6B **20**
Ash Gro. BD11: B'haw..................3C **46**
Ash Gro. LS18: Hors.....................1C **18**
Ash Gro. LS28: Pud...................... 1G **37**
Ash Gro. LS6: Leeds.................... 2D **30**
Ashgrove BD10: B'ford..................4A **16**
Ashgrove M. LS13: Leeds........... 1H **27**
Ash Hill Dr. LS17: Shad.............. 5H **15**
Ash Hill Gdns. LS17: Shad.......... 5H **15**
Ash Hill Gth. LS17: Shad............ 5H **15**
Ash Hill La. LS17: Shad.............. 5H **15**
Ash Ho. LS15: Leeds.................... 1G **43**
Ashington Cl. BD2: B'ford............1A **26**
Ashlea Ct. LS13: Leeds................1C **28**
.....................................*(off Ashlea Ga.)*
Ashlea Ga. LS13: Leeds...............2C **28**
Ashlea Grn. LS13: Leeds..............2C **28**
Ashleigh Gdns. LS26: Oult...........3C **54**
Ashleigh Rd. LS16: Leeds............ 3G **19**
Ashley Av. LS9: Leeds..................3C **32**
Ashley Ct. LS16: Leeds................ 2H **19**
....*(off Otley Rd.)*
Ashley Grn. LS12: Leeds............. 1H **39**
Ashley Ind. Est. LS7: Leeds......... 2G **31**
Ashley Rd. LS9: Leeds..................3B **32**
Ashley Ter. LS9: Leeds.................3C **32**
Ash M. BD10: B'ford......................4A **16**
Ash Rd. LS16: Leeds.....................4A **12**
Ash Rd. LS6: Leeds.......................1A **30**
Ashroyd LS26: Rothw.................. 5H **53**
Ash Ter. LS6: Leeds......................6B **20**
Ashtofts Mt. LS20: Guis................. 4G **7**
Ashton Av. LS8: Leeds..................2B **32**
Ashton Ct. LS8: Leeds..................2C **32**
Ashton Cres. WF3: Car.................6F **53**
Ashton Gro. LS8: Leeds................3B **32**
Ashton Mt. LS8: Leeds..................3B **32**
Ashton Pl. LS8: Leeds...................3B **32**
Ashton Rd. LS8: Leeds..................2C **32**
Ashton Rd. Ind. Est. LS8: Leeds...2C **32**
Ashton St. LS8: Leeds...................2B **32**
Ashton Ter. LS8: Leeds..................3B **32**
Ashton Ter. WF3: Rob H................5D **52**
Ashton Vw. LS8: Leeds..................3B **32**
Ash Tree App. LS14: Leeds.......... 1D **34**
Ash Tree Bank LS14: Leeds......... 6D **24**
...............................*(off Swarcliffe Av.)*
Ash Tree Cl. LS14: Leeds............. 6D **24**
Ash Tree Gdns. LS14: Leeds........ 6D **24**
Ash Tree Gro. LS14: Leeds.......... 6D **24**
Ash Tree Vw. LS14: Leeds........... 6D **24**
..................................*(off Stanks Gdns.)*
Ash Tree Wlk. LS14: Leeds.......... 6D **24**
.............................*(off Ash Tree Gdns.)*
Ash Vw. LS6: Leeds.......................6B **20**
Ash Vw. WF3: E Ard...................... 4G **57**
Ash Vs. LS15: Leeds..................... 1D **34**
Ashville Av. LS6: Leeds.................2B **30**
Ashville Gro. LS6: Leeds...............2B **30**
Ashville Rd. LS4: Leeds.................2B **30**
Ashville Rd. LS6: Leeds.................2B **30**
Ashville Ter. LS28: Fars................3F **27**
....*(off New St.)*
Ashville Ter. LS6: Leeds................2B **30**
Ashville Vw. LS6: Leeds................3C **30**
Ashwood LS14: Leeds....................2B **24**
Ashwood Dr. LS27: Gil...................2B **48**
Ashwood Gdns. LS27: Gil..............2B **48**
Ashwood Gro. LS27: Gil................2C **48**
Ashwood Pde. LS27: Gil.................2B **48**
..............................*(off Ashwood Gdns.)*
Ashwood Pde. LS9: Leeds..............6A **32**
..............................*(off Ashwood Gdns.)*
Ashwood St. BD4: B'ford................6A **36**
Ashwood Ter. LS6: Leeds.............. 1D **30**
Ashwood Vs. LS6: Leeds............... 1D **30**
Asket Av. LS14: Leeds................... 6G **23**
Asket Cl. LS14: Leeds.................... 5G **23**
Asket Cres. LS14: Leeds................ 6G **23**
Asket Dr. LS14: Leeds.................... 5G **23**
Asket Fold LS14: Leeds.................. 5G **23**
Asket Gdns. LS8: Leeds..................5F **23**
Asket Gth. LS14: Leeds.................. 6G **23**
Asket Grn. LS14: Leeds.................. 6G **23**
Asket Hill LS8: Leeds......................4F **23**
Asket Pl. LS14: Leeds..................... 6G **23**
Asket Row LS14: Leeds................... 5G **23**
Asket Wlk. LS14: Leeds.................. 6G **23**
Askey Cres. LS27: Morl..................1A **56**
Askrigg Ct. LS29: Men.................... 3D **6**
Aspect 14 LS7: Leeds........ 1F **5** (4G **31**)
Aspect Gdns. LS28: Pud..................5E **27**
Aspect Ter. LS28: Pud.....................5E **27**
Aspen Ct. WF3: Ting.......................2A **56**
Aspen Mt. LS16: Leeds....................1E **19**
Aspen Vw. LS14: Leeds...................3C **24**
Aspen Way LS14: Leeds...................3C **24**
Asquith Av. LS27: Morl....................3E **49**
Asquith Av. Bus. Pk. LS27: Gil.....3E **49**
Asquith Cl. LS27: Morl.....................4F **49**
Asquith Dr. LS27: Morl.....................4F **49**
Asquith Ho. LS6: Leeds...................2F **31**
Assembly St. LS2: Leeds... 5F **5** (6G **31**)
Assisi Pl. LS10: Leeds......................3A **42**
Aster Gro. LS14: Leeds.................... 4H **33**
Astley Av. LS26: Swil........................ 6G **45**
Astley La. LS26: Swil......................... 6H **45**
Astley La. Ind. Est. LS26: Swil..... 1H **55**
Astley Way LS26: Swil...................... 1H **55**
Aston Av. LS13: Leeds..................... 3D **28**
Aston Cres. LS13: Leeds..................3E **29**
Aston Dr. LS13: Leeds......................3E **29**
Aston Gro. LS13: Leeds....................3E **29**
Aston Mt. LS13: Leeds......................3E **29**
Aston Pl. LS13: Leeds.......................3E **29**
Aston Rd. LS13: Leeds...................... 3D **28**
Aston St. LS13: Leeds....................... 3D **28**
Aston Ter. LS13: Leeds......................3E **29**
Aston Vw. LS13: Leeds...................... 3D **28**
Astor Gro. LS13: Leeds......................3A **28**
Astoria Ct. LS8: Leeds.......................6C **22**
Astor St. LS13: Leeds.........................3A **28**
Astra Bus. Pk. LS11: Leeds............. 5G **41**
Astura Ct. LS7: Leeds.........................6F **21**
Atha Cl. LS11: Leeds...........................6E **41**
Atha Cres. LS11: Leeds.......................6E **41**
Atha Ho. LS2: Leeds.........1D **4** (3G **31**)
......................................*(off Carlton Hill)*
Atha St. LS11: Leeds...........................6E **41**
Athens LS20: Guis................................4F **7**
Athlone Gro. LS12: Leeds..................6A **30**
Athlone St. LS12: Leeds.....................6A **30**
Athlone Ter. LS12: Leeds....................6A **30**
ATKINSON HILL....................................3B 42
Atkinson Quay LS10: Leeds.................2A **42**
Atkinson St. LS10: Leeds.....................2A **42**
Atlanta St. LS13: Leeds........................3A **28**
Atlantic Apts. LS1: Leeds....................... 5C **4** (6F **31**)
................................*(off Wellington St.)*
Attlee Gro. WF1: Outw.........................6E **59**
Aubrey Ct. LS11: Leeds...................... 2D **40**
Augusta Ct. LS26: Rothw.....................5A **54**
AUSTHORPE..5E 35
Austhorpe Av. LS15: Leeds..................6E **35**
Austhorpe Ct. LS15: Leeds...................6E **35**
Austhorpe Dr. LS15: Leeds...................6E **35**
Austhorpe Gdns. LS15: Leeds..............5F **35**
Austhorpe Gro. LS15: Leeds.................6E **35**
Austhorpe La. LS15: Leeds................. 4D **34**
Austhorpe Rd. LS15: Leeds...................3C **34**
Austhorpe Vw. LS15: Leeds................. 5D **34**
Austin Hall LS7: Leeds..........................2F **31**
Authorpe Rd. LS6: Leeds..................... 5D **20**
Autumn Av. LS6: Leeds........................3C **30**
Autumn Cl. BD11: Drig......................... 3H **47**
Autumn Cres. LS18: Hors.................... 4D **18**
Autumn Gro. LS6: Leeds......................3C **30**
Autumn Pl. LS6: Leeds..........................3C **30**
Autumn St. LS6: Leeds..........................3C **30**
Autumn Ter. LS6: Leeds........................3C **30**
Auty Cres. WF3: Stly............................ 6H **59**
Auty M. WF3: Stly................................. 6H **59**
Auty Sq. LS27: Morl.............................. 6H **49**
....*(off High St.)*
Avenue, The LS15: Leeds Newsam Grn. Rd........................ 5D **44**
Avenue, The LS15: Swil Newsam Grn. Rd........................ 5D **44**
Avenue, The LS15: Leeds Sandbed La.................................. 2D **34**
Avenue, The BD10: B'ford..................6A **8**
Avenue, The BD17: Esh......................6A **8**
Avenue, The LS15: Scho......................3F **25**
Avenue, The LS17: Leeds.................... 4D **12**
Avenue, The LS18: Hors...................... 2H **17**
Avenue, The LS8: Leeds.......................3C **22**
Avenue, The LS9: Leeds.... 5H **5** (6A **32**)
Avenue, The WF3: Ting.........................3E **57**
Avenue Ct. LS17: Leeds....................... 4D **12**
Avenue Cres. LS8: Leeds......................1B **32**
Avenue Gdns. LS17: Leeds................... 4D **12**
Avenue Hill LS8: Leeds..........................1A **32**
Avenue Lawns LS17: Leeds.................. 4D **12**
Avenue St. BD4: B'ford..........................6A **36**
Avenue Ter. LS19: Yead..........................2F **9**
Avenue Victoria LS8: Leeds..................3C **22**
Avenue Wlk. LS2: Leeds........................2E **31**
Avenue Wlk. LS6: Leeds........................2E **31**
Aviary Gro. LS12: Leeds........................5A **30**
Aviary Mt. LS12: Leeds..........................5A **30**
Aviary Pl. LS12: Leeds...........................5A **30**
Aviary Rd. LS12: Leeds..........................5A **30**
Aviary Row LS12: Leeds.........................5A **30**

62 A-Z Leeds

Aviary St. – Bk. Glenthorpe Ter.

Aviary St. LS12: Leeds ... 5A **30**
Aviary Ter. LS12: Leeds ... 5A **30**
Aviary Vw. LS12: Leeds ... 5A **30**
Avocet Gth. LS10: Leeds ... 4H **51**
Avon Cl. LS17: Shad ... 5H **15**
Avon Ct. LS17: Shad ... 4G **15**
Avondale Ct. LS17: Leeds ... 6H **13**
Avondale Dr. WF3: Stly ... 6G **59**
Avondale St. LS13: Leeds ... 4C **28**
Axis Ct. LS27: Gil ... 4E **49**
Aylesford Mt. LS15: Leeds ... 2F **35**
Ayresome Av. LS8: Leeds ... 1C **22**
Ayresome Ter. LS8: Leeds ... 1B **22**
Aysgarth Cl. LS9: Leeds ... 6B **32**
Aysgarth Ct. LS29: Men ... 3D **6**
Aysgarth Dr. LS9: Leeds ... 6B **32**
Aysgarth Fold LS10: Leeds ... 5G **51**
Aysgarth Pl. LS9: Leeds ... 6B **32**
Aysgarth Wlk. LS9: Leeds ... 6B **32**
Ayton Ho. BD4: B'ford ... 6B **36**
Azalea Av. LS14: Leeds ... 4H **33**

B

Bachelor La. LS18: Hors ... 2C **18**
Bk. Airlie Av. LS8: Leeds ... 1B **32** *(off Airlie Av.)*
Bk. Airlie Pl. LS8: Leeds ... 1B **32** *(off Airlie Pl.)*
Bk. Albert Gro. LS6: Leeds ... 5B **20**
Bk. Albert Ter. LS6: Leeds ... 3C **30** *(off Springrove Ter.)*
Bk. Alcester Pl. LS8: Leeds ... 1B **32** *(off Alcester Pl.)*
Bk. Alcester Rd. LS8: Leeds ... 1B **32** *(off Alcester Rd.)*
Bk. Alcester Ter. LS8: Leeds ... 1B **32** *(off Hill Top Av.)*
Bk. Allerton Ter. LS7: Leeds ... 4G **21**
Bk. Alma St. LS19: Yead ... 2E **9** *(off Alma St.)*
Bk. Archery Pl. LS2: Leeds ... 3F **31** *(off Archery Rd.)*
Bk. Archery Rd. LS2: Leeds ... 3F **31** *(off Archery Rd.)*
Bk. Archery St. LS2: Leeds ... 3F **31** *(off Archery Rd.)*
Bk. Archery Ter. LS2: Leeds ... 3F **31** *(off Archery Rd.)*
Bk. Ash Gro. LS6: Leeds ... 2D **30**
Bk. Ashley Av. LS9: Leeds ... 3C **32** *(off Ashley Rd.)*
Bk. Ashley St. LS9: Leeds ... 3C **32** *(off Ashley Rd.)*
Bk. Ashville Av. LS6: Leeds ... 2C **30** *(off Cardigan Rd.)*
Bk. Ashville Gro. LS6: Leeds ... 2B **30** *(off Cardigan Rd.)*
Bk. Ashville Rd. LS6: Leeds ... 2B **30** *(off Cardigan Rd.)*
Bk. Ashville Ter. LS6: Leeds ... 2B **30** *(off Cardigan Rd.)*
Bk. Ashwood Ter. LS6: Leeds ... 1D **30**
Bk. Aston Pl. LS13: Leeds ... 3E **29** *(off Aston Rd.)*
Bk. Aston Rd. LS13: Leeds ... 3D **28**
Bk. Aston St. LS13: Leeds ... 3D **28** *(off Ashton Mt.)*
Bk. Aston Ter. LS13: Leeds ... 3E **29** *(off Aston Av.)*
Bk. Aston Vw. LS13: Leeds ... 3E **29** *(off Aston Av.)*
Bk. Athlone Av. LS12: Leeds ... 6A **30**
Bk. Athlone Gro. LS12: Leeds ... 6A **30** *(off Athlone St.)*
Bk. Athlone Ter. LS12: Leeds ... 6A **30** *(off Athlone St.)*
Bk. Atlanta St. LS13: Leeds ... 3A **28** *(off Fairfield Av.)*
Bk. Austhorpe Rd. LS15: Leeds ... 3C **34** *(off Austhorpe Rd.)*
Bk. Autumn Rd. LS6: Leeds ... 3C **30** *(off Autumn Gro.)*
Bk. Autumn Ter. LS6: Leeds ... 3C **30** *(off Alexandra Rd.)*
Bk. Aviary Rd. LS12: Leeds ... 5A **30** *(off Aviary Gro.)*
Bk. Bailey's Pl. LS16: Leeds ... 5B **20**
Bk. Baldovan Ter. LS8: Leeds ... 1B **32** *(off Baldovan Ter.)*
Bk. Bank Ter. LS28: Stan ... 3G **27**
Bk. Banstead St. LS8: Leeds ... 2B **32** *(off Harehills Rd.)*
Bk. Barden Pl. LS12: Leeds ... 6G **29** *(off Conference Rd.)*
Bk. Barkly Gro. LS11: Leeds ... 5E **41** *(off Theodore St.)*
Bk. Barkly Pde. LS11: Leeds ... 6E **41** *(off Barkly Dr.)*
Bk. Barkly Ter. LS11: Leeds ... 5E **41** *(off Barkly Dr.)*
Bk. Barrowby Vw. LS15: Leeds ... 6E **35**
Bk. Bath Rd. LS13: Leeds ... 3C **28** *(off Cross Bath Rd.)*
Bk. Beamsley Gro. LS6: Leeds ... 3C **30** *(off Harold Gro.)*
Bk. Beamsley Mt. LS6: Leeds ... 3C **30** *(off Royal Pk. Rd.)*
Bk. Beamsley Ter. LS6: Leeds ... 3C **30** *(off Royal Pk. Rd.)*
Bk. Beechwood Gro. LS4: Leeds ... 2B **30**
Bk. Beechwood Rd. LS4: Leeds ... 2B **30** *(off Beechwood Pl.)*
Bk. Bellbrooke Gro. LS9: Leeds ... 3D **32** *(off Bellbrooke St.)*
Bk. Bellbrooke Pl. LS9: Leeds ... 3D **32** *(off Bellbrooke St.)*
Bk. Bellbrooke Ter. LS9: Leeds ... 3D **32** *(off Coldcotes Av.)*
Bk. Belvedere Av. LS11: Leeds ... 5F **41** *(off Harlech Rd.)*
Bk. Bentley Av. LS6: Leeds ... 5D **20** *(off Bentley Mt.)*
Bk. Bentley Gro. LS6: Leeds ... 5D **20** *(off Bentley Mt.)*
Bk. Berkeley Av. LS8: Leeds ... 2C **32** *(off Berkeley Rd.)*
Bk. Berkeley Ter. LS8: Leeds ... 2C **32** *(off Berkeley Rd.)*
Bk. Blenheim Av. LS2: Leeds ... 3F **31**
Bk. Blenheim Ter. LS2: Leeds ... 3F **31**
Bk. Boundary Ter. LS3: Leeds ... 4C **30** *(off Woodsley Rd.)*
Bk. Branch Pl. LS12: Leeds ... 3G **39** *(off Branch Rd.)*
Bk. Breary Av. LS18: Hors ... 2D **18**
Bk. Breary Ter. LS18: Hors ... 2D **18** *(off Breary Av.)*
Bk. Bright St. LS28: Stan ... 3H **27**
Bk. Broad La. LS13: Leeds ... 1D **28**
Bk. Broomfield Cres. LS6: Leeds ... 1B **30**
Bk. Broomfield Pl. LS6: Leeds ... 2B **30** *(off Newport Rd.)*
Bk. Broomfield Rd. LS6: Leeds ... 2B **30** *(off Newport Rd.)*
Bk. Broughton Av. LS9: Leeds ... 3C **32** *(off Foundry App.)*
Bk. Broughton Ter. LS9: Leeds ... 3C **32** *(off Foundry App.)*
Bk. Brudenell Gro. LS6: Leeds ... 2D **30** *(off Royal Pk. Rd.)*
Bk. Brudenell Mt. LS6: Leeds ... 2C **30** *(off Royal Pk. Rd.)*
Bk. Brudenell Rd. LS6: Leeds ... 2C **30** *(off Thornville Rd.)*
Bk. Brunswick St. LS2: Leeds ... 2F **5** (4G **31**)
Bk. Burchett Gro. LS6: Leeds ... 1E **31** *(off Hartley Av.)*
Bk. Burchett Pl. LS6: Leeds ... 1E **31** *(off Hartley Av.)*
Bk. Burley Hill LS4: Leeds ... 3A **30**
Bk. Burley Lodge Rd. LS6: Leeds ... 3C **30** *(off Chiswick St.)*
Bk. Burley Lodge Ter. LS6: Leeds ... 4C **30** *(off Burley Lodge Ter.)*
Bk. Burley St. LS3: Leeds .. 3A **4** (5E **31**) *(off Burley St.)*
Bk. Burlington Pl. LS11: Leeds ... 5F **41** *(off Tempest Rd.)*
Bk. Burlington Rd. LS11: Leeds ... 5F **41** *(off Harlech Av.)*
Bk. Burton Cres. LS6: Leeds ... 5B **20**
Bk. Burton Ter. LS11: Leeds ... 4G **41**
Bk. Camberley St. LS11: Leeds ... 4F **41** *(off Camberley St.)*
Bk. Carberry Pl. LS6: Leeds ... 3C **30** *(off Carberry Rd.)*
Bk. Carberry Rd. LS6: Leeds ... 3C **30** *(off Chiswick St.)*
Bk. Carberry Ter. LS6: Leeds ... 3C **30** *(off Carberry Rd.)*
Bk. Carter Mt. LS15: Leeds ... 5C **34** *(off Carter La.)*
Bk. Carter Ter. LS15: Leeds ... 4C **34** *(off Carter La.)*
Bk. Chapel La. LS6: Leeds ... 1B **30** *(off Broomfield Rd.)*
Bk. Charlton Rd. LS9: Leeds ... 6C **32**
Bk. Chatsworth Rd. LS8: Leeds ... 2C **32** *(off Harehills La.)*
Bk. Chestnut Av. LS15: Leeds ... 3D **34** *(off Railway Rd.)*
Bk. Chiswick Ter. LS6: Leeds ... 3C **30** *(off Carberry Rd.)*
Bk. Christ Chu. Vw. LS12: Leeds. 5H **29** *(off Stanningley Rd.)*
Bk. Church La. LS16: Leeds ... 4B **12**
Bk. Church La. LS5: Leeds ... 1G **29** *(off Hesketh Rd.)*
Bk. Claremont Av. LS3: Leeds ... 2A **4** (4E **31**) *(off Woodhouse Sq.)*
Bk. Claremont Gro. LS3: Leeds ... 2A **4** (4E **31**) *(off Woodhouse Sq.)*
Bk. Claremont St. LS26: Oult ... 3C **54**
Bk. Claremont Ter. LS3: Leeds ... 2A **4** (4E **31**) *(off Kendal La.)*
Bk. Clarence Rd. LS18: Hors ... 4B **18**
Bk. Clarence St. LS13: Leeds ... 4C **28**
Bk. Clarkson Vw. LS6: Leeds ... 1E **31** *(off Quarry St.)*
Bk. Cliff Mt. LS6: Leeds ... 1E **31** *(off Cliff Mt. Ter.)*
Bk. Clifton Ter. LS9: Leeds ... 3D **32** *(off Clifton Av.)*
Bk. Clipston Av. LS6: Leeds ... 5D **20** *(off Clipston Av.)*
Bk. Clovelly Pl. LS11: Leeds ... 4F **41** *(off Rowland Rd.)*
Bk. Colenso Mt. LS11: Leeds ... 3D **40** *(off Cleveleys Av.)*
Bk. Colenso Rd. LS11: Leeds ... 3D **40** *(off Cleveleys Av.)*
Bk. Colton Rd. LS12: Leeds ... 6A **30**
Bk. Colwyn Vw. LS11: Leeds ... 5F **41** *(off Colwyn Av.)*
Bk. Conway St. LS8: Leeds ... 2B **32** *(off Harehills Rd.)*
Bk. Cowper Gro. LS9: Leeds ... 2C **32** *(off Ashley Rd.)*
Bk. Cowper St. LS7: Leeds ... 2A **32** *(off Cross Cowper St.)*
Bk. Craggwood Rd. LS18: Hors ... 4C **18**
Bk. Cranbrook Av. LS11: Leeds ... 4E **41** *(off Wickham St.)*
Bk. Cranbrook Ter. LS11: Leeds ... 4E **41** *(off Hird St.)*
Bk. Cromer Ter. LS2: Leeds ... 1B **4** (3E **31**)
Bk. Cross Flatts Av. LS11: Leeds ... 5E **41** *(off Theodore St.)*
Bk. Cross Flatts Cres. LS11: Leeds ... 5D **40** *(off Wooler St.)*
Bk. Cross Flatts Gro. LS11: Leeds ... 5E **41** *(off Wooler Dr.)*
Bk. Cross Flatts Mt. LS11: Leeds ... 5E **41** *(off Wooler Gro.)*
Bk. Cross Flatts Pl. LS11: Leeds ... 5D **40** *(off Wooler St.)*
Bk. Cross Flatts Row LS11: Leeds ... 5D **40** *(off Wooler St.)*
Bk. Cross Grn. Cres. LS9: Leeds .. 1B **42** *(off Cross Grn. La.)*
Bk. Cross Grn. La. LS9: Leeds ... 1B **42** *(off Cross Grn. Rd.)*
Bk. Dalton Gro. LS11: Leeds ... 5E **41** *(off Cross Flatts Av.)*
Bk. Dalton Rd. LS11: Leeds ... 5E **41**
Bk. Dawlish Av. LS9: Leeds ... 5D **32** *(off Ivy Av.)*
Bk. Dawlish Mt. LS9: Leeds ... 5D **32** *(off Ivy Av.)*
Bk. Dawlish Rd. LS9: Leeds ... 5D **32** *(off Dawlish Cres.)*
Bk. De Lacy Mt. LS5: Leeds ... 6G **19** *(off Morris La.)*
Bk. Delph Mt. LS6: Leeds ... 1E **31** *(off Delph La.)*
Bk. Dent St. LS9: Leeds ... 6B **32** *(off Kippax Mt.)*
Bk. Devonshire La. LS8: Leeds ... 1C **22**
Bk. Dewsbury Dr. LS11: Leeds ... 5G **41** *(off Dewsbury Rd.)*
Bk. Dorset Mt. LS8: Leeds ... 1C **32** *(off Dorset St.)*
Bk. Dorset Rd. LS8: Leeds ... 1C **32** *(off Dorset Av.)*
Bk. Dorset Ter. LS8: Leeds ... 2C **32** *(off Harehills La.)*
Bk. East Pk. Rd. LS9: Leeds ... 6C **32** *(off Garton Rd.)*
Bk. Ecclesburn Gro. LS9: Leeds .. 6D **32** *(off Ivy St.)*
Bk. Ecclesburn St. LS9: Leeds ... 6C **32** *(off Park Pde.)*
Bk. Edinburgh Rd. LS12: Leeds .. 5G **29** *(off Moorfield Rd.)*
Bk. Elford Pl. LS8: Leeds ... 2B **32** *(off Roundhay Rd.)*
Bk. Ellers Gro. LS8: Leeds ... 1B **32** *(off Ellers Gro.)*
Bk. Ellers Rd. LS8: Leeds ... 1B **32** *(off Ellers Rd.)*
Bk. Elsworth St. LS12: Leeds ... 6B **30**
Bk. Eric St. LS13: Leeds ... 6C **18**
Bk. Eshald Pl. LS26: W'frd ... 3D **54**
Bk. Esmond Ter. LS12: Leeds ... 6A **30**
Bk. Estcourt Av. LS6: Leeds ... 6A **20** *(off Canterbury Dr.)*
Bk. Estcourt Ter. LS6: Leeds ... 1A **30** *(off Canterbury Dr.)*
Bk. Fairford Pl. LS11: Leeds ... 4G **41**
Bk. Featherbank Ter. LS18: Hors ... 4B **18**
Bk. Garton Rd. LS9: Leeds ... 6C **32** *(off East Pk. Rd.)*
Bk. Garton Ter. LS9: Leeds ... 6C **32** *(off East Pk. Pde.)*
Bk. Gathorne St. LS7: Leeds ... 2A **32** *(off Gathorne St.)*
Bk. Gillett La. LS26: Rothw ... 4H **53**
Bk. Glebe Ter. LS16: Leeds ... 5B **20** *(off Weetwood La.)*
Bk. Glenthorpe Ter. LS9: Leeds ... 5C **32** *(off Walford Rd.)*

A-Z Leeds 63

Bk. Glossop St. LS6: Leeds ... 1F **31** *(off Elm St.)*
Bk. Gordon Ter. LS6: Leeds ... 5D **20** *(off Gordon Vw.)*
Bk. Graham Gro. LS4: Leeds ... 2B **30**
Bk. Granby Gro. LS6: Leeds ... 1B **30** *(off Granby Rd.)*
Bk. Grange Av. LS7: Leeds ... 1H **31** *(off Grange Av.)*
Bk. Grange Cres. LS7: Leeds ... 1A **32** *(off Hamilton Ter.)*
Bk. Grange Ter. LS7: Leeds ... 1H **31** *(off Nassau Pl.)*
Bk. Grange Vw. LS7: Leeds ... 1A **32** *(off Nassau Pl.)*
Bk. Graveley St. LS15: Leeds ... 5A **34** *(off Primrose La.)*
Back Grn. LS27: Chur ... 2A **50**
Bk. Greenhow Wlk. LS4: Leeds ... 3B **30** *(off Greenhow Wlk.)*
Bk. Greenmount Ter. LS11: Leeds ... 4F **41** *(off Greenmount La.)*
Bk. Grosvenor Ter. LS6: Leeds ... 1D **30** *(off Cliff La.)*
Bk. Grove Gdns. LS6: Leeds ... 5C **20** *(off Grove Av.)*
Bk. Grovehall Av. LS11: Leeds ... 6E **41**
Bk. Grovehall Dr. LS11: Leeds ... 6E **41**
Bk. Haigh Av. LS26: Rothw ... 2E **53**
Bk. Haigh St. LS26: Rothw ... 2E **53**
Bk. Haigh Vw. LS26: Rothw ... 2E **53**
Bk. Halliday Gro. LS12: Leeds ... 5G **29**
Bk. Halliday Pl. LS12: Leeds ... 5G **29**
Bk. Hamilton Av. LS7: Leeds ... 1A **32** *(off Nassau Pl.)*
Bk. Hamilton Vw. LS7: Leeds ... 1A **32** *(off Hamilton Ter.)*
Bk. Harehills Av. LS7: Leeds ... 1A **32** *(off Nassau Pl.)*
Bk. Harehills Pk. Vw. LS9: Leeds ... 3D **32** *(off Foundry App.)*
Bk. Harehills Pl. LS8: Leeds ... 2B **32** *(off Harehills Pl.)*
Bk. Harehills Rd. LS8: Leeds ... 2B **32** *(off Harehills Pl.)*
Bk. Hares Av. LS8: Leeds ... 1B **32** *(off Hares Av.)*
Bk. Hares Mt. LS8: Leeds ... 1A **32** *(off Hares Rd.)*
Bk. Hares Ter. LS8: Leeds ... 1B **32** *(off Hares Ter.)*
Bk. Hares Vw. LS8: Leeds ... 1A **32** *(off Hares Rd.)*
Bk. Harold Gro. LS6: Leeds ... 3C **30** *(off Cardigan Rd.)*
Bk. Hartley Av. LS6: Leeds ... 1F **31** *(off Burchett Ter.)*
Bk. Hartley Gro. LS6: Leeds ... 1E **31** *(off Glossop Vw.)*
Bk. Hartley St. LS27: Morl ... 6A **50**
Bk. Hawksworth Gro. LS5: Leeds ... 5D **18**
Bk. Headingley Av. LS6: Leeds ... 6A **20** *(off Canterbury Dr.)*
Bk. Headingley Mt. LS6: Leeds ... 6A **20** *(off Canterbury Dr.)*
Bk. Heathfield Ter. LS6: Leeds ... 5B **20** *(off Heathfield Ter.)*
Bk. Heathfield Ter. LS6: Leeds ... 5B **20** *(off Heathfield Terrace)*
Bk. Heddon St. LS6: Leeds ... 5C **20** *(off Brookfield Rd.)*
Bk. Hessle Av. LS6: Leeds ... 2C **30** *(off Walmsley Rd.)*
Bk. Hessle Mt. LS6: Leeds ... 2C **30** *(off Brundenell Rd.)*
Bk. Hessle Ter. LS6: Leeds ... 2C **30** *(off Walmsley Rd.)*
Bk. Hessle Vw. LS6: Leeds ... 2C **30** *(off Welton Rd.)*
Bk. Highbury Ter. LS6: Leeds ... 5C **20** *(off Highbury Mt.)*
Bk. Highfield Rd. LS13: Leeds ... 3D **28** *(off Aston Mt.)*
Bk. High St. LS19: Yead ... 2D **8**
Bk. Highthorne Gro. LS12: Leeds ... 5G **29** *(off Highthorne St.)*
Bk. Highthorne St. LS12: Leeds ... 5G **29** *(off Armley Ridge Rd.)*
Bk. Hillcrest Av. LS7: Leeds ... 1A **32** *(off Grange Av.)*
Bk. Hillcrest Vw. LS7: Leeds ... 1A **32** *(off Hillcrest Pl.)*
Bk. Hilltop Av. LS8: Leeds ... 1B **32** *(off Shepherd's La.)*
Bk. Hill Top Mt. LS8: Leeds ... 1B **32** *(off Hill Top Mt.)*
Bk. Hilton Pl. LS8: Leeds ... 1B **32** *(off Hilton Pl.)*
Bk. Hilton Rd. LS8: Leeds ... 1B **32** *(off Avenue Cres.)*
Bk. Hollyshaw Ter. LS15: Leeds ... 5C **34**
Bk. Holywell La. LS17: Shad ... 4F **15**
Backhouse Yd. LS14: Leeds ... 1B **34**
Bk. Hovingham Gro. LS8: Leeds ... 1C **32** *(off Sandhurst Mt.)*
Bk. Hovingham Mt. LS8: Leeds ... 1C **32** *(off Dorset Av.)*
Bk. Hovingham Ter. LS8: Leeds ... 1C **32** *(off Dorset Av.)*
Bk. Hyde Ter. LS2: Leeds ... 1A **4** (4E **31**)
Bk. Ibbetson Pl. LS1: Leeds ... 1C **4** (4F **31**) *(off Fenton St.)*
Bk. Ingledew Cres. LS8: Leeds ... 1D **22**
Bk. Ivy Av. LS9: Leeds ... 5C **32** *(off Ivy Av.)*
Bk. Ivy Gro. LS9: Leeds ... 6D **32** *(off Victoria Av.)*
Bk. Ivy Mt. LS9: Leeds ... 5C **32** *(off Ivy Vw.)*
Bk. Ivy St. LS9: Leeds ... 5C **32** *(off Ivy Av.)*
Bk. Karnac Rd. LS8: Leeds ... 1B **32** *(off Nice St.)*
Bk. Kelso Rd. LS2: Leeds ... 1A **4** (3D **30**)
Bk. Kendal La. LS3: Leeds ... 2A **4** (4E **31**) *(off Kendal Rd.)*
Bk. Kennerleigh Wlk. LS15: Leeds ... 4C **34** *(off Kingswear Pde.)*
Bk. Kensington Ter. LS6: Leeds ... 2D **30**
Bk. Kings Av. LS6: Leeds ... 3C **30** *(off Alexandra Rd.)*
Bk. Kitson St. LS9: Leeds ... 6B **32** *(off Kippax Mt.)*
Bk. Knowle Mt. LS4: Leeds ... 2B **30** *(off Stanmore Hill)*
Bk. Lake St. LS10: Leeds ... 5H **41**
Bk. Lambton Gro. LS8: Leeds ... 1B **32** *(off Lambton Gro.)*
Bk. Landseer Av. LS13: Leeds ... 2E **29** *(off Victoria Pk. Av.)*
Bk. Landseer Gro. LS13: Leeds ... 2E **29** *(off Victoria Pk. Av.)*
Bk. Landseer Ter. LS13: Leeds ... 2E **29** *(off Victoria Pk. Av.)*
Back La. BD11: Drig ... 2H **47**
Back La. LS11: Leeds ... 6D **40**
Back La. LS12: N Far ... 5C **38**
Back La. LS13: Leeds ... 4D **28**
Back La. LS18: Hors ... 3B **18**
Back La. LS19: Yead ... 3C **8**
Back La. LS20: Guis ... 4E **7**
Back La. LS28: Fars ... 2F **27**
Back La. WF3: Loft ... 2E **59**
Bk. Langdale Gdns. LS6: Leeds ... 1A **30** *(off Canterbury Dr.)*
Bk. Langdale Ter. LS6: Leeds ... 1A **30** *(off Canterbury Dr.)*
Bk. Laurel Mt. LS7: Leeds ... 6H **21**
Bk. Linden Gro. LS11: Leeds ... 4G **41** *(off Linden Gro.)*
Bk. Lodge La. LS11: Leeds ... 5F **41** *(off Stratford Ter.)*
Bk. Lombard St. LS19: Raw ... 5C **8**
Bk. Longroyd Ter. LS11: Leeds ... 4G **41** *(off Burton Av.)*
Bk. Low La. LS18: Hors ... 2D **18** *(off Bk. Breary Av.)*
Bk. Lucas St. LS6: Leeds ... 1E **31** *(off Delph La.)*
Bk. Lunan Pl. LS8: Leeds ... 1B **32** *(off Lunan Pl.)*
Bk. Lunan Ter. LS8: Leeds ... 1B **32** *(off Lunan Ter.)*
Bk. Mafeking Av. LS11: Leeds ... 6E **41** *(off Dewsbury Rd.)*
Bk. Mafeking Mt. LS11: Leeds ... 6E **41**
Bk. Manor Dr. LS6: Leeds ... 1C **30** *(off Manor Av.)*
Bk. Manor Gro. LS7: Leeds ... 5H **21** *(off St Martin's Dr.)*
Bk. Markham Av. LS8: Leeds ... 1B **32** *(off Markham Av.)*
Bk. Marshall Av. LS15: Leeds ... 3D **34** *(off Railway Rd.)*
Bk. Marshall St. LS15: Leeds ... 3C **34** *(off Austhorpe Rd.)*
Bk. Marshall Ter. LS15: Leeds ... 3C **34** *(off Railway Rd.)*
Bk. Mary St. WF3: E Ard ... 3A **58**
Bk. Masham St. LS12: Leeds ... 6B **30** *(off Bk. Middle Cross St.)*
Bk. Maud Av. LS11: Leeds ... 5F **41** *(off Maud Pl.)*
Bk. Mayville Av. LS6: Leeds ... 2C **30** *(off Mayville Rd.)*
Bk. Mayville Pl. LS6: Leeds ... 2C **30** *(off Cardigan La.)*
Bk. Mayville St. LS6: Leeds ... 2C **30** *(off Mayville St.)*
Bk. Mayville Ter. LS6: Leeds ... 2C **30** *(off Mayville Rd.)*
Bk. Meadow Vw. LS6: Leeds ... 2C **30** *(off Brundenell Rd.)*
Bk. Melbourne Gro. LS13: Leeds ... 3C **28** *(off Hough La.)*
Bk. Methley Dr. LS7: Leeds ... 5H **21**
Bk. Mexborough Av. LS7: Leeds ... 1H **31** *(off Savile Av.)*
Bk. Mexborough Dr. LS7: Leeds ... 1H **31** *(off Savile Av.)*
Bk. Mexborough Gro. LS7: Leeds ... 1H **31** *(off Savile Av.)*
Bk. Mexborough St. LS7: Leeds ... 1H **31** *(off Savile Av.)*
Bk. Meynell Av. LS26: Rothw ... 4G **53**
Bk. Middle Cross St. LS12: Leeds ... 6B **30**
Bk. Middleton Vw. LS11: Leeds ... 4E **41**
Bk. Midland Rd. LS6: Leeds ... 2D **30** *(off Hyde Pk. Ter.)*
Bk. Milan Av. LS8: Leeds ... 2B **32** *(off Milan Rd.)*
Bk. Milan Rd. LS8: Leeds ... 2B **32** *(off Harehills Rd.)*
Bk. Milan St. LS8: Leeds ... 2C **32** *(off Harehills La.)*
Bk. Mitford Rd. LS12: Leeds ... 6B **30**
Bk. Model Rd. LS12: Leeds ... 6B **30**
Bk. Model Ter. LS12: Leeds ... 6B **30**
Bk. Model Vw. LS12: Leeds ... 6B **30**
Bk. Monk Bri. Dr. LS6: Leeds ... 5D **20** *(off Bentley Mt.)*
Bk. Monk Bri. St. LS6: Leeds ... 5D **20** *(off Monk Bri. St.)*
Bk. Montpelier Ter. LS6: Leeds ... 1E **31** *(off Cliff Rd.)*
Bk. Moorfield Ter. LS12: Leeds ... 5G **29**
Bk. Moorland Ter. LS2: Leeds ... 3E **31**
Bk. Morritt Dr. LS15: Leeds ... 5H **33**
Bk. Mount Pleasant LS10: Leeds ... 4G **51**
Bk. Mount Vw. LS6: Leeds ... 1D **30** *(off Regent Pk. Ter.)*
Bk. Nansen St. LS13: Leeds ... 3A **28** *(off Fairfield Av.)*
Bk. Newport Gdns. LS6: Leeds ... 2B **30** *(off Newport Rd.)*
Bk. Newport Mt. LS6: Leeds ... 2B **30** *(off Newport Rd.)*
Bk. Newport Pl. LS6: Leeds ... 2B **30** *(off Newport Rd.)*
Bk. Newton Gro. LS7: Leeds ... 1H **31**
Bk. New York St. LS2: Leeds ... 5G **5** (6H **31**)
Bk. Nice Vw. LS8: Leeds ... 1B **32** *(off Nice Vw.)*
Bk. Norman Mt. LS5: Leeds ... 1G **29** *(off Morris La.)*
Bk. Norman Pl. LS8: Leeds ... 1C **22** *(off Norton Rd.)*
Bk. Norman Ter. LS8: Leeds ... 1C **22** *(off Norton Rd.)*
Bk. Northbrook St. LS7: Leeds ... 4H **21** *(off Northbrook St.)*
Bk. North Pk. Av. LS8: Leeds ... 3B **22**
Bk. Norwood Gro. LS6: Leeds ... 2C **30** *(off Norwood Mt.)*
Bk. Norwood Pl. LS6: Leeds ... 2C **30** *(off Norwood Mt.)*
Bk. Norwood Rd. LS6: Leeds ... 2C **30** *(off Norwood Vw.)*
Bk. Norwood Ter. LS6: Leeds ... 2C **30**
Bk. Nowell Cres. LS9: Leeds ... 4D **32** *(off Harehills La.)*
Bk. Nowell Mt. LS9: Leeds ... 4D **32** *(off Harehills La.)*
Bk. Nowell Pl. LS9: Leeds ... 4D **32** *(off Harehills La.)*
Bk. Nowell Ter. LS9: Leeds ... 4D **32** *(off Harehills La.)*
Bk. Nunington St. LS12: Leeds ... 5B **30** *(off Armley Pk. Rd.)*
Bk. Nunington Vw. LS12: Leeds ... 4A **30** *(off Nunnington Vw.)*
Bk. Nunroyd Rd. LS17: Leeds ... 2H **21** *(off Nunroyd Ter.)*
Bk. Nursery Mt. LS10: Leeds ... 6A **42** *(off Woodville Mt.)*
Bk. Oakfield Ter. LS6: Leeds ... 5C **20** *(off Brookfield Rd.)*
Bk. Oakley St. WF3: Thpe H ... 2A **58**
Bk. Oakley Ter. LS11: Leeds ... 5G **41** *(off Garnet Rd.)*
Bk. Oak Rd. LS7: Leeds ... 6H **21** *(off St Mary's Rd.)*
Bk. Oakwood Av. LS8: Leeds ... 5D **22** *(off Oakwood Av.)*
Bk. Oakwood Dr. LS8: Leeds ... 5D **22** *(off Oakwood Boundary Rd.)*
Bk. Osmondthorpe La. LS9: Leeds ... 5E **33** *(off Cross Osmondthorpe La.)*
Bk. Outwood La. LS18: Hors ... 4C **18**
Bk. Overdale Ter. LS15: Leeds ... 5A **34** *(off Cross St.)*
Bk. Oxford Pl. LS1: Leeds ... 3C **4** (5F **31**) *(off Oxford Row)*
Bk. Oxford St. WF3: E Ard ... 3A **58**
Bk. Park Cres. LS8: Leeds ... 1D **22**
Bk. Parkfield Pl. LS11: Leeds ... 4E **41** *(off Parkfield Row)*
Bk. Parkfield Rd. LS11: Leeds ... 4E **41** *(off Parkfield Row)*
Bk. Park Vw. LS11: Leeds ... 4E **41** *(off Dawson Rd.)*
Bk. Park Vw. Av. LS4: Leeds ... 2B **30**
Bk. Parkville Rd. LS13: Leeds ... 2C **28**

Barden Gro. – Belle Isle Cir.

Barden Gro. LS12: Leeds 6G **29**
Barden Ho. LS29: Men 3C **6**
Barden Mt. LS12: Leeds 6G **29**
Barden Pl. LS12: Leeds 6G **29**
Barden Ter. LS12: Leeds 6G **29**
Bardon Hall Gdns. LS16: Leeds 3A **20**
Bardon Hall M. LS16: Leeds 3A **20**
Bardwell Ct. WF3: Stly 6G **59**
Barfield Av. LS19: Yead 3C **8**
Barfield Cres. LS17: Leeds 4B **14**
Barfield Dr. LS19: Yead 3C **8**
Barfield Gro. LS17: Leeds 4C **14**
Barfield Mt. LS17: Leeds 4C **14**
Barham Ter. BD10: B'ford 1A **26**
Barker Hill LS12: Gil 6B **38**
Barker Pl. LS13: Leeds 4D **28**
Barkers Well Fold LS12: N Far 4D **38**
Barkers Well Gth. LS12: N Far 4E **39**
Barkers Well Ga. LS12: N Far 4E **39**
Barkers Well Lawn LS12: N Far 4E **39**
Barkly Av. LS11: Leeds 6E **41**
Barkly Dr. LS11: Leeds 6E **41**
Barkly Gro. LS11: Leeds 5E **41**
Barkly Pde. LS11: Leeds 6E **41**
Barkly Pl. LS11: Leeds 6E **41**
Barkly Rd. LS11: Leeds 5D **40**
Barkly St. LS11: Leeds 6E **41**
Barkly Ter. LS11: Leeds 6E **41**
Bar La. LS18: Hors 3G **17**
Barlby Way LS8: Leeds 5E **23**
Barleycorn Yd. LS12: Leeds 6H **29**
Barley Fld. Ct. LS15: Leeds 5A **34**
Barley Grange LS15: B Elm 5H **25**
Barley M. WF3: Rob H 6D **52**
Barnard Cl. LS15: Leeds 2E **35**
Barnard Way LS15: Leeds 2E **35**
BARNBOW CARR 6H **25**
Barnbow La. LS15: Leeds 1H **35**
Barnbrough St. LS4: Leeds 3A **30**
Barn Cl. LS29: Men 1B **6**
Barncroft Cl. LS14: Leeds 4H **23**
Barncroft Ct. LS14: Leeds 5G **23**
Barncroft Dr. LS14: Leeds 5G **23**
Barncroft Gdns. LS14: Leeds 5H **23**
Barncroft Grange LS14: Leeds 5G **23**
Barncroft Hgts. LS14: Leeds 4G **23**
Barncroft Mt. LS14: Leeds 5G **23**
Barncroft Ri. LS14: Leeds 5H **23**
Barncroft Rd. LS14: Leeds 5H **23**
Barncroft Towers LS14: Leeds 5G **23**
Barn Emsley's Farm, The 4C **8**
Barnet Gro. LS27: Morl 6G **49**
Barnet Rd. LS12: Leeds 6A **30**
Barnstaple Way BD4: B'ford 5A **36**
Barnswick Vw. LS16: Leeds 5E **11**
Baron Cl. LS11: Leeds 3E **41**
Baronscourt LS15: Leeds 5D **34**
Baronsmead LS15: Leeds 5C **34**
Baronsway LS15: Leeds 5C **34**
Barrack Rd. LS7: Leeds 2H **31**
Barrack St. LS7: Leeds 3G **31**
Barraclough Bldgs. BD10: B'ford 4A **16**
Barraclough Yd. LS26: Rothw 4G **53**
Barran Ct. LS8: Leeds 2B **32**
Barras Fold LS12: Leeds 1H **39**
Barras Gth. Ind. Est. LS12: Leeds 1H **39**
Barras Gth. Pl. LS12: Leeds 1H **39**
Barras Gth. Rd. LS12: Leeds 1H **39**
Barras Pl. LS12: Leeds 1H **39**
Barras St. LS12: Leeds 1H **39**
Barras Ter. LS12: Leeds 1H **39**
Barrington Gdns. LS15: Leeds 4F **35**
Barrington Gro. LS15: Leeds 4F **35**
Barrington Way LS15: Leeds 4F **35**
BARROWBY 5H **35**
Barrowby Av. LS15: Leeds 6E **35**
Barrowby Carr Dr. LS15: Gar 5G **35**
Barrowby Cl. LS29: Men 1D **6**
Barrowby Cres. LS15: Leeds 5E **35**
Barrowby Dr. LS15: Leeds 6F **35**
Barrowby Gdns. LS15: Leeds 5F **35**
Barrowby La. LS15: Leeds 5E **35**
Barrowby La. LS25: Gar 5G **35**
Barrowby La. LS25: Leeds 5G **35**
Barrowby Rd. LS15: Leeds 6F **35**
Barthorpe Av. LS17: Leeds 3F **21**
Barthorpe Cl. BD4: B'ford 5B **36**
Barthorpe Cres. LS17: Leeds 3G **21**
Barton Ct. LS15: Leeds 6C **34**
Barton Gro. LS11: Leeds 3E **41**
Barton Hill LS11: Leeds 3E **41**
Barton Mt. LS11: Leeds 3E **41**
Barton Pl. LS11: Leeds 3E **41**
Barton Rd. LS11: Leeds 3E **41**
Barton Ter. LS11: Leeds 3E **41**
Barton Vw. LS11: Leeds 3E **41**
Barton Way LS27: Morl 6E **49**
Barwick Ct. LS27: Morl 4H **49**
Barwick Rd. LS15: Leeds 2B **34**
Basilica LS1: Leeds 4E **5** (5G **31**)
(off King Charles St.)
Batcliffe Dr. LS6: Leeds 5A **20**
Batcliffe Mt. LS6: Leeds 6A **20**
Bateson St. BD10: B'ford 4A **16**
Bath Cl. LS13: Leeds 3C **28**
Bath Gro. LS13: Leeds 3C **28**
Bath La. LS13: Leeds 4C **28**
Bath Rd. LS11: Leeds 1E **41**
Bath Rd. LS13: Leeds 4C **28**
Batley Rd. WF3: W Ard 5B **56**
Batter La. LS19: Raw 5E **9**
Battlefield Vw. BD11: B'haw 2D **46**
BAWN 2F **39**
Bawn App. LS12: Leeds 2E **39**
Bawn Av. LS12: Leeds 1E **39**
Bawn Chase LS12: Leeds 1E **39**
Bawn Dr. LS12: Leeds 1E **39**
Bawn Gdns. LS12: Leeds 1E **39**
Bawn La. LS12: Leeds 1E **39**
Bawn Path LS12: Leeds 1F **39**
(off Bawn Av.)
Bawn Va. LS12: Leeds 1E **39**
(off Bawn Gdns.)
Bawn Wlk. LS12: Leeds 1F **39**
(off Bawn Gdns.)
Baxendale Dr. LS13: Leeds 5B **18**
Bay Horse La. LS14: S'cft 2H **15**
Bay Horse La. LS17: Leeds 2H **15**
Bay Horse La. LS17: S'cft 2H **15**
Bay Horse Yd. LS1: Leeds 4F **5** (5G **31**)
(off Briggate)
Bay Horse Yd. LS28: Fars 2F **27**
Bayonne LS20: Guis 4F **7**
(off Silver Cross Way)
Bayswater Cres. LS8: Leeds 2B **32**
Bayswater Gro. LS8: Leeds 2B **32**
Bayswater Mt. LS8: Leeds 2B **32**
Bayswater Pl. LS8: Leeds 2B **32**
Bayswater Rd. LS8: Leeds 2A **32**
Bayswater Row LS8: Leeds 2B **32**
Bayswater Ter. LS8: Leeds 2B **32**
Bayswater Vw. LS8: Leeds 2B **32**
Bayton La. LS18: Hors 4G **9**
Bayton La. LS19: Hors 3F **9**
Bayton La. LS19: Yead 3F **9**
Beacon Av. LS27: Morl 1A **56**
Beacon Gro. LS27: Morl 1A **56**
Beacon Vw. LS27: Morl 1A **56**
(off Tingley Comn.)
Beamsley Cl. LS29: Men 2C **6**
Beamsley Ct. LS29: Men 3C **6**
Beamsley Cft. LS29: Men 3C **6**
Beamsley Gro. LS6: Leeds 3C **30**
Beamsley Mt. LS6: Leeds 3C **30**
Beamsley Pl. LS6: Leeds 3C **30**
Beamsley Ter. LS6: Leeds 3C **30**
Beamsley Wlk. LS29: Men 2C **6**
Bearing Av. LS11: Leeds 5G **41**
Bear Pit Gdns. LS6: Leeds 2B **30**
(off Chapel La.)
Beaumont Av. LS8: Leeds 1C **22**
Beaumont Cl. WF3: Stly 6H **59**
Beaumont Sq. LS28: Pud 1F **37**
Beaumont St. WF3: Stly 6H **59**
Beck Bottom LS28: Cal 5A **16**
Beck Bottom LS28: Fars 1G **27**
Beckbury Cl. LS28: Fars 3F **27**
Beckbury St. LS28: Fars 3F **27**
Beckers Av. WF17: Birs 6B **48**
Becket La. WF3: Loft 1D **58**
Beckett Ct. LS15: Leeds 1D **44**
BECKETT PK. 5B **20**
Becketts, The LS6: Leeds 5D **20**
(off Monk Bri. Rd.)
Beckett's Pk. Cres. LS6: Leeds 6A **20**
Beckett's Pk. Dr. LS6: Leeds 6A **20**
Beckett's Pk. Rd. LS6: Leeds 6B **20**
Beckett St. LS9: Leeds 4A **32**
Beckhill App. LS7: Leeds 5E **21**
Beckhill Av. LS7: Leeds 5E **21**
Beckhill Chase LS7: Leeds 5E **21**
Beckhill Cl. LS7: Leeds 5E **21**
Beckhill Dr. LS7: Leeds 4E **21**
Beckhill Fold LS7: Leeds 4E **21**
Beckhill Gdns. LS7: Leeds 5E **21**
Beckhill Gth. LS7: Leeds 5E **21**
Beckhill Ga. LS7: Leeds 5E **21**
Beckhill Grn. LS7: Leeds 5E **21**
Beckhill Gro. LS7: Leeds 5E **21**
Beckhill Lawn LS7: Leeds 5E **21**
Beckhill Pl. LS7: Leeds 4E **21**
Beckhill Row LS7: Leeds 4E **21**
Beckhill Va. LS7: Leeds 4E **21**
Beckhill Vw. LS7: Leeds 5E **21**
Beckhill Wlk. LS7: Leeds 4E **21**
Beck Rd. LS8: Leeds 1B **32**
Beckside Gdns. LS16: Leeds 4B **20**
Beckside Vw. LS27: Morl 5A **50**
Beck Vw. LS26: Oult 4D **54**
Beck Way WF3: E Ard 3B **58**
Beckwith Dr. BD10: B'ford 6A **16**
Bedale LS29: Men 3C **6**
Bedale WF3: W Ard 3B **56**
Bedale Ct. LS27: Morl 5C **50**
Bedale Dr. LS27: Morl 5C **50**
Bedale St. LS27: Morl 5C **50**
Bedford Chambers LS1: Leeds 4D **4** (5F **31**)
(off Bedford St.)
Bedford Cl. LS16: Leeds 6E **11**
Bedford Ct. LS8: Leeds 5E **23**
Bedford Dr. LS16: Leeds 6E **11**
Bedford Fld. LS6: Leeds 1E **31**
Bedford Gdns. LS16: Leeds 6E **11**
Bedford Gth. LS16: Leeds 6E **11**
Bedford Grn. LS16: Leeds 6E **11**
Bedford Gro. LS16: Leeds 1E **19**
Bedford Mt. LS16: Leeds 1E **19**
(not continuous)
Bedford Pl. LS16: Leeds 6E **11**
Bedford Pl. LS20: Guis 5G **7**
(off Otley Rd.)
Bedford Row LS10: Leeds 3H **41**
Bedford St. LS1: Leeds 4D **4** (5F **31**)
Bedford Vw. LS16: Leeds 6E **11**
Beech Av. LS12: Leeds 5A **30**
Beech Av. LS18: Hors 4C **18**
Beech Av. LS8: Leeds 2E **33**
Beech Av. WF3: Stly 6H **59**
Beech Cl. LS16: Leeds 4A **12**
Beech Ct. LS14: Leeds 3G **33**
Beech Cres. LS9: Leeds 2F **33**
Beech Cft. WF3: Loft 2G **59**
Beechcroft Cl. LS11: Leeds 6B **40**
Beechcroft Mead LS17: Leeds 5C **14**
Beechcroft Vw. LS11: Leeds 6B **40**
Beech Dr. LS12: Leeds 5A **30**
Beech Dr. LS14: Leeds 3G **33**
Beech Dr. LS18: Hors 4B **18**
Beeches, The BD11: B'haw 4C **46**
Beeches, The LS20: Guis 3G **7**
Beeches, The LS28: Pud 5D **26**
Beechfield LS12: N Far 4D **38**
Beech Gro. LS26: Rothw 3H **53**
Beech Gro. LS27: Morl 6F **49**
Beech Gro. LS29: Men 2C **6**
Beech Gro. LS6: Leeds 5B **20**
Beech Gro. LS8: Leeds 2E **33**
Beech Gro. Gdns. LS26: Oult 4C **54**
Beech Gro. Ter. LS2: Leeds 3E **31**
Beech Ho. LS16: Leeds 3A **20**
Beech La. LS9: Leeds 2E **33**
Beech Lees LS28: Fars 1E **27**
Beech M. LS8: Leeds 2E **33**
Beech Mt. LS9: Leeds 2F **33**
Beech Ri. LS9: Leeds 2F **33**
Beechroyd LS28: Pud 1G **37**
Beech St. LS27: Morl 6F **49**
Beech St. WF3: Ting 2C **56**
Beech Tree Av. LS5: Leeds 2F **29**
Beech Wlk. BD11: B'haw 5D **46**
Beech Wlk. LS16: Leeds 1B **20**
Beech Wlk. LS9: Leeds 2F **33**
Beech Way LS14: Leeds 4C **24**
BEECHWOOD 5H **23**
BEECHWOOD 6B **10**
Beechwood LS26: W'frd 2C **54**
Beechwood Av. BD11: Drig 2F **47**
Beechwood Av. LS4: Leeds 2B **30**
Beechwood Cen. LS26: W'frd 2C **54**
(off Beechwood)
Beechwood Cl. LS17: Shad 5G **15**
Beechwood Cl. LS18: Hors 6A **10**
Beechwood Ct. LS14: Leeds 5G **23**
Beechwood Ct. LS16: Leeds 4H **11**
Beechwood Ct. LS4: Leeds 2B **30**
(off Beechwood Gro.)
Beechwood Cres. LS4: Leeds 2B **30**
Beechwood Gro. BD11: Drig 2F **47**
Beechwood Gro. LS4: Leeds 2B **30**
Beechwood Mt. LS4: Leeds 2B **30**
Beechwood Pl. LS4: Leeds 2B **30**
Beechwood Rd. LS4: Leeds 2B **30**
Beechwood Row LS4: Leeds 2B **30**
Beechwood St. LS28: Stan 4E **27**
Beechwood St. LS4: Leeds 2B **30**
Beechwood Ter. LS4: Leeds 2B **30**
Beechwood Vw. LS4: Leeds 2B **30**
Beechwood Wlk. LS4: Leeds 2B **30**
Beecroft Cl. LS13: Leeds 2A **28**
Beecroft Cres. LS13: Leeds 2B **28**
Beecroft Gdns. LS13: Leeds 2A **28**
Beecroft Mt. LS13: Leeds 2A **28**
Beecroft St. LS5: Leeds 2G **29**
BEESTON 6D **40**
BEESTON HILL 3E **41**
Beeston Pk. Cft. LS11: Leeds 5C **40**
Beeston Pk. Gth. LS11: Leeds 5C **40**
Beeston Pk. Gro. LS11: Leeds 5C **40**
Beeston Pk. Pl. LS11: Leeds 5C **40**
BEESTON PARK SIDE 1E **51**
Beeston Pk. Ter. LS11: Leeds 5C **40**
Beeston Rd. LS11: Leeds 5D **40**
BEESTON ROYDS 5H **39**
Beeston Royds Ind. Est. LS12: Leeds 4A **40**
Beevers Ct. LS16: Leeds 1G **19**
BEGGARINGTON HILL 5B **56**
Belford Cl. BD4: B'ford 4A **36**
Belford Ct. LS6: Leeds 2C **20**
Belfrey Cl. LS26: Rothw 5A **54**
Belfry, The LS19: Yead 3E **9**
Belfry Ct. WF1: Outw 6E **59**
Belfry Rd. LS9: Leeds 2C **42**
Belgrave M. LS19: Raw 5C **8**
Belgrave Retail Pk. 4G **27**
Belgrave St. LS2: Leeds 3E **5** (5G **31**)
Belgravia Gdns. LS8: Leeds 4E **23**
Belinda St. LS10: Leeds 3A **42**
Bellbrooke Av. LS9: Leeds 3D **32**
Bellbrooke Gro. LS9: Leeds 3D **32**
Bellbrooke Pl. LS9: Leeds 3D **32**
Bellbrooke St. LS9: Leeds 3C **32**
BELLE ISLE 1A **52**
Belle Isle Cir. LS10: Leeds 1A **52**

66 A-Z Leeds

Belle Isle Cl. – Boocock St.

Belle Isle Cl. LS10: Leeds............1A **52**
Belle Isle Pde. LS10: Leeds..........6A **42**
Belle Isle Rd. LS10: Leeds...........5A **42**
Belle Vue Av. LS15: Scho 4F **25**
Belle Vue Av. LS8: Leeds.............5F **23**
Belle Vue Ct. LS3: Leeds 4D **30**
.................................(off Consort Ter.)
Belle Vue Dr. LS28: Fars..............2E **27**
Belle Vue Est. LS15: Scho 5F **25**
Belle Vue Rd. LS15: Scho..............5F **25**
Belle Vue Rd. LS3: Leeds 4D **30**
Belle Vue Ter. LS20: Guis............... 5G **7**
Belle Vue Ter. LS27: Gil 3D **48**
Bell Gro. LS13: Leeds....................2C **28**
Bell La. LS13: Leeds.......................2C **28**
Bellmount Cl. LS13: Leeds........... 2D **28**
Bellmount Gdns. LS13: Leeds......1C **28**
Bellmount Grn. LS13: Leeds.......... 2D **28**
Bellmount Pl. LS13: Leeds............1C **28**
Bellmount Vw. LS13: Leeds 2D **28**
Bell Rd. LS13: Leeds 2C **28**
Bell St. LS9: Leeds 3H **5** (5H **31**)
Bell Wood Ct. LS28: Pud 1F **37**
BELL WOOD RDBT. 3G **43**
Belmont Gro. LS19: Raw 4E **9**
Belmont Gro. LS2: Leeds... 2B **4** (4E **31**)
Belmont Ter. WF3: Thpe H............1B **58**
Belvedere Av. LS11: Leeds.............5F **41**
Belvedere Av. LS17: Leeds.......... 5H **13**
Belvedere Ct. LS17: Leeds............5A **14**
Belvedere Ct. LS7: Leeds...............6A **22**
...............................(off Harehills La.)
Belvedere Ct. WF1: Outw 6E **59**
Belvedere Gdns. LS17: Leeds 5A **14**
Belvedere Gro. LS17: Leeds......... 5H **13**
Belvedere Mt. LS11: Leeds 5F **41**
Belvedere Rd. LS17: Leeds 5H **13**
Belvedere Ter. LS11: Leeds...........5F **41**
Belvedere Vw. LS17: Leeds..........5A **14**
Benbow Av. BD10: B'ford 6A **16**
Bennet Ct. LS15: Leeds 5D **34**
Bennett Rd. LS6: Leeds...................6B **20**
Bennetts Yd. LS26: Rothw............ 5G **53**
Benson Gdns. LS12: Leeds 1H **39**
Benson St. LS7: Leeds 1G **5** (3H **31**)
Bentcliffe Av. LS17: Leeds 1H **21**
Bentcliffe Cl. LS17: Leeds.............2A **22**
Bentcliffe Ct. LS17: Leeds.............2A **22**
Bentcliffe Dr. LS17: Leeds.............1A **22**
Bentcliffe Gdns. LS17: Leeds.......2A **22**
Bentcliffe Gro. LS17: Leeds...........2A **22**
Bentcliffe La. LS17: Leeds 2H **21**
Bentcliffe Mt. LS17: Leeds.............2A **22**
Bentley Ct. LS26: W'frd 2C **54**
Bentley Ct. LS7: Leeds 5D **20**
Bentley Gdns. LS7: Leeds 5D **20**
Bentley Gro. LS6: Leeds 5D **20**
Bentley La. LS26: Oult................. 4D **54**
Bentley La. LS6: Leeds.................. 5D **20**
Bentley La. LS7: Leeds.................. 5D **20**
Bentley M. LS6: Leeds................... 5D **20**
Bentley Mt. LS6: Leeds 5D **20**
Bentley Pde. LS6: Leeds............... 5D **20**
Bentley Sq. LS26: Oult...................4C **54**
Benton Pk. Av. LS19: Raw..............4E **9**
Benton Pk. Cres. LS19: Raw 4E **9**
Benton Pk. Dr. LS19: Raw 4E **9**
Benton Pk. Rd. LS19: Raw 4E **9**
Benyon Pk. Way LS12: Leeds.......3B **40**
Beringa LS12: Leeds 5A **4** (6E **31**)
Berkeley Av. LS8: Leeds.................2C **32**
Berkeley Ct. LS2: Leeds 1A **4** (4D **30**)
Berkeley Ct. LS8: Leeds 2C **32**
............................(off Chatsworth Rd.)
Berkeley Cres. LS8: Leeds 2C **32**
Berkeley Gro. LS8: Leeds...............2C **32**
Berkeley Ho. BD4: B'ford..............4A **36**
.................................(off Stirling Cres.)
Berkeley Mt. LS8: Leeds 2C **32**
Berkeley Rd. LS8: Leeds.................2C **32**
Berkeley St. LS8: Leeds.................2C **32**
Berkeley Ter. LS8: Leeds...............2C **32**
Berkeley Vw. LS8: Leeds................2C **32**
Berking Av. LS9: Leeds 5B **32**
Berking Row LS9: Leeds................5B **32**
Bernard St. LS26: W'frd 3D **54**
Bertha St. LS28: Fars 3F **27**
Bertrand St. LS11: Leeds 2E **41**
Bessbrook St. LS10: Leeds 4H **41**
Beulah Gro. LS6: Leeds 2F **31**
Beulah Mt. LS6: Leeds 2F **31**
Beulah St. LS6: Leeds 2F **31**
Beulah Ter. LS15: Leeds................3C **34**
...............................(off Austhorpe Rd.)
Beulah Ter. LS6: Leeds..................1F **31**
....................................(off Beulah Gro.)
Beulah Vw. LS6: Leeds...................2F **31**
Beverley Av. LS11: Leeds..............4F **41**
Beverley Ct. LS17: Leeds 1H **21**
Beverley Ct. LS28: Fars 3F **27**
Beverley Mt. LS11: Leeds...............4F **41**
..................................(off Lady Pit Lane)
Beverley Sq. LS11: Leeds...............4F **41**
Beverley St. BD4: B'ford.................2A **36**
Beverley Ter. LS11: Leeds 4F **41**
Beverley Vw. LS11: Leeds...............4F **41**
..............................(off Fulham Street)
Bevin Cl. WF1: Outw.........................6E **59**
Bevin Cres. WF1: Outw....................6E **59**
Bewerley Cft. LS11: Leeds 3F **41**
Bewerley M. LS29: Men 2C **6**
...................................(off Melbeck Cl.)
Bewick Gro. LS10: Leeds 2B **52**
Bexley Av. LS8: Leeds 3B **32**
Bexley Gro. LS8: Leeds 3B **32**
Bexley Hall LS12: Leeds.................6A **30**
....(off Hall Rd.)
Bexley Mt. LS8: Leeds......................3B **32**
Bexley Pl. LS8: Leeds.......................3B **32**
Bexley Rd. LS8: Leeds......................3B **32**
Bexley Ter. LS8: Leeds......................3B **32**
Bexley Vw. LS8: Leeds......................3B **32**
Beza Ct. LS10: Leeds..................... 5H **41**
Beza Rd. LS10: Leeds...................... 4H **41**
Beza St. LS10: Leeds 4H **41**
Biddenden Rd. LS15: Leeds 3F **35**
Bidder Dr. WF3: E Ard..................... 2G **57**
Bideford Av. LS8: Leeds 6B **14**
Bideford Mt. BD4: B'ford.................4A **36**
BIERLEY MARSH 2B **46**
Big Depot Climbing Cen. 2C **40**
Bill Bowes Ct. LS29: Men................ 1D **6**
Billey La. LS12: Leeds 2E **39**
Billingbauk Ct. LS13: Leeds.......... 4D **28**
Billingbauk Dr. LS13: Leeds.......... 4D **28**
Billing Ct. LS19: Raw...........................6F **9**
Billing Dr. LS19: Raw........................ 6G **9**
Billington Cl. LS13: Leeds................5B **18**
Billing Vw. LS19: Raw 6F **9**
Billingwood Dr. LS19: Raw...............6F **9**
Bingham Pl. WF3: Loft.....................6C **58**
Bingley Rd. LS29: Men......................2A **6**
Bingley St. LS3: Leeds 4A **4** (5D **30**)
Binks St. WF1: Outw............................6E **59**
Birch Av. LS15: Leeds........................5A **34**
Birch Ct. BD11: B'haw 3D **46**
Birch Cres. LS15: Leeds.....................5A **34**
Birches, The LS20: Guis 3G **7**
Birchfield Av. LS27: Gil......................3C **48**
Birchfields Av. LS14: Leeds 3C **24**
Birchfields Cl. LS14: Leeds 4C **24**
Birchfields Ct. LS14: Leeds.............3C **24**
Birchfields Cres. LS14: Leeds........3C **24**
Birchfields Gth. LS14: Leeds...........4C **24**
Birchfields Ri. LS14: Leeds.............4C **24**
Birch Hill Ri. LS18: Hors...................3E **19**
Birch Ho. LS7: Leeds 4H **21**
Birch M. LS16: Leeds 1B **20**
Birchroyd LS26: Rothw................... 5H **53**
Birchtree Way LS16: Leeds..........1E **19**
Birchwood Av. LS17: Leeds 6C **14**
Birchwood Hill LS17: Leeds..........5C **14**
Birchwood M. LS17: Leeds............5C **14**
Birchwood Mt. LS17: Leeds 5C **14**
Birfed Cres. LS4: Leeds.................. 2H **29**
Birkdale Cl. LS17: Leeds..................5F **13**
Birkdale Dr. LS17: Leeds 5E **13**
Birkdale Grn. LS17: Leeds..............5F **13**
Birkdale Gro. LS17: Leeds..............5E **13**
Birkdale Mt. LS17: Leeds 5F **13**
Birkdale Pl. LS17: Leeds 5E **13**
Birkdale Ri. LS17: Leeds 5E **13**
Birkdale Wlk. LS17: Leeds...............5E **13**
Birkdale Way LS17: Leeds 5F **13**
BIRKENSHAW 4C **46**
BIRKENSHAW BOTTOMS.......................5E **47**
Birkenshaw La. BD11: B'haw 4D **46**
Birkhill Cres. BD11: B'haw........... 4D **46**
Birk La. LS27: Morl............................5E **49**
Birksland Moor BD11: B'haw...... 6D **46**
Birkwith Cl. LS14: Leeds................3B **24**
Birstall La. BD11: Drig.................... 4G **47**
Birstall Pk. Ct. WF17: Birs 6H **47**
Birstall Shop. Pk. 5A **48**
Bishopgate St.
LS1: Leeds 5D **4** (6F **31**)
Bishops Way LS14: Leeds........... 6G **23**
Bishop Way WF3: Ting 3D **56**
Bismarck Ct. LS11: Leeds...............3F **41**
Bismarck Dr. LS11: Leeds 3F **41**
Bismarck St. LS11: Leeds 3F **41**
Bismarck Way LS11: Leeds 3F **41**
Bittern Ri. LS27: Morl 6A **50**
Black Bull St. LS10: Leeds 1H **41**
Blackburn Ct. LS26: Rothw 4H **53**
Blackburn Ga. LS27: Morl 6E **49**
Blackett St. LS28: Cal 4D **16**
Blackgate M. WF3: Ting..................2C **56**
BLACK GATES..2D **56**
Blackgates Ct. WF3: Ting............ 3D **56**
Blackgates Cres. WF3: Ting........ 3D **56**
Blackgates Dr. WF3: Ting............. 3D **56**
Blackgates Fold WF3: Ting 3D **56**
Blackgates Ri. WF3: Ting.............. 3D **56**
Blackman La. LS2: Leeds.. 1D **4** (3F **31**)
Blackman La. LS7: Leeds................3F **31**
BLACK MOOR 5E **13**
BLACKMOOR..2H **15**
Blackmoor Ct. LS17: Leeds........ 4D **12**
Blackmoor La. LS17: Bard 1H **15**
Blackmoor La. LS17: S'cft 1H **15**
Black Moor Rd. LS17: Leeds....... 6D **12**
Blackpool Gro. LS12: Leeds........ 3G **39**
Blackpool Pl. LS12: Leeds........... 3G **39**
Blackpool St. LS12: Leeds 3G **39**
Blackpool Ter. LS12: Leeds......... 3G **39**
Blackpool Vw. LS12: Leeds..........3F **39**
Black Shepherd's La.
LS7: Leeds 1A **32**
...........................(off Shepherd's Gro.)
Blacksmith M. WF3: Rob H 6D **52**
Blackthorn Av. LS14: Leeds 3A **24**
Blackthorn Ct. LS10: Leeds......... 1H **51**
Blackwell Ct. LS27: Morl..............6E **49**
Blackwell Dr. LS27: Morl...............6E **49**
Blackwood Av. LS16: Leeds........ 6D **10**
Blackwood Gdns. LS16: Leeds ... 6D **10**
Blackwood Gro. LS16: Leeds...... 6D **10**
Blackwood Mt. LS16: Leeds 6D **10**
Blackwood Ri. LS16: Leeds 6D **10**
Blairsville Gdns. LS13: Leeds 1B **28**
Blairsville Gro. LS13: Leeds.........1C **28**
Blake Cres. LS20: Guis.................. 5H **7**
Blake Gro. LS7: Leeds 5H **21**
Blakeney Gro. LS10: Leeds 6H **41**
Blakeney Rd. LS10: Leeds 6H **41**
Blandford Gdns. LS2: Leeds..........3F **31**
Blandford Gro. LS2: Leeds 3F **31**
.........................(off Bk. Blenheim Ter.)
Blayds Gth. LS26: W'frd 2A **54**
Blayd's M. LS1: Leeds....... 6E **5** (6G **31**)
Blayds St. LS9: Leeds......................6B **32**
Blayd's Yd. LS1: Leeds...... 6E **5** (6G **31**)
Bleaberry Cl. LS9: Leeds 5F **33**
Blencarn Cl. LS14: Leeds............. 1H **33**
Blencarn Cres. LS14: Leeds 1H **33**
Blencarn Dr. LS14: Leeds............ 1H **33**
Blencarn Gdns. LS14: Leeds....... 1H **33**
Blencarn Vw. LS14: Leeds 1H **33**
Blencartha Cres. LS9: Leeds........5F **33**
Blenheim Av. LS2: Leeds.................3F **31**
Blenheim Ct. LS2: Leeds 3F **31**
...............................(off Blackman La.)
Blenheim Cres. LS2: Leeds 3F **31**
................................(off Blenheim Av.)
Blenheim Gro. LS2: Leeds..............3F **31**
Blenheim Sq. LS2: Leeds.................3F **31**
Blenheim Ter. LS2: Leeds...............3F **31**
.........................(off Bk. Blenheim Ter.)
Blenheim Ter. LS27: Morl 3G **49**
Blenheim Vw. LS2: Leeds................3F **31**
Blenheim Wlk. LS2: Leeds 3F **31**
Blenkinsop Av. LS10: Leeds........ 5H **51**
Blenkinsop Dr. LS10: Leeds 5A **52**
Blenkinsop Way LS10: Leeds.......5A **52**
Bletchley Av. LS18: Hors 4G **17**
Bletchley Cl. LS18: Hors.................4F **17**
Bletchley Ct. LS18: Hors..................4F **17**
Bletchley Fold LS18: Hors 4F **17**
Bletchley Rd. LS18: Hors.................3F **17**
Bletchley Way LS18: Hors..............3F **17**
Blind La. BD11: Drig 2H **47**
Blind La. LS17: Shad 5G **15**
Blind La. WF3: E Ard..........................6E **57**
Blossom Ct. LS19: Yead 3D **8**
Blucher St. BD4: B'ford 1A **36**
Bluebell Ct. LS14: Leeds 3A **24**
Bluebell Rd. WF3: E Ard 3A **58**
Blue Hill Cres. LS12: Leeds......... 1G **39**
Blue Hill Grange LS12: Leeds...... 2G **39**
Blue Hill Gro. LS12: Leeds............ 1G **39**
Blue Hill La. LS12: Leeds 1G **39**
Blundell St. LS1: Leeds 2C **4** (4F **31**)
Boar La. LS1: Leeds 5E **5** (6G **31**)
Bobby Collins Way
LS11: Leeds...4C **40**
Bodington Av. LS16: Leeds 1H **19**
Bodington Way LS16: Leeds 1A **20**
Bodley Ter. LS4: Leeds 4B **30**
Bodmin App. LS10: Leeds...............4E **51**
Bodmin Chase LS10: Leeds 3E **51**
Bodmin Cres. LS10: Leeds..............4E **51**
Bodmin Cft. LS10: Leeds..................4F **51**
Bodmin Gdns. LS10: Leeds 5E **51**
Bodmin Gth. LS10: Leeds.................5E **51**
Bodmin Hill LS10: Leeds 3E **51**
Bodmin Pl. LS10: Leeds 5F **51**
.................................(not continuous)
Bodmin Rd. LS10: Leeds 3D **50**
Bodmin Sq. LS10: Leeds 5E **51**
Bodmin St. LS10: Leeds 5E **51**
Bodmin Ter. LS10: Leeds..................5E **51**
Bodmin Wlk. LS10: Leeds 3E **51**
Bodylines Gym Leeds.......3H **5** (4A **32**)
..................(within Mabgate Mills Ind. & Commercial Cen.)
Body Mania Fitness.............................4G **53**
....(off Marsh St.)
Boggart Hill LS14: Leeds............ 5G **23**
Boggart Hill Cres. LS14: Leeds ... 5G **23**
Boggart Hill Dr. LS14: Leeds 5G **23**
Boggart Hill Gdns.
LS14: Leeds 5G **23**
Boggart Hill Rd. LS14: Leeds 5G **23**
Bog La. LS15: Leeds........................ 6G **25**
Bog La. LS15: Scho........................... 6G **25**
Boldmere Rd. LS15: Leeds........... 6G **33**
Bolton Grange LS19: Yead 3E **9**
Bolton Rd. LS19: Yead.........................3E **9**
Bonaire LS12: Leeds 5A **4** (6D **30**)
Bond Ct. LS1: Leeds 4D **4** (5F **31**)
......................................(off Park Row)
Bond St. LS1: Leeds 4D **4** (5F **31**)
Bond St. LS15: Leeds 3E **35**
Bonham Ct. LS27: Morl 5G **49**
....(off Queen St.)
Boocock St. LS28: Stan.................. 4G **27**
....(off Varley St.)

A-Z Leeds 67

Bookbinders, The – Broadway Dr.

Bookbinders, The
LS2: Leeds ... 5G 5 (6H 31)
... (off Bk. York St.)
Booth Holme Cl. BD4: B'ford ... 1D 46
Boothroyd Dr. LS6: Leeds ... 6D 20
Booth's Yd. LS28: Pud ... 5G 27
Borrough Av. LS8: Leeds ... 3A 22
Borrough Vw. LS8: Leeds ... 3A 22
Borrowdale Cl. LS12: Leeds ... 3F 29
Borrowdale Ct. LS29: Men ... 3D 6
Borrowdale Cres. LS12: Leeds ... 3F 29
Borrowdale Cft. LS19: Yead ... 2D 8
Borrowdale Ter. LS14: Leeds ... 2H 33
Boston Av. LS5: Leeds ... 2F 29
Boston Exchange Ct.
LS4: Leeds ... 2A 30
Boston Towers LS9: Leeds ... 4A 32
... (off Lindsey Gdns.)
Bottoms La. BD11: B'haw ... 5D 46
Boulevard, The LS10: Leeds ... 1H 41
Boulevard, The LS12: Leeds ... 4B 40
Boulevard, The LS28: Fars ... 3F 27
Boulevard Ri. LS10: Leeds ... 5A 52
Boundary Cl. LS15: Leeds ... 6E 35
Boundary Farm Rd.
LS17: Leeds ... 6E 13
Bourse, The LS1: Leeds ... 5E 5 (6G 31)
... (off Boar La.)
Bouverie Ct. LS9: Leeds ... 1A 42
Bowater Ct. BD4: B'ford ... 5B 36
Bowcliffe Rd. LS10: Leeds ... 3B 42
Bower Rd. LS15: Leeds ... 2E 35
Bowfell Cl. LS14: Leeds ... 1A 34
Bowland Cl. LS15: Leeds ... 6G 33
Bowling Grn. Ter.
LS11: Leeds ... 2F 41
Bowling Grn. Vw. BD11: Drig ... 3G 47
Bowman La.
LS10: Leeds ... 6G 5 (6H 31)
Bowness Av. BD10: B'ford ... 1A 26
Bowood Av. LS7: Leeds ... 4E 21
Bowood Cres. LS7: Leeds ... 4E 21
Bowood Gro. LS7: Leeds ... 4E 21
Bow St. LS9: Leeds ... 6A 32
Boyd Av. BD3: B'ford ... 4A 26
Boyds Mill LS9: Leeds ... 1A 42
Bracken Ct. LS12: Leeds ... 2C 40
Bracken Ct. LS17: Leeds ... 2G 21
Bracken Edge LS8: Leeds ... 6B 22
Bracken Grn. WF3: E Ard ... 3A 58
Bracken Hill LS17: Leeds ... 2G 21
Brackenhurst Dr. LS17: Leeds ... 1G 21
Brackenhurst Pl. LS17: Leeds ... 1G 21
Bracken Pk. LS14: S'cft ... 1H 15
Brackenwood Cl. LS8: Leeds ... 4A 22
Brackenwood Ct. WF1: Outw ... 6F 59
Brackenwood Dr. LS8: Leeds ... 3A 22
Brackenwood Grn. LS8: Leeds ... 3A 22
Brackenwood Rd. WF1: Outw ... 6F 59
Bradburn Rd. WF3: Rob H ... 6C 52
Bradfield Av. LS27: Morl ... 6E 49
Bradfield Gdns. LS27: Morl ... 6E 49
Bradford & Heckmondwike Rd.
BD4: E Bier ... 1B 46
Bradford & Wakefield Rd.
BD4: B'ford ... 2E 47
Bradford Golf Course ... 6C 6
Bradford La. BD3: B'ford ... 6A 26
Bradford Plaza BD3: B'ford ... 5A 26
Bradford Rd. BD11: Drig
Buttercup Way ... 4B 48
Bradford Rd. BD11: Drig
Woodview ... 2F 47
Bradford Rd. BD11: B'haw ... 5C 46
Bradford Rd. BD19: Gom ... 5C 46
Bradford Rd. BD3: B'ford ... 4B 26
Bradford Rd. BD4: E Bier ... 1B 46
Bradford Rd. LS20: Guis ... 4E 7
Bradford Rd. LS27: Gil ... 4B 48
Bradford Rd. LS28: Pud ... 4E 27
Bradford Rd. LS28: Stan ... 4E 27
Bradford Rd. LS29: Men ... 1D 6
Bradford Rd. WF2: Carr G ... 6A 58
... (not continuous)
Bradford Rd. WF2: Wren ... 6A 58
... (not continuous)
Bradford Rd. WF3: E Ard ... 2B 56
Bradford Rd. WF3: Ting ... 2B 56
BRADLEY HILL ... 2A 28
Bradley Hill Vw. LS28: Stan ... 3A 28
... (off Swinnow La.)
Bradley La. LS28: Pud ... 6D 26
Bradley Ter. LS17: Leeds ... 5C 14
Bradley Vw. LS27: Morl ... 4A 50
Bradstock Gdns. LS27: Morl ... 3G 49
Bragg Ct. LS16: Leeds ... 1A 20
Braithwaite Row LS10: Leeds ... 5A 42
Braithwaite St. LS11: Leeds ... 1D 40
Bramall Ho. BD3: B'ford ... 5B 26
... (off Chapman Rd.)
Bramble App. LS14: Leeds ... 4C 24
Bramble Ct. WF1: Outw ... 6C 58
Bramble M. LS17: Leeds ... 4E 15
Bramble Sq. WF3: E Ard ... 3B 58
Brambling M. LS27: Morl ... 5A 50
Bramham Gdns. LS15: Leeds ... 4F 35
Bramham Pk. Ct. LS10: Leeds ... 6H 51
Bramleigh Dr. LS27: Morl ... 3G 49
Bramleigh Gro. LS27: Morl ... 3G 49
BRAMLEY ... 2D 28
Bramley Baths ... 2B 28
Bramley Cen. ... 2D 28
Bramley Cl. WF3: E Ard ... 4G 57
Bramley Station (Rail)
West Yorkshire ... 4B 28
Bramley's Yd. LS1: Leeds . 4F 5 (5G 31)
... (off The Headrow)
Bramstan Av. LS13: Leeds ... 2A 28
Bramstan Cl. LS13: Leeds ... 2A 28
Bramstan Gdns. LS13: Leeds ... 2A 28
Brancepeth Pl. LS12: Leeds ... 6C 30
Branch Cl. LS12: Leeds ... 3G 39
Branch End LS27: Gil ... 2E 49
Branch Pl. LS12: Leeds ... 3G 39
Branch Rd. LS12: Leeds
Beech Dr. ... 5A 30
Branch Rd. LS12: Leeds
Branch Pl. ... 3G 39
Branch Rd. LS27: Gil ... 2D 48
Branch St. LS12: Leeds ... 3G 39
Brander App. LS9: Leeds ... 4E 33
Brander Cl. LS9: Leeds ... 4F 33
Brander Dr. LS9: Leeds ... 4E 33
Brander Gro. LS9: Leeds ... 4E 33
Brander Rd. LS9: Leeds ... 3F 33
Brander St. LS9: Leeds ... 3F 33
Brandling Ct. LS10: Leeds ... 4G 51
Brandling Cres. LS10: Leeds ... 6H 51
BRANDON ... 4G 15
Brandon Cl. LS17: Leeds ... 2H 23
Brandon Ct. LS17: Leeds ... 4D 14
Brandon Cres. LS17: Leeds ... 2G 15
Brandon Golf Course ... 4F 15
Brandon Ho. BD4: B'ford ... 5A 36
... (off Fontmell Cl.)
Brandon La. LS17: Leeds ... 2H 15
Brandon La. LS17: Wike ... 1F 15
Brandon Rd. LS3: Leeds ... 3A 4 (5E 31)
Brandon St. LS12: Leeds ... 6D 30
Brandon Ter. LS17: Leeds ... 4D 14
Brandon Vw. LS17: Shad ... 4F 15
Brandon Way LS7: Leeds ... 6H 21
Brandon Way Cres. LS7: Leeds ... 6A 22
Branksome Pl. LS6: Leeds ... 3C 30
Branksome St. LS6: Leeds ... 3C 30
... (off Queen's Rd.)
Branksome Ter. LS6: Leeds ... 3C 30
... (off Queen's Rd.)
Bransby Cl. LS28: Fars ... 3G 27
Bransby Ct. LS28: Fars ... 3G 27
Bransby Ri. LS28: Fars ... 2G 27
Bransdale Av. LS20: Guis ... 5G 7
Bransdale Cl. LS20: Guis ... 5G 7
Bransdale Gdns. LS20: Guis ... 5G 7
Bransdale Gth. LS20: Guis ... 5G 7
Brantford St. LS7: Leeds ... 5H 21
Branwell Av. LS20: Guis ... 4F 7
Branwell Av. WF17: Birs ... 6G 47
Branwell Cl. LS20: Guis ... 4F 7
Branwell Rd. LS20: Guis ... 4F 7
Branwell Wlk. WF17: Birs ... 6H 47
Brathay Gdns. LS14: Leeds ... 2A 34
Braunstone Ct. LS29: Men ... 1B 6
Brayshaw Rd. WF3: E Ard ... 5G 57
Brayton App. LS14: Leeds ... 6C 24
Brayton Cl. LS14: Leeds ... 6C 24
Brayton Gth. LS14: Leeds ... 6D 24
Brayton Grange LS14: Leeds ... 6D 24
Brayton Grn. LS14: Leeds ... 6D 24
Brayton Gro. LS14: Leeds ... 6C 24
Brayton Pl. LS14: Leeds ... 6D 24
Brayton Sq. LS14: Leeds ... 6D 24
Brayton Ter. LS14: Leeds ... 6C 24
Brayton Wlk. LS14: Leeds ... 6C 24
Breary Av. LS18: Hors ... 2D 18
... (not continuous)
Breary Ter. LS18: Hors ... 2D 18
Breary Wlk. LS18: Hors ... 2D 18
Brecks La. LS26: Swil ... 3H 45
Brecon App. LS9: Leeds ... 4F 33
Brecon Ct. LS9: Leeds ... 4F 33
Brecon Ri. LS9: Leeds ... 4F 33
Brendon Ct. BD4: B'ford ... 4A 36
Brendon Wlk. BD4: B'ford ... 5A 36
Brentwood Ct. LS16: Leeds ... 3G 19
Brentwood Gro. LS12: Leeds ... 6A 30
Brentwood St. LS12: Leeds ... 6A 30
Brentwood Ter. LS12: Leeds ... 6A 30
Brett Gdns. LS11: Leeds ... 3F 41
Brewery Pl. LS10: Leeds ... 6G 5 (6H 31)
... (off Kendell St.)
Brewery Wharf LS10: Leeds
Brewery Pl. ... 6G 5 (6H 31)
Brewery Wharf LS10: Leeds
Waterloo St. ... 6F 5 (6G 31)
... (off Waterloo St.)
Brian Cres. LS15: Leeds ... 2B 34
Brian Pl. LS15: Leeds ... 2B 34
BRIANSIDE ... 2A 34
Brian Vw. LS15: Leeds ... 2B 34
Briar Cl. LS28: Fars ... 3F 27
Briardene LS26: Oult ... 5C 54
Briarfield Gdns. LS27: Gil ... 3C 48
Briarlea Cl. LS19: Yead ... 4B 8
Briarmains Rd. WF17: Birs ... 6H 47
Briarsdale Ct. LS8: Leeds ... 2E 33
Briarsdale Cft. LS8: Leeds ... 2E 33
Briarsdale Gth. LS8: Leeds ... 2D 32
Briarsdale Hgts. LS9: Leeds ... 2E 33
Briarsdale M. LS8: Leeds ... 2D 32
Briarwood Cl. WF1: Outw ... 6F 59
Brick Mill Rd. LS28: Pud ... 1H 37
Brick St. LS9: Leeds ... 5H 5 (6H 31)
Bridge, The LS10: Leeds ... 6F 5 (6G 31)
... (off Waterloo St.)
Bridge Ct. LS11: Leeds ... 2E 41
Bridge Ct. LS27: Morl ... 6H 49
Bridge End LS1: Leeds ... 5E 5 (6G 31)
Bridge End LS11: Leeds ... 6F 5 (6G 31)
... (off Water La.)
Bridge Fold LS5: Leeds ... 1F 29
Bridge Pl. LS18: Hors ... 1C 18
Bridge Rd. LS11: Leeds ... 2E 41
Bridge Rd. LS13: Leeds ... 6G 17
Bridge Rd. LS5: Leeds ... 1F 29
Bridge St. LS2: Leeds ... 4G 5 (5H 31)
Bridge St. LS27: Morl ... 6H 49
Bridge St. M. LS27: Morl ... 6H 49
... (off Quarry La.)
Bridge Ter. LS27: Morl ... 6H 49
Bridge Vw. LS13: Leeds ... 6G 17
Bridgewater Ct. LS6: Leeds ... 5D 20
Bridgewater Pl. LS11: Leeds ... 1F 41
Bridgewater Rd. LS9: Leeds ... 2A 42
Bridge Wood Cl. LS18: Hors ... 2D 18
Bridge Wood Vw. LS18: Hors ... 1D 18
Bridge Works LS27: Morl ... 6G 49
Bridle Path LS15: Leeds ... 3A 34
Bridle Path Rd. LS17: Leeds ... 4F 15
Bridle Path Wlk. LS15: Leeds ... 3A 34
Bridleway LS27: Chur ... 2H 49
Briggate LS1: Leeds ... 5E 5 (6G 31)
Brigg Ho. LS3: Leeds ... 4D 30
Brigg Mill Ct. LS28: Pud ... 5H 27
Briggs Bldgs. LS27: Morl ... 5H 49
... (off Melbourne St.)
Brighton Av. LS27: Morl ... 4F 49
Brighton Cliff LS13: Leeds ... 3C 28
Brighton Gro. LS13: Leeds ... 4D 28
Bright St. LS27: Morl ... 5F 49
Bright St. LS28: Stan ... 3H 27
Bright St. WF3: E Ard ... 3H 57
Brignall Cft. LS9: Leeds ... 4B 32
Brignall Gth. LS9: Leeds ... 4B 32
Brignall Way LS9: Leeds ... 4B 32
Brinsmead Ct. LS26: Rothw ... 2H 53
Bristol St. LS7: Leeds ... 1H 5 (4H 31)
Britannia Cl. LS28: Stan ... 3H 27
Britannia Ct. LS13: Leeds ... 5A 28
Britannia Gdns. LS28: Pud ... 5H 27
Britannia Ho. LS1: Leeds ... 4C 4 (6F 31)
... (off York Pl.)
Britannia M. LS28: Pud ... 5A 28
Britannia Rd. LS27: Morl ... 6F 49
Britannia Sq. LS27: Morl ... 6F 49
Britannia St. LS1: Leeds ... 5C 4 (6F 31)
Britannia St. LS28: Stan ... 3H 27
Broadcasting Pl.
LS2: Leeds ... 1D 4 (3F 31)
... (off Woodhouse La.)
Broadcroft Chase WF3: Ting ... 4C 56
Broadcroft Dr. WF3: Ting ... 4C 56
Broadcroft Gro. WF3: Ting ... 3C 56
Broadcroft Way WF3: Ting ... 3C 56
Broadfield Cl. BD4: B'ford ... 6A 36
Broadfields LS18: Hors ... 2D 18
Broad Gate ... 3E 5 (5G 31)
Broadgate Av. LS18: Hors ... 2D 18
Broadgate Ct. LS18: Hors ... 3D 18
Broadgate Cres. LS18: Hors ... 3C 18
Broadgate Dr. LS18: Hors ... 2D 18
Broadgate La. LS18: Hors ... 2C 18
Broadgate M. LS18: Hors ... 3D 18
Broadgate Ri. LS18: Hors ... 3D 18
Broadgate Wlk. LS18: Hors ... 3C 18
Broadlands Av. LS28: Pud ... 6H 27
Broadlands Ct. LS28: Pud ... 6H 27
Broadlands Gdns. LS28: Pud ... 6A 28
Broadlands Pl. LS28: Pud ... 6H 27
Broadlands Vw. LS28: Pud ... 6A 28
Broadland Way WF3: Loft ... 3E 59
Broad La. LS13: Leeds ... 1C 28
Broad La. LS28: Leeds ... 3A 28
Broad La. LS5: Leeds ... 2F 29
Broad La. Cl. LS13: Leeds ... 1E 29
Broadlea Av. LS13: Leeds ... 1E 29
Broadlea Cl. LS13: Leeds ... 1E 29
Broadlea Cres. LS13: Leeds ... 1E 29
Broadlea Gdns. LS13: Leeds ... 1E 29
Broadlea Gro. LS13: Leeds ... 1E 29
Broadlea Hill LS13: Leeds ... 1E 29
Broadlea Mt. LS13: Leeds ... 2F 29
Broadlea Oval LS13: Leeds ... 1E 29
Broadlea Pl. LS13: Leeds ... 2E 29
Broadlea Rd. LS13: Leeds ... 1E 29
Broadlea St. LS13: Leeds ... 1E 29
Broadlea Ter. LS13: Leeds ... 1E 29
Broadlea Vw. LS13: Leeds ... 1D 28
Broadmeadows WF1: Outw ... 6E 59
Broadstone Way BD4: B'ford ... 6A 36
Broad St. LS28: Fars ... 2E 27
Broad Wlk. LS2: Leeds ... 2E 31
Broadway LS15: Leeds ... 1H 43
Broadway LS18: Hors ... 5G 17
Broadway LS20: Guis ... 5D 6
Broadway LS5: Leeds ... 4E 19
Broadway Av. LS6: Leeds ... 3C 30
Broadway Dr. LS18: Hors ... 3B 18

68 A-Z Leeds

Calverley La. – Chapel Fold

Calverley La. LS28: Fars 5E **17**
(not continuous)
Calverley Moor Av. LS28: Pud 4C **26**
Calverley Rd. LS26: Oult 4C **54**
Calverley St. LS1: Leeds 2C **4** (4F **31**)
Calverley Ter. LS13: Leeds 2B **28**
Camberley Cl. LS28: Pud 1G **37**
Camberley Mt. BD4: B'ford 3A **36**
Camberley St. LS11: Leeds 4G **41**
Camberley Way LS28: Pud 1G **37**
Cambrian St. LS11: Leeds 3E **41**
Cambrian Ter. LS11: Leeds 3E **41**
Cambridge Cl. LS27: Morl 4H **49**
Cambridge Ct. LS27: Morl 5H **49**
Cambridge Dr. LS13: Leeds 2B **28**
Cambridge Gdns. LS13: Leeds 2B **28**
Cambridge Rd. LS6: Leeds 2F **31**
Cambridge St. LS20: Guis 4G **7**
Campbell St. LS28: Stan 3F **27**
CAMP FIELD 1F **41**
CAMP TOWN 5F **13**
Canada Cres. LS19: Raw 5E **9**
Canada Dr. LS19: Raw 4E **9**
Canada Rd. LS19: Raw 4E **9**
Canada Ter. LS19: Raw 5E **9**
Canalbank Vw. LS13: Leeds 6H **17**
Canal Cl. BD10: B'ford 3A **16**
Canal Ct. WF3: Loft 5F **59**
Canal Gdns. 2D **22**
Canal La. WF3: Loft 5E **59**
Canal La. WF3: Stly 5E **59**
Canal Pl. LS12: Leeds 6D **30**
Canal Rd. LS12: Leeds 5A **30**
Canal Rd. LS13: Leeds 5G **17**
Canal St. LS12: Leeds 6C **30**
Canal Wlk. WF3: Stly 5H **59**
Canal Wharf LS11: Leeds 6C **4** (6F **31**)
Canal Wharf LS5: Leeds 2F **29**
Candle Ho. LS1: Leeds 6C **4** (6F **31**)
(off Wharf App.)
Cannon Wlk. LS2: Leeds 3E **31**
Canonbury Ter. LS11: Leeds 4C **40**
Canter, The LS10: Leeds 6H **51**
Canterbury Dr. LS6: Leeds 1A **30**
Canterbury Rd. LS6: Leeds 1A **30**
Cape Ind. Est. LS28: Fars 2G **27**
Capel Ct. LS28: Cal 5D **16**
Capel St. LS28: Cal 5D **16**
Capitol Blvd. LS27: Morl 2A **56**
Capitol Cl. LS27: Morl 1A **56**
Capitol Pde. LS6: Leeds 4D **20**
Caraway Ct. LS6: Leeds 2D **20**
Caraway Dr. LS6: Leeds 2D **20**
Caraway M. LS6: Leeds 2D **20**
Carberry Pl. LS6: Leeds 3C **30**
Carberry Rd. LS6: Leeds 3C **30**
Carberry Ter. LS6: Leeds 3C **30**
(off Carberry Rd.)
Carden Av. LS15: Leeds 6G **33**
Carden Gro. LS15: Leeds 6G **33**
Carden Pl. LS15: Leeds 5G **33**
Carden Rd. BD4: B'ford 2A **36**
Cardigan Ct. LS6: Leeds 1C **30**
Cardigan Flds. Rd. LS4: Leeds 4A **30**
Cardigan Grn. LS13: Leeds 2D **28**
Cardigan La. LS4: Leeds 3B **30**
(not continuous)
Cardigan La. LS6: Leeds 2C **30**
Cardigan Rd. LS6: Leeds 1B **30**
Cardigan Ter. WF3: E Ard 3A **58**
Cardigan Trad. Est. LS4: Leeds 4B **30**
Cardinal Av. LS11: Leeds 1D **50**
Cardinal Ct. LS11: Leeds 6C **40**
Cardinal Cres. LS11: Leeds 1D **50**
Cardinal Gdns. LS11: Leeds 1C **50**
Cardinal Gro. LS11: Leeds 1C **50**
Cardinal Rd. LS11: Leeds 1C **50**
Cardinal Sq. LS11: Leeds 6C **40**
Cardinal Wlk. LS11: Leeds 6C **40**
Cardwell Rd. LS14: Leeds 6H **23**
Carisbrooke Rd. LS16: Leeds 4H **19**
Carlisle Av. LS19: Yead 3E **9**
Carlisle Dr. LS28: Pud 1F **37**
Carlisle Gro. LS28: Pud 1F **37**
Carlisle Rd. LS10: Leeds 1H **41**
Carlisle Rd. LS28: Pud 1F **37**
Carlisle St. LS28: Stan 4E **27**
CARLTON 6F **53**
Carlton Av. LS28: Pud 6G **27**
Carlton Carr LS7: Leeds 3G **31**
Carlton Cl. LS7: Leeds 3G **31**
(off Carlton Ri.)
Carlton Ct. BD11: B'haw 5C **46**
Carlton Ct. LS12: Leeds 3C **40**
Carlton Cft. LS7: Leeds 3G **31**
(off Carlton Gdns.)
Carlton Dr. LS20: Guis 3H **7**
Carlton Gdns. LS7: Leeds 3G **31**
Carlton Gth. LS17: Leeds 4C **14**
Carlton Gth. LS7: Leeds 3G **31**
Carlton Ga. LS7: Leeds 3G **31**
Carlton Grange LS19: Yead 2E **9**
Carlton Grn. LS26: Rothw 5G **53**
Carlton Gro. LS7: Leeds 3G **31**
Carlton Hill LS2: Leeds 1E **5** (3G **31**)
Carlton Hill LS7: Leeds 3G **31**
Carlton La. LS20: Guis 3H **7**
Carlton La. LS26: Rothw 5F **53**
Carlton La. WF3: Loft 2E **59**
Carlton M. LS20: Guis 4G **7**
Carlton Moor M. LS10: Leeds 4B **52**
Carlton Mt. LS19: Yead 1E **9**
Carlton Pde. LS7: Leeds 3G **31**
(off Carlton Wlk.)
Carlton Pl. LS7: Leeds 3G **31**
Carlton Ri. LS28: Pud 6G **27**
Carlton Ri. LS7: Leeds 3G **31**
Carlton Row LS12: Leeds 6G **29**
Carlton Ter. LS19: Yead 2E **9**
Carlton Ter. LS28: Pud 5G **27**
Carlton Trad. Est. LS12: Leeds 5B **30**
Carlton Vw. LS7: Leeds 3G **31**
Carlton Wlk. LS7: Leeds 3G **31**
Carnegie Sports Cen. 5H **19**
Carr Beck Ri. BD10: B'ford 4A **16**
Carr Bottom Rd. BD10: B'ford 4A **16**
Carr Bri. Av. LS16: Leeds 6D **10**
Carr Bri. Cl. LS16: Leeds 6D **10**
Carr Bri. Dr. LS16: Leeds 6D **10**
Carr Bri. Vw. LS16: Leeds 6D **10**
Carr Cl. LS19: Raw 6F **9**
Carr Crofts LS12: Leeds 6H **29**
CARR CROFTS 6H **29**
Carr Crofts Dr. LS12: Leeds 6H **29**
CARR GATE 6A **58**
Carr Ga. Cres. WF2: Carr G 6H **57**
Carr Ga. Dr. WF2: Carr G 6H **57**
Carr Ga. Mt. WF2: Carr G 6H **57**
Carr Hill Av. LS28: Cal 5C **16**
Carr Hill Dr. LS28: Cal 5C **16**
Carr Hill Gro. LS28: Cal 5C **16**
Carr Hill Nook LS28: Cal 5C **16**
Carr Hill Ri. LS28: Cal 5C **16**
Carr Hill Rd. LS28: Cal 5C **16**
Carrholm Cres. LS7: Leeds 4F **21**
Carrholm Dr. LS7: Leeds 4F **21**
Carrholm Gro. LS7: Leeds 4F **21**
Carrholm Mt. LS7: Leeds 4F **21**
Carrholm Rd. LS7: Leeds 4F **21**
Carrholm Vw. LS7: Leeds 4F **21**
Carriage Dr. BD19: Gom 6D **46**
Carriage Dr., The LS8: Leeds 2E **23**
Carriageworks, The 3D **4** (5F **31**)
Carrick Dr. BD3: B'ford 5B **26**
Carrington Ter. LS20: Guis 5F **7**
Carr La. LS19: Raw 6F **9**
Carr La. WF3: Car 6G **53**
Carr Mnr. Av. LS17: Leeds 3F **21**
Carr Mnr. Cres. LS17: Leeds 2F **21**
Carr Mnr. Cft. LS17: Leeds 4F **21**
Carr Mnr. Dr. LS17: Leeds 3F **21**
Carr Mnr. Gdns. LS17: Leeds 3F **21**
Carr Mnr. Gth. LS17: Leeds 2F **21**
Carr Mnr. Gro. LS17: Leeds 3F **21**
Carr Mnr. Mt. LS17: Leeds 3F **21**
Carr Mnr. Pde. LS17: Leeds 3F **21**
Carr Mnr. Pl. LS17: Leeds 3F **21**
Carr Mnr. Rd. LS17: Leeds 4F **21**
Carr Mnr. Vw. LS17: Leeds 2F **21**
Carr Mnr. Wlk. LS17: Leeds 4F **21**
Carr Mills LS7: Leeds 1F **31**
Carr Moor Side LS11: Leeds 4G **41**
Carr Moor St. LS10: Leeds 5H **41**
Carr Pl. LS7: Leeds 3G **31**
Carr Rd. LS28: Cal 4B **16**
Carr Wood Cl. LS28: Cal 5C **16**
Carr Wood Gdns. LS28: Cal 5C **16**
Carr Wood Way LS28: Cal 4C **16**
Carson Gro. LS27: Morl 6E **49**
Carter Av. LS15: Leeds 5C **34**
Carter La. LS15: Leeds 4C **34**
Carter Mt. LS15: Leeds 5C **34**
Carter Ter. LS15: Leeds 4C **34**
Cartier Ho. LS10: Leeds 1H **41**
Cartmell Ct. LS15: Leeds 6F **33**
Cartmell Dr. LS15: Leeds 6F **33**
Cartwright Av. LS20: Guis 4G **7**
Casson Av. WF3: E Ard 2F **57**
Casson Dr. WF3: E Ard 2F **57**
Casson Gro. WF3: E Ard 2F **57**
Castlefields LS26: Rothw 4D **52**
Castle Ga. LS26: Oult 3G **59**
Castle Grange LS19: Yead 3F **9**
Castle Gro. Av. LS6: Leeds 4B **20**
Castle Gro. Dr. LS6: Leeds 5B **20**
Castle Head Cl. WF3: Loft 3E **59**
Castle Head La. WF3: Loft 4B **58**
Castle Head La. WF3: Thpe H 3B **58**
Castle Ings Cl. LS12: N Far 4D **38**
Castle Ings Dr. LS12: N Far 4D **38**
Castle Ings Gdns. LS12: N Far 4D **38**
Castle Lodge Av. LS26: Rothw 2D **52**
Castle Lodge Ct. LS26: Rothw 3E **53**
Castle Lodge Gdns.
LS26: Rothw 3D **52**
Castle Lodge Gth. LS26: Rothw 2E **53**
Castle Lodge M. LS26: Rothw 3E **53**
Castle Lodge Sq. LS26: Rothw 2E **53**
Castle Lodge Way LS26: Rothw 3D **52**
Castle Rd. LS26: Rothw 4F **53**
Castle St. LS1: Leeds 4B **4** (5E **31**)
Castleton Cl. LS12: Leeds 6D **30**
Castleton Rd. LS12: Leeds 5C **30**
Castle Vw. LS17: Leeds 2F **21**
Castlewood Cl. LS18: Hors 3D **18**
Catalina LS12: Leeds 6A **4** (6E **31**)
Cathcart St. LS6: Leeds 2E **31**
Catherine Gro. LS11: Leeds 4F **41**
Catherines Wlk. LS18: Hors 4C **18**
Cautley Rd. LS9: Leeds 1B **42**
Cavalier App. LS9: Leeds 1B **42**
Cavalier Cl. LS9: Leeds 1B **42**
Cavalier Ct. LS9: Leeds 1B **42**
Cavalier Dr. BD10: B'ford 3A **16**
Cavalier Gdns. LS9: Leeds 1B **42**
Cavalier Ga. LS9: Leeds 1B **42**
Cavalier Grn. LS9: Leeds 1B **42**
CAVALIER HILL 6A **32**
Cavalier M. LS9: Leeds 1B **42**
Cavalier Vw. LS9: Leeds 1B **42**
Cave La. WF3: E Ard 3H **57**
Cavendish App. BD11: Drig 3G **47**
Cavendish Ct. BD11: Drig 3G **47**
(off Cavendish App.)
Cavendish Dr. LS20: Guis 5F **7**
Cavendish Gro. LS20: Guis 5F **7**
Cavendish M. BD11: Drig 3G **47**
Cavendish M. LS17: Leeds 5H **13**
Cavendish Pl. LS28: Stan 4F **27**
Cavendish Ri. LS28: Pud 6A **28**
Cavendish Rd.
LS2: Leeds 1C **4** (3F **31**)
Cavendish Rd. LS20: Guis 5F **7**
Cavendish Sq. LS28: Stan 4G **27**
Cavendish St. LS19: Yead 2E **9**
Cavendish St. LS28: Pud 6A **28**
Cavendish St. LS3: Leeds 5D **30**
Caythorpe Rd. LS16: Leeds 4H **19**
Cecil Gro. LS12: Leeds 5A **30**
Cecil Mt. LS12: Leeds 5A **30**
Cecil Rd. LS12: Leeds 5A **30**
Cecil St. LS12: Leeds 5A **30**
Cedar Av. LS12: Leeds 6A **30**
Cedar Cl. LS12: Leeds 6A **30**
Cedar Ct. LS17: Leeds 1H **21**
(off Harrogate Rd.)
Cedar Ct. LS26: W'frd 2E **55**
Cedar Dr. LS14: Leeds 3G **33**
Cedar Mt. LS12: Leeds 6H **29**
Cedar Pk. LS26: Rothw 2D **52**
Cedar Pl. LS12: Leeds 6H **29**
Cedar Rd. LS12: Leeds 6H **29**
Cedar St. LS12: Leeds 6H **29**
Cedar Ter. LS12: Leeds 6H **29**
Cemetery La. WF3: Car 2E **59**
Cemetery Rd. LS11: Leeds 3E **41**
Cemetery Rd. LS19: E Car 2E **9**
Cemetery Rd. LS19: Yead 2E **9**
Cemetery Rd. LS28: Pud 5E **27**
Centaur Ho. LS1: Leeds 3B **4** (5E **31**)
Central Arc. LS1: Leeds 5F **5** (6G **31**)
Central Pk. LS11: Leeds 1F **41**
Central Rd. LS1: Leeds 5F **5** (6G **31**)
Central St. LS1: Leeds 4C **4** (5F **31**)
Central Village Leeds
LS1: Leeds 1C **4** (4F **31**)
(off Woodhouse La.)
Central Village Twr.
LS1: Leeds 1C **4** (4F **31**)
(off Woodhouse La.)
Centre 27 Bus. Pk. WF17: Birs 6B **48**
Century Flds. LS13: Leeds 4C **28**
Century Way LS15: Leeds 6F **35**
Chaddlewood Cl. LS18: Hors 2C **18**
Chadwick St.
LS10: Leeds 6G **5** (1H **41**)
Chadwick St. Sth. LS10: Leeds 1H **41**
Chalfont Rd. LS16: Leeds 3H **19**
Chalice Cl. LS10: Leeds 2A **52**
Chalner Av. LS27: Morl 6F **49**
Chalner Cl. LS27: Morl 6F **49**
Chancellor Ct.
LS2: Leeds 5F **5** (6G **31**)
Chancellor St. LS6: Leeds 2F **31**
Chancel Sq. LS6: Leeds 2D **20**
Chandlers, The
LS2: Leeds 6G **5** (6H **31**)
(off The Calls)
Chandlers Cl. WF1: Outw 6D **58**
Chandlers Wharf LS13: Leeds 5G **17**
Chandos Av. LS8: Leeds 3A **22**
Chandos Fold LS8: Leeds 4A **22**
Chandos Gdns. LS8: Leeds 3A **22**
Chandos Gth. LS8: Leeds 3A **22**
Chandos Grn. LS8: Leeds 3A **22**
Chandos M. LS8: Leeds 3A **22**
Chandos Pl. LS8: Leeds 3B **22**
Chandos Ter. LS8: Leeds 3B **22**
Chandos Wlk. LS8: Leeds 3A **22**
Change All. LS1: Leeds 4E **5** (5G **31**)
(off Albion Pl.)
Chantrell Ct. LS2: Leeds 5G **5** (6H **31**)
Chantrey Cl. LS14: Leeds 6H **23**
Chantry Ct. LS27: Morl 4H **49**
Chantry Cft. LS15: Leeds 6D **34**
Chantry Gth. LS15: Leeds 6D **34**
Chapel, The LS26: Oult 4C **54**
(off Calverley Rd.)
CHAPEL ALLERTON 5F **21**
CHAPEL ALLERTON HOSPITAL 6A **22**
Chapel Allerton Tennis,
Squash & Gym 4G **21**
Chapel Ct. BD4: E Bier 2B **46**
Chapel Ct. LS15: Leeds 5A **34**
Chapel Fold LS11: Leeds 5C **40**
Chapel Fold LS12: Leeds 6A **30**
(off Wesley Rd.)
Chapel Fold LS15: Leeds 5A **34**

70 A-Z Leeds

Chapel Fold – Clark Gro.

Chapel Fold LS17: Shad 5G **15**
Chapel Fold LS28: Pud 1G **37**
.... (off Littlemoor Rd.)
Chapel Fold LS6: Leeds 2B **30**
Chapel Grn. LS28: Pud 1F **37**
Chapel Hill LS10: Leeds 4H **51**
Chapel Hill LS19: Yead 2D **8**
Chapel Hill LS27: Morl 4G **49**
Chapel La. LS12: Leeds 6A **30**
Chapel La. LS12: N Far 2D **38**
Chapel La. LS19: Yead 2D **8**
Chapel La. LS6: Leeds 1B **30**
Chapel Lofts LS27: Morl 5H **49**
.... (off Commercial St.)
Chapel Pl. LS6: Leeds 6B **20**
Chapel Rd. LS7: Leeds 6H **21**
Chapel Sq. LS6: Leeds 6B **20**
.... (off Chapel St.)
Chapel St. LS13: Leeds 6G **17**
Chapel St. LS15: Leeds 5A **34**
Chapel St. LS19: Raw 5D **8**
Chapel St. LS28: Cal 4D **16**
Chapel St. LS28: Stan 4G **27**
Chapel St. LS6: Leeds 6B **20**
Chapel St. WF3: Car 6F **53**
Chapel St. WF3: E Ard 4G **57**
Chapel St. WF3: Stly 6G **59**
Chapel St. WF3: Ting 2D **56**
Chapel Ter. LS6: Leeds 6B **20**
.... (off Chapel St.)
Chapeltown LS28: Pud 1F **37**
CHAPELTOWN **1H 31**
Chapeltown Bus. Cen.
LS7: Leeds 1H **31**
.... (off Chapeltown Rd.)
Chapeltown Rd. LS7: Leeds 2H **31**
Chapel Vw. LS17: Shad 5G **15**
Chapel Vw. LS27: Gil 1C **48**
Chapel Yd. LS15: Leeds 5A **34**
.... (off Chapel St.)
Chapel Yd. LS15: Leeds 1D **44**
.... (off Meynell Rd.)
Chapel Yd. LS26: Oult 4C **54**
Chapman Rd. BD3: B'ford 5B **26**
Charles Apts.
LS3: Leeds 3A **4** (5E **31**)
.... (off Hanover Sq.)
Charles Av. BD3: B'ford 6A **26**
Charles Av. LS9: Leeds 1B **42**
Charles Av. WF1: Outw 6D **58**
Charles Gro. LS26: Oult 3C **54**
Charles Morris Hall LS2: Leeds ... 4E **31**
Charles St. LS18: Hors 3B **18**
Charles St. LS27: Morl 5H **49**
Charles St. LS28: Fars 2F **27**
Charlotte Cl. WF17: Birs 6H **47**
Charlotte Gro. LS15: Leeds 5B **34**
Charlton Gro. LS9: Leeds 6C **32**
Charlton Pl. LS9: Leeds 6C **32**
Charlton Rd. LS9: Leeds 6C **32**
Charlton St. LS9: Leeds 6C **32**
Charnley Dr. LS7: Leeds 5A **22**
Chartist's Ct. LS27: Morl 6G **49**
.... (off Gt. Northern St.)
Chartists Way LS27: Morl 6G **49**
Chartwell Ct. LS17: Leeds 4D **14**
.... (off Shadwell La.)
Charville Gdns. LS17: Shad 6H **15**
Chase, The LS19: Raw 5C **8**
Chase, The WF3: Stly 5H **59**
Chase, The WF3: Ting 2C **56**
Chase Av. LS27: Morl 2A **56**
Chase Ct. LS27: Morl 2A **56**
Chase La. WF3: E Ard 3G **57**
Chatswood Av. LS11: Leeds 1D **50**
Chatswood Cres. LS11: Leeds 1D **50**
Chatswood Dr. LS11: Leeds 6D **40**
Chatsworth Av. LS28: Pud 5C **26**
Chatsworth Cl. LS8: Leeds 2C **32**
Chatsworth Cres. LS28: Pud 5C **26**
Chatsworth Dr. LS28: Pud 5C **26**
Chatsworth Fall LS28: Pud 5C **26**
Chatsworth Ind. Est.
LS12: Leeds 1B **40**
Chatsworth M. LS27: Morl 6A **50**
Chatsworth Ri. LS28: Pud 5C **26**
Chatsworth Rd. LS28: Pud 5C **26**
Chatsworth Rd. LS8: Leeds 2C **32**
Chaucer Av. LS28: Pud 1H **37**
Chaucer Av. WF3: Stly 5G **59**
Chaucer Gdns. LS28: Pud 1H **37**
Chaucer Gro. LS28: Pud 1H **37**
Cheapside LS27: Morl 4G **49**
.... (off Chapel Hill)
Chellow Ter. BD11: B'haw 5D **46**
Chelsea Cl. LS12: Leeds 1A **40**
Chelsfield Ct. LS15: Leeds 2F **35**
Chelsfield Way LS15: Leeds 2F **35**
Cheltenham St. LS12: Leeds 1B **40**
Chelwood Av. LS8: Leeds 6B **14**
Chelwood Cres. LS8: Leeds 1B **22**
Chelwood Dr. LS8: Leeds 6B **14**
Chelwood Gro. LS8: Leeds 6B **14**
Chelwood Mt. LS8: Leeds 6B **14**
Chelwood Pl. LS8: Leeds 6A **14**
Chenies Cl. LS14: Leeds 4G **33**
Chepstow Dr. LS10: Leeds 6H **51**
Cherry Blossom Ri.
LS14: Leeds 4H **33**
Cherry Cl. LS14: Leeds 3G **33**
Cherry Ct. LS19: Yead 3D **8**
Cherry Ct. LS6: Leeds 5D **20**
Cherry Ct. LS9: Leeds 4A **32**
.... (off Cherry Row)
Cherry Gro. LS6: Leeds 6D **20**
Cherry Lea Ct. LS19: Raw 4D **8**
Cherry Pl. LS9: Leeds 4A **32**
Cherry Ri. LS14: Leeds 3C **24**
Cherry Row LS9: Leeds 2H **5** (4A **32**)
Cherry Tree Av. BD10: B'ford 4A **16**
Cherry Tree Ct. WF3: E Ard 4G **57**
Cherry Tree Cres. LS28: Fars 2F **27**
Cherry Tree Dr. LS28: Fars 2F **27**
Cherry Tree Fold LS28: Fars 2F **27**
Cherry Tree Wlk.
LS2: Leeds 5F **5** (6G **31**)
.... (off Crown St.)
Cherry Tree Wlk. WF3: E Ard 4G **57**
Cherrywood Cl. LS14: Leeds 2B **24**
Cherrywood Gdns. LS14: Leeds ... 2B **24**
Chervana Ct. BD4: B'ford 3A **36**
Chesney Av. LS10: Leeds 3H **41**
Chester St. LS12: Leeds 5A **30**
Chesterton Ct. LS15: Leeds 1D **44**
Chestnut Av. LS15: Leeds 3D **34**
Chestnut Av. LS6: Leeds 2C **30**
Chestnut Dr. LS16: Leeds 4H **11**
Chestnut Gdns. LS12: Leeds 1A **40**
Chestnut Gdns. LS27: Chur 2G **49**
Chestnut Gro. LS26: W'frd 3E **55**
Chestnut Gro. LS28: Cal 5D **16**
Chestnut Gro. LS6: Leeds 2C **30**
Chestnut La. LS14: Leeds 3G **33**
Chestnut Pl. LS6: Leeds 2C **30**
Chestnut Ri. LS12: Leeds 1H **39**
Chestnut St. LS6: Leeds 2C **30**
Chestnut Vw. LS27: Chur 2G **49**
Chestnut Way LS16: Leeds 4H **11**
Chevin Av. LS29: Men
Bradford Rd. 1D **6**
Chevin End LS29: Guis 2D **6**
Chevin End LS29: Men 2D **6**
Chevin End Rd. LS20: Guis 2F **7**
Chevington Ct. LS19: Raw 6C **8**
Chevin Ho. LS29: Men 2D **6**
.... (off High Royds Dr.)
Chichester St. LS12: Leeds 5A **30**
Chiltern Ct. LS13: Leeds 6G **17**
Chilver Dr. BD4: B'ford 5C **36**
Chippendale Ct. LS29: Men 1D **6**
Chirton Gro. LS8: Leeds 6C **22**
Chiswick St. LS6: Leeds 3C **30**
Chiswick Ter. LS6: Leeds 3C **30**
.... (off Carberry Rd.)
Chorley La. LS2: Leeds 2B **4** (4E **31**)
Chorley La. LS3: Leeds 3B **4** (5E **31**)
Christ Chu. Av. LS12: Leeds 5H **29**
Christ Chu. Mt. LS12: Leeds 5H **29**
Christ Chu. Pde. LS12: Leeds 5H **29**
Christ Chu. Pl. LS12: Leeds 5H **29**
Christ Chu. Rd. LS12: Leeds 5H **29**
Christ Chu. Ter. LS12: Leeds 5H **29**
Christ Chu. Vw. LS12: Leeds 5H **29**
Christiana Ter. LS27: Morl 4H **49**
Christopher Rd. LS6: Leeds 2E **31**
Church Av. LS18: Hors 2B **18**
Church Av. LS26: Swil 5G **45**
Church Av. LS27: Gil 1C **48**
Church Av. LS6: Leeds 4D **20**
Church Cl. LS14: Leeds 1B **34**
.... (not continuous)
Church Cl. LS26: Swil 5G **45**
Church Ct. LS19: Yead 3D **8**
Church Ct. LS27: Morl 4G **49**
Church Cres. LS17: Leeds 6G **13**
Church Cres. LS18: Hors 2B **18**
Church Cres. LS19: Yead 3C **8**
Church Cres. LS26: Swil 6H **45**
Church Cft. LS29: Men 1B **6**
Church Cft. WF3: Loft 3E **59**
Chu. Farm Cl. BD4: B'ford 6F **37**
Chu. Farm Cl. WF3: Loft 3E **59**
Church Farm Gth. LS17: Shad 5H **15**
Churchfield Cft. LS26: Rothw 4H **53**
Churchfield Gro. LS26: Rothw 3G **53**
Churchfield La. LS26: Rothw 3G **53**
Churchfield Rd. LS26: Rothw 4G **53**
Church Gdns. BD11: Drig 2H **47**
Church Gdns. LS17: Leeds 6H **13**
Church Gdns. LS27: Gil 2C **48**
Church Ga. LS18: Hors 2B **18**
Churchgate LS27: Gil 2C **48**
Church Gro. LS18: Hors 2B **18**
Church Gro. LS6: Leeds 4C **20**
Church Hill Gdns. LS28: Stan 3H **27**
Church Hill Grn. LS28: Stan 3H **27**
Church Hill Mt. LS28: Stan 3H **27**
Churchill Gdns. LS2: Leeds 3F **31**
.... (off Bk. Blenheim Ter.)
Churchill Ho. BD4: B'ford 3A **36**
.... (off Tyersal La.)
Church La. LS15: Leeds 3C **34**
Church La. LS16: Leeds 5A **12**
Church La. LS18: Hors 2B **18**
Church La. LS2: Leeds 5G **5** (6H **31**)
Church La. LS26: Meth 6H **55**
Church La. LS26: Swil 6F **45**
Church La. LS28: Pud 6G **27**
Church La. LS6: Leeds 4D **20**
Church La. LS7: Leeds 5H **21**
Church La. WF1: Outw 6D **58**
Church La. WF3: E Ard 4G **57**
Church La. WF3: W Ard 4B **56**
Church La. Av. WF1: Outw 6D **58**
Church M. LS5: Leeds 5E **19**
Church Mt. LS18: Hors 2B **18**
Church Rd. LS12: Leeds 6A **30**
Church Rd. LS18: Hors 3B **18**
Church Rd. LS9: Leeds 6A **32**
.... (off Cross Catherine St.)
Church Rd. WF3: Stly 6H **59**
Church Row LS2: Leeds 5G **5** (6H **31**)
Churchside Vs. LS26: Meth 6H **55**
Church St. LS10: Leeds 3H **41**
Church St. LS19: Yead 3C **8**
Church St. LS20: Guis 4G **7**
Church St. LS26: Rothw 4G **53**
Church St. LS26: W'frd 2C **54**
Church St. LS27: Gil 2C **48**
Church St. LS27: Morl 4G **49**
Church St. LS5: Leeds 1G **29**
Church Vw. LS16: Leeds 4A **12**
Church Vw. LS29: Men 1B **6**
Church Vw. LS5: Leeds 1H **29**
Church Wlk. LS2: Leeds 5G **5** (6H **31**)
Church Way LS27: Morl 4G **49**
Church Wood Av. LS16: Leeds 5A **20**
Church Wood Av. LS6: Leeds 5H **19**
Church Wood Mt. LS16: Leeds 4A **20**
Church Wood Rd. LS16: Leeds 5A **20**
Churchyard Dr. WF3: E Ard 3G **57**
CHURWELL **1A 50**
CITY **5H 49**
City Bloc Indoor Climbing Wall ... **2H 41**
City Ct. LS27: Morl 5H **49**
.... (off South Pde.)
City Ga. LS3: Leeds 5D **30**
City Golf Course **4A 30**
City Limits LS27: Morl 5H **49**
.... (off Lewisham Vw.)
City Link Ind. Pk. BD4: B'ford 1A **36**
City Mills LS27: Morl 5H **49**
.... (off Peel St.)
City Pk. Ind. Est. LS12: Leeds 4A **40**
City Reach LS3: Leeds 5D **30**
Cityside LS1: Leeds 2D **4** (4F **31**)
City Sq. LS1: Leeds 5D **4** (6F **31**)
City Varieties Music Hall .. **4E 5 (5G 31)**
City Vw. LS11: Leeds 5D **40**
.... (off Kirk Beston Rd.)
City Wlk. LS11: Leeds 1F **41**
City West One Office Pk.
LS12: Leeds 4B **40**
Clapgate La. LS10: Leeds 4B **52**
Clapham Av. LS16: Leeds 1A **20**
Clapham Dene Rd. LS15: Leeds ... 4B **34**
Clara Dr. LS28: Cal 4B **16**
Clara St. LS28: Fars 3F **27**
Claremont LS28: Pud 6H **27**
Claremont Av.
LS3: Leeds 2A **4** (4E **31**)
Claremont Ct. LS6: Leeds 5C **20**
Claremont Cres. LS6: Leeds 6D **20**
Claremont Dr. LS6: Leeds 5C **20**
Claremont Gdns. LS28: Fars 3F **27**
Claremont Gro. LS28: Pud 6G **27**
Claremont Gro.
LS3: Leeds 2A **4** (4E **31**)
Claremont Pl. LS12: Leeds 6G **29**
Claremont Rd. LS6: Leeds 5C **20**
Claremont St. LS12: Leeds 6G **29**
Claremont St. LS26: Oult 3C **54**
Claremont Ter. LS12: Leeds 6G **29**
Claremont Vw. LS26: Oult 3C **54**
Claremont Vw.
LS3: Leeds 2A **4** (4E **31**)
Claremont Vs.
LS2: Leeds 2B **4** (4E **31**)
.... (off Clarendon Rd.)
Claremount LS6: Leeds 5C **20**
Clarence Dock
LS10: Leeds 6H **5** (1H **41**)
Clarence Dr. LS18: Hors 4B **18**
Clarence Gdns. LS18: Hors 4B **18**
Clarence Gro. LS18: Hors 4B **18**
Clarence Ho. LS10: Leeds 1H **41**
Clarence M. LS18: Hors 4B **18**
Clarence Rd. LS10: Leeds 1A **42**
Clarence Rd. LS18: Hors 4B **18**
Clarence St. LS13: Leeds 4C **28**
Clarence Ter. LS28: Pud 5G **27**
Clarendon Ho.
LS2: Leeds 2A **4** (4E **31**)
Clarendon Pl.
LS2: Leeds 1A **4** (3E **31**)
Clarendon Quarter LS3: Leeds 4D **30**
Clarendon Rd.
LS2: Leeds 1A **4** (3E **31**)
Clarendon Ter. LS27: Chur 1A **50**
Clarendon Ter. LS28: Pud 1G **37**
Clarendon Way
LS2: Leeds 2B **4** (4E **31**)
Clarion Camp LS29: Men 1F **7**
Clark Av. LS9: Leeds 6B **32**
Clark Cres. LS9: Leeds 6B **32**
Clarke Rd. WF3: W Ard 6C **56**
Clarke St. LS28: Cal 5D **16**
Clark Gro. LS9: Leeds 1B **42**

A-Z Leeds 71

Name	Grid
Clark La. LS9: Leeds	6B 32
...... (not continuous)	
Clark Mt. LS9: Leeds	6B 32
Clark Rd. LS9: Leeds	1B 42
Clark Row LS9: Leeds	1B 42
Clarkson Ter. LS27: Chur	1A 50
Clarkson Vw. LS6: Leeds	1E 31
Clark Spring Cl. LS27: Morl	2G 49
Clark Spring Ct. LS27: Morl	2H 49
Clark Spring Ri. LS27: Morl	2H 49
Clark Ter. LS9: Leeds	6B 32
Clark Vw. LS9: Leeds	1B 42
Clay Pit La. LS2: Leeds	2E 5 (4G 31)
Clay Pit La. LS7: Leeds	1F 5 (4G 31)
Clayton Bus. Cen. LS10: Leeds	4A 42
Clayton Cl. LS10: Leeds	5B 42
Clayton Ct. LS10: Leeds	5B 42
Clayton Ct. LS16: Leeds	3F 19
Clayton Dr. LS10: Leeds	5B 42
Clayton Grange LS16: Leeds	3F 19
Clayton Gro. LS19: Yead	2D 8
Clayton Ri. WF1: Outw	6D 58
Clayton Rd. LS10: Leeds	5B 42
Claytons Cl. LS26: Meth	6H 55
Clayton St. LS26: Rothw	4H 53
Clayton Way LS10: Leeds	5B 42
Clayton Wood Bank	
LS16: Leeds	2F 19
Clayton Wood Cl. LS16: Leeds	2F 19
Clayton Wood Ct. LS16: Leeds	2F 19
Clayton Wood Ri. LS16: Leeds	2F 19
Clayton Wood Rd. LS16: Leeds	2E 19
Clearings, The LS10: Leeds	1H 51
Cleasby Rd. LS29: Men	2C 6
Cleeve Hill LS19: Raw	5D 8
Clement Ter. LS26: Rothw	5G 53
Cleveleys Av. LS11: Leeds	3D 40
Cleveleys Ct. LS11: Leeds	3D 40
...... (off Cleveleys Av.)	
Cleveleys Mt. LS11: Leeds	3D 40
Cleveleys Rd. LS11: Leeds	3D 40
Cleveleys St. LS11: Leeds	3D 40
...... (off Cleveleys Rd.)	
Cleveleys Ter. LS11: Leeds	3D 40
Cliff Ct. LS6: Leeds	1D 30
Cliffdale Rd. LS7: Leeds	1F 31
Cliffdale Rd. Light Ind. Est.	
LS7: Leeds	1F 31
Cliffe Ct. LS19: Yead	2E 9
...... (off High St.)	
Cliffe Dr. LS19: Raw	6C 8
Cliffe La. LS19: Raw	1E 17
Cliffe Pk. Chase LS12: Leeds	1G 39
Cliffe Pk. Cl. LS12: Leeds	1G 39
Cliffe Pk. Cres. LS12: Leeds	1G 39
Cliffe Pk. Dr. LS12: Leeds	1G 39
Cliffe Pk. Mt. LS12: Leeds	1G 39
Cliffe Pk. Ri. LS12: Leeds	1F 39
Cliffe Pk. Way LS27: Morl	6D 48
Cliffe Ter. WF3: Rob H	6C 52
Cliffe Vw. LS27: Morl	6D 48
Cliff La. LS6: Leeds	1D 30
Cliff Mt. LS6: Leeds	1E 31
Cliff Mt. Ter. LS6: Leeds	1E 31
Clifford Dr. LS29: Men	2D 6
Clifford Pl. LS27: Chur	2H 49
Cliff Rd. LS6: Leeds	1E 31
Cliff Rd. Gdns. LS6: Leeds	1E 31
Cliff Side Gdns. LS6: Leeds	1E 31
Cliff Ter. LS6: Leeds	1E 31
Clifton Av. LS9: Leeds	4C 32
Clifton Av. WF3: Stly	5G 59
Clifton Ct. LS28: Pud	5G 27
...... (off Clifton Rd.)	
Clifton Dr. LS28: Pud	5G 27
Clifton Gro. LS9: Leeds	4C 32
Clifton Hill LS28: Pud	5G 27
Clifton M. LS28: Pud	5G 27
Clifton Mt. LS9: Leeds	3C 32
Clifton Pl. LS28: Pud	5H 27
Clifton Rd. LS28: Pud	5G 27
Clifton Ter. LS9: Leeds	4C 32

Name	Grid
Climax Works LS11: Leeds	5G 41
Clipston Av. LS6: Leeds	5D 20
Clipston Mt. LS6: Leeds	5D 20
Clipston St. LS6: Leeds	5D 20
Clipston Ter. LS6: Leeds	5D 20
Clive Mt. Ho. LS5: Leeds	2F 29
...... (off Broad La.)	
Cloberry St. LS2: Leeds	1A 4 (3E 31)
Clock Bldgs. LS8: Leeds	1C 32
Clock Twr. LS29: Men	3D 6
Close, The LS17: Leeds	4E 13
Close, The LS20: Guis	5E 7
Close, The LS9: Leeds	6A 32
Close, The WF3: E Ard	4H 57
Cloth Dr. LS28: Fars	1F 27
Cloth Hall St. LS1: Leeds	5F 5 (6G 31)
Clough St. LS27: Morl	5H 49
Clovelly Av. LS11: Leeds	4F 41
Clovelly Gro. LS11: Leeds	4F 41
Clovelly Pl. LS11: Leeds	4F 41
Clovelly Row LS11: Leeds	4F 41
Clovelly Ter. LS11: Leeds	4F 41
Clover Cl. LS14: Leeds	4H 33
Clover Ct. LS28: Cal	5C 16
Clover Cres. LS28: Cal	4C 16
Club La. LS13: Leeds	6G 17
Club Row LS19: Yead	2E 9
Club Row LS7: Leeds	4G 21
Clumpcliffe LS26: Meth	6D 54
Clyde App. LS12: Leeds	1C 40
Clyde Chase LS12: Leeds	1C 40
...... (off Clyde App.)	
Clyde Ct. LS12: Leeds	1C 40
...... (off Copley St.)	
Clyde Gdns. LS12: Leeds	1C 40
Clyde Grange LS12: Leeds	1C 40
...... (off Clyde Vw.)	
Clyde Vw. LS12: Leeds	1C 40
Clyde Wlk. LS12: Leeds	1C 40
Coach Rd. LS12: N Far	4E 39
Coach Rd. LS20: Guis	6F 7
Coach Rd. LS26: Swil	1F 55
Coach Rd. WF1: Outw	6E 59
Coal Hill Dr. LS13: Leeds	1H 27
Coal Hill Fold LS13: Leeds	1H 27
Coal Hill Gdns. LS13: Leeds	1H 27
Coal Hill Ga. LS13: Leeds	1H 27
Coal Hill Grn. LS13: Leeds	1H 27
Coal Hill La. LS13: Leeds	2H 27
Coal Hill La. LS28: Fars	1G 27
Coal Rd. LS17: Wike	1F 15
Cobden Av. LS12: Leeds	3F 39
Cobden Gro. LS12: Leeds	3F 39
Cobden M. LS27: Morl	4G 49
Cobden Pl. LS12: Leeds	3F 39
Cobden Rd. LS12: Leeds	3F 39
Cobden St. LS12: Leeds	3F 39
Cobden St. LS27: Morl	4G 49
Cobden Ter. LS12: Leeds	3F 39
Cobham Wlk. LS15: Leeds	3F 35
Cockburn Cl. LS11: Leeds	4G 41
Cockburn Way LS11: Leeds	4G 41
Cockcroft Ho. LS6: Leeds	2B 30
...... (off Chapel La.)	
Cockcroft M. LS6: Leeds	2B 30
...... (off Chapel La.)	
COCKERSDALE	1A 48
Cockshott Cl. LS12: Leeds	4F 29
Cockshott Dr. LS12: Leeds	4F 29
Cockshott Hill LS28: Fars	2F 27
Cockshott La. LS12: Leeds	4F 29
...... (not continuous)	
Colby Ri. LS15: Leeds	6G 33
Coldcotes Av. LS9: Leeds	3D 32
Coldcotes Cir. LS9: Leeds	3E 33
Coldcotes Cl. LS9: Leeds	3E 33
Coldcotes Cres. LS9: Leeds	3F 33
Coldcotes Dr. LS9: Leeds	3E 33
Coldcotes Gth. LS9: Leeds	3F 33
Coldcotes Gro. LS9: Leeds	3F 33
Coldcotes Vw. LS9: Leeds	3F 33
Coldcotes Wlk. LS9: Leeds	3F 33

Name	Grid
Coldwell Rd. LS15: Leeds	4B 34
Coldwell Sq. LS15: Leeds	4B 34
Coleman St. LS12: Leeds	1D 40
Colenso Gdns. LS11: Leeds	2D 40
Colenso Gro. LS11: Leeds	3D 40
Colenso Mt. LS11: Leeds	3D 40
Colenso Pl. LS11: Leeds	3D 40
Colenso Rd. LS11: Leeds	3D 40
Colenso Ter. LS11: Leeds	3D 40
Coleridge Cl. LS26: Oult	6C 54
Coleridge La. LS28: Pud	2H 37
College Ct. LS27: Gil	3D 48
College Lawns LS12: Leeds	5F 29
College Rd. LS27: Gil	3D 48
College Vw. LS12: Leeds	6F 29
Colley Gdns. WF3: Stly	5H 59
Colliers La. LS17: Shad	5G 15
Colliery App. WF3: Loft	5D 58
Collindale Cl. BD10: B'ford	5A 16
Collin Rd. LS14: Leeds	4H 33
Colmore Gro. LS12: Leeds	2B 40
Colmore Rd. LS12: Leeds	2B 40
Colmore St. LS12: Leeds	1B 40
Coltman Way LS14: Leeds	6H 23
COLTON	1D 44
Colton Ct. LS15: Leeds	6D 34
Colton Cft. LS15: Leeds	6D 34
Colton Gth. LS15: Leeds	6D 34
Colton La. LS15: Leeds	6D 34
Colton Lodges LS15: Leeds	6E 35
Colton Mill LS15: Leeds	6F 35
Colton Retail Pk.	6E 35
Colton Rd. LS12: Leeds	6A 30
Colton Rd. LS15: Leeds	6C 34
Colton Rd. E. LS15: Leeds	1E 45
Colton St. LS12: Leeds	6A 30
Colville Ter. LS11: Leeds	3F 41
Colville Ter. WF3: Thpe H	2A 58
Colwyn Av. LS11: Leeds	5F 41
Colwyn Mt. LS11: Leeds	5F 41
Colwyn Pl. LS11: Leeds	5F 41
Colwyn Rd. LS11: Leeds	5F 41
Colwyn Ter. LS11: Leeds	5F 41
Colwyn Vw. LS11: Leeds	5F 41
Combined Court Leeds	3C 4 (5F 31)
Commercial Rd. LS5: Leeds	1G 29
Commercial St.	
LS1: Leeds	4E 5 (5G 31)
Commercial St. LS26: Rothw	4G 53
Commercial St. LS27: Morl	5G 49
Commercial Vs. LS28: Pud	1F 37
Commercial Way LS28: Pud	5H 27
Common La. WF3: E Ard	3F 57
Common Rd. WF3: Stly	4H 59
Compton Av. LS9: Leeds	3C 32
Compton Cres. LS9: Leeds	3C 32
Compton Pl. LS9: Leeds	3C 32
Compton Rd. LS9: Leeds	3C 32
Compton Row LS9: Leeds	3C 32
Compton Ter. LS9: Leeds	3C 32
Compton Vw. LS9: Leeds	3C 32
Concept LS7: Leeds	4G 21
Concept Pl. LS3: Leeds	4D 30
Concordia St. LS1: Leeds	6E 5 (6G 31)
Concord St. LS2: Leeds	2G 5 (4H 31)
Concourse Ho. LS11: Leeds	1D 50
...... (off Dewsbury Rd.)	
Coney Warren La. WF3: Stly	3G 59
Conference Gro. LS12: Leeds	6G 29
Conference Pl. LS12: Leeds	6G 29
Conference Rd. LS12: Leeds	6G 29
Conference Ter. LS12: Leeds	6G 29
Congress Mt. LS12: Leeds	6G 29
Congress St. LS12: Leeds	6G 29
Coniston Av. LS6: Leeds	6C 20
Coniston Ct. WF3: Loft	5D 58
Coniston Gdns. LS15: Leeds	1G 43
Coniston Rd. LS26: W'frd	2C 54
Coniston Way LS26: W'frd	3C 54
Consort St. LS3: Leeds	4D 30
Consort Ter. LS3: Leeds	4D 30
Consort Vw. LS3: Leeds	4D 30

Name	Grid
Consort Wlk. LS3: Leeds	4D 30
...... (not continuous)	
Constable Gro. WF3: Stly	5G 59
Constable Rd. WF3: Ting	3C 56
Constance Gdns. LS7: Leeds	3F 31
Constance Way LS7: Leeds	3F 31
Conway Av. LS8: Leeds	2B 32
Conway Dr. LS8: Leeds	2B 32
Conway Gro. LS8: Leeds	2B 32
Conway Mt. LS8: Leeds	2B 32
Conway Pl. LS8: Leeds	2B 32
Conway Rd. LS8: Leeds	2B 32
Conway St. LS28: Stan	4F 27
Conway St. LS8: Leeds	2B 32
Conway Ter. LS8: Leeds	2B 32
Conway Vw. LS8: Leeds	2B 32
COOKRIDGE	4D 10
Cookridge Av. LS16: Leeds	3E 11
Cookridge Dr. LS16: Leeds	3D 10
Cookridge Gro. LS16: Leeds	3E 11
Cookridge Hall Golf Course	3F 11
Cookridge La. LS16: Leeds	1D 10
Cookridge St. LS1: Leeds	3D 4 (5F 31)
Cookridge St. LS2: Leeds	2D 4 (5F 31)
Co-operation St. LS12: Leeds	3G 39
Co-operative St. LS27: Chur	1A 50
Co-operative St. LS27: Morl	4G 49
Co-operative St. WF3: Loft	2E 59
Cooper Hill LS28: Pud	2H 37
Copeland St. BD4: B'ford	2A 36
Copgrove Cl. BD4: B'ford	4A 36
Copgrove Ct. BD4: B'ford	4A 36
Copgrove Rd. BD4: B'ford	4A 36
Copgrove Rd. LS8: Leeds	1C 32
Copley Hill LS12: Leeds	1C 40
Copley Hill Trad. Est.	
LS12: Leeds	2C 40
Copley Hill Way LS12: Leeds	2C 40
Copley La. WF3: Rob H	5D 52
Copley St. LS12: Leeds	1C 40
Copley Yd. LS12: Leeds	1C 40
Copper Beech Av. LS13: Leeds	2E 29
Copperfield Av. LS9: Leeds	1B 42
Copperfield Cres. LS9: Leeds	1B 42
Copperfield Dr. LS9: Leeds	1B 42
Copperfield Gro. LS9: Leeds	1B 42
Copperfield Mt. LS9: Leeds	1C 42
Copperfield Pl. LS9: Leeds	1B 42
Copperfield Row LS9: Leeds	1B 42
Copperfield Ter. LS9: Leeds	1B 42
Copperfield Vw. LS9: Leeds	1B 42
Copperfield Wlk. LS9: Leeds	1B 42
Coppice, The LS19: Yead	4B 8
Coppice Grange LS19: Yead	1D 8
Coppice Head LS26: Rothw	4H 53
Coppice Way LS8: Leeds	5C 22
Coppice Wood Av. LS19: Yead	1C 8
Coppice Wood Av. LS20: Guis	1C 8
Coppice Wood Av. LS20: Yead	1C 8
Coppice Wood Cl. LS20: Guis	1C 8
Coppice Wood Cres. LS19: Yead	1C 8
Coppice Wood Gro. LS20: Guis	1C 8
Coppice Wood Ri. LS19: Yead	1D 8
Copplestone Wlk. BD4: B'ford	5A 36
Coppy La. LS13: Leeds	1C 28
Copse, The WF3: E Ard	4F 57
Copt Royd Gro. LS19: Yead	2C 8
Cordingley Cl. BD4: B'ford	6A 36
Cordingley St. BD4: B'ford	6A 36
Core Shop. Cen., The	4E 5 (5G 31)
Corner Ho. Shops LS17: Leeds	1H 21
Corn Mill LS29: Men	1D 6
Corn Mill App. LS28: Pud	6E 27
Corn Mill Ct. LS13: Leeds	5D 28
Cornmill Ho. LS14: Leeds	2H 33
Cornmill Vw. LS18: Hors	3E 19
Cornstone Fold LS12: Leeds	6C 28
Cornus Gdns. LS10: Leeds	1H 51
Cornwall Cl. LS26: Rothw	3F 53
Cornwall Cres. LS26: Rothw	3F 53
Coronation Pde. LS15: Leeds	1F 43
...... (not continuous)	

Coronation St. – Cross Louis St.

Coronation St. WF3: Car..............6F 53
Corporation St. LS27: Morl..........4F 49
Corson Ct. LS6: Leeds..................6C 20
Cote, The LS28: Fars....................3E 27
Cotefields Av. LS28: Fars.............2E 27
Cote La. LS28: Fars......................3E 27
Cote La. LS28: Stan......................3E 27
Coteroyd Av. LS27: Chur..............1A 50
Coteroyd Dr. LS27: Chur..............2A 50
Cotswold Dr. LS26: Rothw............3F 53
Cotswold Rd. LS26: Rothw............3G 53
Cottage Rd. BD10: B'ford..............4A 16
Cottage Rd. LS6: Leeds.................5B 20
Cottage Road Cinema
Headingley...................................5B 20
Cotterdale LS29: Men.................... 2D 6
..................................(off Clifford Dr.)
Cotterdale Vw. LS15: Leeds........ 1G 43
COTTINGLEY..................................6B 40
Cottingley App. LS11: Leeds.......6B 40
Cottingley Chase LS11: Leeds.....6A 40
Cottingley Ct. LS11: Leeds...........6B 40
Cottingley Cres. LS11: Leeds.......6B 40
Cottingley Dr. LS11: Leeds...........5A 40
Cottingley Fold LS11: Leeds........5A 40
Cottingley Gdns. LS11: Leeds......6B 40
Cottingley Grn. LS11: Leeds.........6B 40
Cottingley Gro. LS11: Leeds.........6B 40
Cottingley Hall Crematorium.......5B 40
Cottingley Hgts. LS11: Leeds.......6B 40
Cottingley Rd. LS11: Leeds..........5A 40
Cottingley Springs LS27: Gil....... 6G 39
Cottingley Station (Rail)..............6A 40
Cottingley Towers LS11: Leeds....6B 40
Cottingley Va. LS11: Leeds...........6B 40
Cotton St. LS9: Leeds........5H 5 (6A 32)
Coultas Cl. LS29: Men.................... 1D 6
County Arc. LS1: Leeds.....4F 5 (5G 31)
Coupland Pl. LS11: Leeds.............3F 41
Coupland Rd. LS11: Leeds............3F 41
Coupland St. LS11: Leeds.............4F 41
Court, The LS17: Leeds.................4D 12
Court, The WF3: Loft.....................2D 58
Courtenay Cl. BD3: B'ford.............6A 26
Courtenays LS14: Leeds...............1B 34
Courtyard, The LS12: Leeds.........4F 29
Courtyards, The LS14: Leeds.......4B 24
Coverdale Cl. LS12: Leeds............3F 29
Coverley Gth. LS19: Yead.............. 6H 7
Coverley Ri. LS19: Yead................. 6H 7
Cow Cl. Gro. LS12: Leeds.............3F 39
Cow Cl. Rd. LS12: Leeds...............3F 39
Cowley Rd. LS13: Leeds............... 6H 17
Cowper Av. LS9: Leeds..................3C 32
Cowper Cres. LS9: Leeds..............3C 32
Cowper Gro. LS8: Leeds................2C 32
Cowper Mt. LS9: Leeds..................3C 32
Cowper Rd. LS9: Leeds..................3C 32
Cowper St. LS7: Leeds.................. 1H 31
Cowper Ter. LS9: Leeds.................3C 32
Crab La. LS12: Leeds.....................5A 30
Crabtree Way WF3: W Ard............ 3D 56
Cragg Av. LS18: Hors.....................3B 18
Cragg Hill LS18: Hors....................3C 18
Cragg Rd. LS18: Hors.....................3C 18
Cragg Ter. LS18: Hors....................3B 18
.... (not continuous)
Cragg Ter. LS19: Raw.................... 1D 16
Craggwell Ter. LS18: Hors............4C 18
.... (off Wood La.)
Craggwood Cl. LS18: Hors...........4C 18
Cragg Wood Dr. LS19: Raw...........1C 16
Craggwood Rd. LS18: Hors...........4C 18
Craggwood Ter. LS18: Hors...........4C 18
.... (off Craggwood Rd.)
Crag Hill LS16: Leeds.....................2C 10
Crag Hill Av. LS16: Leeds..............2E 11
Crag Hill Vw. LS16: Leeds..............3E 11
Crag La. LS17: Leeds.....................4C 12
Cragside Cl. LS5: Leeds.................4E 19
Cragside Cres. LS5: Leeds............4E 19
Cragside Gdns. LS5: Leeds............4E 19
Cragside Gro. LS5: Leeds............. 5D 18
Cragside Mt. LS5: Leeds................4E 19
Cragside Pl. LS5: Leeds.................4E 19
Cragside Wlk. LS5: Leeds............. 5D 18
Craigmore Ct. BD4: B'ford.............5B 36
Cranbrook Av. LS11: Leeds...........4E 41
Cranbrook Vw. LS28: Pud..............2A 38
Cranewells Dr. LS15: Leeds......... 1D 44
Cranewells Grn. LS15: Leeds.......1C 44
Cranewells Ri. LS15: Leeds...........1C 44
Cranewells Va. LS15: Leeds..........1C 44
Cranewells Vw. LS15: Leeds.........6C 34
Cranmer Bank LS17: Leeds..........6E 13
Cranmer Cl. LS17: Leeds...............6E 13
Cranmer Gdns. LS17: Leeds..........6E 13
Cranmer Ri. LS17: Leeds...............5E 13
Cranmer Rd. LS17: Leeds..............6E 13
.... (not continuous)
Cranmore Cres. LS10: Leeds........4A 52
Cranmore Dr. LS10: Leeds............4B 52
Cranmore Gdns. LS10: Leeds........4A 52
Cranmore Gth. LS10: Leeds...........4A 52
Cranmore Grn. LS10: Leeds...........4A 52
Cranmore Gro. LS10: Leeds...........4A 52
Cranmore La. LS10: Leeds.............4B 52
Cranmore Ri. LS10: Leeds..............4B 52
Cranmore Rd. LS10: Leeds.............4A 52
Craven Ct. LS11: Leeds..................6C 40
Craven Pk. LS29: Men......................1B 6
Craven Rd. LS6: Leeds....................2F 31
Crawshaw Av. LS28: Pud................6H 27
Crawshaw Cl. LS28: Pud.................6G 27
Crawshaw Gdns. LS28: Pud...........6H 27
Crawshaw Hill LS28: Pud................6G 27
Crawshaw Pk. LS28: Pud.................6G 27
Crawshaw Ri. LS28: Pud.................1G 37
Crawshaw Rd. LS28: Pud................6G 27
Crescent, The BD11: B'haw...........2C 46
Crescent, The LS13: Leeds............2C 28
Crescent, The LS15: Leeds............5B 34
Crescent, The LS16: Leeds............. 5G 11
Crescent, The LS17: Leeds............ 3D 12
Crescent, The LS18: Hors.............. 2H 17
Crescent, The LS20: Guis.................5E 7
Crescent, The LS28: Pud................ 5H 27
Crescent, The LS29: Men................. 1D 6
Crescent, The LS6: Leeds...............2E 31
.... (off Woodhouse La.)
Crescent, The WF3: Ting................3E 57
Crescent Av. LS26: Rothw..............2H 53
Crescent Bungs. WF3: Thpe H.... 1H 57
Crescent Ct. LS17: Leeds.............. 3D 12
Crescent Gdns. LS17: Leeds.......... 5H 13
Crescent Grange LS11: Leeds...... 3G 41
Crescent Towers LS11: Leeds...... 3G 41
Crescent Vw. LS17: Leeds.............. 3D 12
Crest, The LS26: Swil..................... 6G 45
Cricketers, The LS5: Leeds............ 1H 29
Cricketers Fold LS17: Shad........... 5G 15
Cricketers Grn. LS19: Yead.............3E 9
Cricketers Ter. LS12: Leeds...........6A 30
Cricketers Vw. LS17: Shad............. 5G 15
Cricketers Wlk. LS15: Leeds..........6E 35
Cricklegate LS15: Leeds.................5B 34
CRIMBLES.......................................6H 27
Crimbles Ct. LS28: Pud................... 6H 27
Crimbles Pl. LS28: Pud.................... 6H 27
Crimbles Rd. LS28: Pud................... 6H 27
Crimbles Ter. LS28: Pud.................. 6H 27
Cripple Syke LS18: Hors..................1C 18
Crispin Ho. LS2: Leeds......3G 5 (5H 31)
...................................(off Trafalgar St.)
Crocus Dr. BD11: Drig....................... 3H 47
Croft, The BD11: Drig...................... 4G 47
Croft, The LS15: Leeds....................4B 34
Croft, The LS26: Oult........................4C 54
Croft, The WF3: W Ard.....................6B 56
Croft Av. LS28: Fars..........................2F 27
Croft Av. WF3: E Ard........................ 4H 57
Croft Bank BD11: B'haw...................4C 46
Croft Bri. LS26: Oult.........................4C 54
Croft Cl. LS29: Men...........................1B 6
Croft Cotts. LS12: N Far..................4E 39
Croft Ct. LS18: Hors..........................2C 18
Croft Ct. LS29: Men............................1C 6
Croftdale Gro. LS15: Leeds............ 3D 34
Croft Dr. LS29: Men.............................1C 6
Crofters Lea LS19: Yead....................3B 8
Croft Head LS20: Guis......................... 4G 7
Croft Ho. LS28: Stan......................... 5G 27
...................................(off Croft Ho. Ct.)
Croft Ho. Av. LS27: Morl................. 4H 49
Croft Ho. Cl. LS27: Morl.................. 3H 49
Croft Ho. Ct. LS28: Pud................... 5G 27
Croft Ho. Dr. LS27: Morl.................. 4H 49
Croft Ho. Gdns. LS27: Morl.............. 4H 49
Croft Ho. Gro. LS27: Morl................ 4H 49
Croft Ho. La. LS27: Morl.................. 4H 49
Croft Ho. M. LS27: Morl................... 4H 49
Croft Ho. Mt. LS27: Morl.................. 3H 49
Croft Ho. Ri. LS27: Morl................... 3H 49
Croft Ho. Rd. LS27: Morl.................. 4H 49
Croft Ho. Vw. LS27: Morl.................. 4H 49
Croft Ho. Wlk. LS27: Morl................ 3H 49
Croft Ho. Way LS27: Morl................. 3H 49
Crofton Ri. LS17: Shad..................... 5H 15
Crofton Ter. LS17: Shad................... 5H 15
Croft Pk. LS29: Men............................1B 6
Croft Ri. LS29: Men.............................1C 6
Croft's Ct. LS1: Leeds........ 4D 4 (5F 31)
Croftside Cl. LS14: Leeds................2B 34
Croft St. BD11: B'haw.......................4C 46
....(not continuous)
Croft St. LS28: Fars............................2F 27
Croft Ter. LS12: N Far........................4E 39
Cft. Way LS29: Men.............................1C 6
Cromack Vw. LS28: Pud....................6E 27
Cromer Pl. LS2: Leeds........................3E 31
....(not continuous)
Cromer Rd. LS2: Leeds...... 1A 4 (3E 31)
Cromer St. LS2: Leeds....... 1A 4 (3E 31)
Cromer Ter. LS2: Leeds..... 1A 4 (4E 31)
Crompton Dr. LS27: Morl..................3F 49
Crompton Way BD10: B'ford........3A 16
Cromwell Ct. BD11: Drig.................4F 47
Cromwell Hgts. LS9: Leeds............4A 32
..................................(off Thealby Lawn)
Cromwell M. LS9: Leeds..................4A 32
Cromwell Mt. LS10: Leeds.............. 1H 51
Cromwell Mt. LS9: Leeds................4A 32
Cromwell St. LS9: Leeds... 3H 5 (5A 32)
Crooklands LS20: Guis..................... 4G 7
..................................(off Kelcliffe La.)
Cropper Ga. LS1: Leeds..... 4A 4 (5E 31)
Crosby Av. LS11: Leeds.................... 3D 40
Crosby Pl. LS11: Leeds......................2E 41
Crosby Rd. LS11: Leeds.................... 3D 40
Crosby St. LS11: Leeds..................... 2D 40
Crosby Ter. LS11: Leeds....................2E 41
Crosby Vw. LS11: Leeds....................2E 41
Crosland M. LS15: Scho.................... 6G 25
Cross Albert Pl. LS12: Leeds.........1B 40
Cross Arc. LS1: Leeds....... 4F 5 (5G 31)
...........................(off King Edward St.)
Cross Aston Gro. LS13: Leeds......3E 29
Cross Av. LS26: Rothw...................... 2H 53
Cross Aysgarth Mt. LS9: Leeds....5B 32
Cross Banstead St. LS8: Leeds....2B 32
Cross Bath Rd. LS13: Leeds.........3C 28
Cross Belgrave St.
LS2: Leeds...................... 3F 5 (5G 31)
Cross Bellbrooke Av.
LS9: Leeds.................................... 3D 32
............................(off Bellbrooke Av.)
Cross Bell St. LS9: Leeds..3H 5 (5H 31)
....(off Bell St.)
Cross Bentley La. LS6: Leeds...... 5D 20
Cross Burley Lodge Rd.
LS6: Leeds.....................................3C 30
.............................(off Broadway Av.)
Cross Cardigan Ter. LS4: Leeds...4A 30
Cross Catherine St. LS9: Leeds...6A 32
Cross Chancellor St. LS6: Leeds..2F 31
Cross Chapel St. LS6: Leeds........6B 20
Cross Chestnut Gro. LS6: Leeds..2C 30
.............................(off Chestnut Gro.)
Cross Cliff Rd. LS6: Leeds........... 1D 30
Cross Conway Mt. LS8: Leeds.....2B 32
Cross Cowper St. LS7: Leeds....... 2H 31
Cross Dawlish Gro. LS9: Leeds... 5D 32
Cross Easy Rd. LS9: Leeds............1B 42
Cross Elford St. LS8: Leeds..........2B 32
..................................(off Elford Gro.)
Crossfield St. LS2: Leeds...............2E 31
Cross Flatts Av. LS11: Leeds.........5E 41
Cross Flatts Cres. LS11: Leeds... 5D 40
Cross Flatts Dr. LS11: Leeds....... 4D 40
Cross Flatts Gro. LS11: Leeds..... 5D 40
Cross Flatts Mt. LS11: Leeds........5E 41
Cross Flatts Pde. LS11: Leeds.... 5D 40
Cross Flatts Pk. 4E 41
Cross Flatts Pl. LS11: Leeds........ 5D 40
Cross Flatts Rd. LS11: Leeds....... 5D 40
Cross Flatts Row LS11: Leeds..... 5D 40
Cross Flatts St. LS11: Leeds........ 5D 40
Cross Flatts Ter. LS11: Leeds...... 5D 40
Cross Francis St. LS7: Leeds...... 2H 31
CROSS GATES.................................3C 34
Cross Gates Av. LS15: Leeds.......2C 34
Cross Gates La. LS15: Leeds.......2B 34
Cross Gates Rd. LS15: Leeds.......3A 34
.... (not continuous)
Crossgates Shop. Cen...................3C 34
Cross Gates Station (Rail)...........4C 34
Cross Glen Rd. LS16: Leeds.........4A 20
Cross Granby Ter. LS6: Leeds......6B 20
Cross Grange Av. LS7: Leeds.......2A 32
Cross Grasmere St.
LS12: Leeds...................................6B 30
CROSS GREEN................................2C 42
Cross Grn. BD4: B'ford...................3A 36
Cross Grn. App. LS9: Leeds..........2C 42
Cross Grn. Av. LS9: Leeds.............1B 42
Cross Grn. Cl. LS9: Leeds..............2C 42
Cross Grn. Ct. LS9: Leeds............. 2D 42
Cross Grn. Cres. LS9: Leeds.........1B 42
Cross Grn. Dr. LS9: Leeds.............2C 42
Cross Grn. Gth. LS9: Leeds............2C 42
Cross Grn. Gro. LS9: Leeds...........1B 42
Cross Grn. Ind. Est. LS9: Leeds... 2D 42
Cross Grn. Ind. Pk. LS9: Leeds.....1E 43
Cross Grn. La. LS15: Leeds...........5A 34
Cross Grn. La. LS9: Leeds.............1A 42
Cross Grn. Ri. LS9: Leeds..............2C 42
Cross Grn. Rd. LS9: Leeds.............1B 42
Cross Grn. Row LS6: Leeds...........4C 20
Cross Grn. Va. LS9: Leeds.............3C 42
Cross Grn. Way LS9: Leeds...........2C 42
Cross Greenwood Mt.
LS6: Leeds......................................4C 20
Crosshall Ct. LS27: Morl.................6F 49
Crosshall M. LS27: Morl.................6F 49
Cross Hartley Av. LS6: Leeds........1E 31
.....................................(off Lucas Pl.)
Cross Heath Gro. LS11: Leeds......4C 40
Cross Henley Rd. LS13: Leeds......3C 28
Cross Hill LS11: Leeds...................6C 40
Cross Hilton Gro. LS8: Leeds........1B 32
Cross Ingledew Cres.
LS8: Leeds...................................... 1D 22
Cross Ingram Rd. LS11: Leeds ... 2D 40
Cross Kelso Rd.
LS2: Leeds.......................1A 4 (4D 30)
Crossland Ct. LS11: Leeds............1E 41
Crossland Rd. LS27: Chur............ 2H 49
Crossland Ter. LS11: Leeds.......... 4G 41
Cross La. LS12: Leeds
Privilege St..................................... 6H 29
Cross La. LS12: Leeds
Stonebridge La...............................2E 39
Cross La. BD11: B'haw................... 2D 46
Cross La. BD4: B'haw..................... 2D 46
Cross La. LS20: Guis........................ 1H 7
Cross Lea Farm Rd. LS5: Leeds...4F 19
Cross Lidgett Pl. LS8: Leeds.........3B 22
Cross Louis St. LS7: Leeds.......... 2H 31

A-Z Leeds 73

Cross Maude St. – Dolphin Rd.

Cross Maude St. LS2: Leeds 5G **5** (6H **31**) *(off Maude St.)*
Cross Mitford Rd. LS12: Leeds 6B **30**
Cross Myrtle St. LS11: Leeds 2G **41**
Cross Osmondthorpe La. LS9: Leeds 5E **33**
Cross Pk. St. LS15: Leeds 5A **34**
Cross Peel St. LS27: Morl 5H **49**
Cross Quarry St. LS6: Leeds 1E **31**
Cross Regent Pk. Av. LS6: Leeds 1D **30** *(off Regent Pk. Av.)*
Cross Reginald Mt. LS7: Leeds 1H **31**
Cross Rd. LS18: Hors 3A **18**
Cross Roseville Rd. LS8: Leeds 2A **32** *(off Bayswater Rd.)*
Cross Roundhay Av. LS8: Leeds 6B **22**
Cross Row LS15: Swil C 1G **45**
Cross St Michaels La. LS6: Leeds 1B **30**
Cross Speedwell St. LS6: Leeds 2F **31**
Cross Stamford St. LS7: Leeds 1H **5** (4H **31**)
Cross St. LS15: Leeds 5A **34**
Cross St. LS26: Rothw 4G **53**
Cross St. WF3: E Ard 3A **58**
Cross Ter. LS26: Rothw 4G **53**
Cross Valley Dr. LS15: Leeds 4B **34**
Cross Wingham St. LS7: Leeds 3H **31**
Cross Woodstock St. LS2: Leeds 3F **31** *(off Blenheim Wlk.)*
Cross Woodview St. LS11: Leeds 5F **41** *(off Woodview St.)*
Cross York St. LS2: Leeds 5G **5** (6H **31**)
Crown Av. WF3: E Ard 3F **57**
Crown Ct. LS2: Leeds 5F **5** (6G **31**)
Crow Nest Dr. LS11: Leeds 5C **40**
Crow Nest La. LS11: Leeds 5B **40**
Crow Nest M. LS11: Leeds 5C **40**
Crown Ho. LS1: Leeds 3C **4** (5F **31**) *(off Gt. George St.)*
Crown Pl. LS28: Pud 5H **27**
CROWN POINT 6G **5** (6H **31**)
Crown Point Rd. LS10: Leeds 1G **41**
Crown Point Rd. LS2: Leeds 6G **5** (6H **31**)
Crown Point Rd. LS9: Leeds 5H **5** (6H **31**)
Crown Point Shop. Pk. 1G **41**
Crown St. LS2: Leeds 5F **5** (6G **31**)
Crown St. Bldg. LS2: Leeds 5F **5** (6G **31**) *(off Crown St.)*
Crowther Av. LS28: Cal 5B **16**
Crowther Pl. LS6: Leeds 2F **31**
Crowther St. BD10: B'ford 4A **16**
Crowthers Yd. LS28: Pud 1G **37**
Crowtrees Ct. LS19: Raw 5E **9**
Crow Trees Pk. LS19: Raw 5D **8**
Croxall Dr. WF3: Stly 6G **59**
Croydon St. LS11: Leeds 1D **40**
Crozier Ho. LS10: Leeds 1H **41**
Cudbear St. LS10: Leeds 1H **41**
Cumberland Ct. LS6: Leeds 2B **30**
Cumberland Rd. LS6: Leeds 1D **30**
Cunningham Ct. WF3: Rob H 5C **52**
Curlew Ri. LS27: Morl 6B **50**
Cusworth Ct. LS15: Leeds 4G **35**
Cusworth Gth. LS15: Leeds 4G **35**
Cutler Pl. BD4: B'ford 3A **36**
Cypress Point LS7: Leeds 1G **5** (4H **31**) *(off Leylands Rd.)*
Czar St. LS11: Leeds 1E **41**

D

Daffil Av. LS27: Chur 2H **49**
Daffil Grange M. LS27: Morl 2H **49**
Daffil Grange Way LS27: Morl 2H **49**
Daffil Gro. LS27: Chur 2H **49**
Daffil Rd. LS27: Chur 2H **49**
Dahlia Gro. BD11: Drig 3H **47**
Daisyfield Grange LS13: Leeds 4D **28** *(off Rossefield App.)*
Daisyfield Rd. LS13: Leeds 3D **28**
Daisy Hill LS27: Morl 4A **50**
DAISY HILL 4A **50**
Daisy Hill Av. LS27: Morl 3A **50**
Daisy Hill Cl. LS27: Morl 3H **49**
Daisy Hill Ct. LS27: Morl 4A **50**
Daisy Hill M. LS27: Morl 4A **50**
Daisy La. WF3: E Ard 3B **58**
Daisy Pl. LS14: Leeds 4H **33**
Daisy Row LS13: Leeds 4D **28**
Daisy Va. M. WF3: Thpe H 2A **58**
Daisy Va. Ter. WF3: Thpe H 2A **58**
Dalby Way LS10: Leeds 5A **52**
Dale Cl. LS20: Guis 5D **6**
Dale Pk. Av. LS16: Leeds 5D **10**
Dale Pk. Cl. LS16: Leeds 5D **10**
Dale Pk. Gdns. LS16: Leeds 5D **10**
Dale Pk. Ri. LS16: Leeds 5D **10**
Dale Pk. Vw. LS16: Leeds 5D **10**
Dale Pk. Wlk. LS16: Leeds 5D **10**
Dale Rd. BD11: Drig 6A **38**
Dales Dr. LS20: Guis 5D **6**
Daleside Av. LS28: Pud 5C **26**
Daleside Cl. LS28: Pud 4B **26**
Daleside Gro. LS28: Pud 5C **26**
Daleside Rd. LS28: Pud 4B **26**
Dales Way LS20: Guis 5D **6**
Dale Vw. BD11: Drig 3H **47**
Dale Vs. LS18: Hors 4D **18**
Dalton Av. LS11: Leeds 5E **41**
Dalton Gro. LS11: Leeds 5E **41**
Dalton Rd. LS11: Leeds 5E **41**
Dam La. LS19: Yead 2E **9**
Damon Av. BD10: B'ford 1A **26**
Danby Ct. WF3: Rob H 5C **52**
Danby Wlk. LS9: Leeds 6B **32**
Danecourt Rd. BD4: B'ford 4A **36**
Dane Hill Dr. BD4: B'ford 3A **36**
Daniel Ct. BD4: B'ford 5B **36**
Darcy Ct. LS15: Leeds 5C **34**
Darfield Av. LS8: Leeds 2C **32**
Darfield Cres. LS8: Leeds 2C **32**
Darfield Gro. LS8: Leeds 2B **32**
Darfield Pl. LS8: Leeds 2C **32**
Darfield Rd. LS8: Leeds 2C **32**
Darfield St. LS8: Leeds 2C **32**
Darfield Vs. LS8: Leeds 3C **32** *(off Darfield Cres.)*
Dark La. WF17: Birs 6H **47**
Dark Neville St. LS1: Leeds 6D **4** (6F **31**) *(off Granary Wharf)*
Darkwood Cl. LS17: Leeds 5C **14**
Darkwood Way LS17: Leeds 5C **14**
Darley Av. LS10: Leeds 2H **51**
Darnley La. LS15: Leeds 1C **44**
Darnley Rd. LS16: Leeds 4H **19**
Darren St. BD4: B'ford 1A **36**
Dartmouth Av. LS27: Morl 6G **49**
Dartmouth M. LS27: Morl 6F **49**
Dartmouth Pk. 6E **49**
Dartmouth Way LS11: Leeds 5G **41**
David Lloyd Leisure Leeds 1F **21**
David St. LS11: Leeds 1F **41**
Davies Av. LS8: Leeds 3B **22**
Dawlish Av. LS9: Leeds 5D **32**
Dawlish Cres. LS9: Leeds 5D **32**
Dawlish Gro. LS9: Leeds 6D **32**
Dawlish Mt. LS9: Leeds 5D **32**
Dawlish Pl. LS9: Leeds 5D **32**
Dawlish Rd. LS9: Leeds 5D **32**
Dawlish Row LS9: Leeds 5D **32**
Dawlish St. LS9: Leeds 5D **32**
Dawlish Ter. LS9: Leeds 5D **32**
Dawlish Wlk. LS9: Leeds 5D **32**
Dawson Hill LS27: Morl 4G **49**
Dawson La. BD4: B'ford Keeper La. 5G **37**
Dawson La. LS26: Rothw 3G **53**
Dawson Rd. LS11: Leeds 4E **41**
Dawsons Cnr. LS28: Stan 3E **27**
Dawsons Ct. LS14: Leeds 1B **34**
Dawsons Mdw. LS28: Stan 3E **27**
Dawsons Sq. LS28: Fars 3D **26**
Dawsons Ter. LS28: Stan 3E **27**
Dawson St. LS28: Stan 4F **27**
Dawson St. WF3: Ting 2B **56**
Dawson Vw. LS27: Morl 4B **50**
Dealtry Cl. LS15: Leeds 1F **45**
Dealtry Rd. LS15: Leeds 1F **45**
Dean Av. LS8: Leeds 5C **22**
Dean Ct. LS8: Leeds 5C **22**
Deanfield Av. LS27: Morl 3F **49**
Dean Hall Cl. LS27: Morl 5F **49**
Dean Head LS18: Hors 1A **10**
Deanhurst Gdns. LS27: Gil 3D **48**
Deanhurst Ind. Cen. LS27: Gil 3D **48**
Dean La. LS18: Hors 1A **10**
Dean La. LS18: Yead 1A **10**
Dean La. LS20: Hawk 5B **6**
Dean M. LS18: Hors 1B **10**
Dean Pk. Av. BD11: Drig 2G **47**
Dean Pk. Dr. BD11: Drig 2G **47**
Dean Pastures BD11: Drig 3G **47**
Deansway LS27: Morl 3F **49**
Deanswood Cl. LS17: Leeds 6E **13**
Deanswood Dr. LS17: Leeds 6D **12**
Deanswood Gdns. LS17: Leeds 6D **12**
Deanswood Gth. LS17: Leeds 6E **13**
Deanswood Grn. LS17: Leeds 6D **12**
Deanswood Hill LS17: Leeds 6D **12**
Deanswood Pl. LS17: Leeds 6E **13**
Deanswood Ri. LS17: Leeds 6E **13**
Deanswood Vw. LS17: Leeds 6E **13**
Dean Vw. WF17: Birs 6H **47**
Deepdale LS29: Men 3C **6**
Deighton Vw. LS6: Leeds 2C **20**
De Lacies Ct. LS26: W'frd 2A **54**
De Lacies Rd. LS26: W'frd 2A **54**
De Lacy Mt. LS5: Leeds 1G **29**
Delius Av. BD10: B'ford 6A **16**
Delph Ct. LS6: Leeds 1E **31**
Delph End LS28: Pud 6D **26**
DELPH END 6D **26**
Delph Hill LS28: Pud 5G **27** *(off Clifton Hill)*
Delphinium Gro. LS16: Leeds 1B **20**
Delph La. LS6: Leeds 1E **31**
Delph Mt. LS6: Leeds 1E **31**
Delph Vw. LS6: Leeds 1E **31**
Denbigh App. LS9: Leeds 3F **33**
Denbigh Cft. LS9: Leeds 3F **33**
Denbigh Hgts. LS9: Leeds 3F **33**
Denbrook Av. BD4: B'ford 6B **36**
Denbrook Cl. BD4: B'ford 6B **36**
Denbrook Cres. BD4: B'ford 1B **46**
Denbrook Wlk. BD4: B'ford 6B **36**
Denbrook Way BD4: B'ford 6B **36**
Denbury Mt. BD4: B'ford 5A **36**
Denby Ho. BD4: B'ford 6B **36**
Dence Grn. BD4: B'ford 2A **36**
Dence Pl. LS15: Leeds 5G **33**
Dene Ho. Ct. LS2: Leeds 3F **31**
Deneway LS28: Stan 3E **27**
Denham Av. LS27: Morl 6G **49**
Denison Hall LS3: Leeds 2A **4** (4E **31**)
Denison Rd. LS3: Leeds 3A **4** (5E **31**)
Denison St. LS19: Yead 2D **8**
Dennil Cres. LS15: Leeds 1D **34**
Dennil Rd. LS15: Leeds 2D **34**
Dennison Fold BD4: B'ford 2A **36**
Dennistead Cres. LS6: Leeds 6B **20**
Denshaw Dr. LS27: Morl 5A **50**
Denshaw Gro. LS27: Morl 5A **50**
Denshaw La. WF3: Ting 6D **50**
Denton Av. LS8: Leeds 3B **22**
Denton Gro. LS8: Leeds 3B **22**
Denton Ho. LS14: Leeds 5G **23** *(off Kingsdale Ct.)*
Denton Row LS12: Leeds 1G **39**
Denton Ter. LS27: Morl 6G **49**
Dent St. LS9: Leeds 6B **32**
Derby Pl. BD3: B'ford 6A **26**
Derby Pl. LS19: Raw 5D **8** *(off North St.)*
Derby Rd. BD3: B'ford 6A **26**
Derby Rd. LS19: Raw 5D **8**
Derbyshire St. LS10: Leeds 4B **42**
Derby Ter. BD10: B'ford 3A **16**
Derry Hill LS29: Men 2B **6**
Derry Hill Gdns. LS29: Men 1B **6**
Derry La. LS29: Men 1B **6**
Derwent Av. LS26: W'frd 3C **54**
Derwent Dr. LS16: Leeds 5B **12**
Derwent Pl. LS11: Leeds 1E **41**
Derwent Vw. LS11: Leeds 1E **41**
Derwentwater Gro. LS6: Leeds 6A **20**
Derwentwater Ter. LS6: Leeds 6B **20**
Detroit Av. LS15: Leeds 5D **34**
Detroit Dr. LS15: Leeds 5E **35**
Devon Cl. LS2: Leeds 3F **31**
Devon Rd. LS2: Leeds 3F **31**
Devonshire Av. LS8: Leeds 2C **22**
Devonshire Cl. LS8: Leeds 1C **22** (not continuous)
Devonshire Cres. LS8: Leeds 2C **22**
Devonshire Gdns. LS2: Leeds 2F **31**
Devonshire La. LS8: Leeds 1C **22**
Devonshire Pl. LS19: Yead 2D **8**
Devro Ct. LS9: Leeds 3D **42**
Dewhirst Pl. BD4: B'ford 2A **36**
Dewsbury Rd. LS11: Leeds Meadow La. 1G **41**
Dewsbury Rd. LS11: Leeds Park Wood Cl. 2D **50**
Dewsbury Rd. BD19: Gom 6D **46**
Dewsbury Rd. LS27: Leeds 5D **50**
Dewsbury Rd. LS27: Morl 5D **50**
Dewsbury Rd. WF12: Dew 5A **56**
Dewsbury Rd. WF12: E Ard 5A **56**
Dewsbury Rd. WF3: Ting 3B **56** (not continuous)
Diadem Dr. LS14: Leeds 4G **33**
Dial St. LS9: Leeds 1B **42**
Dibb La. LS19: Yead 6H **7**
Dib Cl. LS8: Leeds 6F **23**
Dib La. LS8: Leeds 6F **23**
Dickinson St. LS18: Hors 1C **18**
Dick La. BD3: B'ford 6A **26**
Dick La. BD4: B'ford 3A **36**
Dick's Gth. Rd. LS29: Men 1B **6**
Digby Rd. LS29: Men 1C **6**
Digpal Rd. LS27: Chur 6A **40**
Dinsdale Bldgs. LS19: Yead 3C **8**
Discovery Way LS2: Leeds 1B **4** (4F **31**)
Disraeli Gdns. LS11: Leeds 3F **41**
Disraeli Ter. LS11: Leeds 3F **41**
Dixon Ct. LS12: N Far 4H **39**
Dixon La. LS12: Leeds 2A **40**
Dixon La. Rd. LS12: Leeds 2A **40**
Dobson Av. LS11: Leeds 4G **41**
Dobson Gro. LS11: Leeds 4G **41**
Dobson Pl. LS11: Leeds 4G **41**
Dobsons Row WF3: Car 1F **59**
Dobson Ter. LS11: Leeds 4G **41**
Dobson Vw. LS11: Leeds 4G **41**
Dock Grn. Ct. LS9: Leeds 3B **32** *(off Ashley Rd.)*
Dockside, The LS10: Leeds 1H **41**
Dock St. LS10: Leeds 6F **5** (6G **31**)
Dodgson Av. LS7: Leeds 2A **32**
Dolly La. LS9: Leeds 4A **32**
Dolly La. Bus. Cen. LS9: Leeds 3A **32**
Dolphin Ct. LS13: Leeds 4B **28**
Dolphin Ct. LS9: Leeds 6A **32**
Dolphin La. WF3: Thpe H 2A **58** (not continuous)
Dolphin Rd. LS10: Leeds 4A **52**

74 A-Z Leeds

Featherbank La. – Gainsborough Way

Featherbank La. LS18: Hors ... 3B **18**
Featherbank Mt. LS18: Hors ... 3B **18**
Featherbank Ter. LS18: Hors ... 4B **18**
Featherbank Wlk. LS18: Hors ... 4B **18**
Felcourt Dr. BD4: B'ford ... 5A **36**
Felcourt Fold BD4: B'ford ... 5A **36**
Felnex Cl. LS9: Leeds ... 2E **43**
Felnex Cres. LS9: Leeds ... 2E **43**
Felnex Rd. LS9: Leeds ... 2D **42**
Felnex Sq. LS9: Leeds ... 2D **42**
Felnex Trad. Est. LS9: Leeds ... 2E **43**
Felnex Way LS9: Leeds ... 2E **43**
Fencote Cres. BD2: B'ford ... 2A **26**
Fenton Av. LS26: W'frd ... 2B **54**
Fenton Cl. LS26: W'frd ... 2B **54**
Fenton Ga. LS10: Leeds ... 5A **52**
Fenton Pl. LS10: Leeds ... 5A **52**
Fenton Rd. WF3: Stly ... 4H **59**
Fentonsgate WF3: Loft ... 2E **59**
Fenton St. LS1: Leeds ... 1D **4** (4F **31**)
Fenton St. WF3: Ting ... 2D **56**
Fernbank Av. LS13: Leeds ... 2H **27**
Fernbank Cl. LS13: Leeds ... 2H **27**
Fernbank Dr. LS13: Leeds ... 2H **27**
Fernbank Gdns. LS13: Leeds ... 2H **27**
Fernbank Pl. LS13: Leeds ... 2H **27**
Fernbank Rd. LS13: Leeds ... 2H **27**
Fernbank Ter. LS19: Yead ... 2C **8**
... *(off Park Av.)*
Fernbank Wlk. LS13: Leeds ... 2H **27**
Ferncliffe Rd. LS13: Leeds ... 3C **28**
Ferncliffe Ter. LS13: Leeds ... 3B **28**
Fern Cft. LS14: S'cft ... 2H **15**
Ferndene Av. WF17: Birs ... 6H **47**
Ferndene Wlk. WF17: Birs ... 6H **47**
Fern Gro. LS5: Leeds ... 1G **29**
... *(off Tordoff Pl.)*
Fernlea LS26: Rothw ... 3H **53**
Fernlea Ct. LS12: Leeds ... 6D **28**
Fern Lea Vw. LS28: Stan ... 3G **27**
Fern Ter. LS28: Stan ... 3G **27**
Fern Way LS14: S'cft ... 2H **15**
Fernwood LS8: Leeds ... 2C **22**
Fernwood Ct. LS8: Leeds ... 2C **22**
Ferriby Cl. BD2: B'ford ... 2A **26**
Ferriby Towers LS9: Leeds ... 4A **32**
... *(off Granville Rd.)*
Fewston Av. LS9: Leeds ... 1B **42**
... (not continuous)
Fewston Ct. LS9: Leeds ... 1B **42**
Field End LS15: Leeds ... 6A **34**
Fld. End Cl. LS15: Leeds ... 6A **34**
Fld. End Ct. LS15: Leeds ... 6A **34**
Fld. End Cres. LS15: Leeds ... 6A **34**
Fld. End Gdns. LS15: Leeds ... 6A **34**
Fld. End Gth. LS15: Leeds ... 6A **34**
Fld. End Grn. LS15: Leeds ... 6A **34**
Fld. End Gro. LS15: Leeds ... 5B **34**
Fld. End Mt. LS15: Leeds ... 6A **34**
Fld. End Rd. LS15: Leeds ... 6A **34**
Fieldgate Rd. BD10: B'ford ... 4A **16**
Fieldhead WF17: Birs ... 6G **47**
Fieldhead Cres. WF17: Birs ... 6G **47**
Fieldhead Dr. LS20: Guis ... 5E **7**
Fieldhead Gro. LS20: Guis ... 5E **7**
Fld. Head La. BD11: Drig ... 4G **47**
Fieldhead Pde. WF17: Birs ... 6H **47**
Fieldhead Rd. LS20: Guis ... 5E **7**
Fieldhead Ter.
LS7: Leeds ... 1E **5** (3G **31**)
Fieldhouse Cl. LS17: Leeds ... 1G **21**
Fieldhouse Dr. LS17: Leeds ... 1G **21**
Fieldhouse Gro. LS28: Fars ... 3E **27**
Fieldhouse Lawn LS17: Leeds ... 1G **21**
Fieldhouse Wlk. LS17: Leeds ... 1G **21**
... (not continuous)
Fielding Ct. LS27: Morl ... 4F **49**
Fielding Ga. LS12: Leeds ... 5B **30**
Fielding Ga. M. LS12: Leeds ... 5A **30**
Fielding Way LS27: Morl ... 4F **49**
Fieldmoor Lodge LS28: Pud ... 1G **37**
Fld. Pk. Grange LS27: Gil ... 3D **48**
Fields, The WF3: Loft ... 2F **59**
Fieldside Cl. BD4: B'ford ... 5B **36**
Field Ter. LS15: Leeds
Cross St. ... 5A **34**
Field Ter. LS15: Leeds
Hermon Rd. ... 4B **34**
Field Vw. LS26: Oult ... 4D **54**
Fieldway Av. LS13: Leeds ... 1A **28**
Fieldway Chase LS26: Oult ... 4D **54**
Fieldway Cl. LS13: Leeds ... 1A **28**
Fieldway Ri. LS13: Leeds ... 1A **28**
Fifth Av. LS26: Rothw ... 2A **54**
Fillingfir Dr. LS16: Leeds ... 3F **19**
Fillingfir Rd. LS16: Leeds ... 3F **19**
Fillingfir Wlk. LS16: Leeds ... 3F **19**
Finch Dr. LS15: Leeds ... 1F **45**
Finchley Way LS27: Morl ... 6G **49**
Findon Ter. BD10: B'ford ... 1A **26**
Fink Hill LS18: Hors ... 3A **18**
Finkle Ct. LS27: Gil ... 3C **48**
Finkle La. LS27: Gil ... 3C **48**
Finsbury Rd. LS1: Leeds ... 1C **4** (4F **31**)
Fir Av. LS16: Leeds ... 4A **12**
Firbank Gro. LS15: Leeds ... 1G **43**
First Av. LS12: Leeds ... 6B **30**
First Av. LS19: Raw ... 4E **9**
First Av. LS26: Rothw ... 2H **53**
First Av. LS28: Stan ... 4G **27**
First Av. Ind. Est. LS28: Stan ... 4G **27**
Firth Av. LS11: Leeds ... 5E **41**
Firth Cl. WF3: Stly ... 6G **59**
Firth Gro. LS11: Leeds ... 5E **41**
Firth Mt. LS11: Leeds ... 5E **41**
Firth Rd. LS11: Leeds ... 5E **41**
Firth St. LS9: Leeds ... 1H **5** (4A **32**)
Firth Ter. LS9: Leeds ... 1H **5** (4A **32**)
Firth Vw. LS11: Leeds ... 5E **41**
Fir Tree App. LS17: Leeds ... 5F **13**
Fir Tree Cl. LS17: Leeds ... 5G **13**
Fir Tree Gdns. LS17: Leeds ... 5F **13**
Fir Tree Grn. LS17: Leeds ... 5G **13**
Fir Tree Gro. LS17: Leeds ... 6G **13**
Fir Tree La. LS17: Leeds ... 6H **13**
Fir Tree Ri. LS17: Leeds ... 6G **13**
Fir Tree Va. LS17: Leeds ... 6G **13**
Fish St. LS1: Leeds ... 4F **5** (5G **31**)
Fitness and Physique ... **4H 51**
... *(within Middleton District Cen.)*
Fitzroy Dr. LS8: Leeds ... 5B **22**
Flats, The LS19: Yead ... 3E **9**
Flawith Dr. BD2: B'ford ... 3A **26**
Flax Mill Rd. LS10: Leeds ... 4A **42**
Flax Pl. LS9: Leeds ... 6H **5** (6A **32**)
Flaxton Cl. LS11: Leeds ... 4F **41**
Flaxton Ct. BD4: B'ford ... 1A **36**
Flaxton Gdns. LS11: Leeds ... 4F **41**
Flaxton Grn. BD2: B'ford ... 3A **26**
Flaxton St. LS11: Leeds ... 4F **41**
Flaxton Vw. LS11: Leeds ... 4F **41**
Fleet La. LS26: Meth ... 5G **55**
Fleet La. LS26: Oult ... 4D **54**
Fleet St. LS15: Leeds ... 3E **35**
Fleet Thro' Rd. LS18: Hors ... 5B **18**
Flexbury Av. LS27: Morl ... 6G **49**
Flinton Gro. BD2: B'ford ... 2A **26**
Floral Av. LS7: Leeds ... 5G **21**
Florence Av. LS9: Leeds ... 3C **32**
Florence Gro. LS9: Leeds ... 3C **32**
Florence Mt. LS9: Leeds ... 3C **32**
Florence Pl. LS9: Leeds ... 3C **32**
Florence St. LS9: Leeds ... 3C **32**
Florence Ter. LS27: Morl ... 5H **49**
... *(off Gillroyd Pde.)*
Flossmore Way LS27: Gil ... 2C **48**
Flower Chase LS20: Guis ... 4H **7**
Flower Cl. LS19: Yead ... 2C **8**
Flower Ct. LS18: Hors ... 4B **18**
Flower Gth. LS18: Hors ... 3B **18**
... *(off Stanhope Dr.)*
Flower Mt. LS19: Yead ... 2E **9**
... *(off Alexandra Ter.)*
Focus Way LS19: Raw ... 4D **8**
Fold, The LS15: Leeds ... 1E **35**
Folkton Holme BD2: B'ford ... 3A **26**
Folly Hall Mt. WF3: Ting ... 3C **56**
Folly Hall Rd. WF3: Ting ... 3C **56**
Folly La. LS11: Leeds ... 3F **41**
Fontmell Cl. BD4: B'ford ... 5A **36**
Football LS19: Yead ... 2E **9**
Football World Leeds ... **2D 42**
Forber Gro. BD4: B'ford ... 2A **36**
Forber Pl. LS15: Leeds ... 6G **33**
Forbes Ho. BD4: B'ford ... 4A **36**
... *(off Stirling Cres.)*
Forest Bank LS27: Gil ... 2C **48**
Forest Ridge WF3: E Ard ... 2G **57**
Forest Yd. LS10: Leeds ... 5A **52**
Forge La. LS12: Leeds ... 5B **30**
Forge Row LS12: N Far ... 4D **38**
Forman's Dr. WF3: Rob H ... 6C **52**
Forrester Ct. WF3: Rob H ... 6D **52**
Forster Loft LS12: Leeds ... 3H **39**
Forster M. LS12: Leeds ... 3G **39**
Forster Pl. LS12: Leeds ... 3G **39**
Forster St. LS10: Leeds ... 2A **42**
Forsythia Av. WF3: E Ard ... 3G **57**
Forth Ct. LS11: Leeds ... 1E **41**
Forum Leisure Cen., The,
Leeds ... **4H 5 (5H 31)**
Foster Cl. LS27: Morl ... 4G **49**
Foster Cres. LS27: Morl ... 4G **49**
Foster Sq. LS10: Leeds ... 1H **51**
Foster St. LS27: Morl ... 4G **49**
Foster Ter. LS13: Leeds ... 2D **28**
Foston Cl. BD2: B'ford ... 3A **26**
Foston La. BD2: B'ford ... 3A **26**
Foundry, The LS3: Leeds ... 3A **4** (5D **30**)
... *(off Cavendish St.)*
Foundry App. LS9: Leeds ... 3D **32**
Foundry Av. LS8: Leeds ... 2D **32**
Foundry Av. LS9: Leeds ... 2D **32**
Foundry Dr. LS9: Leeds ... 2D **32**
Foundry Ind. Est. LS28: Stan ... 4G **27**
Foundry La. LS14: Leeds ... 2G **33**
Foundry La. LS28: Stan ... 3G **27**
Foundry La. LS9: Leeds ... 2F **33**
Foundry Mill Cres. LS14: Leeds ... 2H **33**
Foundry Mill Dr. LS14: Leeds ... 2G **33**
... (not continuous)
Foundry Mill Gdns.
LS14: Leeds ... 6G **23**
Foundry Mill Mt. LS14: Leeds ... 2H **33**
Foundry Mill St. LS14: Leeds ... 2G **33**
Foundry Mill Ter. LS14: Leeds ... 2H **33**
Foundry Mill Vw. LS14: Leeds ... 2H **33**
Foundry Mill Wlk. LS14: Leeds ... 2H **33**
Foundry Pl. LS9: Leeds ... 2D **32**
Foundry Rd. LS28: Stan ... 4G **27**
Foundry Sq. LS11: Leeds ... 1F **41**
... *(off Foundry St.)*
Foundry St. LS11: Leeds ... 1F **41**
Foundry St. LS9: Leeds ... 5H **5** (6A **32**)
Foundry Wlk. LS8: Leeds ... 2C **32**
Fountain Ct. LS18: Hors ... 6A **10**
Fountain Ct. LS27: Morl ... 5E **49**
Fountain Hall LS27: Morl ... 6F **49**
... *(off Fountain St.)*
Fountain St. LS1: Leeds ... 3B **4** (5E **31**)
Fountain St. LS27: Chur ... 1A **50**
Fountain St. LS27: Morl ... 6F **49**
Fourteenth Av. LS12: Leeds ... 1B **40**
Fourth Av. LS26: Rothw ... 2A **54**
Fowler's Pl. LS28: Stan ... 3G **27**
Foxcroft Cl. LS6: Leeds ... 6H **19**
Foxcroft Gth. LS6: Leeds ... 6H **19**
Foxcroft Grn. LS6: Leeds ... 6H **19**
Foxcroft Mt. LS6: Leeds ... 6H **19**
Foxcroft Rd. LS6: Leeds ... 6H **19**
Foxcroft Wlk. LS6: Leeds ... 6H **19**
Foxcroft Way LS6: Leeds ... 6H **19**
Foxglove Av. LS8: Leeds ... 5E **23**
Foxglove Rd. WF17: Birs ... 6G **47**
Foxhill Av. LS16: Leeds ... 2A **20**
Foxhill Ct. LS16: Leeds ... 2A **20**
Foxhill Cres. LS16: Leeds ... 2B **20**
Foxhill Dr. LS16: Leeds ... 2A **20**
Foxhill Grn. LS16: Leeds ... 2B **20**
Foxhill Gro. LS16: Leeds ... 2B **20**
Foxhills, The LS16: Leeds ... 5D **10**
Foxholes Cres. LS28: Cal ... 5D **16**
Foxholes La. LS28: Cal ... 5D **16**
Foxton Gdns. LS27: Morl ... 6F **49**
Fox Way LS10: Leeds ... 2A **42**
Foxwood LS8: Leeds ... 3E **23**
Foxwood Av. LS8: Leeds ... 6G **23**
Foxwood Cl. LS8: Leeds ... 6G **23**
Foxwood Farm Way LS8: Leeds .. 6G **23**
Foxwood Gro. LS8: Leeds ... 6G **23**
Foxwood Ri. LS8: Leeds ... 6G **23**
Foxwood Wlk. LS8: Leeds ... 6G **23**
Fraisthorpe Mead BD2: B'ford ... 3A **26**
Frances Lupton Ho. LS6: Leeds .. 1D **30**
... *(off Victoria Gdns.)*
Frances St. LS28: Fars ... 3F **27**
Francis Ct. LS7: Leeds ... 2H **31**
... *(off Francis St.)*
Francis Gro. LS11: Leeds ... 4F **41**
Francis St. LS7: Leeds ... 2H **31**
Frankland Gro. LS7: Leeds ... 2A **32**
Frankland Pl. LS7: Leeds ... 2A **32**
... (not continuous)
Frank Parkinson Ct. LS20: Guis ... 4G **7**
... *(off W. Villa Rd.)*
Frank Parkinson Homes
LS20: Guis ... 4G **7**
... *(off Lands La.)*
Fraser Av. LS18: Hors ... 3H **17**
Fraser Rd. LS28: Cal ... 5B **16**
Fraser St. LS9: Leeds ... 4B **32**
Frederick Av. LS9: Leeds ... 1C **42**
Frederick St. LS28: Fars ... 2E **27**
Freeman Gdns. LS9: Leeds ... 6B **32**
Freemantle Pl. LS15: Leeds ... 6G **33**
Freemont St. LS13: Leeds ... 3A **28**
Freestone M. LS12: Leeds ... 6C **28**
Fremantle Gro. BD4: B'ford ... 2A **36**
Frensham Av. LS27: Morl ... 6F **49**
Frodingham Vs. BD2: B'ford ... 3A **26**
Frontline Cl. LS8: Leeds ... 5C **22**
Front Row LS11: Leeds ... 1F **41**
... (not continuous)
Front St. LS11: Leeds ... 1F **41**
Fuchsia Cft. LS26: W'frd ... 3E **55**
Fulford Wlk. BD2: B'ford ... 3A **26**
Fulham Pl. LS11: Leeds ... 4F **41**
Fulham Sq. LS11: Leeds ... 4F **41**
... *(off Fulham St.)*
Fulham St. LS11: Leeds ... 4F **41**
Fullers Ho. LS9: Leeds ... 6H **5** (6A **32**)
... *(off East St.)*
Fulmar Ct. LS10: Leeds ... 4H **51**
Fulneck LS28: Pud ... 3F **37**
FULNECK ... **2G 37**
Fulneck Cl. LS11: Leeds ... 2E **51**
Fulneck Ct. LS28: Pud ... 2H **37**
Fulneck Golf Course ... **3F 37**
Fulneck M. LS28: Pud ... 2H **37**
Fulton Pl. LS16: Leeds ... 4A **20**
Furnace La. BD11: B'haw ... 3C **46**
Future Bodies Gym Morley ... **4G 49**
... *(off Bank Av.)*

G

Gable End Ter. LS28: Pud ... 6H **27**
Gables, The LS17: Leeds ... 5C **14**
Gables, The LS18: Hors ... 1C **18**
Gabriel Ct. LS10: Leeds ... 3H **41**
... *(off Hunslet Grn. Way)*
Gainsborough Av. LS16: Leeds ... 4H **11**
Gainsborough Dr. LS16: Leeds ... 4H **11**
Gainsborough Flds. LS12: N Far .. 4E **39**
... *(off Coach Rd.)*
Gainsborough Pl. LS12: N Far ... 4E **39**
... *(off Coach Rd.)*
Gainsborough Way WF3: Stly ... 6G **59**

A-Z Leeds 77

Gaitskell Wlk. – Granby Gro.

Gaitskell Wlk. LS11: Leeds 2E **41**
Gala Bingo Bradford 6A **36**
Gallagher Leisure Pk. 5B **26**
Gallops, The LS27: Morl 2A **56**
Galloway Ct. LS28: Pud 5C **26**
Galloway Gdns. LS28: Stan 4D **26**
Galloway Grange LS28: Pud 4D **26**
Galloway Grn. LS28: Pud 5D **26**
Galloway La. LS28: Pud 4C **26**
Galloway Rd. BD10: B'ford 4A **16**
Gamble Hill LS13: Leeds 5D **28**
GAMBLE HILL 5D **28**
Gamble Hill Chase LS13: Leeds .. 5D **28**
Gamble Hill Cl. LS13: Leeds 5D **28**
Gamble Hill Cft. LS13: Leeds 5D **28**
.... *(off Gamble Hill Vw.)*
Gamble Hill Cross LS13: Leeds ... 5D **28**
.... *(off Gamble Hill Lawn)*
Gamble Hill Dr. LS13: Leeds 5D **28**
Gamble Hill Fold LS13: Leeds 5D **28**
.... *(off Gamble Hill Lawn)*
Gamble Hill Grange
LS13: Leeds 5D **28**
.... *(off Gamble Hill Dr.)*
Gamble Hill Grn. LS13: Leeds 5D **28**
Gamble Hill Lawn LS13: Leeds ... 5D **28**
Gamble Hill Path LS13: Leeds 5D **28**
.... *(off Gamble Hill Grn.)*
Gamble Hill Pl. LS13: Leeds 5D **28**
Gamble Hill Ri. LS13: Leeds 5D **28**
Gamble Hill Va. LS13: Leeds 5D **28**
Gamble Hill Vw. LS13: Leeds 5D **28**
Gamble Hill Wlk. LS13: Leeds 5D **28**
.... *(off Gamble Hill Ri.)*
Gamble La. LS12: Leeds 1C **38**
Gambles Hill LS28: Fars 2F **27**
Gang, The LS12: Leeds 6A **30**
.... *(off Town St.)*
Ganners Cl. LS13: Leeds 1C **28**
Ganners Gth. LS13: Leeds 1D **28**
Ganners Grn. LS13: Leeds 1C **28**
Ganners Gro. LS13: Leeds 1D **28**
Ganners Hill LS13: Leeds 1D **28**
Ganners La. LS13: Leeds 1C **28**
Ganners Mt. LS13: Leeds 1C **28**
Ganners Ri. LS13: Leeds 1D **28**
Ganners Rd. LS13: Leeds 1C **28**
Ganners Wlk. LS13: Leeds 1C **28**
Ganners Way LS13: Leeds 1C **28**
Ganton Cl. LS6: Leeds 1F **31**
Gardeners Ct. LS10: Leeds 3H **41**
Garden Ho. La. WF3: Ting 3E **57**
Gardenhurst LS6: Leeds 1B **30**
Gardens, The LS10: Leeds 5G **51**
Gardens, The LS28: Fars 2E **27**
Gardens, The LS3: Leeds... 1A **4** (4D **30**)
Garden Vw. Ct. LS8: Leeds 2D **22**
GARFORTH BRIDGE 2H **45**
Gargrave App. LS9: Leeds 5B **32**
Gargrave Ct. LS9: Leeds 4B **32**
Gargrave Pl. LS9: Leeds 4B **32**
Garibaldi St. BD3: B'ford 6A **26**
.... (not continuous)
Garland Dr. LS15: Leeds 6D **34**
Garmont M. LS7: Leeds 5H **21**
Garmont Rd. LS7: Leeds 5H **21**
Garnet Av. LS11: Leeds 4G **41**
Garnet Cres. LS11: Leeds 4G **41**
Garnet Gro. LS11: Leeds 4G **41**
Garnet Pde. LS11: Leeds 4G **41**
Garnet Pl. LS11: Leeds 4G **41**
Garnet Rd. LS11: Leeds 5G **41**
Garnet Ter. LS11: Leeds 4G **41**
Garnet Vw. LS11: Leeds 4G **41**
Garth, The LS9: Leeds 6A **32**
Garth Av. LS17: Leeds 2F **21**
Garth Dr. LS17: Leeds 2F **21**
Garth Gro. LS29: Men 1C **6**
Garth Rd. LS17: Leeds 2F **21**
Garth Wlk. LS17: Leeds 2F **21**
Garton Av. LS9: Leeds 6C **32**
Garton Gro. LS9: Leeds 6C **32**
Garton Rd. LS9: Leeds 6C **32**
Garton Ter. LS9: Leeds 6C **32**
Garton Vw. LS9: Leeds 6C **32**
Gascoigne Rd. WF3: Thpe H 2A **58**
Gate Ho. Ct. LS26: W'frd 2E **55**
Gateland Dr. LS17: Shad 5G **15**
Gateland La. LS17: Shad 6G **15**
Gateway, The LS26: Rothw 5G **53**
Gate Way Dr. LS19: Yead 2C **8**
Gateway E. LS9: Leeds 5H **5** (6H **31**)
.... *(off Marsh La.)*
Gateway Nth. LS9: Leeds .. 5H **5** (6H **31**)
.... *(off Crown Point Rd.)*
Gateways WF1: Outw 6E **59**
Gateway Sth. LS9: Leeds .. 6H **5** (6H **31**)
.... *(off Marsh La.)*
Gateway W. LS9: Leeds 6H **5** (6H **31**)
.... *(off East St.)*
Gathorne Cl. LS8: Leeds 2A **32**
Gathorne St. LS8: Leeds 2A **32**
.... (not continuous)
Gathorne Ter. LS8: Leeds 2A **32**
.... (not continuous)
Gaunts Pl. LS28: Fars 2G **27**
Gavin Cl. BD3: B'ford 6A **26**
Gelderd Bus. Pk. LS12: Leeds 3B **40**
Gelderd Cl. LS12: Leeds 3B **40**
Gelderd La. LS12: Leeds 3B **40**
Gelderd Motor Pk. LS12: Leeds ... 4A **40**
Gelderd Pl. LS12: Leeds 1C **40**
Gelderd Rd. LS12: Gil 6H **39**
Gelderd Rd. LS12: Leeds 6H **39**
Gelderd Rd. LS27: Gil 4C **48**
Gelderd Trad. Est. LS12: Leeds 2C **40**
Gelder Rd. LS12: Leeds 6H **29**
Gemini Bus. Pk. LS7: Leeds 2H **31**
Genista Dr. LS10: Leeds 1H **51**
George Mann Rd. LS10: Leeds 4C **42**
George Mann Way LS10: Leeds ... 4B **42**
George St. LS19: Raw 5D **8**
George St. LS2: Leeds 4F **5** (5G **31**)
George St. WF1: Outw 6D **58**
Georgian Sq. LS13: Leeds 6G **17**
Gerard Av. LS27: Morl 5F **49**
Ghyll Beck Dr. LS19: Raw 6G **9**
Ghyll Mt. LS19: Yead 3B **8**
Ghyll Rd. LS6: Leeds 5G **19**
Ghyll Royd LS20: Guis 6G **7**
.... (not continuous)
Ghyllroyd LS19: Yead 4C **8**
Ghyllroyd Av. BD11: B'haw 4D **46**
Ghyllroyd Dr. BD11: B'haw 4D **46**
Gibraltar Island Rd.
LS10: Leeds 3B **42**
Gibraltar Rd. LS28: Pud 6D **26**
Gibson Dr. LS15: Leeds 6C **34**
Gilbert Chase LS5: Leeds 2G **29**
Gilbert Cl. LS5: Leeds 2H **29**
Gilbert Mt. LS5: Leeds 2H **29**
Gilbert St. LS28: Fars 3F **27**
GILDERSOME 2C **48**
Gildersome Cross LS27: Gil 3C **48**
Gildersome La. LS12: Gil 6B **38**
Gildersome La. LS12: N Far 6B **38**
Gildersome La. LS27: Gil 1B **48**
Gildersome Spur LS27: Gil 4D **48**
GILDERSOME STREET 4B **48**
Gilhusum Rd. LS27: Gil 3D **48**
Gillett Dr. LS26: Rothw 4H **53**
Gillett La. LS26: Rothw 4H **53**
Gillingham Grn. BD4: B'ford 4A **36**
Gill La. LS19: Yead 5A **8**
GILLROYD 5A **50**
Gillroyd Mt. LS27: Morl 5A **50**
Gillroyd Pde. LS27: Morl 6H **49**
Gillroyd Pl. LS27: Morl 5H **49**
Gillroyd Ter. LS27: Morl 5A **50**
Gills, The LS27: Morl 5A **50**
Gillstead Ho. LS14: Leeds 5H **23**
.... *(off Kingsdale Ct.)*
Gilpin Pl. LS12: Leeds 1B **40**
Gilpin St. LS12: Leeds 1B **40**
Gilpin Ter. LS12: Leeds 1B **40**
Gilpin Vw. LS12: Leeds 1B **40**
Gilwell Ct. WF3: Thpe H 1B **58**
Gipsy Hill LS26: W'frd 3B **54**
Gipsy La. LS11: Leeds 1E **51**
Gipsy La. LS26: W'frd 3B **54**
Gipsy Mead LS26: W'frd 3B **54**
Gipsy St. BD3: B'ford 5A **26**
GIPTON 2D **32**
Gipton App. LS9: Leeds 4E **33**
Gipton Av. LS7: Leeds 2A **32**
Gipton Ga. E. LS9: Leeds 2E **33**
Gipton Ga. W. LS9: Leeds 2D **32**
Gipton Lodge LS8: Leeds 1C **32**
.... *(off Copgrove Rd.)*
Gipton Sq. LS9: Leeds 4F **33**
Gipton St. LS8: Leeds 2A **32**
GIPTON WOOD 6D **22**
Gipton Wood Av. LS8: Leeds 6D **22**
Gipton Wood Cres. LS8: Leeds 6D **22**
Gipton Wood Gro. LS8: Leeds 6D **22**
Gipton Wood Pl. LS8: Leeds 6D **22**
Gipton Wood Rd. LS8: Leeds 6D **22**
Glade, The LS28: Stan 3C **26**
Gladedale Av. LS8: Leeds 2E **33**
Glade Wlk. LS10: Leeds 5B **52**
Gladstone Ct. LS28: Stan 3H **27**
.... *(off Gladstone Ter.)*
Gladstone Cres. LS19: Raw 4D **8**
Gladstone Ho. BD4: B'ford 3A **36**
.... *(off Tyersal La.)*
Gladstone Rd. LS19: Raw 5D **8**
Gladstone St. LS28: Fars 2F **27**
Gladstone Ter. LS27: Morl 5G **49**
Gladstone Ter. LS28: Stan 3H **27**
Gladstone Vs. LS17: Shad 6G **15**
Glanville Ter. LS26: Rothw 4G **53**
Glasshouse St. LS10: Leeds 2H **41**
Glasshouse Vw. LS10: Leeds 5F **51**
Glastonbury Ct. BD4: B'ford 3A **36**
Glebe Av. LS5: Leeds 1H **29**
Glebe Ct. LS26: Rothw 4C **52**
Glebelands Dr. LS6: Leeds 5B **20**
Glebe Mt. LS28: Pud 1G **37**
Glebe Pl. LS5: Leeds 1H **29**
Glebe St. LS28: Pud 1G **37**
Glebe Ter. LS16: Leeds 4B **20**
GLEDHOW 4B **22**
Gledhow Av. LS8: Leeds 3B **22**
Gledhow Ct. LS7: Leeds 4A **22**
Gledhow Grange Vw.
LS8: Leeds 4B **22**
Gledhow Grange Wlk.
LS8: Leeds 4B **22**
Gledhow La. LS7: Leeds 4H **21**
Gledhow La. LS8: Leeds 4A **22**
Gledhow La. End LS7: Leeds 4H **21**
Gledhow Mt. LS8: Leeds 3A **32**
Gledhow Pk. Av. LS7: Leeds 5A **22**
Gledhow Pk. Cres. LS7: Leeds 5A **22**
Gledhow Pk. Dr. LS7: Leeds 5H **21**
Gledhow Pk. Gro. LS7: Leeds 5A **22**
Gledhow Pk. Rd. LS7: Leeds 5A **22**
Gledhow Pk. Vw. LS7: Leeds 5A **22**
Gledhow Pl. LS8: Leeds 3A **32**
Gledhow Ri. LS8: Leeds 5D **22**
Gledhow Rd. LS8: Leeds 3A **32**
Gledhow Ter. LS8: Leeds 3A **32**
Gledhow Towers LS8: Leeds 4A **22**
Gledhow Valley Rd.
LS17: Leeds 3G **21**
Gledhow Valley Rd. LS7: Leeds .. 3H **21**
Gledhow Valley Rd. LS8: Leeds ... 5B **22**
Gledhow Wood Av. LS8: Leeds 4B **22**
Gledhow Wood Cl. LS8: Leeds 4A **22**
Gledhow Wood Ct. LS8: Leeds 6C **22**
Gledhow Wood Gro. LS8: Leeds ... 4B **22**
Gledhow Wood Rd. LS8: Leeds 4B **22**
Glencoe Vw. LS9: Leeds 1B **42**
Glen Ct. LS27: Morl 6H **49**
Glendale Gdns. LS27: Morl 6H **49**
Glen Dene LS29: Men 1D **6**
Glendower Pk. LS16: Leeds 1B **20**
Gleneagles Dr. LS26: Rothw 5A **54**
Gleneagles Rd. LS17: Leeds 5F **13**
Glenfield Cvn. Pk. LS17: Bard
Bardsey 1H **15**
Glen Gro. LS27: Morl 6H **49**
Glenholme Rd. LS28: Fars 3E **27**
Glenhurst BD4: B'ford 6A **36**
Glenlea Cl. LS28: Stan 2A **28**
Glenlea Gdns. LS28: Stan 2A **28**
Glenmere Mt. LS19: Yead 2F **9**
Glen Mt. LS27: Morl 6H **49**
Glen Mt. LS29: Men 2D **6**
Glenmount Ter. LS27: Morl 1A **56**
Glen Rd. LS16: Leeds 4A **20**
Glen Rd. LS27: Morl 6H **49**
Glenroyd Cl. LS28: Pud 6E **27**
Glensdale Gro. LS9: Leeds 6B **32**
Glensdale Mt. LS9: Leeds 6B **32**
Glensdale Rd. LS9: Leeds 6B **32**
Glensdale St. LS9: Leeds 6B **32**
Glensdale Ter. LS9: Leeds 6B **32**
Glenthorpe Av. LS9: Leeds 5C **32**
Glenthorpe Cres. LS9: Leeds 5C **32**
Glenthorpe Ter. LS9: Leeds 5C **32**
Glenvale Cl. LS14: Leeds 6G **23**
Glen Vw. LS27: Morl 6H **49**
Global Av. LS11: Leeds 6C **40**
Global Ct. LS11: Leeds 1C **50**
Globe Rd. LS11: Leeds 6A **4** (6E **31**)
Glossop Gro. LS6: Leeds 1F **31**
.... *(off Glossop Vw.)*
Glossop Mt. LS6: Leeds 1F **31**
Glossop St. LS6: Leeds 1F **31**
Glossop Vw. LS6: Leeds 1F **31**
Gloucester Ct. LS12: Leeds 6C **30**
Gloucester Ter. LS12: Leeds 5C **30**
Glover Way LS11: Leeds 5G **41**
Goals Soccer Cen. Leeds 4A **30**
Goffee Way LS27: Chur 1A **50**
Golden Bank LS18: Hors 2C **18**
Golden Ter. LS12: Leeds 3G **39**
Goldsmith Dr. WF3: Rob H 6D **52**
Gomersall Ho. BD11: Drig 3F **47**
Goodman St. LS10: Leeds 2A **42**
Goodrick La. LS17: Leeds 3F **13**
Goodwin Rd. LS12: Leeds 1A **40**
Goodwood LS10: Leeds 6H **51**
Goody Cross La. LS26: Swil 5H **45**
Goody Cross Va. LS26: Swil 5H **45**
Goosedale Ct. BD4: B'ford 6C **36**
Gordon Dr. LS6: Leeds 5C **20**
Gordon Pl. LS6: Leeds 5D **20**
Gordon St. WF3: E Ard 3A **58**
Gordon Ter. LS6: Leeds 5D **20**
Gordon Vw. LS6: Leeds 5D **20**
Gorse Lea LS10: Leeds 1H **51**
Gotts Pk. Av. LS12: Leeds 4F **29**
Gotts Pk. Cres. LS12: Leeds 4F **29**
Gotts Pk. Golf Course 4G **29**
Gotts Pk. Vw. LS12: Leeds 3F **29**
Gotts Rd. LS12: Leeds 5A **4** (6D **30**)
Gower St. LS2: Leeds 3G **5** (5H **31**)
Grace Causier St. LS26: Meth 6H **55**
Grace St. LS1: Leeds 4B **4** (5E **31**)
Grafton St. LS7: Leeds 2F **5** (4G **31**)
Grafton Vs. LS15: Leeds 1D **34**
Graham Av. LS4: Leeds 2B **30**
Graham Gro. LS4: Leeds 2B **30**
Graham Ho. LS5: Leeds 2F **29**
.... *(off Broad La.)*
Graham Mt. LS4: Leeds 2B **30**
Graham St. LS4: Leeds 2B **30**
Graham Ter. LS4: Leeds 2B **30**
Graham Vw. LS4: Leeds 2B **30**
Graham Wlk. LS27: Gil 2D **48**
Graingers Way LS12: Leeds 6D **30**
Granary Wharf
LS1: Leeds 6D **4** (6F **31**)
Granby Av. LS6: Leeds 6B **20**
Granby Cl. LS6: Leeds 1B **30**
Granby Gro. LS6: Leeds 1B **30**

78 A-Z Leeds

Granby Mt. – Grove Rd.

Granby Mt. LS6: Leeds 6B **20**
Granby Pl. LS6: Leeds 6B **20**
Granby Rd. LS6: Leeds 1B **30**
Granby St. LS6: Leeds 6B **20**
Granby Ter. LS6: Leeds 6B **20**
Granby Vw. LS6: Leeds 6B **20**
Grand Arc. LS1: Leeds 3F **5** (5G **31**)
(off New Briggate)
Grandstand Rd. WF2: Carr G 6A **58**
Grandstand Rd. WF3: Loft 6C **58**
Grand Theatre & Opera House 3F **5** (5G **31**)
Grange, The LS11: Leeds 5E **41**
Grange, The LS12: Leeds 4F **29**
Grange, The LS13: Leeds 4C **28**
Grange, The LS28: Pud 5G **27**
Grange, The LS6: Leeds 6C **20**
Grange, The WF3: Car 6F **53**
Grange Av. BD3: B'ford 5B **26**
Grange Av. BD4: E Bier 1C **46**
Grange Av. LS19: Yead 3E **9**
Grange Av. LS29: Men 1B **6**
Grange Av. LS7: Leeds 1A **32**
Grange Bldgs. LS27: Morl 1A **56**
(off Hodgson St.)
Grange Cl. LS10: Leeds 3H **41**
Grange Cl. LS18: Hors 3H **17**
Grange Ct. LS15: Scho 5F **25**
Grange Ct. LS17: Leeds 4G **13**
Grange Ct. LS26: W'frd 2C **54**
Grange Ct. LS6: Leeds 6D **20**
Grange Cres. LS19: Yead 3E **9**
Grange Cres. LS7: Leeds 1A **32**
Grange Cft. LS17: Leeds 4G **13**
Grange Dr. LS18: Hors 3H **17**
Grange Farm Cl. LS29: Men 1B **6**
Grangefield Ind. Est. LS28: Stan 4G **27**
Grangefield Rd. LS28: Stan 3G **27**
(not continuous)
Grange Flds. Mt. LS10: Leeds 2B **52**
Grange Flds. Rd. LS10: Leeds 3B **52**
Grange Flds. Way LS10: Leeds 3B **52**
Grange Gro. BD3: B'ford 5B **26**
Grange Holt LS17: Leeds 4G **13**
Grange Mt. LS19: Yead 3E **9**
Grange Pk. Av. LS8: Leeds 6F **23**
Grange Pk. Cl. LS27: Morl 2H **49**
Grange Pk. Cl. LS8: Leeds 6G **23**
Grange Pk. Ct. LS27: Morl 2H **49**
(off Grange Pk. Dr.)
Grange Pk. Cres. LS8: Leeds 6F **23**
Grange Pk. Dr. LS27: Morl 2H **49**
Grange Pk. Gro. LS8: Leeds 6F **23**
Grange Pk. M. LS27: Chur 2H **49**
Grange Pk. M. LS27: Morl 2H **49**
Grange Pk. M. LS8: Leeds 6F **23**
Grange Pk. Pl. LS8: Leeds 6F **23**
Grange Pk. Ri. LS8: Leeds 6F **23**
Grange Pk. Rd. LS8: Leeds 6F **23**
Grange Pk. Ter. LS8: Leeds 6G **23**
Grange Pk. Wlk. LS8: Leeds 6F **23**
Grange Pk. Way LS27: Morl 2H **49**
Grange Rd. LS10: Leeds 3H **41**
Grange Rd. LS19: Yead 3E **9**
Grange Rd., The LS16: Leeds 2H **19**
Grange St. LS27: Chur 1A **50**
Grange Ter. LS19: Yead 3E **9**
(off Grange Rd.)
Grange Ter. LS27: Morl 2H **49**
Grange Ter. LS28: Pud 5G **27**
Grange Ter. LS7: Leeds 1H **31**
Grange Vw. BD3: B'ford 5B **26**
Grange Vw. LS15: Leeds 1D **44**
Grange Vw. LS28: Pud 5G **27**
Grange Vw. LS7: Leeds 1A **32**
Grange Vw. Gdns. LS17: Leeds 2H **23**
Grangewood Ct. LS16: Leeds 2H **19**
Grangewood Ct. WF1: Outw 6F **59**
Grangewood Gdns. LS16: Leeds 2H **19**
Granhamthorpe LS13: Leeds 3C **28**
Granny Av. LS27: Chur 1A **50**
Granny La. LS12: Leeds 2G **39**
Granny Pl. LS27: Chur 1A **50**
Grant Av. LS7: Leeds 3A **32**
Grantham Towers LS9: Leeds 4A **32**
(off Lindsey Gdns.)
Granton Rd. LS7: Leeds 6H **21**
Grant Row LS16: Leeds 1A **20**
Granville Rd. LS9: Leeds 4A **32**
Granville St. LS28: Pud 5E **27**
Granville St. LS28: Stan 3H **27**
Granville Ter. LS19: Yead 2E **9**
Granville Ter. LS20: Guis 3H **7**
Grape St. LS10: Leeds 2H **41**
Grasmere Cl. LS12: Leeds 1B **40**
Grasmere Ct. LS12: Leeds 6B **30**
Grasmere Rd. LS12: Leeds 1B **40**
GRAVELEYTHORPE 5A **34**
Graveleythorpe Ri. LS15: Leeds 4B **34**
Graveleythorpe Rd. LS15: Leeds 4B **34**
Gray Ct. LS15: Leeds 5D **34**
Grayrigg Cl. LS15: Leeds 6G **33**
Grayshon St. BD11: Drig 4G **47**
Grayson Crest LS4: Leeds 2H **29**
Grayson Hgts. LS4: Leeds 2H **29**
Grayswood Dr. BD4: B'ford 3A **36**
Gt. Exhibition Way LS5: Leeds 5D **18**
Gt. George St. LS1: Leeds 3C **4** (5E **31**)
Gt. George St. LS2: Leeds 3D **4** (5F **31**)
Gt. Northern St. LS27: Morl 6G **49**
Gt. Wilson St. LS11: Leeds 1F **41**
Greaves Yd. LS28: Pud 2G **37**
Greek St. LS1: Leeds 4D **4** (5F **31**)
Green, The BD4: E Bier 2B **46**
Green, The LS14: Leeds 1A **34**
(not continuous)
GREEN, THE 1B **34**
Green, The LS17: Leeds 1A **22**
Green, The LS18: Hors 3B **18**
Green, The LS19: Yead 2D **8**
(off Town St.)
Green, The LS20: Guis 5G **7**
Green, The LS27: Gil 2D **48**
Green, The LS28: Fars 1F **27**
GREEN, THE 1F **27**
Greenacre Pk. LS19: Raw 4D **8**
Greenacre Pk. Av. LS19: Raw 4D **8**
Greenacre Pk. M. LS19: Raw 4E **9**
Greenacre Pk. Ri. LS19: Raw 4D **8**
Greenacres Dr. WF17: Birs 6H **47**
Grn. Bank WF3: Loft 2F **59**
Greenbanks Av. LS18: Hors 1C **18**
Greenbanks Cl. LS18: Hors 1C **18**
Greenbanks Dr. LS18: Hors 1B **18**
GREENBOTTOM 5G **7**
Grn. Chase LS6: Leeds 4C **20**
Green Cl. LS6: Leeds 4D **20**
Green Ct. LS15: Scho 4F **25**
Green Ct. LS17: Leeds 1H **21**
Green Cres. LS6: Leeds 4C **20**
Greencroft M. LS20: Guis 4G **7**
Grn. Dragon Yd. LS1: Leeds 4D **4** (5F **31**)
(off The Headrow)
Greenfield Av. LS20: Guis 6D **6**
Greenfield Av. LS27: Gil 2B **48**
Greenfield Ct. LS16: Leeds 5H **11**
Greenfield Dr. LS27: Gil 2B **48**
Greenfield La. LS20: Guis 6C **6**
Greenfield Rd. LS9: Leeds 6A **32**
Greengate LS26: Oult 3C **54**
GREENGATES 4A **16**
Greenhead Rd. LS16: Leeds 3H **19**
Grn. Hill Chase LS12: Leeds 1H **39**
Grn. Hill Cl. LS12: Leeds 4F **29**
Grn. Hill Cres. LS12: Leeds 1H **39**
Grn. Hill Cft. LS12: Leeds 1H **39**
Grn. Hill Dr. LS13: Leeds 4E **29**
Grn. Hill Gdns. LS12: Leeds 1H **39**
Grn. Hill Holt LS12: Leeds 1H **39**
Grn. Hill La. LS12: Leeds 2G **39**
Grn. Hill Mt. LS13: Leeds 4E **29**
Grn. Hill Pl. LS13: Leeds 4E **29**
Grn. Hill Rd. LS12: Leeds 4F **29**
Grn. Hill Rd. LS13: Leeds 4E **29**
Greenhills LS19: Raw 6E **9**
Grn. Hill Way LS13: Leeds 4E **29**
Greenholme Ct. BD4: B'ford 5B **36**
Greenhouse LS11: Leeds 3F **41**
(off Beeston Rd.)
Greenhow Cl. LS4: Leeds 3B **30**
Greenhow Gdns. LS4: Leeds 3B **30**
Greenhow Rd. LS4: Leeds 3B **30**
Greenhow Wlk. LS4: Leeds 3B **30**
Greenland Ct. LS26: Oult 4C **54**
Green La. LS11: Leeds 6D **40**
Green La. LS12: Leeds 1C **40**
Green La. LS12: N Far 2C **38**
Green La. LS14: Leeds 3A **24**
Green La. LS15: Leeds 4B **34**
Green La. LS16: Leeds 5D **10**
Green La. LS18: Hors 4B **18**
Green La. LS19: Yead 4D **8**
Green La. LS28: Pud 1F **37**
Green La. WF3: Loft 2E **59**
Grn. Lea LS26: Oult 3B **54**
Greenlea Av. LS19: Yead 3B **8**
Greenlea Cl. LS19: Yead 4B **8**
Greenlea Fold LS19: Yead 4B **8**
Greenlea Mt. LS19: Yead 3B **8**
Greenlea Rd. LS19: Yead 3B **8**
Greenleigh Ct. LS28: Fars 3D **26**
Greenmoor Av. LS12: Leeds 6D **28**
Greenmoor Av. WF3: Loft 2E **59**
Greenmoor Cl. WF3: Loft 2E **59**
Greenmoor Ct. WF3: Car 2E **59**
Greenmoor Ct. WF3: Loft 2E **59**
Greenmoor Cres. WF3: Loft 2F **59**
Greenmount Ct. LS11: Leeds 4F **41**
(off Fulham St.)
Greenmount La. LS11: Leeds 4F **41**
Greenmount Pl. LS11: Leeds 4F **41**
Greenmount St. LS11: Leeds 4F **41**
Greenmount Ter. LS11: Leeds 4F **41**
Greenock Pl. LS12: Leeds 5G **29**
Greenock Rd. LS12: Leeds 5G **29**
Greenock St. LS12: Leeds 5G **29**
Greenock Ter. LS12: Leeds 5G **29**
Green Pk. LS14: Leeds 4B **24**
Green Pk. LS17: Leeds 1A **22**
Grn. Pasture Cl. LS9: Leeds 5E **33**
Grn. Quarter LS9: Leeds 1B **42**
Green Rd. LS6: Leeds 3B **20**
Grn. Row LS6: Leeds 4C **20**
Greenroyd Av. BD19: Hun 6A **46**
Greenshank M. LS27: Morl 5B **50**
Greenshaw Ct. LS20: Guis 4F **7**
(off Branwell Av.)
Greenshaw M. LS20: Guis 4F **7**
(off Branwell Av.)
Greenshaw Ter. LS20: Guis 4F **7**
Greenside LS19: Yead 4C **8**
(off Warm La.)
Greenside LS28: Pud 1F **37**
Greenside Av. LS12: Leeds 2H **39**
Greenside Cl. LS12: Leeds 2A **40**
Greenside Ct. LS27: Gil 2C **48**
Greenside Dr. LS12: Leeds 2A **40**
Greenside Gro. LS28: Pud 1F **37**
Greenside Rd. LS12: Leeds 2A **40**
Greenside Ter. LS12: Leeds 2H **39**
Greenside Wlk. LS12: Leeds 2H **39**
Green Ter. LS11: Leeds 4G **41**
Green Ter. LS20: Guis 5G **7**
Greenthorpe Ct. LS13: Leeds 6E **29**
Greenthorpe Hill LS13: Leeds 6E **29**
Greenthorpe Mt. LS13: Leeds 5E **29**
Greenthorpe Rd. LS13: Leeds 5E **29**
Greenthorpe St. LS13: Leeds 6E **29**
Greenthorpe Wlk. LS13: Leeds 5E **29**
Greentop LS28: Pud 1F **37**
Grn. Top LS12: Leeds 2H **39**
Grn. Top Gdns. LS12: Leeds 2H **39**
Green Vw. LS6: Leeds 4C **20**
Greenview Cl. LS9: Leeds 3E **33**
Greenview Ct. LS8: Leeds 3C **22**
Greenview Mt. LS9: Leeds 3E **33**
Greenville Av. LS12: Leeds 2H **39**
Greenville Gdns. LS12: Leeds 2H **39**
Greenway LS15: Leeds 4C **34**
Greenway LS20: Guis 6E **7**
Greenway Cl. LS15: Leeds 4C **34**
Greenwell Ct. LS9: Leeds 5E **33**
Greenwood Cl. LS13: Leeds 5B **18**
Greenwood Ct. LS6: Leeds 3C **20**
Greenwood Mt. LS6: Leeds 4C **20**
Greenwood Pk. LS6: Leeds 4C **20**
Greenwood Rd. WF3: Ting 3D **56**
Greenwood Row LS28: Pud 6H **27**
Grenfell Dr. BD3: B'ford 5A **26**
Grenfell Ter. BD3: B'ford 5A **26**
Gresley Ho. LS18: Hors 6C **10**
(off Sussex Av.)
Greyshiels Av. LS6: Leeds 1A **30**
Greyshiels Cl. LS6: Leeds 1A **30**
Greystone Mt. LS15: Leeds 6G **33**
Greystones Ct. LS17: Leeds 5G **13**
Greystones Ct. LS8: Leeds 4E **23**
Griff Ho. La. WF3: E Ard 3F **57**
Grimthorpe Av. LS6: Leeds 6A **20**
Grimthorpe Pl. LS6: Leeds 6A **20**
Grimthorpe St. LS6: Leeds 6A **20**
Grimthorpe Ter. LS6: Leeds 6B **20**
Grosmont Pl. LS13: Leeds 2C **28**
Grosmont Rd. LS13: Leeds 3C **28**
Grosmont Ter. LS13: Leeds 2C **28**
Grosvenor Casino Leeds, Wellington Bri. St. 4A **4** (5D **30**)
Grosvenor Ct. LS16: Leeds 5D **10**
Grosvenor Gdns. LS6: Leeds 1D **30**
Grosvenor Hill LS7: Leeds 3G **31**
Grosvenor Ho. LS17: Leeds 1H **21**
(off Harrogate Rd.)
Grosvenor M. LS19: Raw 5C **8**
Grosvenor Mt. LS6: Leeds 1D **30**
Grosvenor Pk. LS7: Leeds 4G **21**
Grosvenor Pk. Gdns. LS6: Leeds 1D **30**
Grosvenor Rd. LS6: Leeds 1D **30**
Grosvenor Ter. LS6: Leeds 1D **30**
Grove, The BD10: B'ford Galloway Rd. 4A **16**
Grove, The LS17: Leeds 4D **12**
Grove, The LS18: Hors 3B **18**
Grove, The LS19: Yead 3D **8**
Grove, The LS26: Swil 5H **45**
Grove, The LS27: Gil 2D **48**
Grove, The LS28: Pud 6F **27**
Grove, The LS8: Leeds 5F **23**
Grove, The WF3: E Ard 3F **57**
Grove Av. LS28: Pud 6F **27**
Grove Av. LS6: Leeds 5C **20**
Grove Ct. LS28: Pud 6F **27**
Grove Ct. LS6: Leeds 5C **20**
Grove Farm Cl. LS16: Leeds 5F **11**
Grove Farm Cres. LS16: Leeds 6E **11**
Grove Farm Cft. LS16: Leeds 5E **11**
Grove Farm Dr. LS16: Leeds 5E **11**
Grove Gdns. LS6: Leeds 5C **20**
Grovehall Av. LS11: Leeds 6D **40**
Grovehall Dr. LS11: Leeds 6D **40**
Grovehall Pde. LS11: Leeds 6D **40**
Grovehall Rd. LS11: Leeds 6D **40**
Grove Ho. LS7: Leeds 1A **32**
(off Woodland Gro.)
Grove Ho. Ct. LS8: Leeds 5F **23**
(off Nth. Grove Cl.)
Grove La. LS6: Leeds 5B **20**
Grove Pk. LS6: Leeds 6D **20**
Grove Ri. LS17: Leeds 4D **12**
Grove Rd. LS10: Leeds 4A **42**
Grove Rd. LS15: Leeds 6A **34**
Grove Rd. LS18: Hors 3B **18**

A-Z Leeds 79

Grove Rd. – Haw Av.

Grove Rd. LS28: Pud 6F **27**
Grove Rd. LS29: Men 1C **6**
Grove Rd. LS6: Leeds 6C **20**
Grove St. LS1: Leeds 4A **4** (5E **31**)
(off Lisbon St.)
Grove St. LS28: Stan 3G **27**
Grove Ter. BD11: B'haw 5C **46**
Grove Ter. LS28: Pud 6F **27**
Grovewood LS6: Leeds 5B **20**
Grunberg Pl. LS6: Leeds 6B **20**
Grunberg St. LS6: Leeds 6B **20**
GT Karting 4C **32**
Guardian M. LS12: Leeds 2A **40**
(off Lynwood Gth.)
Guilderland Way LS27: Gil 3D **48**
Guillemot App. LS27: Morl 6B **50**
GUISELEY 4G **7**
Guiseley AFC 4E **7**
Guiseley Dr. LS29: Men 3D **6**
Guiseley Retail Pk. 5G **7**
Guiseley Station (Rail) 4F **7**
Guiseley Theatre 5G **7**
Guppy Wlk. LS27: Morl 6E **49**
Gurbax Ct. BD3: B'ford 6A **26**
Gwynne Av. BD3: B'ford 4A **26**
Gym, The, Leeds 4E **5** (5G **31**)
(within The Core)
Gym Health & Fitness Club, The, Leeds 3C **32**
Gypsy Wood Cl. LS15: Leeds 6D **34**
Gypsy Wood Crest LS15: Leeds 6D **34**

H

Haddon Av. LS4: Leeds 3A **30**
Haddon Pl. LS4: Leeds 3A **30**
Haddon Rd. LS4: Leeds 3A **30**
Hadleigh Ct. LS17: Leeds 1H **21**
Hadley's Ct. LS27: Gil 3D **48**
(off Gelderd Rd.)
Haigh Av. LS26: Rothw 2E **53**
Haigh Gdns. LS26: Rothw 2E **53**
Haigh Hall BD10: B'ford 4A **16**
Haigh Hall Rd. BD10: B'ford 4A **16**
HAIGH MOOR 5C **56**
Haigh Moor Av. WF3: W Ard 5C **56**
Haigh Moor Cres. WF3: W Ard 5C **56**
Haigh Moor Rd. WF3: W Ard 6C **56**
Haigh Moor Vw. WF3: W Ard 5C **56**
Haigh Pk. Rd. LS10: Leeds 5D **42**
Haigh Rd. LS26: Rothw 3G **53**
Haighside LS26: Rothw 3E **53**
Haighside Cl. LS26: Rothw 3E **53**
Haighside Dr. LS26: Rothw 3E **53**
Haighside Way LS26: Rothw 3E **53**
Haigh Ter. LS26: Rothw 2E **53**
Haigh Vw. LS26: Rothw 2E **53**
Haigh Wood Cres. LS16: Leeds 6D **10**
Haigh Wood Grn. LS16: Leeds 1D **18**
Haigh Wood Rd. LS16: Leeds 6C **10**
Haines Pk. LS7: Leeds 3A **32**
Hainsworth Ct. LS28: Fars 2F **27**
(off Ebenezer St.)
Hainsworth Sq. LS28: Fars 2F **27**
Hainsworth St. LS12: Leeds 1C **40**
Hainsworth St. LS26: Rothw 5G **53**
Halcyon Hill LS7: Leeds 3G **21**
Hales Rd. LS12: Leeds 2H **39**
Halesworth Cres. BD4: B'ford 4A **36**
Haley's Yd. LS13: Leeds 2C **28**
Half Mile LS13: Leeds 3H **27**
HALF MILE 2H **27**
Half Mile Cl. LS28: Stan 3H **27**
Half Mile Ct. LS28: Stan 3H **27**
Half Mile Gdns. LS13: Leeds 3H **27**
Half Mile Grn. LS28: Stan 3H **27**
Half Mile Gro. LS13: Leeds 2H **27**
Half Mile La. LS13: Leeds 2H **27**
Half Mile La. LS28: Fars 2H **27**
Hall, The LS7: Leeds 4G **21**
Hallamfield LS20: Guis 5G **7**
Hallam St. LS20: Guis 5F **7**
Hall Ct. LS7: Leeds 1H **31**
Hall Gro. LS6: Leeds 3D **30**
Halliday Av. LS12: Leeds 5G **29**
Halliday Ct. BD3: B'ford 5B **26**
Halliday Dr. LS12: Leeds 5G **29**
Halliday Gro. LS12: Leeds 5G **29**
Halliday Mt. LS12: Leeds 5G **29**
Halliday Pl. LS12: Leeds 5G **29**
Halliday Rd. LS12: Leeds 5G **29**
Halliday St. LS28: Pud 5G **27**
Hall La. LS12: Leeds 6A **30**
Hall La. LS12: N Far 1C **38**
Hall La. LS16: Leeds 3E **11**
Hall La. LS18: Hors 3H **17**
Hall La. LS7: Leeds 6H **21**
Hall Pk. Av. LS18: Hors 2A **18**
Hall Pk. Cl. LS18: Hors 2A **18**
Hall Pk. Gth. LS18: Hors 2A **18**
Hall Pk. Mt. LS18: Hors 2A **18**
Hall Pk. Ri. LS18: Hors 2A **18**
Hall Pl. LS9: Leeds 6B **32**
Hall Rd. LS12: Leeds 6A **30**
Hall Rd. LS26: Swil 6H **45**
Hall Sq. LS28: Cal 4D **16**
Hall Way LS12: Leeds 2F **29**
Hallwood Grn. BD10: B'ford 6A **16**
HALTON 5H **33**
Halton Dr. LS15: Leeds 5A **34**
Halton Hill LS15: Leeds 5H **33**
HALTON MOOR 6G **33**
Halton Moor Av. LS9: Leeds 1F **43**
Halton Moor Rd. LS15: Leeds 1G **43**
Halton Moor Rd. LS9: Leeds 1C **42**
(not continuous)
Hamilton Av. LS7: Leeds 1A **32**
Hamilton Gdns. LS7: Leeds 2H **31**
Hamilton Pl. LS7: Leeds 2A **32**
Hamilton Ter. LS7: Leeds 1A **32**
Hamilton Vw. LS7: Leeds 1A **32**
Hammerton Gro. LS28: Pud 6H **27**
Hammerton St. LS28: Pud 6G **27**
Hammond Cres. BD11: Drig 2F **47**
Hammond St. LS9: Leeds 1A **42**
Hampton Cres. LS9: Leeds 6B **32**
(off Long La. Cl.)
Hampton Pl. LS9: Leeds 6B **32**
Hampton Ter. LS9: Leeds 6B **32**
Hanley Rd. LS27: Morl 6G **49**
Hanover Av. LS3: Leeds 2A **4** (5E **31**)
Hanover Ct. LS27: Morl 4H **49**
Hanover Ho. LS19: Yead 2E **9**
(off Harper La.)
Hanover La. LS3: Leeds 3B **4** (5E **31**)
Hanover Mt. LS3: Leeds 2A **4** (4E **31**)
Hanover Sq. LS3: Leeds 2A **4** (4E **31**)
Hanover Wlk. LS3: Leeds 3B **4** (5E **31**)
Hanover Way LS3: Leeds 3A **4** (5E **31**)
Hansby Av. LS14: Leeds 6B **24**
Hansby Bank LS14: Leeds 6B **24**
Hansby Cl. LS14: Leeds 1B **34**
Hansby Dr. LS14: Leeds 6B **24**
Hansby Gdns. LS14: Leeds 1B **34**
Hansby Ga. LS14: Leeds 6B **24**
Hansby Grange LS14: Leeds 6B **24**
Hansby Pl. LS14: Leeds 1B **34**
Harborough Grn. BD10: B'ford 3A **16**
Harcourt Dr. LS27: Morl 4F **49**
Harcourt Pl. LS1: Leeds 4A **4** (5D **30**)
Harden Gro. BD10: B'ford 2A **26**
Harding Vs. LS11: Leeds 2E **41**
Hardrow Grn. LS12: Leeds 2B **40**
Hardrow Gro. LS12: Leeds 2B **40**
Hardrow Rd. LS12: Leeds 2A **40**
Hardrow Ter. LS12: Leeds 2B **40**
Hardwick Ct. LS13: Leeds 5B **18**
Hardwick Cft. LS7: Leeds 5H **21**
Hardwick Way LS15: Leeds 4F **35**
Hardy Av. LS27: Chur 1A **50**
Hardy Ct. LS27: Morl 5H **49**
Hardy Gro. LS11: Leeds 4E **41**
Hardy St. LS11: Leeds 4E **41**
Hardy St. LS27: Morl 5H **49**
Hardy Ter. LS11: Leeds 4F **41**
Hardy Vw. LS11: Leeds 4E **41**
Hare Farm Av. LS12: Leeds 6D **28**
Hare Farm Cl. LS12: Leeds 5D **28**
Harefield E. LS15: Leeds 6G **33**
Harefield W. LS15: Leeds 6G **33**
HAREHILLS 3D **32**
Harehills Av. LS7: Leeds 1A **32**
Harehills Av. LS8: Leeds 1A **32**
HAREHILLS CORNER 1B **32**
Harehills La. LS7: Leeds 6A **22**
Harehills La. LS8: Leeds 1C **32**
Harehills La. LS9: Leeds 2C **32**
Harehills Pk. Av. LS9: Leeds 3D **32**
Harehills Pk. Cotts. LS9: Leeds 3E **33**
Harehills Pk. Rd. LS9: Leeds 3D **32**
Harehills Pk. Ter. LS9: Leeds 3D **32**
Harehills Pk. Vw. LS9: Leeds 3D **32**
Harehills Pl. LS8: Leeds 2B **32**
Harehills Rd. LS8: Leeds 1B **32**
Hare La. LS28: Pud 2G **37**
Hare Pk. Mt. LS12: Leeds 6C **28**
Hares Av. LS8: Leeds 1B **32**
Hares Mt. LS8: Leeds 1A **32**
Hares Rd. LS8: Leeds 1A **32**
Hares Ter. LS8: Leeds 1B **32**
Hares Vw. LS8: Leeds 1B **32**
Harewood Ct. LS14: Leeds 1A **34**
Harewood Ct. LS17: Leeds 2H **21**
Harewood Cft. LS15: Leeds 4F **35**
Harewood Dr. BD10: B'ford 3A **16**
Harewood St. LS2: Leeds 4F **5** (5G **31**)
Harewood Way LS13: Leeds 5B **28**
Hargrave Cres. LS29: Men 1B **6**
Hargreaves Av. WF3: Stly 6G **59**
Hargreaves Cl. LS27: Morl 2F **49**
Hargreaves St. LS26: Rothw 4H **53**
Harker Ter. LS28: Stan 4F **27**
Harland Sq. LS2: Leeds 2E **31**
(off Moorfield St.)
Harlech Av. LS11: Leeds 5F **41**
Harlech Cres. LS11: Leeds 5F **41**
Harlech Gro. LS11: Leeds 5F **41**
Harlech Mt. LS11: Leeds 5E **41**
Harlech Pk. Ct. LS11: Leeds 5F **41**
Harlech Rd. LS11: Leeds 5F **41**
Harlech St. LS11: Leeds 5F **41**
Harlech Ter. LS11: Leeds 5F **41**
Harley Cl. LS13: Leeds 5A **28**
Harley Ct. LS13: Leeds 5A **28**
Harley Dr. LS13: Leeds 5A **28**
Harley Gdns. LS13: Leeds 5A **28**
Harley Grn. LS13: Leeds 5A **28**
Harley Ri. LS13: Leeds 5A **28**
Harley Rd. LS13: Leeds 5A **28**
Harley Ter. LS13: Leeds 5A **28**
Harley Vw. LS13: Leeds 5A **28**
Harley Wlk. LS13: Leeds 5A **28**
Harlington Ct. LS27: Morl 6G **49**
Harlington Rd. LS27: Morl 6G **49**
Harlow Ct. LS8: Leeds 4E **23**
Harold Av. LS6: Leeds 3C **30**
Harold Gdns. LS27: Morl 5A **50**
Harold Gro. LS6: Leeds 3C **30**
Harold Mt. LS6: Leeds 3C **30**
Harold Pl. LS6: Leeds 3C **30**
Harold Rd. LS6: Leeds 3C **30**
Harold Sq. LS6: Leeds 3C **30**
Harold St. LS6: Leeds 3C **30**
Harold Ter. LS6: Leeds 3C **30**
Harold Vw. LS6: Leeds 3C **30**
Harold Wlk. LS6: Leeds 3C **30**
Harper Ga. BD4: B'ford 3B **36**
Harper La. LS19: Yead 3D **8**
Harper Rock LS19: Yead 3D **8**
(off Harper La.)
Harper St. LS2: Leeds 5G **5** (6H **31**)
Harper Ter. LS19: Yead 3D **8**
(off Harper La.)
Harrier Way LS27: Morl 5B **50**
Harriet St. LS7: Leeds 2H **31**
Harrison & Potter Trust Homes, The LS2: Leeds 2F **5** (4G **31**)
(off Lovell Pk. Rd.)
Harrison Cres. LS9: Leeds 4F **33**
Harrison Potter Trust Almshouses LS2: Leeds 2E **31**
(off Raglan Rd.)
Harrison's Av. LS28: Stan 3H **27**
Harrison St. LS1: Leeds 3F **5** (5G **31**)
Harrogate Pde. LS17: Leeds 1H **21**
Harrogate Rd. BD10: B'ford 5A **16**
Harrogate Rd. LS17: Leeds 2G **21**
Harrogate Rd. LS19: B'hpe 1G **9**
Harrogate Rd. LS19: Raw 5D **8**
(not continuous)
Harrogate Rd. LS19: Yead 1G **9**
Harrogate Rd. LS19: Yead 5D **8**
(not continuous)
Harrogate Rd. LS7: Leeds 3G **21**
Harrogate Vw. LS17: Leeds 4E **15**
Harrowby Cres. LS16: Leeds 4H **19**
Harrowby Rd. LS16: Leeds 4H **19**
Harthill LS27: Gil 2D **48**
Harthill Av. LS27: Gil 2D **48**
Harthill Cl. LS27: Gil 2D **48**
Harthill La. LS27: Gil 2D **48**
Harthill Paddock LS27: Gil 2D **48**
Harthill Pde. LS27: Gil 2D **48**
(off Town St.)
Harthill Ri. LS27: Gil 2D **48**
Hartland Rd. BD4: B'ford 3A **36**
Hartley Av. LS6: Leeds 1E **31**
Hartley Bus. Pk. BD4: B'ford 1A **36**
Hartley Cres. LS6: Leeds 1E **31**
Hartley Gdns. LS6: Leeds 1F **31**
Hartley Gro. LS6: Leeds 1E **31**
Hartley Hill LS2: Leeds 2F **5** (4G **31**)
Hartley Pl. LS27: Morl 6H **49**
Hartley's Bldgs. LS27: Morl 6H **49**
Hartley St. LS27: Chur 2H **49**
Hartley St. LS27: Morl 5H **49**
Hartley's Yd. LS12: Leeds 6H **29**
Hartwell Rd. LS6: Leeds 3C **30**
Harwill App. LS27: Chur 2A **50**
Harwill Av. LS27: Chur 2A **50**
Harwill Cft. LS27: Chur 2A **50**
Harwill Gro. LS27: Chur 2A **50**
Harwill Ri. LS27: Chur 2A **50**
Harwill Rd. LS27: Chur 2A **50**
Haslewood Cl. LS9: Leeds 5A **32**
Haslewood Ct. LS9: Leeds 5B **32**
Haslewood Dene LS9: Leeds 5B **32**
Haslewood Dr. LS9: Leeds 5A **32**
Haslewood Gdns. LS9: Leeds 5B **32**
Haslewood Grn. LS9: Leeds 5B **32**
Haslewood M. LS9: Leeds 5B **32**
Haslewood Pl. LS9: Leeds 5B **32**
Haslewood Sq. LS9: Leeds 5B **32**
Haslewood Vw. LS9: Leeds 5B **32**
Hastings Ct. LS17: Shad 5G **15**
Hathaway Dr. LS14: Leeds 2B **24**
Hathaway La. LS14: Leeds 3B **24**
Hathaway M. LS14: Leeds 2B **24**
Hathaway Wlk. LS14: Leeds 3B **24**
Hauxwell Dr. LS19: Yead 3D **8**
Havana Residence LS2: Leeds 2F **5** (4G **31**)
(off Wade La.)
Haven, The LS15: Leeds 5D **34**
Haven Chase LS16: Leeds 6E **11**
Haven Cl. LS16: Leeds 5F **11**
Haven Ct. LS16: Leeds 6F **11**
Haven Cft. LS16: Leeds 6F **11**
Haven Gdns. LS16: Leeds 6E **11**
Haven Gth. LS16: Leeds 6E **11**
Haven Grn. LS16: Leeds 6E **11**
Haven Mt. LS16: Leeds 6E **11**
Haven Ri. LS16: Leeds 6E **11**
Haven Vw. LS16: Leeds 6E **11**
Havercroft LS12: Leeds 2E **39**
Havercroft Gdns. LS12: Leeds 2E **39**
Haw Av. LS19: Yead 1E **9**

80 A-Z Leeds

Highfield Pl. – Hopefield Dr.

Highfield Pl. LS27: Morl 6H **49**
Highfield Rd. LS13: Leeds 3D **28**
Highfield Rd. LS28: Pud 5E **27**
Highfield St. LS13: Leeds 3D **28**
Highfield St. LS28: Pud 5E **27**
Highfield Ter. LS19: Raw 6E **9**
Highfield Ter. LS28: Pud 5E **27**
Highfield Vw. LS12: Leeds 2B **40**
.... *(off Hardrow Grn.)*
Highfield Vw. LS27: Gil 2E **49**
Highfold LS19: Yead 4C **8**
High Ga. St. LS10: Leeds 3A **42**
Highland Ct. LS15: Leeds 1F **43**
Highlands LS17: Leeds 4A **14**
Highlands Cl. LS10: Leeds 1B **52**
Highlands Dr. LS10: Leeds 1B **52**
Highlands Gro. LS10: Leeds 1B **52**
Highlands Wlk. LS10: Leeds 1B **52**
Highlea Cl. LS19: Yead 4B **8**
High Mill Bus. Pk. LS27: Morl 6G **49**
High Moor Av. LS17: Leeds 1A **22**
High Moor Cl. LS17: Leeds 6A **14**
High Moor Ct. LS17: Leeds 1A **22**
High Moor Cres. LS17: Leeds 6A **14**
High Moor Dr. LS17: Leeds 6A **14**
High Moor Gro. LS17: Leeds 6A **14**
High Ridge Av. LS26: Rothw 2F **53**
High Ridge Ct. LS26: Rothw 3G **53**
High Ridge Pk. LS26: Rothw 2F **53**
High Royds Ct. LS29: Men 3D **6**
High Royds Dr. LS29: Men 2C **6**
High Royds Fold LS29: Men 3D **6**
High St. LS19: Yead 2D **8**
High St. LS28: Fars 2F **27**
Highthorne Ct. LS17: Leeds 5B **14**
Highthorne Dr. LS17: Leeds 5B **14**
Highthorne Gro. LS12: Leeds 5G **29**
Highthorne Gro. LS17: Leeds 5C **14**
Highthorne Mt. LS17: Leeds 5B **14**
Highthorne St. LS12: Leeds 5G **29**
Highthorne Vw. LS12: Leeds 5G **29**
Highway LS20: Guis 4D **6**
Highways LS14: Leeds 4G **33**
Highwood Av. LS17: Leeds 6G **13**
High Wood Ct. LS6: Leeds 6C **20**
Highwood Cres. LS17: Leeds 6G **13**
Highwood Gro. LS17: Leeds 1G **21**
High Woodlands WF3: E Ard 4G **57**
High Wood Rd. WF17: Birs 5A **48**
Hillary Pl. LS2: Leeds 1C **4** (3F **31**)
Hill Ct. Av. LS13: Leeds 1C **28**
Hillcourt Cft. LS13: Leeds 1C **28**
Hill Ct. Dr. LS13: Leeds 1C **28**
Hill Ct. Fold LS13: Leeds 1C **28**
Hill Ct. Gro. LS13: Leeds 1C **28**
Hill Ct. Vw. LS13: Leeds 1B **28**
Hill Cres. LS19: Raw 4E **9**
Hill Crest LS26: Swil 6G **45**
Hillcrest LS27: Gil 1B **48**
Hillcrest Av. LS7: Leeds 2A **32**
Hill Crest Cl. LS26: Swil 6F **45**
Hillcrest Ct. LS16: Leeds 5E **11**
Hillcrest Mt. LS16: Leeds 5E **11**
Hillcrest Pl. LS7: Leeds 1A **32**
Hillcrest Ri. LS16: Leeds 5D **10**
Hillcrest Vw. LS7: Leeds 1A **32**
HILL END 5E 29
Hill End Cl. LS12: Leeds 5F **29**
Hill End Cres. LS12: Leeds 5F **29**
Hill End Rd. LS12: Leeds 5F **29**
HILLFOOT 5D 26
Hillfoot Av. LS28: Pud 5D **26**
Hillfoot Cotts. LS28: Pud 5C **26**
Hillfoot Cres. LS28: Pud 5D **26**
Hillfoot Dr. LS28: Pud 5D **26**
Hillfoot Ri. LS28: Pud 5D **26**
HILL GREEN 5G 37
Hill Grn. Ct. BD4: B'ford 5G **37**
Hillidge Rd. LS10: Leeds 3H **41**
Hillidge Sq. LS10: Leeds 3H **41**
Hillingdon Way LS17: Leeds 3E **13**
Hillings La. LS20: Hawk 4A **6**
Hillings La. LS20: Men 4A **6**
Hillings La. LS29: Men 1A **6**
Hill Ri. Av. LS13: Leeds 1C **28**
Hill Ri. Gro. LS13: Leeds 1C **28**
Hillside Av. LS20: Guis 2F **7**
Hillside Bldgs. LS11: Leeds 4E **41**
.... *(off Beeston Rd.)*
Hillside Ct. LS29: Men 1B **6**
Hillside Ct. LS7: Leeds 4A **22**
Hillside Gro. LS28: Pud 6H **27**
Hill Side Mt. LS28: Stan 3G **27**
Hillside Mt. LS28: Pud 6A **28**
Hillside Ri. LS20: Guis 2F **7**
Hillside Rd. LS7: Leeds 4H **21**
Hillside Vw. LS28: Pud 6A **28**
Hill St. LS11: Leeds 4F **41**
Hill St. LS9: Leeds 4A **32**
Hillthorpe LS28: Pud 2G **37**
Hillthorpe Ct. LS10: Leeds 6G **51**
Hillthorpe Ri. LS28: Pud 2G **37**
Hillthorpe Rd. LS28: Pud 2G **37**
Hillthorpe Sq. LS28: Pud 2G **37**
Hillthorpe St. LS28: Pud 2G **37**
Hillthorpe Ter. LS28: Pud 2G **37**
HILL TOP 5F 29
HILL TOP 3C 20
Hill Top Av. LS8: Leeds 1B **32**
Hill Top Cl. LS12: Leeds 5F **29**
Hill Top Cl. WF3: W Ard 5C **56**
Hill Top Ct. WF3: W Ard 5C **56**
Hill Top Gdns. WF3: W Ard 5C **56**
Hill Top Grn. WF3: W Ard 5B **56**
Hill Top Gro. WF3: W Ard 5C **56**
Hill Top La. WF3: W Ard 6B **56**
Hill Top Mt. LS8: Leeds 1B **32**
Hill Top Pl. LS6: Leeds 3D **30**
Hill Top Pl. LS8: Leeds 1B **32**
Hill Top Rd. LS12: Leeds 5F **29**
Hill Top Rd. LS6: Leeds 3D **30**
Hill Top St. LS6: Leeds 3D **30**
Hill Top Vw. WF3: W Ard 5B **56**
Hill Top Vs. WF3: W Ard 5B **56**
Hill Vw. Av. LS7: Leeds 4H **21**
Hill Vw. Mt. LS7: Leeds 4H **21**
Hill Vw. Pl. LS7: Leeds 4H **21**
Hillview Ri. BD4: B'ford 3A **36**
Hill Vw. Ter. LS7: Leeds 4H **21**
Hillway LS20: Guis 6E **7**
Hilton Gro. LS8: Leeds 6B **22**
Hilton Pl. LS8: Leeds 1B **32**
Hilton Rd. LS8: Leeds 1B **32**
Hilton St. LS8: Leeds 1B **32**
Hilton Ter. LS8: Leeds 1B **32**
Hindle Pl. LS27: Chur 2H **49**
Hindscarth Way LS9: Leeds 5F **33**
Hindwell Gro. LS14: Leeds 2C **24**
Hinsley Ct. LS6: Leeds 6C **20**
Hird St. LS11: Leeds 4E **41**
Hirst's Yd. LS1: Leeds 5F **5** (6G **31**)
.... *(off Call La.)*
HMP Leeds 6B **30**
Hobberley La. LS17: Leeds 5H **15**
Hobberley La. LS17: Shad 5H **15**
Hobson Cl. LS27: Morl 4A **50**
Hodgson Av. BD3: B'ford 5A **26**
Hodgson Av. LS17: Leeds 6C **14**
Hodgson Cres. LS17: Leeds 6C **14**
Hodgson La. BD11: B'haw 2D **46**
Hodgson La. BD11: Drig 3F **47**
Hodgson Pl. LS27: Chur 2H **49**
Hodgson St. LS27: Morl 2A **56**
HOLBECK 2E 41
Holbeck La. LS11: Leeds 1D **40**
Holbeck Moor Rd. LS11: Leeds 2E **41**
Holborn App. LS6: Leeds 2E **31**
Holborn Central LS6: Leeds 2E **31**
.... *(off Rampart Rd.)*
Holborn Ct. LS6: Leeds 2F **31**
Holborn Gdns. LS6: Leeds 2E **31**
Holborn Grn. LS6: Leeds 2E **31**
Holborn Gro. LS6: Leeds 2E **31**
Holborn St. LS6: Leeds 2F **31**
Holborn Ter. LS6: Leeds 2F **31**
Holborn Towers LS6: Leeds 2F **31**
Holborn Vw. LS6: Leeds 2E **31**
Holborn Wlk. LS6: Leeds 2E **31**
Holden Ing Way WF17: Birs 5A **48**
Holdforth Cl. LS12: Leeds 6C **30**
Holdforth Gdns. LS12: Leeds 6C **30**
Holdforth Grn. LS12: Leeds 6C **30**
Holdforth Pl. LS12: Leeds 6C **30**
Holdsworth Pl. LS12: Leeds 6H **29**
Holland St. BD4: B'ford 1A **36**
Hollerton La. WF3: W Ard 3D **56**
Hollies, The LS12: Leeds 6A **30**
Hollies Cl. LS13: Leeds 2C **28**
Hollies Pk. Ct. LS16: Leeds 3B **20**
Hollin Ct. LS16: Leeds 4B **20**
Hollin Cres. LS16: Leeds 4B **20**
Hollin Dr. LS16: Leeds 4B **20**
Hollin Gdns. LS16: Leeds 4A **20**
Hollingbourne Rd. LS15: Leeds 3F **35**
Hollings, The LS26: Meth 6H **55**
Hollin Hill Av. LS8: Leeds 6E **23**
Hollin Hill Cotts. LS8: Leeds 6E **23**
Hollin Hill Dr. LS8: Leeds 6E **23**
Hollin La. LS16: Leeds 4B **20**
Hollin M. LS16: Leeds 4B **20**
Hollin Mt. LS16: Leeds 4A **20**
HOLLIN PK. 6F 23
Hollin Pk. Av. LS8: Leeds 6F **23**
Hollin Pk. Ct. LS28: Cal 5C **16**
Hollin Pk. Cres. LS8: Leeds 6F **23**
Hollin Pk. Dr. LS28: Cal 5C **16**
Hollin Pk. Mt. LS8: Leeds 5F **23**
Hollin Pk. Pde. LS8: Leeds 6E **23**
Hollin Pk. Pl. LS8: Leeds 6E **23**
Hollin Pk. Rd. LS28: Cal 5C **16**
Hollin Pk. Rd. LS8: Leeds 6E **23**
Hollin Pk. Ter. LS8: Leeds 6E **23**
Hollin Pk. Vw. LS8: Leeds 6E **23**
Hollin Rd. LS16: Leeds 4B **20**
Hollins Hill LS20: Guis 6E **7**
HOLLINTHORPE 3G 45
Hollin Vw. LS16: Leeds 4B **20**
Hollis Pl. LS3: Leeds 4D **30**
Holly Av. LS16: Leeds 6D **10**
Holly Bank LS20: Guis 4F **7**
Holly Bank LS6: Leeds 5B **20**
Holly Cl. LS10: Leeds 5F **51**
Holly Ct. LS20: Guis 5F **7**
Holly Ct. WF1: Outw 6E **59**
Holly Ct. WF3: W Ard 5C **56**
Holly Cres. WF3: E Ard 3B **58**
Hollycroft Ct. LS16: Leeds 6G **11**
Holly Dr. LS16: Leeds 6D **10**
Holly Pk. LS18: Hors 2H **17**
Holly Pk. Mills LS28: Cal 5C **16**
Hollyshaw Cres. LS15: Leeds 5C **34**
Hollyshaw Gro. LS15: Leeds 5C **34**
Hollyshaw La. LS15: Leeds 4C **34**
Hollyshaw St. LS15: Leeds 5C **34**
Hollyshaw Ter. LS15: Leeds 5C **34**
Hollyshaw Wlk. LS15: Leeds 4C **34**
Holly Tree La. LS15: Leeds 1E **45**
Holly Way LS14: Leeds 3G **33**
Hollywell Gro. LS12: Leeds 5H **29**
Hollywell La. LS12: Leeds 6H **29**
Hollywood Bowl Leeds 4B 30
Holme Bank BD4: B'ford 3B **36**
Holme Bank Cl. BD4: B'ford 5B **36**
Holme Farm Ct. LS12: N Far 4D **38**
Holmefield Vw. BD4: B'ford 3B **36**
Holme La. BD4: B'ford 4B **36**
Holmelea Cft. LS6: Leeds 4C **20**
Holmes St. LS11: Leeds 1G **41**
HOLME VILLAGE 4B 36
Holme Well Rd. LS10: Leeds 4A **52**
HOLME WOOD 4A 36
Holmfield Dr. LS8: Leeds 2C **22**
Holmsley Crest LS26: W'frd 2A **54**
Holmsley Fld. Ct. LS26: Oult 3C **54**
Holmsley Fld. La. LS26: Oult 3B **54**
Holmsley Gth. LS26: W'frd 2B **54**
Holmsley Grn. LS26: W'frd 2B **54**
Holmsley La. LS26: W'frd 3A **54**
Holmsley Wlk. LS26: Oult 3B **54**
Holmwood LS8: Leeds 1C **22**
Holmwood Av. LS6: Leeds 3C **20**
Holmwood Cl. LS6: Leeds 3D **20**
Holmwood Cres. LS6: Leeds 3D **20**
Holmwood Dr. LS6: Leeds 3C **20**
Holmwood Gro. LS6: Leeds 3D **20**
Holmwood Mt. LS6: Leeds 3D **20**
Holmwood Vw. LS6: Leeds 3C **20**
Holroyd St. LS7: Leeds 3H **31**
Holsworthy Rd. BD4: B'ford 5A **36**
Holt Av. LS16: Leeds 4A **12**
Holt Cl. LS16: Leeds 5A **12**
Holt Cres. LS16: Leeds 4F **11**
Holtdale App. LS16: Leeds 4E **11**
Holtdale Av. LS16: Leeds 4F **11**
Holtdale Cl. LS16: Leeds 4F **11**
Holtdale Cft. LS16: Leeds 4F **11**
Holtdale Dr. LS16: Leeds 4E **11**
Holtdale Fold LS16: Leeds 4F **11**
Holtdale Gdns. LS16: Leeds 4F **11**
Holtdale Gth. LS16: Leeds 4F **11**
Holtdale Grn. LS16: Leeds 4F **11**
Holtdale Gro. LS16: Leeds 4E **11**
Holtdale Lawn LS16: Leeds 4F **11**
Holtdale Pl. LS16: Leeds 4F **11**
Holtdale Rd. LS16: Leeds 4F **11**
Holtdale Vw. LS16: Leeds 4F **11**
Holtdale Way LS16: Leeds 4F **11**
Holt Dr. LS16: Leeds 4G **11**
Holt Farm Cl. LS16: Leeds 4F **11**
Holt Farm Ri. LS16: Leeds 4F **11**
Holt Gdns. LS16: Leeds 4A **12**
Holt Gth. LS16: Leeds 4G **11**
Holt Ga. LS16: Leeds 4G **11**
Holt Grn. LS16: Leeds 4G **11**
Holt La. LS16: Leeds 4E **11**
Holt La. Ct. LS16: Leeds 5H **11**
HOLT PK. 4F 11
Holt Pk. Active 5F 11
Holt Pk. App. LS16: Leeds 4G **11**
Holt Pk. Av. LS16: Leeds 4G **11**
Holt Pk. Cl. LS16: Leeds 4G **11**
Holt Pk. Cres. LS16: Leeds 4F **11**
Holt Pk. District Cen. 4F **11**
Holt Pk. Dr. LS16: Leeds 4G **11**
Holt Pk. Gdns. LS16: Leeds 4G **11**
Holt Pk. Ga. LS16: Leeds 4G **11**
Holt Pk. Grange LS16: Leeds 4G **11**
Holt Pk. Grn. LS16: Leeds 4G **11**
Holt Pk. Gro. LS16: Leeds 4F **11**
Holt Pk. La. LS16: Leeds 4G **11**
Holt Pk. Ri. LS16: Leeds 4G **11**
Holt Pk. Rd. LS16: Leeds 4G **11**
Holt Pk. Va. LS16: Leeds 4G **11**
Holt Pk. Vw. LS16: Leeds 4F **11**
Holt Pk. Way LS16: Leeds 4G **11**
Holt Ri. LS16: Leeds 4G **11**
Holt Rd. LS16: Leeds 4G **11**
Holts Crest Way LS12: Leeds 5D **30**
Holt Va. LS16: Leeds 4G **11**
Holt Wlk. LS16: Leeds 4G **11**
Holt Way LS16: Leeds 4G **11**
Holybrook Av. BD10: B'ford 5A **16**
Holybrook Gdns. BD10: B'ford 5A **16**
Holywell Dr. BD10: B'ford 6A **16**
Holywell La. LS17: Shad 4F **15**
Holywell Vw. LS17: Shad 4F **15**
Home Farm Dr. LS29: Men 2B **6**
Home Farm M. LS29: Men 2C **6**
Home Lea LS26: Rothw 2F **53**
Home Lea Dr. LS26: Rothw 2F **53**
Honeybourne Rd. LS12: Leeds 4A **40**
Honeysuckle Dr. LS14: Leeds 3A **24**
Hopefield Chase LS26: Rothw 5D **52**
Hopefield Cl. LS26: Rothw 5D **52**
Hopefield Ct. LS26: Rothw 5D **52**
Hopefield Ct. WF3: E Ard 4G **57**
Hopefield Cres. LS26: Rothw 5D **52**
Hopefield Dr. LS26: Rothw 5D **52**

82 A-Z Leeds

Lawns Hall Cl. – Linden Ct.

Lawns Hall Cl. LS16: Leeds......... 6H **11**
Lawns Ho. LS12: N Far................ 2D **38**
......................................*(off Chapel La.)*
Lawns La. LS10: Leeds 4A **42**
Lawns La. LS12: N Far................ 3D **38**
Lawns La. WF2: Carr G.................6A **58**
Lawns Mt. LS12: N Far................ 4D **38**
Lawns Sq. LS12: N Far................ 4D **38**
Lawns Ter. LS12: N Far 4D **38**
Lawns Ter. WF3: E Ard................. 4H **57**
LAWNSWOOD 1G 19
Lawnswood Bus. Pk.
LS16: Leeds 2G **19**
Lawnswood Crematorium.......... 6H **11**
Lawnswood Cres. LS16: Leeds....6A **12**
Lawnswood Gdns. LS16: Leeds.. 1H **19**
Lawnswood Mt. LS16: Leeds.......6A **12**
Lawnswood Va. LS16: Leeds 1A **20**
Lawnswood Vw. LS16: Leeds 1A **20**
Lawrence Av. LS8: Leeds 1E **33**
Lawrence Ct. LS28: Pud 1F **37**
Lawrence Cres. LS8: Leeds..........1E **33**
Lawrence Gdns. LS8: Leeds.........6E **23**
Lawrence Rd. LS8: Leeds.............1E **33**
Lawrence Wlk. LS8: Leeds...........1E **33**
Lawson Ct. LS28: Fars 2G **27**
Lawson St. LS12: Leeds.............. 6H **29**
Lawson Wood Ct. LS6: Leeds...... 2D **20**
Lawson Wood Dr. LS6: Leeds...... 2D **20**
Laycock Pl. LS7: Leeds 2H **31**
Lay Gth. LS26: Rothw 5G **53**
Lay Gth. Cl. LS26: Rothw 4G **53**
Lay Gth. Ct. LS26: Rothw............ 5G **53**
Lay Gth. Fold LS26: Rothw 5G **53**
Lay Gth. Gdns. LS26: Rothw......... 5G **53**
Lay Garth Glade LS26: Rothw 5G **53**
.....................................*(off Lay Garth)*
Lay Gth. Grn. LS26: Rothw........... 5G **53**
Lay Gth. Mead LS26: Rothw 5G **53**
Lay Gth. Pl. LS26: Rothw 5G **53**
Lay Gth. Sq. LS26: Rothw 4G **53**
Layton Av. LS19: Raw.....................6F **9**
Layton Cl. LS19: Raw 1G **17**
Layton Cres. LS19: Raw 6F **9**
Layton Dr. LS19: Raw.................... 6G **9**
Layton La. LS19: Raw.................. 1G **17**
Layton Mt. LS19: Raw 6F **9**
Layton Pk. Av. LS19: Raw 1G **17**
Layton Pk. Cl. LS19: Raw 6F **9**
Layton Pk. Cft. LS19: Raw............ 1G **17**
Layton Pk. Dr. LS19: Raw...............6F **9**
Layton Ri. LS18: Hors.................... 6H **9**
Layton Rd. LS18: Hors................... 6H **9**
Layton Rd. LS19: Raw 6G **9**
Leadwell La. LS26: Rothw........... 5D **52**
Leadwell La. WF3: Rob H 6D **52**
Lea Farm Cres. LS5: Leeds 5F **19**
Lea Farm Dr. LS5: Leeds 4F **19**
Lea Farm Gro. LS5: Leeds............5F **19**
Lea Farm Mt. LS5: Leeds 4F **19**
Lea Farm Pl. LS5: Leeds...............5F **19**
Lea Farm Rd. LS5: Leeds 4E **19**
Lea Farm Row LS5: Leeds 5F **19**
Lea Farm Wlk. LS5: Leeds 4F **19**
Leafield Cl. LS17: Leeds...............1F **21**
Leafield Dr. LS17: Leeds...............1F **21**
Leafield Dr. LS28: Pud................. 2H **37**
Leafield Grange LS17: Leeds 1F **21**
Leafield Pl. LS19: Yead 6H **7**
Leafield Towers LS17: Leeds.......1F **21**
Leafield Vs. LS19: Yead.................. 6H **7**
...................................*(off Leafield Pl.)*
Leah Pl. LS12: Leeds.................... 1D **40**
Leah Row LS12: Leeds................. 1D **40**
Lea Mill Pk. Cl. LS19: Yead 2C **8**
Lea Mill Pk. Dr. LS19: Yead 2C **8**
Leamside Wlk. BD4: B'ford 5A **36**
Lea Pk. Cl. LS10: Leeds 2B **52**
Lea Pk. Cft. LS10: Leeds 2C **52**
Lea Pk. Dr. LS10: Leeds................2B **52**
Lea Pk. Gdns. LS10: Leeds...........2B **52**
Lea Pk. Gth. LS10: Leeds 2B **52**
Lea Pk. Gro. LS10: Leeds 2B **52**
Lea Pk. Va. LS10: Leeds................2C **52**
Leasowe Av. LS10: Leeds.............5A **42**
Leasowe Cl. LS10: Leeds 5A **42**
Leasowe Ct. LS10: Leeds.............5A **42**
.... *(off Springfield Pl.)*
Leasowe Gdns. LS10: Leeds 5B **42**
Leasowe Gth. LS10: Leeds...........5A **42**
Leasowe Rd. LS10: Leeds 5A **42**
Lea Ter. LS17: Leeds.................... 2G **21**
Leathley Av. LS29: Men................. 2D **6**
Leathley Cl. LS29: Men 1D **6**
Leathley Cres. LS29: Men 2D **6**
Leathley La. LS29: Men................. 1D **6**
Leathley Rd. LS10: Leeds............ 2G **41**
Leathley Rd. LS29: Men 1D **6**
Leavens, The BD10: B'ford...........3A **16**
Lea Vw. LS18: Hors 2B **18**
Ledbury Av. LS10: Leeds..............5B **52**
Ledbury Cl. LS10: Leeds 5B **52**
Ledbury Cft. LS10: Leeds..............5B **52**
Ledbury Dr. LS10: Leeds 5B **52**
Ledbury Grn. LS10: Leeds.............5B **52**
Ledbury Gro. LS10: Leeds.............5A **52**
Ledgard Way LS12: Leeds............5A **30**
Ledger La. WF1: Outw 6D **58**
Ledger La. WF3: Loft 2E **59**
Lee Beck Gro. WF3: Stly............. 3G **59**
LEEDS.............................4E 5 (5G 31)
Leeds 27 Ind. Est. LS27: Morl 4E **49**
Leeds & Bradford Rd.
LS13: Leeds 6C **18**
Leeds & Bradford Rd.
LS28: Stan 3H **27**
Leeds & Bradford Rd.
LS5: Leeds 1F **29**
Leeds Aquatic Cen..........................1G 51
Leeds Beckett University
Broadcasting Place 1D 4 (4F 31)
Leeds Beckett University
City Campus......................1D 4 (4F 31)
Leeds Beckett University
Headingley Campus.....................5H 19
Leeds Beckett University
Northern Film School 3D 4 (5F 31)
Leeds Beckett University
Queen Sq..............................2D 4 (4F 31)
.....................................*(off Queen Sq.)*
Leeds Beckett University
The Rose Bowl...............2D 4 (4F 31)
.................................*(off Portland Gate)*
Leeds Beckett University
Tennis Cen. 5H 19
LEEDS BRADFORD AIRPORT 2G 9
Leeds Bus & Coach
Station..............................4G 5 (5H 31)
Leeds Bus. Cen., The
LS27: Morl 4E **49**
LEEDS CHILDREN'S
HOSPITAL 2B 4 (4E 31)
Leeds City Art Gallery.......3D 4 (5F 31)
Leeds City Mus. 2D 4 (4F 31)
Leeds City Office Pk.
LS11: Leeds 1G **41**
Leeds Corn Exchange....... 5F **5** (6G **31**)
.... *(off Call La.)*
LEEDS DENTAL
INSTITUTE 2B 4 (4E 31)
Leeds First Direct Arena ..2E 5 (4G 31)
LEEDS GENERAL
INFIRMARY.......................2C 4 (4F 31)
Leeds Golf Cen...................................1E 15
Leeds Golf Course.........................3F 23
Leeds La. LS26: Swil 2G **45**
Leeds Mus. Discovery Cen. 1A 42
LEEDS NUFFIELD HEALTH
HOSPITAL 3B 4 (5E 31)
Leeds Playhouse..............4H 5 (5H 31)
Leeds Rhinos RLFC.......................1B 30
Leeds Rd. LS15: B Elm 1E **35**
Leeds Rd. LS15: Scho....................1E **35**
Leeds Rd. LS19: Raw 5D **8**
Leeds Rd. LS20: Guis 5G **7**
Leeds Rd. LS26: Meth 6G **55**
Leeds Rd. LS26: Oult..................... 2H **53**
Leeds Rd. LS26: Rothw 2H **53**
Leeds Rd. WF3: Loft 5D **52**
Leeds Rd. WF3: Rob H.................. 5D **52**
Leeds Rugby Academy...................2G 29
Leeds Sailing & Activity Cen. 2E 9
Leeds St Anne's
RC Cathedral...................3D 4 (5F 31)
LEEDS SPIRE HOSPITAL 4C 22
Leeds Station (Rail) 6D 4 (6F 31)
Leeds Student Village
LS3: Leeds 4D **30**
Leeds Thomas Danby
Community Sports Cen. 3H 31
Leeds Trinity University..............6A 10
Leeds United FC...........................4C 40
Leeds University Business School
Western Campus 3D 30
Leeds University Medical Cen......3F 31
...............................*(off Blenheim Wlk.)*
Leeds Valley Pk. LS10: Leeds 1D **52**
Leeds Visitor Info. Cen. 3D 4 (5F 31)
Lee Edge LS10: Leeds 5H **51**
Lee Fair Ct. WF3: W Ard 5B **56**
Lee La. E. LS18: Hors....................1B **18**
Lee La. W. LS18: Hors................... 1H **17**
LEE MOOR 4G 59
Lee Moor La. WF3: Stly 3G **59**
Lee Moor Rd. WF3: Stly............... 4G **59**
LEE MOUNT 5H 59
Lees La. LS28: Fars 1F **27**
Left Bank.......................................3C 30
.................................*(off Cardigan Rd.)*
Leicester Cl. LS7: Leeds...............3F **31**
Leicester Gro. LS7: Leeds 3F **31**
Leicester Pl. LS2: Leeds................3F **31**
Leicester Pl. LS7: Leeds................3F **31**
Leicester Sq. LS15: Leeds............3E **35**
Leigh Av. WF3: Ting.......................3E **57**
Leigh Ct. LS10: Leeds....................5F **51**
Leigh Rd. WF3: Ting 3E **57**
Leighton La. LS1: Leeds.... 3B **4** (5E **31**)
.... *(off Leighton St.)*
Leighton Pl. LS1: Leeds.... 3C **4** (5F **31**)
.... *(off Leighton St.)*
Leighton St. LS1: Leeds 3B **4** (5F **31**)
Leigh Vw. WF3: Ting..................... 3D **56**
Leith Ho. BD4: B'ford 4A **36**
................................*(off Stirling Cres.)*
Lemon Royd Lock LS26: Oult...... 5G **55**
Lemonroyd Marina LS26: Oult 4G **55**
Leng Dr. BD3: B'ford 6B **26**
Lenham Cl. LS27: Morl 6G **49**
Lenhurst Av. LS12: Leeds.............2F **29**
Lennox Gdns. LS15: Leeds...........6C **34**
Lennox Rd. LS4: Leeds..................4B **30**
Lenton Dr. LS11: Leeds 5G **41**
Leodis Ct. LS11: Leeds..................1F **41**
Leodis Ho. LS10: Leeds 6D **42**
Leodis Residences LS6: Leeds 2F **31**
Leodis Way LS10: Leeds 1D **52**
Leopold Gdns. LS7: Leeds............2A **32**
Leopold Gro. LS7: Leeds 2H **31**
Leopold St. LS7: Leeds................. 2H **31**
Lepton Hare Chase
LS10: Leeds 1G **57**
Lepton Pl. LS27: Gil 2D **48**
Leslie Av. LS19: Yead 1E **9**
Leslie Ter. LS6: Leeds....................2E **31**
Levens Bank LS15: Leeds............1F **43**
Levens Cl. LS15: Leeds 1G **43**
Levens Gth. LS15: Leeds.............. 1G **43**
Levens Pl. LS15: Leeds 1G **43**
Leven St. LS14: Leeds.................. 6H **23**
Leventhorpe Ct. LS26: Oult 4C **54**
Leventhorpe Way LS26: Oult........4C **54**
Levita Gro. BD4: B'ford..................3A **36**
Levita Pl. BD4: B'ford 2A **36**
Levita Pl. LS15: Leeds 5G **33**
Lewisham Ct. LS27: Morl 5H **49**
Lewisham Gro. LS27: Morl........... 5H **49**
Lewisham St. LS27: Morl 6E **49**
Lewisham Vw. LS27: Morl............ 5H **49**
Leyburn Av. LS27: Morl 5C **50**
Leyburn Dr. LS27: Morl.................5C **50**
Leyburn Pl. LS27: Morl 5C **50**
THE LEYLANDS................2F 5 (4G 31)
Leylands Rd. LS2: Leeds...2H **5** (4H **31**)
Ley La. LS12: Leeds 5B **30**
Leysholme Cres. LS12: Leeds..... 1G **39**
Leysholme Dr. LS12: Leeds......... 1H **39**
Leysholme Ter. LS12: Leeds........ 1H **39**
Leysholme Vw. LS12: Leeds 1H **39**
Leywell Ter. LS12: Leeds.............. 5G **29**
Liberty Pk. LS1: Leeds 4A **4** (5E **31**)
............................*(off Marlborough St.)*
Liberty Vw. LS27: Morl 4G **49**
.... *(off Chapel Hill)*
Lickless Av. LS18: Hors............... 2D **18**
Lickless Dr. LS18: Hors 2D **18**
Lickless Gdns. LS18: Hors 2D **18**
Lickless Ter. LS18: Hors 2D **18**
Lidget Hill LS28: Pud 6G **27**
Lidgett Av. LS8: Leeds..................4B **22**
Lidgett Ct. LS8: Leeds 3B **22**
Lidgett Cres. LS8: Leeds 3B **22**
Lidgett Gro. LS8: Leeds..................4B **22**
Lidgett Hill LS8: Leeds 4A **22**
Lidgett La. LS17: Leeds................. 2H **21**
Lidgett La. LS8: Leeds....................4B **22**
Lidgett Mt. LS8: Leeds 2B **22**
LIDGETT PK. 3C 22
Lidgett Pk. Av. LS8: Leeds..............2B **22**
Lidgett Pk. Ct. LS8: Leeds..............2B **22**
Lidgett Pk. Gdns. LS8: Leeds 3B **22**
Lidgett Pk. Gro. LS8: Leeds...........3B **22**
Lidgett Pk. M. LS8: Leeds 2C **22**
Lidgett Pk. Rd. LS8: Leeds 2B **22**
.... (not continuous)
Lidgett Pk. Vw. LS8: Leeds 2B **22**
Lidgett Pl. LS8: Leeds 3B **22**
Lidgett Towers LS8: Leeds...........2A **22**
Lidgett Wlk. LS8: Leeds 4B **22**
.... (not continuous)
Lifton Pl. LS2: Leeds 3E **31**
Light, The 3D 4 (5F 31)
Lighthouse Fold WF3: Loft 3E **59**
....................................*(off The Poplars)*
Lilac Ct. LS14: Leeds.................... 3G **33**
Lilacs, The LS20: Guis.................... 4G **7**
Lime Dr. LS14: Leeds.................... 3G **33**
Lime Gro. LS19: Yead 5C **8**
Lime Gro. LS7: Leeds 5H **21**
Lime Pit La. WF3: Stly.................. 6G **59**
Lime Tree Av. LS17: Leeds 1A **22**
Lime Tree Cl. LS26: W'frd............. 3D **54**
Limetree Gro. BD11: B'haw 2C **46**
Limewood App. LS14: Leeds........4A **24**
Limewood Bus. Pk.
LS14: Leeds 5B **24**
Limewood Ct. LS14: Leeds............4A **24**
Limewood Pk. LS14: Leeds............4A **24**
Limewood Rd. LS14: Leeds............5A **24**
Limewood Way LS14: Leeds 5A **24**
Lincoln Ct. LS28: Fars 3F **27**
.... *(off South Dr.)*
Lincoln Grn. Ct. LS9: Leeds..........4A **32**
Lincoln Grn. Rd.
LS9: Leeds 2H **5** (4A **32**)
Lincoln Grn. Shop. Cen. 4A **32**
Lincoln Rd. LS9: Leeds..................4A **32**
Lincoln Towers LS9: Leeds 4A **32**
.....................................*(off Lincoln Rd.)*
Lincombe Bank LS8: Leeds 3A **22**
Lincombe Dr. LS8: Leeds..............3A **22**
Lincombe Mt. LS8: Leeds..............3A **22**
Lincombe Ri. LS8: Leeds...............3A **22**
Lincroft Cres. LS13: Leeds 1D **28**
Lindale Cl. LS10: Leeds 2H **51**
Linden Av. BD3: B'ford 5A **26**
Linden Av. LS11: Leeds 4F **41**
Linden Ct. LS16: Leeds..................4B **20**

86 A-Z Leeds

M

Masham Ct. – Mill St.

Masham Ct. LS6: Leeds 5B **20**
Masham Gro. LS12: Leeds 6B **30**
Masham St. LS12: Leeds....6B **30**
Matrix Ct. LS11: Leeds 5F **41**
Matty La. LS26: Rothw 5D **52**
Maud Av. LS11: Leeds 5E **41**
Maude St. LS2: Leeds....5G **5** (6H **31**)
Maud Pl. LS11: Leeds 5F **41**
Mavis Av. LS16: Leeds 3E **11**
Mavis Gro. LS16: Leeds....4E **11**
Mavis La. LS16: Leeds 3E **11**
Mawcroft Cl. LS19: Yead....4C **8**
Mawcroft Grange Dr.
LS19: Yead....4C **8**
Mawcroft M. LS19: Yead....4D **8**
Maxwell St. LS27: Morl 6F **49**
May Av. LS27: Chur 1A **50**
Maybrook Ind. Pk. LS12: Leeds ...5C **30**
May Ct. LS27: Chur....6A **40**
Mayfair Mt. LS15: Leeds 3E **35**
Mayfield Ct. LS18: Hors....2C **18**
Mayfield Rd. LS15: Leeds....5B **34**
Mayflower Ho. LS10: Leeds 5C **42**
Mayflower Vw. LS15: Leeds....1F **43**
Mayo Cl. LS8: Leeds....5F **23**
May Ter. LS9: Leeds 1B **42**
Maythorne Cl. BD4: B'ford....5B **36**
Mayville Av. LS6: Leeds....2C **30**
Mayville Pl. LS6: Leeds....2C **30**
Mayville Rd. LS6: Leeds....2C **30**
Mayville St. LS6: Leeds....2C **30**
Mayville Ter. LS6: Leeds....2C **30**
Mead Cl. LS15: Leeds....1E **45**
Mead Gro. LS15: Leeds....1E **45**
Meadowbrook Ct. LS27: Morl 6E **49**
Meadow Cl. WF1: Outw 6F **59**
Mdw. Cft. BD11: Drig....3F **47**
Mdw. Cft. LS11: Leeds....2F **41**
Mdw. Cft. LS29: Men....2C **6**
Mdw. Cft. WF1: Outw....6E **59**
Meadowcroft Cl. WF1: Outw 6F **59**
Meadowcroft Ct. WF1: Outw 6F **59**
Meadowcroft M. LS9: Leeds 6A **32**
Meadowcroft Rd. WF1: Outw 6F **59**
Meadow Gth. WF1: Outw....6E **59**
Meadowgate Cft. WF3: Loft 1D **58**
Meadowgate Dr. WF3: Loft....1D **58**
Meadowgate Va. WF3: Loft....2D **58**
Meadowhurst Gdns. LS28: Pud ...6F **27**
Meadow La. LS11: Leeds 1G **41**
Meadow Pk. Cres. LS28: Stan....3D **26**
Meadow Pk. Dr. LS28: Stan....3D **26**
Meadow Rd. BD10: B'ford....3A **16**
Meadow Rd. LS11: Leeds....2F **41**
Meadows, The LS16: Leeds 6A **12**
Meadow Side Rd. WF3: E Ard 2A **58**
Meadow Va. WF1: Outw 6E **59**
Mdw. Valley LS17: Leeds 4F **13**
Meadow Vw. LS28: Pud 6E **27**
Meadow Vw. LS6: Leeds....2C **30**
Meadow Wlk. LS7: Leeds....5A **22**
Mdw. Way LS17: Leeds 4E **13**
Mdw. Way WF3: W Ard 4B **56**
Mead Rd. LS15: Leeds....1E **45**
Mead Vw. BD4: B'ford 4A **36**
Mead Way LS15: Leeds 1E **45**
MEANWOOD....4D **20**
Meanwood Cl. LS7: Leeds....1F **31**
Meanwood Gro. LS6: Leeds 2C **20**
MEANWOOD GROVE....2C **20**
Meanwood Rd. LS6: Leeds....5D **20**
Meanwood Rd. LS7: Leeds....1F **31**
Meanwood St. LS7: Leeds....3G **31**
Meanwood Towers LS6: Leeds 3E **21**
Meanwood Valley Cl.
LS7: Leeds 5D **20**
Meanwood Valley Dr.
LS7: Leeds....5D **20**
Meanwood Valley Grn.
LS7: Leeds....5D **20**
Meanwood Valley Gro.
LS7: Leeds....5D **20**
Meanwood Valley Mt.
LS7: Leeds 5D **20**
Meanwood Valley Urban Farm....6F **21**
Meanwood Valley Wlk.
LS7: Leeds 5D **20**
Mecca Bingo Leeds, Balm Rd. 4H **41**
Mecca Bingo Leeds,
Cross Gates Rd. 3C **34**
Mecca Bingo Leeds,
New York St. 5G **5** (6H **31**)
....*(off New York St.)*
Medeway LS28: Stan....3E **27**
Melbeck Cl. LS29: Men 2C **6**
Melbourne Gro. BD3: B'ford 5A **26**
Melbourne Gro. LS13: Leeds....3C **28**
Melbourne Mills LS27: Morl....5H **49**
....*(off Melbourne St.)*
Melbourne Mill Yd. LS27: Morl ... 5H **49**
....*(off Middleton Rd.)*
Melbourne St. LS13: Leeds....3C **28**
Melbourne St.
LS2: Leeds 2G **5** (4H **31**)
Melbourne St. LS27: Morl 5H **49**
Melbourne St. LS28: Fars....3F **27**
Melcombe Wlk. BD4: B'ford....3A **36**
Melrose Gro. LS18: Hors 3E **19**
Melrose Pl. LS18: Hors....3D **18**
Melrose Pl. LS28: Pud 1F **37**
Melrose Ter. LS18: Hors 3D **18**
Melrose Vs. LS18: Hors 3D **18**
....*(off Melrose Ter.)*
Melrose Wlk. LS18: Hors....3D **18**
Melton Av. LS10: Leeds....5B **52**
Melton Cl. LS10: Leeds....5B **52**
Melton Gth. LS10: Leeds 5B **52**
Melton Ter. BD10: B'ford 1A **26**
Melville Cl. LS6: Leeds....2F **31**
Melville Gdns. LS6: Leeds....1F **31**
Melville Pl. LS6: Leeds....1F **31**
Melville Rd. LS6: Leeds....2F **31**
Memorial Cotts. LS12: N Far....4D **38**
....*(off Lawn La.)*
Memorial Dr. LS6: Leeds....4D **20**
MENSTON....1B **6**
Menston Dr. LS29: Men....2C **6**
Menston Hall LS29: Men....1D **6**
Menston Ho. LS29: Men....2C **6**
....*(off High Royds Dr.)*
Menston Station (Rail)....1C **6**
Merchants Ho.
LS2: Leeds....2G **5** (4H **31**)
....*(off North St.)*
Merchants Quay
LS9: Leeds....6H **5** (6H **31**)
Merchant Way LS15: Leeds 6F **33**
Mercia Way LS15: Leeds....2E **35**
Merlin Cl. LS27: Morl....6A **50**
Merlyn-Rees Av. LS27: Morl....5G **49**
Merrion Cen. 2E **5** (4G **31**)
Merrion Ho. LS2: Leeds....2E **5** (4G **31**)
Merrion Pl. LS1: Leeds....3F **5** (5G **31**)
....(not continuous)
Merrion Pl. LS2: Leeds 5G **31**
Merrion St. LS1: Leeds....3F **5** (5G **31**)
Merrion St. LS2: Leeds....3E **5** (5G **31**)
Merrion Way LS2: Leeds ... 2E **5** (4G **31**)
Merriville LS18: Hors....4D **18**
Merton Av. LS28: Fars....3F **27**
Merton Dr. LS28: Fars 3E **27**
Merton Gdns. LS28: Fars....3E **27**
Methley Dr. LS7: Leeds....5G **21**
Methley Gro. LS7: Leeds 5G **21**
Methley La. LS26: Oult....5C **54**
Methley La. LS7: Leeds 5H **21**
Methley Mt. LS7: Leeds....5H **21**
METHLEY PARK SPIRE
HOSPITAL....6G **55**
Methley Pl. LS7: Leeds....5G **21**
Methley Ter. LS7: Leeds 5H **21**
Methley Vw. LS7: Leeds 5H **21**
Mexborough Av. LS7: Leeds....1H **31**
Mexborough Dr. LS7: Leeds....1H **31**
Mexborough Gro. LS7: Leeds....1H **31**
Mexborough Pl. LS7: Leeds 2H **31**
Mexborough Rd. LS7: Leeds....2H **31**
Mexborough St. LS7: Leeds 1H **31**
Meynell App. LS11: Leeds....2E **41**
Meynell Av. LS26: Rothw....4G **53**
Meynell Ct. LS15: Leeds....6D **34**
Meynell Fold LS15: Leeds 1D **44**
Meynell Hgts. LS11: Leeds....2E **41**
Meynell La. LS15: Leeds 1D **44**
Meynell Mt. LS26: Rothw 4H **53**
Meynell Rd. LS15: Leeds....6D **34**
Meynell Sq. LS11: Leeds....2E **41**
Meynell Wlk. LS11: Leeds....2E **41**
Michael Av. WF3: Stly....6G **59**
Micklefield Ct. LS19: Raw....5D **8**
Micklefield La. LS19: Raw 5C **8**
Micklefield Rd. LS19: Raw....5D **8**
Mickley St. LS12: Leeds....6B **30**
Middlebrook Cl. LS27: Morl 4A **50**
Middlecroft Cl. LS10: Leeds....1B **52**
Middlecroft Rd. LS10: Leeds....1B **52**
Middle Cross St. LS12: Leeds 6B **30**
....(not continuous)
Middle Fold LS9: Leeds....3H **5** (5H **31**)
Middleham Ct. BD4: B'ford....4A **36**
Middleham Moor LS10: Leeds 6H **51**
Middlemoor LS14: Leeds 3B **24**
Middle Rd. LS9: Leeds....5F **43**
Middlethorne Cl. LS17: Leeds....4D **14**
Middlethorne Ct. LS17: Leeds....4C **14**
Middlethorne M. LS17: Leeds 4D **14**
Middlethorne Ri. LS17: Leeds 4C **14**
MIDDLETON....4F **51**
Middleton Av. LS26: Rothw 4C **52**
Middleton Av. LS9: Leeds....4B **32**
Middleton Cl. LS27: Morl....5A **50**
Middleton Cres. LS11: Leeds 5F **41**
Middleton District Cen. 4H **51**
Middleton Gro. LS11: Leeds....6F **41**
Middleton Gro. LS27: Morl 5A **50**
Middleton La. LS26: Rothw 4C **52**
....(not continuous)
Middleton La. WF3: Thpe H....6H **51**
Middleton Leisure Cen. 4H **51**
Middleton Pk. Av. LS10: Leeds....5F **51**
Middleton Pk. Cir. LS10: Leeds 4F **51**
Middleton Pk. Ct. LS10: Leeds 5F **51**
Middleton Pk. Cres.
LS10: Leeds....5G **51**
Middleton Pk. Equestrian Cen.....1G **51**
Middleton Pk. Grn. LS10: Leeds...5F **51**
Middleton Pk. Gro. LS10: Leeds...4F **51**
Middleton Pk. Mt. LS10: Leeds 5F **51**
Middleton Pk. Rd. LS10: Leeds 4F **51**
Middleton Pk. Ter. LS10: Leeds... 5G **51**
Middleton Railway Moor
Road Station....4H **41**
Middleton Railway Park
Halt Station....1H **51**
Middleton Rd. LS10: Leeds 2A **52**
Middleton Rd. LS27: Morl....5H **49**
Middleton Ter. LS27: Morl 5A **50**
Middleton Way LS10: Leeds....3B **52**
Middle Wlk. LS8: Leeds....2E **23**
Midgley Gdns. LS6: Leeds....2E **31**
Midgley Pl. LS6: Leeds....2E **31**
Midgley Ter. LS6: Leeds 2F **31**
Midland Cl. LS10: Leeds....4B **42**
Midland Dr. LS10: Leeds 4B **42**
Midland Gth. LS10: Leeds 4A **42**
Midland Ho. LS26: W'frd 3D **54**
....*(off Midland St.)*
Midland Pas. LS6: Leeds....2D **30**
Midland Pl. LS11: Leeds....1E **41**
Midland Rd. LS10: Leeds 4A **42**
Midland Rd. LS6: Leeds 2D **30**
Midland St. LS26: Oult 3C **54**
Mid Point BD3: B'ford....5B **26**
Mid Point Bus. Pk. BD3: B'ford 5B **26**
Midwinter Row BD11: Drig 3H **47**
Milan Rd. LS8: Leeds....2B **32**
Milan St. LS8: Leeds....2C **32**
MILES HILL....5F **21**
Miles Hill Av. LS7: Leeds....5F **21**
Miles Hill Cres. LS7: Leeds 5F **21**
Miles Hill Gro. LS7: Leeds....5F **21**
Miles Hill Mt. LS7: Leeds 4E **21**
Miles Hill Pl. LS7: Leeds....4F **21**
Miles Hill Rd. LS7: Leeds 4F **21**
Miles Hill Sq. LS7: Leeds....5F **21**
Miles Hill St. LS7: Leeds 5F **21**
Miles Hill Ter. LS7: Leeds 5F **21**
Miles Hill Vw. LS7: Leeds....5F **21**
Milestone Ct. LS28: Stan....3H **27**
Milford Gro. BD19: Gom 6C **46**
Milford Pl. LS4: Leeds 4B **30**
Millard Rd. WF3: W Ard 4F **57**
Millard Way WF3: W Ard 3F **57**
Millbank LS19: Yead 1D **8**
Millbank Ct. LS28: Pud....1H **37**
Millbank Fold LS28: Pud....1H **37**
Millbank Vw. LS28: Pud 1H **37**
Millbeck App. LS27: Morl....5A **50**
Mill Beck Cl. LS28: Fars....1G **27**
Mill Cft. LS27: Gil....2D **48**
Millcroft WF3: Loft....5G **59**
Millcroft Cl. WF3: Loft 5F **59**
Millcroft Ri. WF3: Loft 5G **59**
Mill Dale Ct. BD11: Drig 3H **47**
....*(off Moorside Va.)*
Millennium Ct. LS28: Pud....5H **27**
....*(off Lowtown)*
Millennium Dr. LS11: Leeds 6F **41**
Millennium Sq.
LS2: Leeds 2D **4** (4F **31**)
Millennium Way LS11: Leeds....6F **41**
Millers Dale LS27: Morl....3F **49**
Miller Wlk. LS18: Hors....3F **17**
Mill Fold LS27: Gil 2D **48**
Mill Gth. LS27: Gil....2D **48**
MILL GREEN 6B **24**
Mill Grn. LS12: Leeds 1D **40**
Mill Grn. Cl. LS14: Leeds....6C **24**
Mill Grn. Gdns. LS14: Leeds....6C **24**
Mill Grn. Gth. LS14: Leeds....6C **24**
Mill Grn. Pl. LS14: Leeds 6C **24**
Mill Grn. Rd. LS14: Leeds 6C **24**
Mill Grn. Vw. LS14: Leeds 6C **24**
Mill Hill LS1: Leeds....5E **5** (6G **31**)
Mill Hill LS26: Rothw 4G **53**
Mill Hill LS28: Pud 2G **37**
Mill Hill Grn. LS26: Rothw 4G **53**
Mill Hill Sq. LS26: Rothw....4G **53**
Millington Rd. LS27: Morl 6E **49**
Mill La. BD4: B'ford Tong La.....4H **37**
Mill La. BD11: B'haw....3C **46**
Mill La. LS13: Leeds 2A **28**
Mill La. LS27: Gil 2D **48**
Mill La. WF17: Birs 6B **48**
Mill La. WF3: E Ard....3H **57**
Mill Pit La. LS26: Rothw....2F **53**
Mill Pond Cl. LS6: Leeds 5C **20**
Millpond Gdns. LS12: Leeds 5H **29**
....*(off Eyres Mill Side)*
Mill Pond Gro. LS6: Leeds....5C **20**
Mill Pond La. LS6: Leeds....4C **20**
Mill Pond Sq. LS6: Leeds 4C **20**
Mill Race La. BD4: B'ford....1A **36**
MILL SHAW....6C **40**
Millshaw LS11: Leeds 6B **40**
Millshaw Mt. LS11: Leeds....1C **50**
Millshaw Pk. Av. LS11: Leeds....1B **50**
Millshaw Pk. Cl. LS11: Leeds....1B **50**
Millshaw Pk. Dr. LS11: Leeds 6B **40**
Millshaw Pk. La. LS11: Leeds....1B **50**
Millshaw Pk. Trad. Est.
LS11: Leeds 1C **50**
Millshaw Pk. Way LS11: Leeds....6B **40**
Millshaw Rd. LS11: Leeds....2C **50**
Millside Wlk. LS27: Morl 5A **50**
Mill Sq. LS18: Hors....3F **17**
Mill St. LS27: Morl....6G **49**
Mill St. LS9: Leeds....5H **5** (6A **32**)

A-Z Leeds 89

Millwright St. – Mount Dr.

Millwright St. LS2: Leeds 2H **5** (4H **31**)
Milne Ct. LS15: Leeds 1D **44**
Milner Fold LS28: Pud 2F **37**
Milner Gdns. LS9: Leeds 1B **42**
Milner La. WF3: Rob H 6C **52**
Milner's Rd. LS19: Yead 6H **7**
Milnes St. LS12: Leeds 1C **40**
Milton Ct. WF3: Stly 5H **59**
Milton Dr. LS15: Scho 4F **25**
Milton Ter. LS19: Yead 6H **7**
Milton Ter. LS5: Leeds 1G **29**
Minerva Ind. Est. LS26: W'frd 2E **55**
Minett Ct. LS26: Meth 6H **55**
Minor & Scurr's Yd.
LS1: Leeds 4E **5** (5G **31**)
(off Briggate)
MINOR INJURIES UNIT
(ST GEORGES CENTRE) 4H **51**
Minster Dr. BD4: B'ford 2A **36**
Mirycarr La. LS14: Leeds 1E **25**
Mirycarr La. LS14: T'ner 1E **25**
Miry La. LS19: Yead 2D **8**
Mistress La. LS12: Leeds 5A **30**
Mitford Pl. LS12: Leeds 6B **30**
Mitford Rd. LS12: Leeds 6B **30**
Mitford Ter. LS12: Leeds 6B **30**
Mitford Vw. LS12: Leeds 6B **30**
Modder Av. LS12: Leeds 6H **29**
Modder Pl. LS12: Leeds 6H **29**
Model Av. LS12: Leeds 6B **30**
Model Rd. LS12: Leeds 6B **30**
Model Ter. LS12: Leeds 6B **30**
Monet Cl. LS7: Leeds 5E **21**
Monet Gdns. LS7: Leeds 5E **21**
Monk Bri. Av. LS6: Leeds 5D **20**
Monk Bri. Dr. LS6: Leeds 5D **20**
Monk Bri. Gro. LS6: Leeds 5C **20**
Monk Bri. Mt. LS6: Leeds 5C **20**
Monk Bri. Pl. LS6: Leeds 5C **20**
Monk Bri. Rd. LS6: Leeds 5C **20**
Monk Bri. St. LS6: Leeds 5D **20**
Monk Bri. Ter. LS6: Leeds 5C **20**
Monkswood LS5: Leeds 5F **19**
Monkswood Av. LS14: Leeds 3H **23**
Monkswood Bank LS14: Leeds 3H **23**
Monkswood Cl. LS14: Leeds 3H **23**
Monkswood Dr. LS14: Leeds 3H **23**
Monkswood Ga. LS14: Leeds 3A **24**
Monkswood Grn. LS14: Leeds 3H **23**
Monkswood Hill LS14: Leeds 3H **23**
Monkswood Ho. LS5: Leeds 1F **29**
Monkswood Ri. LS14: Leeds 3H **23**
Monkswood Wlk. LS14: Leeds 3A **24**
Monkwood Rd. WF1: Outw 6D **58**
Monson Av. LS28: Cal 5D **16**
Montagu Av. LS8: Leeds 6D **22**
Montagu Ct. LS8: Leeds 5D **22**
Montagu Cres. LS8: Leeds 6E **23**
Montagu Dr. LS8: Leeds 5D **22**
Montague LS12: Leeds 5A **4** (6D **30**)
(off Gotts Rd.)
Montague Ct. LS12: Leeds 6G **29**
Montagu Gdns. LS8: Leeds 6D **22**
Montagu Gro. LS8: Leeds 6E **23**
Montagu Pl. LS8: Leeds 6D **22**
Montagu Ri. LS8: Leeds 6E **23**
Montagu Vw. LS8: Leeds 6D **22**
Montcalm Cres. LS10: Leeds 5A **42**
Montfort Cl. LS18: Hors 6B **10**
Montgomery Av. LS16: Leeds 4A **20**
Montpelier Ter. LS6: Leeds 1E **31**
Montreal Av. LS7: Leeds 5H **21**
Montreal Ter. LS13: Leeds 5A **28**
Montserrat Rd. BD4: B'ford 6B **36**
MOOR ALLERTON 6G **13**
Moor Allerton Av. LS17: Leeds 1A **22**
Moor Allerton Cen. 1F **21**
Moor Allerton Cres.
LS17: Leeds 1A **22**
Moor Allerton Dr. LS17: Leeds 1A **22**
Moor Allerton Gdns.
LS17: Leeds 1H **21**
Moor Allerton Golf Course 1G **15**
Moor Allerton Hall LS8: Leeds 2B **22**
Moor Allerton Way LS17: Leeds 1A **22**
Moor Av. LS15: Leeds 6H **33**
Moor Av. WF3: Stly 5G **59**
Moor Bank BD4: B'ford 2C **46**
Moorbank Ct. LS6: Leeds 6C **20**
Moor Cl. LS10: Leeds 5H **41**
Moor Ct. WF3: E Ard 3H **57**
Moor Cres. LS11: Leeds 3G **41**
Moor Cres. Chase LS11: Leeds 3G **41**
Moor Cft. LS16: Leeds 5B **12**
Moorcroft Av. BD3: B'ford 4A **26**
Moorcroft Dr. BD4: B'ford 6B **36**
Moorcroft Rd. BD4: B'ford 6B **36**
Moorcroft Ter. BD4: B'ford 6B **36**
Moor Dr. LS28: Pud 2H **37**
Moor Dr. LS6: Leeds 5C **20**
Moorehouse Gro. LS9: Leeds 4A **32**
MOOR END 6G **29**
Moor Farm Gdns. LS7: Leeds 4G **21**
Moorfield BD11: B'haw 5E **47**
Moorfield LS27: Gil 2C **48**
Moorfield Av. BD3: B'ford 4A **26**
Moorfield Av. LS12: Leeds 5G **29**
Moorfield Av. LS29: Men 1B **6**
Moorfield Bus. Pk. LS19: Yead 3F **9**
Moorfield Cl. LS19: Yead 3F **9**
Moorfield Ct. LS19: Yead 3F **9**
Moorfield Cres. LS12: Leeds 5G **29**
Moorfield Cres. LS19: Yead 3E **9**
Moorfield Cres. LS28: Pud 1F **37**
Moorfield Cft. LS19: Yead 3F **9**
Moorfield Dr. LS19: Yead 3F **9**
Moorfield Gdns. LS28: Pud 1E **37**
Moorfield Gro. LS12: Leeds 5G **29**
Moorfield Gro. LS28: Pud 1E **37**
Moorfield Ind. Est. LS19: Yead 2F **9**
Moorfield Rd. LS12: Leeds 5G **29**
Moorfield Rd. LS19: Yead 3F **9**
Moorfields LS13: Leeds 2C **28**
Moorfields LS17: Leeds 1H **21**
Moorfield St. LS12: Leeds 5G **29**
Moorfield St. LS2: Leeds 2E **31**
Moorfield Ter. LS19: Yead 2E **9**
Moor Flatts Av. LS10: Leeds 4G **51**
Moor Flatts Rd. LS10: Leeds 4G **51**
Moorgarth Av. BD3: B'ford 4A **26**
Moor Ga. WF3: E Ard 3H **57**
Moor Grange LS19: Yead 3F **9**
Moor Grange Ct. LS16: Leeds 3F **19**
Moor Grange Dr. LS16: Leeds 3G **19**
Moor Grange Ri. LS16: Leeds 3G **19**
Moor Grange Vw. LS16: Leeds 3G **19**
Moor Gro. LS28: Pud 2H **37**
Moor Gro. WF3: Stly 5G **59**
Moorhaven Ct. LS17: Leeds 6E **13**
MOOR HEAD 1C **48**
Moorhead Vs. LS27: Gil 6B **38**
Moorhouse Av. LS11: Leeds 6D **40**
Moor Ho. Ct. LS17: Leeds 5D **14**
Moorhouse Dr. BD11: B'haw 2B **46**
Moorhouse La. BD11: B'haw 2C **46**
Moorings, The BD10: B'ford 3A **16**
Moorings, The LS10: Leeds 4D **42**
Moorings, The LS17: Leeds 4A **14**
Moor Knoll Cl. WF3: E Ard 3H **57**
Moor Knoll Dr. WF3: E Ard 3G **57**
Moor Knoll Fold WF3: E Ard 2G **57**
Moor Knoll Gdns. WF3: E Ard 2G **57**
Moor Knoll La. WF3: E Ard 2G **57**
Moorland Av. LS20: Guis 4G **7**
Moorland Av. LS27: Gil 1B **48**
Moorland Av. LS6: Leeds 3D **30**
Moorland Cl. LS17: Leeds 2H **21**
Moorland Cl. LS27: Gil 1C **48**
Moorland Cres. LS29: Men
Bradford Rd. 3E **7**
Moorland Cres. LS17: Leeds 2G **21**
Moorland Cres. LS20: Guis 3G **7**
Moorland Cres. LS27: Gil 1B **48**
Moorland Cres. LS28: Pud 5C **26**
Moorland Dr. BD11: B'haw 2D **46**
Moorland Dr. LS17: Leeds 2G **21**
Moorland Dr. LS20: Guis 3G **7**
Moorland Dr. LS28: Pud 4C **26**
Moorland Gdns. BD4: B'ford 2B **36**
Moorland Gdns. LS17: Leeds 2H **21**
Moorland Gth. LS17: Leeds 2G **21**
Moorland Gro. LS17: Leeds 1G **21**
Moorland Gro. LS28: Pud 4C **26**
Moorland Ings LS17: Leeds 2G **21**
Moorland La. BD4: B'ford 2A **36**
Moorland Leys LS17: Leeds 2F **21**
Moorland Pl. WF3: Stly 3H **59**
Moorland Ri. LS17: Leeds 2G **21**
Moorland Rd. BD11: Drig 3G **47**
Moorland Rd. LS28: Pud 4C **26**
Moorland Rd. LS6: Leeds 3D **30**
Moorlands, The LS17: Leeds 5A **14**
Moorlands Av. BD11: B'haw 2C **46**
Moorlands Av. LS19: Yead 3F **9**
Moorlands Dr. LS19: Yead 3F **9**
Moorlands Rd. BD11: B'haw 2C **46**
Moorland Vw. LS13: Leeds 1B **28**
Moorland Vw. LS17: Leeds 1G **21**
Moorland Wlk. LS17: Leeds 1G **21**
Moor La. BD11: B'haw 5E **47**
Moor La. LS20: Guis 2G **7**
Moor La. LS29: Men 1A **6**
Moor Pk. Av. LS6: Leeds 5B **20**
Moor Pk. Dr. LS6: Leeds 5B **20**
Moor Pk. Mt. LS6: Leeds 5B **20**
Moor Pk. Vs. LS6: Leeds 5C **20**
Moor Rd. LS10: Leeds 3H **41**
Moor Rd. LS11: Leeds 3G **41**
Moor Rd. LS6: Leeds 5B **20**
Moor Rd. WF3: Stly 5G **59**
Moor Road Station
Middleton Railway 4H **41**
MOORSIDE 4H **47**
MOORSIDE 1C **28**
Moorside App. BD11: Drig 4H **47**
Moorside Av. BD11: B'haw 2C **46**
Moorside Av. BD11: Drig 4H **47**
Moorside Cl. BD11: Drig 4H **47**
Moorside Cres. BD11: Drig 4G **47**
Moorside Dr. BD11: Drig 4H **47**
Moorside Dr. LS13: Leeds 1C **28**
Moorside Gdns. BD11: Drig 4H **47**
Moorside Grn. BD11: Drig 3H **47**
Moorside Maltings
LS11: Leeds 3G **41**
Moor Side M. BD4: B'ford 1A **46**
Moorside Mt. BD11: Drig 4G **47**
Moorside Pde. BD11: Drig 4H **47**
Moorside Rd. BD11: Drig 4G **47**
Moorside St. LS13: Leeds 1C **28**
Moorside Ter. BD11: Drig 4H **47**
Moorside Ter. LS13: Leeds 1C **28**
Moorside Va. BD11: Drig 3H **47**
Moorside Vw. BD11: Drig 4H **47**
Moorside Wlk. BD11: Drig 3H **47**
Moor Top BD11: Drig 3F **47**
(not continuous)
Moor Top LS12: N Far 5C **38**
MOOR TOP 6H **29**
Moor Top LS20: Guis 2G **7**
MOORTOWN 1H **21**
Moortown Cnr. LS17: Leeds 1H **21**
Moortown Golf Course 4H **13**
Moor Vw. BD4: B'ford 2C **46**
Moor Vw. LS11: Leeds 2E **41**
Moor Vw. LS12: Leeds 6H **29**
Moor Vw. LS19: Yead 2F **9**
Moor Vw. LS6: Leeds 2D **30**
(off Hyde Pk. Rd.)
Moor Vw. Cl. LS29: Men 2C **6**
Moorview Cft. LS29: Men 1B **6**
Moorville Cl. LS11: Leeds 3F **41**
Moorville Ct. LS11: Leeds 3E **41**
Moorville Dr. BD11: B'haw 2C **46**
Moorville Gro. LS11: Leeds 3E **41**
Moorville Rd. LS11: Leeds 3F **41**
Moorway LS20: Guis 4D **6**
Moravia Bank LS28: Pud 2G **37**
(off Fartown)
Moravian Mus. & Settlement 2G **37**
Moresdale La. LS14: Leeds 2H **33**
MORLEY 5G **49**
Morley Av. BD3: B'ford 4A **26**
MORLEY BOTTOMS 4G **49**
MORLEY HOLE 4F **49**
Morley Leisure Cen. 5G **49**
Morley Mkt. 5G **49**
(off Hope St.)
Morley Station (Rail) 4A **50**
Morpeth Pl. LS9: Leeds 6A **32**
Morrell Ct. BD4: B'ford 4A **36**
Morris Av. LS5: Leeds 6G **19**
Morris Cl. LS18: Hors 4F **17**
Morris Fold LS18: Hors 4G **17**
Morris Gro. LS5: Leeds 1G **29**
Morris La. LS5: Leeds 6G **19**
Morris Mt. LS5: Leeds 1G **29**
Morris Pl. LS27: Morl 4F **49**
Morris Vw. LS5: Leeds 1G **29**
Morritt Av. LS15: Leeds 4B **34**
Morritt Dr. LS15: Leeds 5H **33**
Morritt Gro. LS15: Leeds 5H **33**
Mortec Pk. LS15: Leeds 4E **25**
Mortimer Av. BD3: B'ford 4A **26**
Morton Ter. LS20: Guis 4F **7**
Morwick Gro. LS15: Scho 5F **25**
Morwick Ter. LS14: Leeds 3E **25**
Mosedale Dr. LS14: Leeds 2C **24**
Moseley Beck Av. LS16: Leeds 4C **10**
Moseley Beck Cres.
LS16: Leeds 4C **10**
Moseley Beck Dr. LS16: Leeds 4C **10**
Moseley Beck La. LS16: Leeds 3C **10**
Moseley Beck Wlk. LS16: Leeds 4C **10**
Moseley Beck Way LS16: Leeds 4C **10**
Moseley Pl. LS6: Leeds 2F **31**
Moseley Wood App.
LS16: Leeds 5D **10**
Moseley Wood Av. LS16: Leeds 3D **10**
Moseley Wood Bank
LS16: Leeds 4D **10**
Moseley Wood Cl. LS16: Leeds 5D **10**
Moseley Wood Cres.
LS16: Leeds 4D **10**
Moseley Wood Cft. LS16: Leeds 5C **10**
Moseley Wood Dr. LS16: Leeds 4D **10**
Moseley Wood Gdns.
LS16: Leeds 4D **10**
Moseley Wood Grn.
LS16: Leeds 4D **10**
Moseley Wood Gro.
LS16: Leeds 4D **10**
Moseley Wood La. LS16: Leeds 4E **11**
Moseley Wood Ri. LS16: Leeds 4D **10**
Moseley Wood Vw. LS16: Leeds 3E **11**
Moseley Wood Wlk.
LS16: Leeds 4D **10**
Moseley Wood Way
LS16: Leeds 3D **10**
Moss Bri. Rd. LS13: Leeds 6H **17**
Moss Gdns. LS17: Leeds 4E **13**
Moss Lea LS27: Chur 2H **49**
Moss Ri. LS17: Leeds 4E **13**
Moss Valley LS17: Leeds 4E **13**
Motley La. LS20: Guis 3G **7**
Motley Row LS20: Guis 3G **7**
(off Motley La.)
Mount, The LS15: Leeds 4B **34**
Mount, The LS17: Leeds 3F **13**
Mount, The LS19: Raw 6F **9**
Mount, The LS26: Rothw 2H **53**
Mount, The LS27: Chur 2H **49**
(off Elland Rd.)
Mountbatten Av. WF1: Outw 6E **59**
Mountbatten Cres. WF1: Outw 6E **59**
Mountbatten Gro. WF1: Outw 6F **59**
Mountcliffe Vw. LS27: Chur 2H **49**
Mount Dr. LS17: Leeds 3F **13**

90 A-Z Leeds

Mountfields – NEW WORTLEY

Mountfields LS2: Leeds.....1A **4** (4D **30**)
(off Clarendon Rd.)
Mount Gdns. LS17: Leeds 3F **13**
Mt. Pleasant LS10: Leeds........... 4G **51**
Mt. Pleasant LS13: Leeds............1B **28**
Mt. Pleasant LS18: Hors...............3D **18**
(off Broadgate La.)
Mt. Pleasant LS20: Guis 3G **7**
Mt. Pleasant LS28: Stan...............4F **27**
(off Westbourne Pl.)
Mt. Pleasant Av. LS8: Leeds........6B **22**
Mt. Pleasant Ct. LS28: Pud 5G **27**
Mt. Pleasant Gdns. LS8: Leeds 6B **22**
(off Sycamore Av.)
Mt. Pleasant Hgts. LS28: Pud 5G **27**
(off Mt. Pleasant Rd.)
Mt. Pleasant Rd. LS28: Pud 5G **27**
Mt. Pleasant St. LS28: Pud 5H **27**
Mt. Preston LS2: Leeds 1A **4** (4E **31**)
(off Cromer Ter.)
Mt. Preston St.
LS2: Leeds 1A **4** (4E **31**)
Mount Ri. LS17: Leeds 3F **13**
Mount Rd. WF3: Stly................... 5H **59**
Mt. Royal LS18: Hors...................3B **18**
Mt. Tabor St. LS28: Pud...............6E **27**
Mt. Vernon Rd. LS19: Raw 5E **9**
Mount Vw. LS27: Chur................ 2H **49**
Mowbray Chase LS26: W'frd.......2B **54**
Mowbray Ct. LS14: Leeds 2A **34**
Mowbray Cres. LS14: Leeds 2A **34**
Moxon St. WF1: Outw...................6E **59**
Moxon Way WF1: Outw 6E **59**
Moynihan Cl. LS8: Leeds............ 1D **32**
Mozart Way LS27: Chur...............1A **50**
Muir Ct. LS6: Leeds.......................1B **30**
(off Sagar Pl.)
Muirfield Dr. LS26: Rothw 5A **54**
Muirhead Ct. BD4: B'ford 5A **36**
Muirhead Dr. BD4: B'ford 5A **36**
Muirhead Fold BD4: B'ford...........5A **36**
Mulberry Av. LS16: Leeds 5B **12**
Mulberry Gdns. LS26: Meth 6H **55**
Mulberry Gth. LS16: Leeds............6B **12**
Mulberry Ri. LS16: Leeds............5B **12**
Mulberry Rd. LS28: Fars 1F **27**
Mulberry St. LS28: Pud 6G **27**
Mulberry Vw. LS16: Leeds 6B **12**
Mullins Ct. LS9: Leeds..................6B **32**
Munroe Ct. LS11: Leeds...............1B **50**
Murray Av. LS10: Leeds 5A **52**
Murray Cl. LS10: Leeds 5A **52**
Murray Ct. LS18: Hors...................3E **19**
Murray Cres. LS11: Leeds.............2E **41**
Murray Dr. LS10: Leeds..................5A **52**
Murray Vw. LS10: Leeds 5A **52**
Murray Way LS10: Leeds 5A **52**
Murton Cl. LS14: Leeds.................1A **34**
Museum St. LS9: Leeds..................4B **32**
Musgrave Bank LS13: Leeds 3E **29**
Musgrave Bldgs. LS28: Pud......... 5H **27**
Musgrave Ct. LS28: Pud............... 6G **27**
Musgrave Mt. LS13: Leeds...........3E **29**
Musgrave Ri. LS13: Leeds............3E **29**
Musgrave Vw. LS13: Leeds 3E **29**
Musgrove Ho. LS5: Leeds 1F **29**
(off Broad La.)
Mushroom St.
LS9: Leeds 1H **5** (4H **31**)
Myers Dr. LS13: Leeds...................5B **18**

N

Nab La. WF17: Birs........................6A **48**
(not continuous)
Naburn App. LS14: Leeds..............2B **24**
Naburn Chase LS14: Leeds...........4B **24**
Naburn Cl. LS14: Leeds..................4C **24**
Naburn Ct. LS14: Leeds..................3B **24**
Naburn Dr. LS14: Leeds..................4B **24**
Naburn Fold LS14: Leeds...............4C **24**
Naburn Gdns. LS14: Leeds............4B **24**
Naburn Grn. LS14: Leeds 4B **24**
Naburn Pl. LS14: Leeds..................3B **24**
Naburn Rd. LS14: Leeds.................4B **24**
Naburn Vw. LS14: Leeds 4C **24**
Naburn Wlk. LS14: Leeds..............4B **24**
Nancroft Cres. LS12: Leeds 6A **30**
Nancroft Mt. LS12: Leeds...............6A **30**
Nancroft Ter. LS12: Leeds 6A **30**
Nansen Av. LS13: Leeds.................3B **28**
Nansen Gro. LS13: Leeds...............3B **28**
Nansen Mt. LS13: Leeds 3B **28**
Nansen Pl. LS13: Leeds..................3B **28**
Nansen St. LS13: Leeds 3A **28**
Nansen Ter. LS13: Leeds 3B **28**
Nansen Vw. LS13: Leeds.................3B **28**
Napier St. BD3: B'ford 6A **26**
Narrowboat Wharf LS13: Leeds.. 6H **17**
Naseby Gdns. LS9: Leeds..............5A **32**
Naseby Gth. LS9: Leeds 4A **32**
Naseby Grange LS9: Leeds 5A **32**
(off Naseby Gdns.)
Naseby Ho. BD4: B'ford.................6B **36**
Naseby Pl. LS9: Leeds....................5A **32**
Naseby Ter. LS9: Leeds...................5A **32**
Naseby Vw. LS9: Leeds 5A **32**
Naseby Wlk. LS9: Leeds.................5A **32**
Nassau Pl. LS7: Leeds...................2A **32**
Nateby Ri. WF3: Car 6F **53**
National Pk. LS10: Leeds 3A **42**
National Rd. LS10: Leeds 2A **42**
Navigation Ct. LS13: Leeds 5G **17**
Navigation Dr. BD10: B'ford 3A **16**
Navigation Wlk.
LS10: Leeds 6F **5** (6G **31**)
Naylor Av. LS19: Yead 4D **8**
Naylor Ct. LS19: Yead.................... 3D **8**
Naylor Gth. LS6: Leeds............... 6D **20**
Naylor Pl. LS11: Leeds 3F **41**
Neath Gdns. LS9: Leeds 2F **33**
Ned La. BD4: B'ford 3A **36**
Needless Inn La. LS26: W'frd.......2C **54**
Nelson Pl. LS27: Morl 4G **49**
(off Croft Ho. Rd.)
Nepshaw La. LS27: Gil 5D **48**
Nepshaw La. LS27: Morl 4F **49**
Nepshaw La. Nth. LS27: Morl 4E **49**
Nepshaw La. Sth. LS27: Gil..........4E **49**
Neptune St. LS9: Leeds.....6H **5** (6H **31**)
Nesfield Cl. LS10: Leeds 3B **52**
Nesfield Ct. LS10: Leeds 3A **52**
Nesfield Cres. LS10: Leeds 3B **52**
Nesfield Gdns. LS10: Leeds 3A **52**
Nesfield Gth. LS10: Leeds 3A **52**
Nesfield Grn. LS10: Leeds.............3A **52**
Nesfield Rd. LS10: Leeds 3A **52**
Nesfield Vw. LS10: Leeds..............3A **52**
Nesfield Wlk. LS10: Leeds 3A **52**
Nethercliffe Cres. LS20: Guis.........3F **7**
Nethercliffe Rd. LS20: Guis 3F **7**
Netherfield Cl. LS19: Yead 2D **8**
Netherfield Ct. LS20: Guis..............4F **7**
(off Netherfield Rd.)
Netherfield Dr. LS20: Guis..............3F **7**
Netherfield Ri. LS20: Guis..............4F **7**
Netherfield Rd. LS20: Guis.............3F **7**
Netherfield Ter. LS19: Yead........... 2D **8**
Netherfield Ter. LS20: Guis.............4F **7**
(off Netherfield Rd.)
Nethermore Pk.............................4E **7**
NETHERTOWN................................2A **48**
NETHER YEADON 5D **8**
Nettleton Cl. BD4: B'ford 5G **37**
Nettleton Ct. LS15: Leeds.............. 5D **34**
Neville App. LS9: Leeds.................1E **43**
Neville Av. LS9: Leeds....................1E **43**
Neville Cl. LS9: Leeds.....................1E **43**
Neville Gth. LS9: Leeds 1E **43**
Neville Gro. LS26: Swil 5G **45**
Neville Gro. LS9: Leeds 1E **43**
Neville Mt. LS9: Leeds.....................1E **43**
Neville Pde. LS9: Leeds 1E **43**
Neville Pl. LS9: Leeds....................6F **33**
Neville Rd. LS15: Leeds............... 6G **33**
Neville Rd. LS9: Leeds....................5F **33**
Neville Row LS9: Leeds.................1E **43**
Neville Sq. LS9: Leeds 5F **33**
Neville St. LS1: Leeds........ 6D **4** (6F **31**)
Neville St. LS11: Leeds...... 6D **4** (1F **41**)
Neville Ter. LS9: Leeds 1E **43**
Neville Vw. LS9: Leeds 1E **43**
Neville Wlk. LS9: Leeds..................6E **33**
New Adel Av. LS16: Leeds........... 6G **11**
New Adel Gdns. LS16: Leeds 6G **11**
New Adel La. LS16: Leeds 1G **19**
Newark Va. WF3: Rob H 6C **52**
New Bank Ri. BD4: B'ford 4A **36**
New Bank St. LS27: Morl 4H **49**
NEW BLACKPOOL 3G **39**
New Briggate LS1: Leeds.. 3F **5** (5G **31**)
New Briggate LS2: Leeds.. 3F **5** (5G **31**)
NEW BRIGHTON 5G **49**
Newby Cl. LS29: Men 2D **6**
Newby Ct. LS29: Men 2D **6**
Newby Gth. LS17: Leeds 4D **14**
Newcastle Cl. BD11: Drig.............4F **47**
New Centaur Ho.
LS11: Leeds 6D **4** (6F **31**)
New Cote Cotts. LS28: Fars 2G **27**
New Craven Ga. LS11: Leeds...... 2G **41**
New Cres. LS18: Hors...................3B **18**
New Cft. LS18: Hors 3B **18**
Newell Sq. LS28: Pud 1F **37**
(off Smalewell Rd.)
New Fairfield St. LS13: Leeds......3B **28**
New Farmers Hill LS26: W'frd..... 2D **54**
NEW FARNLEY 4D **38**
Newfield Dr. LS29: Men.................1C **6**
New Forest Dr. LS10: Leeds.........5A **52**
New Forest Way LS10: Leeds 5A **52**
Newhall Bank LS10: Leeds 4H **51**
Newhall Chase LS10: Leeds........ 3H **51**
Newhall Cl. LS10: Leeds............... 3H **51**
Newhall Cres. LS10: Leeds 3H **51**
Newhall Cft. LS10: Leeds 2A **52**
Newhall Gdns. LS10: Leeds 4H **51**
Newhall Gth. LS10: Leeds 3H **51**
Newhall Ga. LS10: Leeds 2H **51**
Newhall Grn. LS10: Leeds.............3A **52**
Newhall Gro. LS10: Leeds 2H **51**
Newhall Mt. LS10: Leeds 4H **51**
Newhall Rd. LS10: Leeds 3H **51**
Newhall Wlk. LS10: Leeds.............3A **52**
New Inn St. LS12: Leeds............... 6G **29**
Newlaithes Gdns. LS18: Hors.......4B **18**
Newlaithes Gth. LS18: Hors 5A **18**
Newlaithes Rd. LS18: Hors 5A **18**
Newlands LS28: Fars 3F **27**
Newlands Av. LS19: Yead..............1C **8**
Newlands Cres. LS27: Morl..........5B **50**
Newlands Dr. LS27: Morl..............4B **50**
Newlands Dr. WF3: Stly................ 6G **59**
Newlands Ri. LS19: Yead 2C **8**
Newlands Wlk. WF3: Stly 6G **59**
Newlands Way BD10: B'ford 6A **16**
New La. BD4: B'ford Raikes La. ... 5D **36**
New La. BD11: Drig 1A **48**
New La. BD3: B'ford 1A **36**
New La. LS10: Leeds.......................4F **51**
New La. LS11: Leeds.......................1F **41**
New La. LS27: Gil 1B **48**
New La. WF3: E Ard 3F **57**
(not continuous)
NEWLAY 5B **18**
Newlay Bridle Path LS18: Hors....4B **18**
Newlay Cl. BD10: B'ford................4A **16**
Newlay Gro. LS18: Hors 5B **18**
Newlay La. LS13: Leeds 1C **28**
Newlay La. LS18: Hors 4B **18**
Newlay La. Pl. LS13: Leeds..........1C **28**
Newlay Mt. LS18: Hors...................5B **18**
Newlay Wood Av. LS18: Hors 4C **18**
Newlay Wood Cl. LS18: Hors........4C **18**
Newlay Wood Cres. LS18: Hors ...4C **18**
Newlay Wood Dr. LS18: Hors 4C **18**
Newlay Wood Fold LS18: Hors.....4B **18**
Newlay Wood Gdns. LS18: Hors...4C **18**
Newlay Wood Ri. LS18: Hors.......4C **18**
Newlay Wood Rd. LS18: Hors 4B **18**
New Leeds LS13: Leeds 6B **18**
New Line BD10: B'ford 4A **16**
Newmarket App. LS9: Leeds....... 2D **42**
Newmarket Grn. LS9: Leeds 1D **42**
Newmarket La. LS9: Leeds 2D **42**
New Mkt. St. LS1: Leeds... 5F **5** (6G **31**)
New Moon Apts. LS6: Leeds 6C **20**
New Occupation La. LS28: Pud ...1E **37**
New Pk. Av. LS28: Fars 2G **27**
New Pk. Cl. LS28: Fars.................. 2G **27**
New Pk. Cft. LS28: Fars 2G **27**
New Pk. Gro. LS28: Fars 2F **27**
New Pk. Pl. LS28: Fars.................. 2G **27**
New Pk. St. LS27: Morl...................6F **49**
New Pk. Va. LS28: Fars 2G **27**
New Pk. Vw. LS28: Fars 3G **27**
New Pk. Wlk. LS28: Fars.................3F **27**
New Pk. Way LS28: Fars 2G **27**
New Pepper Rd. LS10: Leeds.......4B **42**
Newport Av. LS13: Leeds 3A **28**
Newport Cres. LS6: Leeds..............2B **30**
Newport Gdns. LS6: Leeds.............2B **30**
Newport Mt. LS6: Leeds..................2B **30**
Newport Rd. LS6: Leeds..................2B **30**
Newport Vw. LS6: Leeds 1B **30**
New Princess St. LS11: Leeds 2F **41**
New Pudsey Sq. LS28: Stan..........4E **27**
New Pudsey Station (Rail) 4E **27**
New Rd. LS19: Yead 6H **7**
New Rd. WF3: Car 6F **53**
New Rd. Side LS18: Hors 3A **18**
New Rd. Side LS19: Raw............... 4D **8**
New Row LS15: Leeds.....................1E **45**
New Row LS28: Cal..........................2B **26**
Newsam Ct. LS15: Leeds 6A **34**
NEWSAM GREEN 5D **44**
Newsam Grn. Rd. LS26: W'frd..... 5D **44**
NEW SCARBOROUGH......................4D **28**
NEW SCARBOROUGH.........................6H **7**
New Scarbro' Rd. LS13: Leeds ... 3D **28**
New Station St.
LS1: Leeds 5D **4** (6F **31**)
Newstead Av. WF1: Outw 6C **58**
New St. LS18: Hors.........................3B **18**
New St. LS28: Fars 4F **27**
New St. LS28: Pud 1F **37**
New St. Cl. LS28: Pud.................... 1G **37**
New St. Gdns. LS28: Pud 1G **37**
New St. Gro. LS28: Pud 1G **37**
New Temple Ga. LS15: Leeds.......1A **44**
Newton Cl. LS26: Rothw................ 5D **52**
Newton Ct. LS26: Rothw................ 5D **52**
Newton Ct. LS8: Leeds.....................5E **23**
Newton Gth. LS7: Leeds..................6A **22**
Newton Gro. LS7: Leeds..................1A **32**
Newton Hill Rd. LS7: Leeds.......... 6H **21**
Newton Lodge Cl. LS7: Leeds 6G **21**
Newton Lodge Dr. LS7: Leeds..... 6G **21**
Newton Pde. LS7: Leeds 6H **21**
Newton Pk. Ct. LS7: Leeds 6A **22**
Newton Pk. Dr. LS7: Leeds.............6A **22**
Newton Pk. Vw. LS7: Leeds 1A **32**
Newton Rd. LS7: Leeds 1H **31**
Newton Sq. LS12: N Far 4D **38**
Newton Ter. LS7: Leeds.................. 5G **21**
Newton Vw. LS7: Leeds.................. 6H **21**
Newton Vs. LS7: Leeds................... 5G **21**
Newton Wlk. LS7: Leeds 1A **32**
NEW TOWN 3A **32**
New Village M. LS27: Chur 1A **50**
(off New Village Way)
New Village Wlk. LS27: Chur 6A **40**
New Village Way LS27: Chur.........6A **40**
New Wlk. LS8: Leeds...................... 2D **22**
New Way LS20: Guis 4D **6**
New Windsor Dr. LS26: Rothw 3H **53**
NEW WORTLEY 6C **30**

A-Z Leeds 91

New York Cotts. – Oakwell Ct.

New York Cotts. LS19: Raw 1F **17**
New York La. LS19: Raw 1F **17**
New York Rd. LS2: Leeds ..3G **5** (5H **31**)
.... (not continuous)
New York Rd. LS9: Leeds ..3H **5** (5H **31**)
New York St. LS2: Leeds ... 5F **5** (6G **31**)
NHS WALK-IN CENTRE
(SHAKESPEARE) **4A 32**
Nice Av. LS8: Leeds 1B **32**
Nice St. LS8: Leeds 1B **32**
Nice Vw. LS8: Leeds 1B **32**
Nicholson Ct. LS8: Leeds 5C **22**
Nickleby Rd. LS9: Leeds 5C **32**
Nijinsky Way LS10: Leeds 6D **42**
Nile St. LS2: Leeds 2G **5** (4H **31**)
Nineveh Gdns. LS11: Leeds 2E **41**
Nineveh Pde. LS11: Leeds 2E **41**
Nineveh Rd. LS11: Leeds 2E **41**
Nippet La. LS9: Leeds 5A **32**
Nixon Av. LS9: Leeds 6D **32**
Nook, The LS17: Leeds 4H **13**
Nook, The WF3: W Ard 5C **56**
Nook Gdns. LS15: Scho 3F **25**
Nook Grn. WF3: W Ard 4D **56**
Nook Rd. LS15: Scho 3F **25**
Nooks, The LS27: Gil 2D **48**
Nook Vw. WF3: W Ard 5C **56**
Noon Cl. WF3: Stly 6G **59**
Nora Pl. LS13: Leeds 2A **28**
Nora Rd. LS13: Leeds 2A **28**
Nora Ter. LS13: Leeds 2A **28**
Norbury Rd. BD10: B'ford 1A **26**
Norfolk Cl. LS26: Oult 4D **54**
Norfolk Cl. LS7: Leeds 4H **21**
Norfolk Dr. LS26: Oult 4D **54**
Norfolk Gdns. LS7: Leeds 4H **21**
Norfolk Grn. LS7: Leeds 4H **21**
Norfolk Mt. LS7: Leeds 4H **21**
Norfolk Pl. LS7: Leeds 4H **21**
Norfolk Ter. LS7: Leeds 4H **21**
Norfolk Vw. LS7: Leeds 4H **21**
Norfolk Wlk. LS7: Leeds 4H **21**
Norman Gro. LS5: Leeds 1G **29**
Norman Mt. LS5: Leeds 1G **29**
Norman Pl. LS8: Leeds 1C **22**
Norman Row LS5: Leeds 1G **29**
Norman St. LS5: Leeds 1G **29**
Norman Ter. LS8: Leeds 1C **22**
Normanton Gro. LS11: Leeds 3E **41**
Normanton Pl. LS11: Leeds 3E **41**
Norman Towers LS16: Leeds 5G **19**
Norman Vw. LS5: Leeds 1G **29**
Normington Ho. LS13: Leeds 6G **17**
Norquest Ind. Pk. WF17: Birs 6A **48**
Nortech Cl. LS7: Leeds 3H **31**
Nth. Broadgate La. LS18: Hors 2C **18**
Northbrook Cft. LS7: Leeds 4H **21**
.... *(off Hill Vw. Mt.)*
Northbrook Pl. LS7: Leeds 4H **21**
Northbrook St. LS7: Leeds 4H **21**
North Cl. LS8: Leeds 5F **23**
Northcote Cres. LS11: Leeds 3F **41**
Northcote Dr. LS11: Leeds 3F **41**
Northcote Grn. LS11: Leeds 3F **41**
Northcote St. LS28: Fars 3F **27**
North Ct. LS2: Leeds 3F **5** (5G **31**)
North Cres. LS2: Leeds 2F **5** (4G **31**)
Northern Ballet Leeds ....**4H 5 (5H 31)**
.... *(off St Cecilia St.)*
Northern St. LS1: Leeds 5B **4** (6E **31**)
Northern St. Apts.
LS1: Leeds 5C **4** (6F **31**)
.... *(off Northern St.)*
Nth. Farm Rd. LS8: Leeds 2D **32**
Nth. Farm Rd. LS9: Leeds 2E **33**
Northfield Av. LS26: Rothw 5E **53**
Northfield Pl. LS26: Rothw 5D **52**
Northgate LS26: Oult 3C **54**
Nth. Grange M. LS6: Leeds 1D **30**
Nth. Grange Mt. LS6: Leeds 6C **20**
Nth. Grange Rd. LS6: Leeds 1C **30**
North Gro. Cl. LS8: Leeds 5F **23**
North Gro. Dr. LS8: Leeds 5F **23**
North Gro. Ri. LS8: Leeds 5F **23**
Nth. Hill Cl. LS8: Leeds 5E **23**
Nth. Hill Ct. LS6: Leeds 6D **20**
Nth. Hill Rd. LS6: Leeds 1D **30**
North La. LS26: Oult 3C **54**
North La. LS26: W'frd 3C **54**
North La. LS6: Leeds 6B **20**
North La. LS8: Leeds 4E **23**
North La. Gdns. LS8: Leeds 5E **23**
Nth. Lingwell Rd. LS10: Leeds 4G **51**
Northolme Av. LS16: Leeds 4H **19**
Northolme Cres. LS16: Leeds 4H **19**
North Pde. LS16: Leeds 3G **19**
North Pde. LS27: Morl 6H **49**
.... *(off Gillroyd Pde.)*
North Pk. Av. LS8: Leeds 3B **22**
North Pk. Gro. LS8: Leeds 3C **22**
North Pk. Pde. LS8: Leeds 2B **22**
North Pk. Rd. LS8: Leeds 3C **22**
.... (not continuous)
Nth. Parkway LS14: Leeds 6G **23**
North Rd. LS15: Leeds 3C **34**
North Rd. LS18: Hors 6B **10**
Northrops Yd. LS28: Pud 6G **27**
Northside Bus. Pk. LS7: Leeds 3H **31**
Northside Retail Pk. 4D **20**
North St. LS19: Raw 5D **8**
North St. LS2: Leeds 2G **5** (4H **31**)
North St. LS28: Stan 5G **27**
North St. LS7: Leeds 3H **31**
North Ter. LS15: Leeds 3C **34**
.... *(off Tranquility Av.)*
North Ter. LS19: Yead 2D **8**
North Vw. LS26: Rothw 4H **53**
.... *(off Royds La.)*
North Vw. LS29: Men 1C **6**
North Vw. LS8: Leeds 5F **23**
North Vw. Ct. LS28: Stan 3G **27**
.... *(off North Vw. St.)*
North Vw. Rd. BD4: B'ford 2C **46**
North Vw. St. LS28: Stan 3G **27**
North Vw. Ter. LS28: Stan 3G **27**
Nth. Way LS8: Leeds 5F **23**
Northwest Bus. Pk. LS6: Leeds 2F **31**
North W. Rd. LS6: Leeds 2F **31**
Northwood Chase LS28: Pud 2H **37**
Northwood Cl. LS26: W'frd 2C **54**
Northwood Cl. LS28: Pud 2H **37**
Northwood Falls LS26: W'frd 2C **54**
Northwood Gdns. LS15: Leeds 6E **35**
Northwood Grn. LS28: Pud 2H **37**
.... *(off Roker La.)*
Northwood Grn. LS28: Pud 2H **37**
Northwood Mt. LS28: Pud 2H **37**
Northwood Pk. LS26: W'frd 2C **54**
Northwood Vw. LS28: Pud 2H **37**
Norton Rd. LS8: Leeds 1C **22**
Norton Way LS27: Morl 3G **49**
Norville Ter. LS6: Leeds 1C **30**
.... *(off Headingley La.)*
Norwich Av. LS10: Leeds 5H **41**
Norwood Av. BD11: B'haw 5D **46**
Norwood Av. LS29: Men 2C **6**
Norwood Cl. LS29: Men 2C **6**
Norwood Ct. LS29: Men 3C **6**
Norwood Cres. BD11: B'haw 5D **46**
Norwood Cres. LS28: Stan 3H **27**
Norwood Cft. LS28: Stan 3H **27**
Norwood Dr. BD11: B'haw 5D **46**
Norwood Dr. LS29: Men 3C **6**
Norwood Fold LS29: Men 2C **6**
Norwood Gro. BD11: B'haw 5D **46**
Norwood Gro. LS6: Leeds 2C **30**
Norwood Mt. LS6: Leeds 2C **30**
Norwood Pl. LS6: Leeds 2C **30**
Norwood Rd. LS6: Leeds 2C **30**
Norwood Ter. LS6: Leeds 2C **30**
Norwood Vw. LS6: Leeds 2C **30**
Noster Gro. LS11: Leeds 4D **40**
Noster Hill LS11: Leeds 4D **40**
Noster Pl. LS11: Leeds 4D **40**
Noster Rd. LS11: Leeds 4D **40**
Noster St. LS11: Leeds 4D **40**
Noster Ter. LS11: Leeds 4D **40**
Noster Vw. LS11: Leeds 4D **40**
Nottingham Cl. WF3: Rob H 6C **52**
Nottingham St. BD3: B'ford 6A **26**
Nova La. WF17: Birs 6F **47**
Nowell App. LS9: Leeds 4D **32**
Nowell Av. LS9: Leeds 4D **32**
Nowell Cl. LS9: Leeds 4D **32**
Nowell Ct. LS9: Leeds 4D **32**
Nowell Cres. LS9: Leeds 4D **32**
Nowell End Row LS9: Leeds 4D **32**
Nowell Gdns. LS9: Leeds 4D **32**
Nowell Gro. LS9: Leeds 4D **32**
Nowell La. LS9: Leeds 4D **32**
Nowell Mt. LS9: Leeds 4D **32**
Nowell Pde. LS9: Leeds 4D **32**
Nowell Pl. LS9: Leeds 4D **32**
Nowell St. LS9: Leeds 4D **32**
Nowell Ter. LS9: Leeds 4D **32**
Nowell Vw. LS9: Leeds 4D **32**
Nowell Wlk. LS9: Leeds 4D **32**
Nuffield Health Guiseley **4E 7**
Nuffield Health Leeds,
The Headrow ....**3D 4 (5F 31)**
.... *(within The Light)*
Nunnington Av. LS12: Leeds 5A **30**
Nunnington St. LS12: Leeds 5A **30**
Nunnington Ter. LS12: Leeds 5A **30**
Nunnington Vw. LS12: Leeds 4A **30**
Nunroyd Av. LS17: Leeds 2H **21**
Nunroyd Av. LS20: Guis 5H **7**
Nunroyd Gro. LS17: Leeds 2H **21**
Nunroyd Lawn LS17: Leeds 2H **21**
Nunroyd Rd. LS17: Leeds 2H **21**
Nunroyd St. LS17: Leeds 2H **21**
Nunroyd Ter. LS17: Leeds 2H **21**
Nunthorpe Rd. LS13: Leeds 6H **17**
Nursery Cl. LS17: Leeds 5G **13**
Nursery Gro. LS17: Leeds 5E **13**
Nursery La. LS17: Leeds 5E **13**
Nursery Mt. LS10: Leeds 6A **42**
Nursery Mt. Rd. LS10: Leeds 5A **42**
Nursery Pit Dr. LS15: Leeds 2F **43**
Nursery Rd. LS20: Guis 2F **7**
Nussey Av. WF17: Birs 6G **47**
Nutting Gro. Ter. LS12: Leeds 2E **39**

O

O2 Academy Leeds ....**2D 4 (4F 31)**
Oak Av. LS27: Morl 6H **49**
Oak Cres. LS15: Leeds 6H **33**
Oakdale Cl. BD10: B'ford 2A **26**
Oakdale Cl. WF3: Loft 5D **58**
Oakdale Dr. BD10: B'ford 2A **26**
Oakdale Gth. LS14: Leeds 2B **24**
Oakdale Mdw. LS14: Leeds 2B **24**
Oakdene LS26: W'frd 2D **54**
Oakdene Cl. LS28: Pud 2H **37**
Oakdene Ct. LS17: Leeds 5C **14**
Oakdene Dr. LS17: Leeds 5C **14**
Oakdene Gdns. LS17: Leeds 5C **14**
Oakdene Va. LS17: Leeds 5C **14**
Oakdene Way LS17: Leeds 5C **14**
Oak Dr. LS10: Leeds 5H **51**
Oak Dr. LS14: Leeds 4C **24**
Oak Dr. LS16: Leeds 1H **19**
Oakfield LS6: Leeds 1C **30**
Oakfield Av. LS26: Rothw 3G **53**
Oakfield Ter. LS18: Hors 3E **19**
.... *(off Woodville St.)*
Oakford Ter. LS18: Hors 2E **19**
Oak Gro. LS14: Leeds 1C **34**
Oak Gro. LS27: Morl 6H **49**
Oakham Gth. LS9: Leeds 6E **33**
Oakham M. LS9: Leeds 6D **32**
Oakhampton Ct. LS8: Leeds 3E **23**
Oakham Way LS9: Leeds 6D **32**
Oak Ho. LS15: Leeds 1G **43**
Oak Ho. LS5: Leeds 1F **29**
Oak Ho. LS7: Leeds 4H **21**
.... *(off Allerton Pk.)*
Oakhurst LS6: Leeds 1C **30**
Oakhurst Av. LS11: Leeds 6D **40**
Oakhurst Gro. LS11: Leeds 6D **40**
Oakhurst Mt. LS11: Leeds 6D **40**
Oakhurst Rd. LS11: Leeds 6D **40**
Oakhurst St. LS11: Leeds 6E **41**
Oaklands WF3: Rob H 6C **52**
Oaklands Av. LS13: Leeds 6G **17**
Oaklands Av. LS16: Leeds 6B **12**
Oaklands Cl. LS16: Leeds 6B **12**
Oaklands Cl. LS8: Leeds 1E **33**
Oaklands Ct. LS8: Leeds 2E **33**
Oaklands Cres. LS8: Leeds 2E **33**
Oaklands Dr. LS16: Leeds 1B **20**
Oaklands Dr. LS8: Leeds 2E **33**
Oaklands Fold LS16: Leeds 6B **12**
Oaklands Fold LS8: Leeds 1E **33**
Oaklands Gro. LS13: Leeds 6G **17**
Oaklands Gro. LS16: Leeds 6A **12**
Oaklands Gro. LS8: Leeds 2E **33**
Oaklands Pl. LS8: Leeds 2E **33**
Oaklands Rd. LS13: Leeds 6G **17**
Oaklands Rd. LS28: Fars 1G **27**
Oaklands St. LS8: Leeds 2E **33**
Oaklea Gdns. LS16: Leeds 1B **20**
Oaklea Hall Cl. LS16: Leeds 1B **20**
Oaklea Rd. LS15: Scho 5F **25**
Oakley Gro. LS11: Leeds 4G **41**
Oakley St. WF3: Thpe H 2A **58**
Oakley Ter. LS11: Leeds 5G **41**
Oakley Vw. LS11: Leeds 5G **41**
Oak Pk. Cl. LS16: Leeds 1E **19**
Oak Pk. Dr. LS16: Leeds 1E **19**
Oak Pk. Gdns. LS15: Scho 5F **25**
Oak Pk. Grn. LS16: Leeds 6E **11**
Oak Pk. La. LS16: Leeds 1E **19**
Oak Pk. M. LS16: Leeds 6E **11**
Oak Pk. Mt. LS16: Leeds 1E **19**
Oak Pk. Ter. LS16: Leeds 1E **19**
Oakridge Av. LS29: Men 1D **6**
Oak Rd. LS12: Leeds 6C **30**
Oak Rd. LS15: Leeds 5H **33**
Oak Rd. LS27: Morl 6F **49**
Oak Rd. LS7: Leeds 6H **21**
Oakroyd LS26: Rothw 5H **53**
Oakroyd Cl. BD11: B'haw 4C **46**
Oakroyd Dr. BD11: B'haw 5C **46**
Oakroyd Fold LS27: Chur 1A **50**
Oakroyd Mt. LS28: Stan 5G **27**
Oakroyd Ter. LS27: Chur 1A **50**
Oakroyd Ter. LS28: Stan 5G **27**
Oaks, The LS10: Leeds 5A **52**
Oaks, The LS20: Guis 3G **7**
Oaks, The LS27: Chur 2H **49**
Oak St. LS27: Chur 2H **49**
Oak St. LS28: Pud 5E **27**
Oak Ter. LS15: Leeds 2D **34**
.... *(off Church La.)*
Oak Tree Bus. Pk. LS14: Leeds 4A **24**
Oak Tree Cl. LS9: Leeds 2E **33**
Oak Tree Ct. LS9: Leeds 2E **33**
.... *(off Oak Tree Pl.)*
Oak Tree Cres. LS9: Leeds 2E **33**
Oak Tree Dr. LS8: Leeds 2E **33**
Oak Tree Gro. LS9: Leeds 2E **33**
Oak Tree La. LS14: Leeds 3G **33**
Oak Tree Mt. LS9: Leeds 2E **33**
Oak Tree Pl. LS9: Leeds 2E **33**
Oak Tree Wlk. LS9: Leeds 2E **33**
Oak Vw. LS16: Leeds 4A **12**
Oakway BD11: B'haw 5D **46**
OAKWELL **6F 47**
Oakwell Av. LS12: Leeds 6B **30**
Oakwell Av. LS8: Leeds 5C **22**
Oakwell Cl. BD11: Drig 4A **48**
Oakwell Ct. LS13: Leeds 2B **28**
Oakwell Ct. LS28: Fars 2F **27**
.... *(off Water La.)*
Oakwell Ct. WF17: Birs 6A **48**
.... (not continuous)

92 A-Z Leeds

Oakwell Cres. – Parkfield Gro.

Oakwell Cres. LS8: Leeds 5C 22
Oakwell Dr. LS8: Leeds 5C 22
Oakwell Gdns. LS8: Leeds 5C 22
Oakwell Gro. LS13: Leeds 2C 28
Oakwell Hall 6F 47
Oakwell Hall Country Pk. 6E 47
Oakwell Ind. Est. WF17: Birs 6A 48
Oakwell Ind. Pk. WF17: Birs 6H 47
Oakwell Mt. LS8: Leeds 5C 22
Oakwell Oval LS8: Leeds 5C 22
Oakwell Rd. BD11: Drig 4A 48
Oakwell Ter. LS28: Fars 2F 27
Oakwell Way WF17: Birs 6A 48
OAKWOOD 5D 22
Oakwood Av. BD11: B'haw 5C 46
Oakwood Av. LS8: Leeds 5D 22
Oakwood Boundary Rd.
LS8: Leeds 5D 22
Oakwood Ct. LS8: Leeds 5E 23
Oakwood Dr. LS26: Rothw 2F 53
Oakwood Dr. LS8: Leeds 5D 22
Oakwood Gdns. LS28: Pud 1G 37
Oakwood Gdns. LS8: Leeds 5D 22
Oakwood Gth. LS8: Leeds 5E 23
Oakwood Grange LS8: Leeds 5E 23
Oakwood Grange La.
LS8: Leeds 5E 23
Oakwood Grn. LS8: Leeds 5E 23
Oakwood Gro. LS8: Leeds 5D 22
Oakwood Ho. LS13: Leeds 5F 17
(off Rodley La.)
Oakwood La. LS8: Leeds 5D 22
Oakwood La. LS9: Leeds 2F 33
Oakwood Mt. LS8: Leeds 5D 22
Oakwood Nook LS8: Leeds 5D 22
Oakwood Pk. LS8: Leeds 6E 23
Oakwood Pl. LS8: Leeds 5D 22
Oakwood Ri. LS8: Leeds 5E 23
Oakwood Ter. LS28: Pud 1G 37
Oakwood Vw. LS8: Leeds 5E 23
Oakwood Wlk. LS8: Leeds 5E 23
Oasby Cft. BD4: B'ford 6A 36
Oast Ho. Cft. WF3: Rob H 6D 52
Oastler Rd. LS28: Cal 5D 16
Oatland Cl. LS7: Leeds 3G 31
Oatland Ct. LS7: Leeds 1F 5 (3G 31)
(not continuous)
Oatland Dr. LS7: Leeds 3G 31
Oatland Gdns. LS7: Leeds 3G 31
Oatland Grn. LS7: Leeds 3G 31
Oatland Hgts. LS7: Leeds 1F 5 (3H 31)
(off Oatland Ct.)
Oatland La. LS7: Leeds 3G 31
Oatland Pl. LS7: Leeds 2G 31
Oatland Rd. LS7: Leeds 3G 31
Oatland Towers
LS7: Leeds 1F 5 (3G 31)
Oban Cl. WF3: Ting 2B 56
Oban Pl. LS12: Leeds 5G 29
Oban St. LS12: Leeds 5H 29
Oban Ter. LS12: Leeds 5H 29
Oban Ter. WF3: Ting 2B 56
Occupation La. LS28: Pud 1E 37
Odda La. LS20: Hawk 4A 6
Oddfellow St. LS27: Morl 5G 49
Oddy Pl. LS6: Leeds 5B 20
Oddy's Fold LS6: Leeds 3C 20
Oddy St. BD4: B'ford 6A 36
Odeon Cinema Bradford 5B 26
Odeon Cinema Leeds,
Thorpe Park 5F 35
Ogden Ho. BD4: B'ford 3B 36
Ogilby Ct. LS26: W'frd 2B 54
Ogilby M. LS26: W'frd 2B 54
O'Grady Sq. LS9: Leeds 6B 32
Old Acre Sq. LS10: Leeds 5G 51
Old Barn Cl. LS17: Leeds 4E 13
Old Brandon La. LS17: Shad 5G 15
Old Cl. LS11: Leeds 1B 50
Old Cornmill, The LS18: Hors 3E 19
Old Farm App. LS16: Leeds 3F 19
Old Farm Cl. LS16: Leeds 3G 19
Old Farm Cross LS16: Leeds 3G 19
Old Farm Dr. LS16: Leeds 3F 19
Old Farm Gth. LS16: Leeds 3G 19
Old Farm Pde. LS16: Leeds 3G 19
Old Farm Wlk. LS16: Leeds 3F 19
Oldfield Av. LS12: Leeds 1A 40
Oldfield Ct. LS7: Leeds 5A 22
Oldfield La. LS12: Leeds 1A 40
Oldfield St. LS12: Leeds 1A 40
Old Fold LS28: Fars 2F 27
Old Hall Rd. WF3: Ting 3D 56
Old Haworth La. LS19: Yead 2D 8
Old Heybeck La. WF3: W Ard 6B 56
Old Hollings Hill LS20: Guis 6E 7
Old La. BD11: B'haw 3C 46
Old La. BD11: Drig 2H 47
Old La. LS11: Leeds 5D 40
Old La. LS20: Hawk 5A 6
Old Marsh LS28: Pud 6E 27
Old Mill Bus. Pk. LS10: Leeds 3B 42
Old Mill La. LS10: Leeds 3A 42
Old Oak Cl. LS16: Leeds 4G 19
Old Oak Dr. LS16: Leeds 4G 19
Old Oak Gth. LS16: Leeds 4F 19
Old Oak Lawn LS16: Leeds 4G 19
Old Orchard, The LS13: Leeds 1B 28
Old Orchard, The LS29: Men 1D 6
(off Station Rd.)
Old Pk. Rd. LS8: Leeds 1D 22
(not continuous)
Old Rd. LS27: Chur 1A 50
Old Rd. LS28: Fars 4E 27
Old Rd. LS28: Stan 4E 27
Oldroyd Cres. LS11: Leeds 5C 40
Old Run Rd. LS10: Leeds 5H 41
Old Run Vw. LS10: Leeds 1H 51
Old School Ho., The LS6: Leeds 1D 30
Old School Lofts LS12: Leeds 6G 29
Old School M. LS27: Chur 1A 50
Old Smithy Ct. LS28: Cal 5D 16
(off Little La.)
Old Whack Ho. La. LS19: Yead 3B 8
Old William St. LS28: Stan
Milestone Ct. 3H 27
Olive Lodge LS18: Hors 2C 18
(off Broadgate La.)
Oliver Ct. BD11: Drig 4F 47
Oliver Hill LS18: Hors 4C 18
Olive Yeates Way LS15: Leeds 3E 35
Olrika Ct. LS7: Leeds 1H 31
Ontario Pl. LS7: Leeds 5H 21
Opal Three LS2: Leeds 2F 5 (4G 31)
(off Jacob Street)
Open University, The
Leeds 5E 5 (6G 31)
(off Trevelyan Sq.)
Orange Tree Gro. WF3: E Ard 4G 57
Orchard Av. WF3: Stly 6H 59
Orchard Cl. WF3: E Ard 5H 57
Orchard Ct. LS16: Leeds 4B 20
(off St Chads Rd.)
Orchard Ct. LS20: Guis 4G 7
(off Orchard La.)
Orchard Cft. LS15: Leeds 3B 34
Orchard Dr. LS28: Pud 5D 26
Orchard Grn. LS15: Scho 5F 25
Orchard Gro. LS29: Men 1D 6
Orchard La. LS20: Guis 4G 7
Orchard M. LS13: Leeds 6G 17
Orchard Mt. LS15: Leeds 3C 34
Orchard Rd. LS15: Leeds 3B 34
Orchards, The LS15: Leeds 3B 34
Orchards, The WF3: W Ard 6B 56
Orchard Sq. LS15: Leeds 3B 34
Orchard Way LS20: Guis 4G 7
Orchard Way LS26: Rothw 3G 53
Orchid Ct. WF3: Loft 1D 58
Orchid Way LS19: Raw 1C 16
Oriental St. LS12: Leeds 6A 30
Orion Cres. LS10: Leeds 2A 52
Orion Dr. LS10: Leeds 2A 52
Orion Gdns. LS10: Leeds 2B 52
Orion Vw. LS10: Leeds 2B 52
Orion Wlk. LS10: Leeds 1B 52
Orion Way LS9: Leeds 2F 43
Ormonde Pl. LS7: Leeds 2G 31
Orrell Gro. LS10: Leeds 5A 52
Orville Gdns. LS6: Leeds 1C 30
Osbourne Ct. LS13: Leeds 4D 28
OSMONDTHORPE 5E 33
Osmondthorpe Cotts.
LS9: Leeds 6E 33
Osmondthorpe La. LS9: Leeds 5E 33
Osmondthorpe Ter. LS9: Leeds 5D 32
Osprey Cl. LS17: Leeds 5B 14
Osprey Gro. LS17: Leeds 5B 14
Osprey Mdw. LS27: Morl 5B 50
Osterley Cres. BD10: B'ford 6A 16
Osterley Gro. BD10: B'ford 6A 16
Oswald Cl. LS20: Guis 4F 7
Oswalds Grn. LS26: Meth 6H 55
Oswaldthorpe Av. BD3: B'ford 4A 26
Otley La. LS19: Yead 2D 8
Otley Old Rd. LS16: Leeds 4E 11
Otley Rd. LS16: Leeds 1H 11
Otley Rd. LS20: Guis 4E 7
Otley Rd. LS6: Leeds 5B 20
Ottawa Pl. LS7: Leeds 5H 21
Otterburn Gdns. LS16: Leeds 6H 11
OULTON 4C 54
Oulton Dr. LS26: Oult 6C 54
Oulton La. LS26: Oult 2C 54
Oulton La. LS26: Rothw 4H 53
Oulton Pk. Golf Course 5B 54
Outgang LS13: Leeds 2D 28
Outgang La. LS13: Leeds 2E 29
Outwood Av. LS18: Hors 4D 18
Outwood Chase LS18: Hors 3D 18
Outwood La. LS18: Hors 4C 18
Outwood Station (Rail) 6C 58
Outwood Wlk. LS18: Hors 4C 18
OUZLEWELL GREEN 2F 59
Ouzlewell Grn. WF3: Loft 1F 59
Oval, The LS10: Leeds 3H 41
Oval, The LS14: Leeds 3H 33
OVAL, THE 3H 33
Oval, The LS20: Guis 5E 7
Oval, The LS26: Rothw 4H 53
Oval, The LS28: Fars 3G 27
Overdale Av. LS17: Leeds 4C 14
Overdale Ter. LS15: Leeds 5A 34
Overland Pk. LS27: Gil 4C 48
Overland Trad. Est. LS27: Gil 4C 48
Over La. LS19: Raw 6E 9
Ovington Dr. BD4: B'ford 6A 36
Owlcotes Dr. LS28: Pud 5E 27
Owlcotes Gdns. LS28: Pud 5E 27
Owlcotes Gth. LS28: Pud 5D 26
Owlcotes La. LS28: Pud 5E 27
Owlcotes La. LS28: Stan 4E 27
(not continuous)
Owlcotes Rd. LS28: Pud 5D 26
Owlcotes Shop. Cen. 4F 27
Owlcotes Ter. LS28: Pud 5E 27
Owler La. WF17: Birs 6G 47
Owlett Mead WF3: Thpe H 2A 58
Owlett Mead Cl. WF3: Thpe H 2A 58
Owl Ridge LS27: Morl 6A 50
Oxendale Cl. LS26: W'frd 3B 54
Oxenford Ct. LS16: Leeds 6G 11
Oxford Av. LS20: Guis 3F 7
Oxford Ct. Apts. LS20: Guis 4G 7
(off Oxford Rd.)
Oxford Pl. LS1: Leeds 3C 4 (5F 31)
Oxford Pl. LS28: Stan 4G 27
Oxford Rd. BD19: Gom 6D 46
Oxford Rd. LS20: Guis 4F 7
Oxford Rd. LS7: Leeds 2G 31
Oxford Row LS1: Leeds 3C 4 (5F 31)
Oxford St. LS20: Guis 4G 7
Oxford St. WF3: E Ard 3A 58
Oxford Vs. LS20: Guis 4G 7
Oxley St. LS9: Leeds 6B 32
Oxton Mt. LS9: Leeds 5B 32
Oxton Way LS9: Leeds 5B 32
Oyster Cl. LS27: Morl 6A 50

P

Pack Horse Yd.
LS1: Leeds 4E 5 (5G 31)
(off Lands La.)
Paddock, The BD4: B'ford 6A 36
(off Tennis Av.)
Paddock, The LS26: Rothw 4G 53
Paddock, The LS6: Leeds 4D 20
Paddock Cl. BD11: Drig 4G 47
Paddock Dr. BD11: Drig 4G 47
Paddock Ri. WF3: E Ard 3F 57
Padstow Av. LS10: Leeds 4E 51
Padstow Gdns. LS10: Leeds 4E 51
Padstow Pl. LS10: Leeds 5E 51
Padstow Row LS10: Leeds 5E 51
Paigton Ct. LS13: Leeds 4D 28
Paisley Gro. LS12: Leeds 5G 29
Paisley Pl. LS12: Leeds 5G 29
Paisley Rd. LS12: Leeds 5G 29
Paisley St. LS12: Leeds 5G 29
Paisley Ter. LS12: Leeds 5G 29
Paisley Vw. LS12: Leeds 5G 29
Palmer Grn. LS28: Fars 2F 27
Palmerston Cl. LS28: Stan 3H 27
Palmerston Ho. BD4: B'ford 3A 36
(off Tyersal La.)
Pansy Ct. LS14: Leeds 4H 33
Parade, The BD4: B'ford 4A 36
Parade, The LS19: Yead 3B 8
(off Westfield Dr.)
Parade, The LS6: Leeds 6B 20
(off North La.)
Paradise Gro. LS18: Hors 3E 19
(off Low La.)
Paradise Pl. LS18: Hors 3E 19
Paradise St. LS28: Fars 2F 27
Parc Mont LS8: Leeds 3E 23
Park & Ride Elland Road 4B 40
Park & Ride King Lane 6F 13
Park & Ride Temple Green 4G 43
Park App. LS15: Leeds 5F 35
Park Av. BD11: Drig 3G 47
Park Av. LS12: Leeds 5H 29
Park Av. LS15: Leeds 3D 34
Park Av. LS19: Raw 5E 9
Park Av. LS19: Yead 2C 8
Park Av. LS26: Swil 6G 45
Park Av. LS27: Morl 6F 49
Park Av. LS28: Pud 6G 27
Park Av. LS8: Leeds 3E 23
Park Av. WF3: Loft 5E 59
Park Cen. LS18: Hors 1C 18
Park Cl. BD11: Drig 3G 47
Park Cl. LS13: Leeds 2C 28
Pk. Copse LS18: Hors 2A 18
Park Cotts. LS8: Leeds 2D 22
Park Cres. LS12: Leeds 5H 29
Park Cres. LS20: Guis 6E 7
Park Cres. LS26: Rothw 3A 54
Park Cres. LS27: Gil 3D 48
Park Cres. LS8: Leeds 2D 22
Parkcroft LS28: Fars 3F 27
Park Cross St.
LS1: Leeds 4C 4 (5F 31)
Pk. Dale LS29: Men 1C 6
Park Dr. LS12: N Far 4G 39
Park Dr. LS18: Hors 3H 17
Park Dr. WF3: Loft 4E 59
Park Edge Cl. LS8: Leeds 4E 23
Parker La. LS26: Meth 6H 55
Parker St. WF3: E Ard 4G 57
Park Farm Ind. Est. LS11: Leeds 1F 51
Park Fld. LS29: Men 1C 6
Parkfield Av. LS11: Leeds 4E 41
Parkfield Cl. LS28: Pud 6F 27
Parkfield Ct. LS14: Leeds 2G 33
Parkfield Ct. LS27: Morl 6F 49
Parkfield Gro. LS11: Leeds 4E 41

A-Z Leeds 93

Pickard Ct. – Quarrie Dene Ct.

Pickard Ct. LS15: Leeds ... 5C **34**
Pickering Mt. LS12: Leeds ... 5B **30**
Pickering St. LS12: Leeds ... 5B **30**
Pickpocket La. LS26: Rothw ... 2A **54**
Pickpocket La. LS26: W'frd ... 2A **54**
Pickup Bus. Pk. LS28: Stan ... 3H **27**
Piebridge Way LS12: Leeds ... 4A **40**
Piece Wood Rd. LS16: Leeds ... 6D **10**
Pigeon Cote Cl. LS14: Leeds ... 5A **24**
Pigeon Cote Rd. LS14: Leeds ... 5A **24**
Pilden La. WF3: E Ard ... 5G **57**
Pilgrim Way LS28: Stan ... 3A **28**
Pilot St. LS9: Leeds ... 1H **5** (4A **32**)
Pinder Av. LS12: Leeds ... 3F **39**
Pinder Gro. LS12: Leeds ... 3F **39**
Pinder St. LS12: Leeds ... 3F **39**
Pinder Vw. LS12: Leeds ... 3F **39**
Pine Ct. LS2: Leeds ... 5F **5** (6H **31**)
Pines, The LS10: Leeds ... 5A **52**
Pines, The LS17: Leeds ... 6D **14**
Pinfold Ct. LS15: Leeds ... 5B **34**
Pinfold Gro. LS15: Leeds ... 5A **34**
Pinfold Hill LS15: Leeds ... 5B **34**
Pinfold La. LS12: Leeds ... 6H **29**
Pinfold La. LS15: Leeds ... 5A **34**
Pinfold La. LS16: Leeds ... 3E **11**
Pinfold Mt. LS15: Leeds ... 6B **34**
Pinfold Rd. LS15: Leeds ... 6B **34**
Pinfold Sq. LS15: Leeds ... 5A **34**
Pipe & Nook La. LS12: Leeds ... 6F **29**
Pipit Mdw. LS27: Morl ... 6A **50**
Pitchstone Ct. LS12: Leeds ... 6D **28**
Pitfall St. LS1: Leeds ... 6F **5** (6G **31**)
Pit Fld. Rd. WF3: Car ... 1F **59**
Pitt Row LS1: Leeds ... 6E **5** (6G **31**)
Place, The LS17: Leeds ... 5H **13**
Place's Rd. LS9: Leeds ... 6A **32**
Plaid Row LS9: Leeds ... 5A **32**
Plane Tree Av. LS17: Leeds ... 5B **14**
Plane Tree Cl. LS17: Leeds ... 5B **14**
Plane Tree Cft. LS17: Leeds ... 5B **14**
Plane Tree Gdns. LS17: Leeds ... 5B **14**
Plane Tree Gro. LS19: Yead ... 3F **9**
Plane Tree Ri. LS17: Leeds ... 5B **14**
Plane Trees Cl. BD19: Hun ... 6A **46**
Plane Tree Vw. LS17: Leeds ... 5B **14**
Plantation, The LS14: Leeds ... 1C **34**
Plantation Av. LS15: Leeds ... 6H **33**
Plantation Av. LS17: Leeds ... 4C **14**
Plantation Gdns. LS17: Leeds ... 4C **14**
Plantation Way LS27: Gil ... 4C **48**
Platform One LS5: Leeds ... 1H **29**
... *(off Station App.)*
Playfair Rd. LS10: Leeds ... 5H **41**
Playground LS12: N Far ... 4D **38**
Playhouse Sq.
LS2: Leeds ... 4H **5** (5H **31**)
Plaza, The LS2: Leeds ... 1E **5** (4G **31**)
... *(off Clay Pit La.)*
Pleasance, The LS26: Swil ... 6G **45**
Pleasant Ct. LS6: Leeds ... 2E **31**
... *(off Woodhouse St.)*
Pleasant Mt. LS11: Leeds ... 2E **41**
Pleasant Pl. LS11: Leeds ... 2E **41**
Pleasant St. LS11: Leeds ... 2E **41**
Pleasant Ter. LS11: Leeds ... 2E **41**
Pleasant Vw. WF3: Loft ... 4B **58**
Pleasant Vw. Ter. WF3: Rob H ... 5D **52**
... *(off Copley La.)*
Plevna St. LS10: Leeds ... 5C **42**
Plover Way LS27: Morl ... 6A **50**
Plowmans Wlk. LS19: Yead ... 3B **8**
Poets Pl. LS18: Hors ... 1C **18**
Pogson's Cotts. LS14: Leeds ... 6B **24**
... *(off York Rd.)*
Point, The LS12: Leeds ... 1D **40**
... *(off Whitehall Pl.)*
Pollard La. LS13: Leeds ... 5B **18**
Pollard St. WF3: Loft ... 5E **59**
Polly Booth Ho. LS15: Leeds ... 3E **35**
Ponderosa Cl. LS8: Leeds ... 2B **32**
Pontefract Av. LS9: Leeds ... 6B **32**
Pontefract La. LS15: Leeds ... 4A **44**
Pontefract La. LS9: Leeds ... 5B **32**
... (not continuous)
Pontefract La. LS9: Swil ... 5B **32**
... (not continuous)
Pontefract La. Cl. LS9: Leeds ... 6B **32**
Pontefract Rd. LS10: Leeds ... 5C **42**
Pontefract Rd. LS26: Rothw ... 1F **53**
Pontefract St. LS9: Leeds ... 6B **32**
Poole Cres. LS15: Leeds ... 3B **34**
Poole Mt. LS15: Leeds ... 4B **34**
Poole Rd. LS15: Leeds ... 3B **34**
Poole Sq. LS15: Leeds ... 4B **34**
Poplar Av. LS15: Leeds ... 3D **34**
Poplar Cl. LS13: Leeds ... 5E **29**
Poplar Ct. LS13: Leeds ... 5E **29**
Poplar Cres. WF3: Ting ... 2A **56**
Poplar Cft. LS13: Leeds ... 5E **29**
Poplar Dr. LS18: Hors ... 3H **17**
Poplar Farm La. LS28: Fars ... 1G **27**
Poplar Gdns. LS13: Leeds ... 5E **29**
Poplar Gth. LS13: Leeds ... 5E **29**
Poplar Ga. LS13: Leeds ... 5E **29**
Poplar Grn. LS13: Leeds ... 5E **29**
Poplar Mt. LS13: Leeds ... 5E **29**
Poplar Pl. LS14: Leeds ... 4C **24**
Poplar Pl. LS28: Pud ... 6D **26**
Poplar Ri. LS13: Leeds ... 4E **29**
Poplars, The LS20: Guis ... 3G **7**
Poplars, The LS6: Leeds ... 1C **30**
Poplars, The WF3: Loft ... 3E **59**
Poplar Sq. LS28: Fars ... 3F **27**
Poplar St. WF3: Loft ... 5E **59**
Poplar Vw. LS12: N Far ... 4G **39**
Poplar Vw. LS13: Leeds ... 5E **29**
Poplar Vw. LS17: Shad ... 6H **15**
Poplar Way LS13: Leeds ... 5E **29**
Poplarwood Gdns. BD10: B'ford ... 6A **16**
Poppleton Ct. WF3: Ting ... 2C **56**
Poppleton Cft. WF3: Ting ... 3C **56**
... *(off Lowry Rd.)*
Poppleton Dr. WF3: Ting ... 2C **56**
Poppleton Ri. WF3: Ting ... 3C **56**
Poppleton Rd. WF3: Ting ... 2C **56**
Poppleton Way WF3: Ting ... 2C **56**
Poppy La. WF3: E Ard ... 3A **58**
Poppy Vw. LS14: Leeds ... 4H **33**
Portage Av. LS15: Leeds ... 6H **33**
Portage Cres. LS15: Leeds ... 6G **33**
Portland Cres.
LS1: Leeds ... 2D **4** (4F **31**)
Portland Ga. LS1: Leeds ... 2D **4** (4F **31**)
... (not continuous)
Portland Ga. LS2: Leeds ... 2D **4** (4F **31**)
Portland Pl. LS6: Leeds ... 1D **30**
Portland Rd. LS12: Leeds ... 1A **40**
Portland St. LS1: Leeds ... 3C **4** (5F **31**)
Portland St. LS28: Pud ... 5A **28**
Portland Way
LS1: Leeds ... 2D **4** (4F **31**)
Portman St. LS28: Cal ... 5D **16**
Post Hill Ct. LS12: Leeds ... 6D **28**
Post Hill Gdns. LS28: Pud ... 6A **28**
Post Hill Vw. LS28: Pud ... 6A **28**
Potovens Ct. WF3: Loft ... 5E **59**
Potovens La. WF1: Outw ... 6D **58**
Potovens La. WF3: Loft ... 6D **58**
POTTERNEWTON ... 1H 31
Potternewton Av. LS7: Leeds ... 5F **21**
Potternewton Ct. LS7: Leeds ... 5G **21**
Potternewton Cres. LS7: Leeds ... 6F **21**
Potternewton Gdns. LS7: Leeds ... 5G **21**
Potternewton Gro. LS7: Leeds ... 5F **21**
Potternewton Hgts. LS7: Leeds ... 5G **21**
Potternewton La. LS7: Leeds ... 5E **21**
Potternewton Mt. LS7: Leeds ... 5F **21**
Potternewton Vw. LS7: Leeds ... 5F **21**
Potters Cft. WF3: Loft ... 5E **59**
POTTERY FIELD ... 1H 41
Pottery La. LS26: W'frd ... 2D **54**
Pottery Rd. LS10: Leeds ... 3H **41**
Poulton Pl. LS11: Leeds ... 4G **41**
Powerleague Leeds, Limewood Approach ... 4A 24
Powerleague Leeds, Wellington Bridge Street ... 5D 30
Premier Way LS26: Oult ... 3H **59**
Preston Pde. LS11: Leeds ... 5E **41**
Preston Vw. LS26: Swil ... 6H **45**
PRIESTHORPE ... 1D 26
Priesthorpe Av. LS28: Stan ... 3D **26**
Priesthorpe Ct. LS28: Fars ... 1F **27**
Priesthorpe La. LS28: Fars ... 2D **26**
Priesthorpe Rd. LS28: Cal ... 1C **26**
... (not continuous)
Priesthorpe Rd. LS28: Fars ... 1C **26**
... (not continuous)
Priestley Cl. LS28: Pud ... 5H **27**
Priestley Ct. LS18: Hors ... 3E **19**
Priestley Ct. LS28: Pud ... 5H **27**
Priestley Dr. LS28: Pud ... 4H **27**
Priestley Gdns. LS28: Pud ... 5H **27**
Priestley Vw. LS28: Pud ... 5H **27**
Priestley Wlk. LS28: Pud ... 5H **27**
Primitive St. WF3: Car ... 6F **53**
Primley Gdns. LS17: Leeds ... 5G **13**
Primley Pk. Av. LS17: Leeds ... 5G **13**
Primley Pk. Cl. LS17: Leeds ... 5H **13**
Primley Pk. Ct. LS17: Leeds ... 4G **13**
Primley Pk. Cres. LS17: Leeds ... 5G **13**
Primley Pk. Dr. LS17: Leeds ... 5G **13**
Primley Pk. Gth. LS17: Leeds ... 4H **13**
Primley Pk. Grn. LS17: Leeds ... 4H **13**
Primley Pk. Gro. LS17: Leeds ... 5G **13**
Primley Pk. La. LS17: Leeds ... 5G **13**
Primley Pk. Mt. LS17: Leeds ... 5H **13**
Primley Pk. Ri. LS17: Leeds ... 5H **13**
Primley Pk. Rd. LS17: Leeds ... 5G **13**
Primley Pk. Vw. LS17: Leeds ... 4G **13**
Primley Pk. Wlk. LS17: Leeds ... 4H **13**
Primley Pk. Way LS17: Leeds ... 4G **13**
Primo Pl. LS8: Leeds ... 2F **33**
Primrose Av. LS15: Leeds ... 5A **34**
Primrose Av. LS26: Swil ... 6H **45**
Primrose Cir. LS7: Leeds ... 3G **31**
Primrose Cl. LS15: Leeds ... 5A **34**
Primrose Ct. LS17: Leeds ... 4H **13**
Primrose Ct. LS20: Guis ... 4G **7**
... *(off Orchard Way)*
Primrose Cres. LS15: Leeds ... 4A **34**
Primrose Dr. LS15: Leeds ... 5A **34**
Primrose Gdns. LS15: Leeds ... 4A **34**
Primrose Gth. LS15: Leeds ... 5H **33**
Primrose Gro. LS15: Leeds ... 4A **34**
Primrose Hill LS28: Stan ... 4G **27**
Primrose Hill Cl. LS26: Swil ... 6H **45**
Primrose Hill Dr. LS26: Swil ... 6H **45**
Primrose Hill Gdns. LS26: Swil ... 6H **45**
Primrose Hill Gth. LS26: Swil ... 1H **55**
Primrose Hill Grn. LS26: Swil ... 1H **55**
Primrose Hill Gro. LS26: Swil ... 6H **45**
Primrose La. LS11: Leeds ... 4G **41**
Primrose La. LS15: Leeds ... 5H **33**
... (not continuous)
Primrose Rd. LS15: Leeds ... 5A **34**
Primrose Wlk. LS27: Chur ... 1A **50**
Primrose Yd. LS26: Oult ... 4C **54**
Prince Edward Gro.
LS12: Leeds ... 3G **39**
Prince Edward Rd.
LS12: Leeds ... 3G **39**
Princes Av. LS8: Leeds ... 4D **22**
Prince's Ct. LS17: Leeds ... 2G **21**
Prince's Gro. LS6: Leeds ... 6B **20**
Princess Ct. LS15: Leeds ... 1D **44**
Princess Ct. LS17: Leeds ... 6H **13**
Princess Flds. LS15: Leeds ... 1D **44**
Princes Sq. LS1: Leeds ... 6C **4** (6F **31**)
Princess St. LS19: Raw ... 5C **8**
Printworks Row LS28: Stan ... 3G **27**
Priory M. WF3: Stly ... 5H **59**
Privilege St. LS12: Leeds ... 6H **29**
Prospect Av. LS13: Leeds ... 2C **28**
Prospect Av. LS28: Pud ... 5F **27**
Prospect Bldgs. WF3: E Ard ... 4G **57**
... *(off Bradford Rd.)*
Prospect Ct. LS27: Morl ... 4G **49**
... *(off Prospect Pl.)*
Prospect Cres. LS10: Leeds ... 4H **41**
Prospect Gdns. LS15: Leeds ... 5B **34**
Prospect Gro. LS28: Pud ... 5F **27**
Prospect La. BD11: B'haw ... 4D **46**
Prospect M. LS27: Morl ... 4G **49**
... *(off Prospect Pl.)*
Prospect Pk. LS14: Leeds ... 4B **24**
Prospect Pk. LS28: Stan ... 4G **27**
Prospect Pl. LS13: Leeds ... 2C **28**
Prospect Pl. LS18: Hors ... 3B **18**
Prospect Pl. LS26: Rothw ... 5H **53**
Prospect Pl. LS27: Morl ... 4G **49**
Prospect Pl. WF3: Loft ... 1D **58**
Prospect Sq. LS28: Fars ... 3F **27**
Prospect St. LS19: Raw ... 6E **9**
Prospect St. LS28: Fars ... 2F **27**
Prospect St. LS28: Pud ... 5E **27**
Prospect Ter. LS13: Leeds
Airedale Mt. ... 6G **17**
Prospect Ter. LS13: Leeds
Prospect Vw. ... 2C **28**
Prospect Ter. LS18: Hors ... 2C **18**
Prospect Ter. LS26: Rothw ... 5H **53**
Prospect Ter. LS28: Fars ... 2F **27**
Prospect Ter. LS9: Leeds ... 6B **32**
... *(off Lavender Wlk.)*
Prospect Vw. LS13: Leeds ... 2C **28**
Prosper St. LS10: Leeds ... 3A **42**
Providence Av. BD10: B'ford ... 3A **16**
Providence Av. LS6: Leeds ... 1E **31**
Providence Ct. LS27: Morl
Bank St. ... 4G **49**
Providence Ct. LS27: Morl
Wide La. ... 6H **49**
Providence Mt. LS27: Morl ... 4G **49**
... *(off Bank St.)*
Providence Pl. LS15: Swil C ... 1G **45**
Providence Pl.
LS2: Leeds ... 1E **5** (4G **31**)
Providence Pl. LS27: Morl ... 5E **49**
Providence Pl. LS28: Stan ... 4G **27**
Providence Rd. LS6: Leeds ... 1E **31**
Providence St. LS28: Fars ... 3F **27**
Providence Ter. LS2: Leeds ... 2E **31**
Providence Works LS27: Morl ... 5D **48**
... *(off Howden Clough Rd.)*
PUDSEY ... 5H 27
Pudsey Bus. Cen. LS28: Pud ... 6H **27**
Pudsey Leisure Cen. ... 6G 27
Pudsey Rd. LS12: Leeds ... 6E **29**
Pudsey Rd. LS13: Leeds ... 6B **28**
Pudsey Rd. LS13: Pud ... 6B **28**
Pudsey Vw. BD4: B'ford ... 2A **36**
Pullman Ct. LS11: Leeds ... 6C **40**
Pullman Ct. LS27: Morl ... 4H **49**
Pullman Cres. LS12: Leeds ... 4A **40**
Pullman Ho. LS11: Leeds ... 6C **40**
Pump La. WF3: W Ard ... 6C **56**
Purbeck Ct. BD4: B'ford ... 5A **36**
PureGym Bradford ... 5B 26
PureGym Bramley ... 4D 28
PureGym Kirkstall ... 1G 29
PureGym Leeds North ... 2E 5 (4G 31)
... *(off Merrion Way)*
PureGym Leeds South ... 5F 5 (6G 31)
Pymont Ct. WF3: Loft ... 2E **59**
Pymont Dr. LS26: W'frd ... 2A **54**
Pymont Gro. LS26: W'frd ... 2B **54**
Pym St. LS10: Leeds ... 2H **41**

Q

Q1 Residence LS2: Leeds ... 2F **5** (4G **31**)
... *(off St Alban's Pl.)*
Q2 Residence LS1: Leeds ... 4B **4** (5E **31**)
Quaker Ho. LS2: Leeds ... 3E **31**
Quakers La. LS19: Raw ... 4D **8**
Quarrie Dene Ct. LS7: Leeds ... 5G **21**

A-Z Leeds 95

Renaissance Ct. – Rossefield Pl.

Renaissance Ct. LS27: Chur ... 1A **50**
Renaissance Dr. LS27: Chur ... 1A **50**
Renison Av. LS15: Leeds ... 1F **45**
Renison Ct. LS15: Leeds ... 1F **45**
Renton Av. LS20: Guis ... 4F **7**
Renton Dr. LS20: Guis ... 5F **7**
Renton Lea LS20: Guis ... 5F **7**
Reservoir Ct. LS28: Cal ... 5C **16**
Reservoir Vw. WF3: E Ard ... 3G **57**
Restmore Av. LS20: Guis ... 3F **7**
Revie Rd. LS11: Leeds ... 4D **40**
Revie Rd. Ind. Est. LS11: Leeds .. 4D **40**
Reyden M. LS12: Leeds ... 1A **40**
Rhodes Ct. LS27: Morl ... 6H **49**
... *(off High St.)*
Rhodes Gdns. WF3: Loft ... 5E **59**
Rhubarb Way WF3: E Ard ... 3F **57**
Rialto Ct. LS13: Leeds ... 6G **17**
Riccall Nook BD10: B'ford ... 5A **16**
Richardshaw Dr. LS28: Stan ... 4G **27**
Richardshaw La. LS28: Pud ... 4G **27**
Richardshaw La. LS28: Stan ... 4G **27**
Richardshaw Rd. LS28: Stan ... 4G **27**
Richardson Cres. LS9: Leeds ... 6D **32**
Richardson Rd. LS9: Leeds ... 6D **32**
Richmond Av. LS6: Leeds ... 1C **30**
Richmond Cl. LS13: Leeds ... 3A **28**
Richmond Cl. LS26: Rothw ... 3H **53**
Richmond Cl. LS27: Morl ... 6G **49**
Richmond Ct. LS13: Leeds ... 6G **17**
Richmond Ct. LS26: Rothw ... 3H **53**
Richmond Cft. LS9: Leeds ... 6B **32**
Richmond Gdns. LS28: Pud ... 6A **28**
Richmond Grn. St. LS9: Leeds ... 6A **32**
... *(off Cross Catherine St.)*
Richmond Gro. BD19: Gom ... 6D **46**
RICHMOND HILL ... 6B **32**
Richmond Hill App. LS9: Leeds ... 6A **32**
Richmond Hill Cl. LS9: Leeds ... 6A **32**
Richmond Ho. LS8: Leeds ... 1D **22**
... *(off Street La.)*
Richmond Mt. LS6: Leeds ... 1C **30**
Richmond Rd. LS28: Fars ... 3E **27**
Richmond Rd. LS6: Leeds ... 1C **30**
Richmond St. LS9: Leeds ... 6H **5** (6A **32**)
Richmond Ter. LS20: Guis ... 4F **7**
Richmond Ter. LS28: Pud ... 6A **28**
Rider Rd. LS6: Leeds ... 1F **31**
Rider St. LS9: Leeds ... 5A **32**
Ridge Cl. LS20: Guis ... 5E **7**
Ridge Gro. LS7: Leeds ... 6E **21**
Ridge Mt. LS6: Leeds ... 1E **31**
Ridge Rd. LS7: Leeds ... 1F **31**
Ridge Ter. LS6: Leeds ... 6C **20**
Ridge Vw. LS13: Leeds ... 5C **28**
Ridgeway LS20: Guis ... 5D **6**
Ridgeway LS8: Leeds ... 5B **22**
Ridgeway Cl. LS8: Leeds ... 5B **22**
Ridgeway Ter. LS6: Leeds ... 1E **31**
... *(off Delph La.)*
Ridings Cl. WF3: Loft ... 5D **58**
Ridings Ct. WF3: Loft ... 5D **58**
Ridings Gdns. WF3: Loft ... 5D **58**
Ridings La. WF3: Loft ... 5D **58**
Ridings M. WF3: Loft ... 5D **58**
Ridings Way WF3: Loft ... 5D **58**
Rigton App. LS9: Leeds ... 5A **32**
Rigton Cl. LS9: Leeds ... 5B **32**
Rigton Dr. LS9: Leeds ... 5A **32**
Rigton Grn. LS9: Leeds ... 5A **32**
Rigton Lawn LS9: Leeds ... 5A **32**
Rigton M. LS9: Leeds ... 5A **32**
Rillbank La. LS3: Leeds ... 4D **30**
Rillbank St. LS3: Leeds ... 4D **30**
... *(off Woodsley Rd.)*
Rillington Mead BD10: B'ford ... 5A **16**
Rimswell Holt BD10: B'ford ... 5A **16**
Ring Hay Rd. BD4: B'ford ... 6C **36**
Ring Rd. Adel LS16: Leeds ... 1B **20**
Ring Rd. Beeston LS11: Leeds ... 6C **40**
Ring Rd. Beeston LS12: Leeds ... 3A **40**
Ring Rd. Beeston Pk. LS10: Leeds ... 3E **51**
Ring Rd. Beeston Pk. LS11: Leeds ... 1E **51**
Ring Rd. Bramley LS13: Leeds ... 5D **28**
Ring Rd. Cross Gates LS15: Leeds ... 2C **34**
Ring Rd. Farnley LS12: Leeds ... 5D **28**
Ring Rd. Farsley LS13: Leeds ... 6F **17**
Ring Rd. Farsley LS13: Pud ... 6F **17**
Ring Rd. Farsley LS28: Fars ... 3D **26**
Ring Rd. Halton LS15: Leeds ... 4C **34**
Ring Rd. Horsforth LS16: Leeds ... 3F **19**
Ring Rd. Horsforth LS18: Hors ... 3E **19**
Ring Rd. Horsforth LS18: Leeds ... 3E **19**
Ring Rd. Lwr. Wortley LS12: Leeds ... 1F **39**
Ring Rd. Meanwood LS16: Leeds ... 1B **20**
Ring Rd. Meanwood LS17: Leeds ... 1C **20**
Ring Rd. Meanwood LS6: Leeds .. 1C **20**
Ring Rd. Middleton LS10: Leeds ... 4H **51**
Ring Rd. Moortown LS17: Leeds .. 1E **21**
Ring Rd. Moortown LS6: Leeds ... 1E **21**
Ring Rd. Seacroft LS14: Leeds ... 3H **23**
Ring Rd. Shadwell LS17: Leeds ... 6E **15**
Ring Rd. Weetwood LS16: Leeds ... 2H **19**
Ring Rd. W. Pk. LS16: Leeds ... 2F **19**
Rington Rd. LS11: Leeds ... 4F **41**
Ringwood Av. LS14: Leeds ... 3H **23**
Ringwood Ct. WF1: Outw ... 6F **59**
Ringwood Cres. LS14: Leeds ... 2A **24**
Ringwood Dr. LS14: Leeds ... 3A **24**
Ringwood Gdns. LS14: Leeds ... 3A **24**
Ringwood Mt. LS14: Leeds ... 3A **24**
Ripley Cl. WF3: E Ard ... 2H **57**
Ripley La. LS20: Guis ... 2G **7**
Ripon Ho. LS28: Fars ... 2F **27**
Rise, The LS5: Leeds ... 6G **19**
Rivendale LS10: Leeds ... 5A **52**
Riverside Ct. LS1: Leeds ... 6F **5** (6G **31**)
Riverside Vw. LS18: Hors ... 4F **17**
Riverside Way LS1: Leeds ... 6B **4** (6E **31**)
Riverside W. LS1: Leeds ... 6A **4** (6E **31**)
River Vw. LS18: Hors ... 2B **18**
Riviera Gdns. LS7: Leeds ... 5G **21**
Roans Brae BD10: B'ford ... 5A **16**
Robb Av. LS11: Leeds ... 6E **41**
Robb St. LS11: Leeds ... 6E **41**
Robert Ho. LS27: Morl ... 4H **49**
... *(off Pullman Ct.)*
Roberts Av. LS9: Leeds ... 3D **32**
Roberts Ct. LS9: Leeds ... 3D **32**
Robertsgate WF3: Loft ... 2D **58**
Robertsgate Sq. WF3: Loft ... 2D **58**
... *(off Robertsgate)*
Roberts Pl. LS9: Leeds ... 4D **32**
Roberts St. LS26: W'frd ... 3C **54**
Roberts Wharf LS9: Leeds ... 6H **5** (1A **42**)
Robin Chase LS28: Pud ... 6H **27**
ROBIN HOOD ... 6D **52**
Robin La. LS28: Pud ... 6G **27**
Robin's Gro. LS26: Rothw ... 4H **53**
Robinwood Ct. LS8: Leeds ... 2C **22**
Rocheford Cl. LS10: Leeds ... 4B **42**
Rocheford Gdns. LS10: Leeds ... 4B **42**
Rocheford Gro. LS10: Leeds ... 4B **42**
Rocheford Wlk. LS10: Leeds ... 4B **42**
Rochester Gdns. LS13: Leeds ... 1H **27**
Rochester Rd. WF17: Birs ... 6G **47**
Rochester Ter. LS6: Leeds ... 1B **30**
Rochester Wynd LS17: Leeds ... 5C **14**
Rock Ct. LS27: Morl ... 4H **49**
Rockery Cft. LS18: Hors ... 1C **18**
Rockery Rd. LS18: Hors ... 1C **18**
Rockfield LS19: Yead ... 2E **9**
... *(off Rockfield Ter.)*
Rockfield Ter. LS19: Yead ... 2E **9**
Rockingham Cl. LS15: Leeds ... 2F **35**
Rockingham Rd. LS15: Leeds ... 2F **35**
Rockingham Way LS15: Leeds ... 2F **35**
Rock La. LS13: Leeds ... 1B **28**
Rockley Hall Yd. LS1: Leeds ... 4F **5** (5G **31**)
... *(off The Headrow)*
Rock Ter. LS15: Leeds ... 5H **33**
Rock Ter. LS27: Morl ... 4H **49**
Rock Ter. WF12: Dew ... 5A **56**
Rockville Ter. LS19: Yead ... 3E **9**
... *(off Rufford Ridge)*
Rockwood Cres. LS28: Cal ... 3C **26**
Rockwood Gro. LS28: Cal ... 2D **26**
Rockwood Hill Ct. LS28: Cal ... 3C **26**
Rockwood Rd. LS28: Cal ... 3C **26**
Roderick St. LS12: Leeds ... 6H **29**
RODLEY ... 6G **17**
Rodley Hall LS13: Leeds ... 6H **17**
... *(off Club La.)*
Rodley La. LS13: Leeds Airedale Quay ... 1A **28**
Rodley La. LS13: Leeds Calverley La. ... 5F **17**
Rodley La. LS28: Cal ... 5E **17**
Rodley Nature Reserve ... 6A **18**
Rods Mills La. LS27: Morl ... 6H **49**
Rods Vw. LS27: Morl ... 6H **49**
Rogers Ct. WF3: Stly ... 5H **59**
Rogers Pl. LS28: Pud ... 5H **27**
Rokeby Gdns. BD10: B'ford ... 5A **16**
Rokeby Gdns. LS6: Leeds ... 6A **20**
Roker La. LS28: Pud ... 2H **37**
ROKER LANE BOTTOM ... 3A **38**
Roman Av. LS8: Leeds ... 1C **22**
Romanby Shaw BD10: B'ford ... 5A **16**
Roman Ct. LS8: Leeds ... 1D **22**
Roman Cres. LS8: Leeds ... 1D **22**
Roman Dr. LS8: Leeds ... 1D **22**
Roman Gdns. LS8: Leeds ... 1C **22**
Roman Gro. LS8: Leeds ... 1C **22**
Roman Mnr. LS13: Leeds ... 3A **28**
Roman Mt. LS8: Leeds ... 1D **22**
Roman Pl. LS8: Leeds ... 1C **22**
Roman Ter. LS8: Leeds ... 1C **22**
Roman Vw. LS8: Leeds ... 1D **22**
Rombalds Av. LS12: Leeds ... 5A **30**
Rombalds Ct. LS29: Men ... 1B **6**
Rombalds Cres. LS12: Leeds ... 4A **30**
Rombalds Cft. LS19: Yead ... 2D **8**
Rombalds Gro. LS12: Leeds ... 5A **30**
Rombalds Pl. LS12: Leeds ... 4A **30**
Rombalds St. LS12: Leeds ... 4A **30**
Rombalds Ter. LS12: Leeds ... 5A **30**
Rombalds Vw. LS12: Leeds ... 4A **30**
Romford Av. LS27: Morl ... 6G **49**
Romney Mt. LS28: Pud ... 2A **38**
Romsey Gdns. BD4: B'ford ... 4A **36**
Romsey M. BD4: B'ford ... 4A **36**
Rona Cft. LS26: Rothw ... 4A **54**
Rook's Nest Rd. WF3: Stly ... 6G **59**
Rookwith Pde. BD10: B'ford ... 5A **16**
Rookwood Av. LS9: Leeds ... 5E **33**
Rookwood Cres. LS9: Leeds ... 5E **33**
Rookwood Cft. LS9: Leeds ... 6E **33**
Rookwood Gdns. LS9: Leeds ... 5E **33**
Rookwood Hill LS9: Leeds ... 5E **33**
Rookwood Mt. LS9: Leeds ... 5E **33**
Rookwood Pde. LS9: Leeds ... 5F **33**
Rookwood Pl. LS9: Leeds ... 5E **33**
Rookwood Rd. LS9: Leeds ... 5E **33**
Rookwood Sq. LS9: Leeds ... 5F **33**
Rookwood St. LS9: Leeds ... 6E **33**
Rookwood Ter. LS9: Leeds ... 5E **33**
Rookwood Va. LS9: Leeds ... 6E **33**
Rookwood Vw. LS9: Leeds ... 5E **33**
Rookwood Wlk. LS9: Leeds ... 5E **33**
ROOMS ... 1F **49**
Rooms Fold LS27: Morl ... 3G **49**
Rooms La. LS27: Gil ... 1F **49**
Rooms La. LS27: Morl ... 1F **49**
Rooms Way LS27: Morl ... 2F **49**
Roper Av. LS8: Leeds ... 3B **22**
Roper Gro. LS8: Leeds ... 3B **22**
Roscoe St. LS7: Leeds ... 3H **31**
Roscoe Ter. LS12: Leeds ... 6H **29**
Roseate Grn. LS27: Morl ... 6A **50**
Rose Av. LS18: Hors ... 4B **18**
Rosebank Cl. LS17: Leeds ... 2H **23**
Rosebank Cres. LS3: Leeds ... 3D **30**
Rosebank Gdns. LS3: Leeds ... 4D **30**
Rosebank Ho. LS3: Leeds ... 3D **30**
Rosebank Rd. LS3: Leeds ... 4D **30**
Rosebank Row LS3: Leeds ... 4D **30**
Rosebery St. LS28: Pud ... 5E **27**
Rosebery Ter. LS28: Stan ... 3H **27**
Rosebud Wlk. LS8: Leeds ... 3A **32**
Rosecliffe Mt. LS13: Leeds ... 2B **28**
Rosecliffe Ter. LS13: Leeds ... 3C **28**
Rosedale LS26: Rothw ... 3H **53**
Rosedale Bank LS10: Leeds ... 6H **41**
Rosedale Ct. BD4: E Bier ... 2A **46**
Rosedale Ct. WF3: W Ard ... 5C **56**
Rosedale Dr. WF3: W Ard ... 5C **56**
Rosedale Gdns. LS10: Leeds ... 6H **41**
... (not continuous)
Rosedale Gdns. WF3: Ting ... 3F **57**
Rosedale Grn. LS10: Leeds ... 6H **41**
Rosedale Wlk. LS10: Leeds ... 6H **41**
Rose Gro. LS26: Rothw ... 3F **53**
Rosemary Av. LS12: Leeds ... 6B **30**
... *(off Armley Gro. Pl.)*
Rosemont Av. LS13: Leeds ... 3C **28**
Rosemont Av. LS28: Pud ... 5H **27**
Rosemont Dr. LS28: Pud ... 5H **27**
Rosemont Gro. LS13: Leeds ... 3B **28**
Rosemont Pl. LS13: Leeds ... 3C **28**
Rosemont Rd. LS13: Leeds ... 3C **28**
Rosemont St. LS13: Leeds ... 3C **28**
Rosemont St. LS28: Pud ... 5H **27**
Rosemont Ter. LS13: Leeds ... 3C **28**
Rosemont Ter. LS28: Pud ... 5H **27**
Rosemont Vw. LS13: Leeds ... 3B **28**
Rosemont Vs. LS28: Pud ... 5H **27**
Rosemont Wlk. LS13: Leeds ... 3C **28**
Rose Mt. BD4: B'ford ... 1C **46**
Rosemount LS7: Leeds ... 5G **21**
... *(off School La.)*
Rose Mt. Pl. LS12: Leeds ... 1B **40**
Roseneath Pl. LS12: Leeds ... 1B **40**
Roseneath St. LS12: Leeds ... 1B **40**
Roseneath Ter. LS12: Leeds ... 1B **40**
Rose St. LS18: Hors ... 3B **18**
Rose Ter. LS18: Hors ... 3A **18**
Roseville Bus. Pk. LS8: Leeds ... 3A **32**
Roseville Rd. LS7: Leeds ... 3A **32**
Roseville Rd. LS8: Leeds ... 1H **5** (3A **32**)
Roseville St. LS8: Leeds ... 3A **32**
Roseville Ter. LS15: Leeds ... 2C **34**
... *(off Church La.)*
Roseville Way LS8: Leeds ... 3A **32**
Rosewood Ct. LS17: Leeds ... 6E **13**
... *(off Cranmer Cl.)*
Rosewood Ct. LS26: Rothw ... 2H **53**
Rosewood Gro. BD4: B'ford ... 2A **36**
Rosgill Dr. LS14: Leeds ... 6H **23**
Rosgill Grn. LS14: Leeds ... 6A **24**
Rosgill Wlk. LS14: Leeds ... 6H **23**
Rossall Rd. LS8: Leeds ... 1B **32**
Rossefield App. LS13: Leeds ... 4D **28**
Rossefield Av. LS13: Leeds ... 3D **28**
Rossefield Chase LS13: Leeds ... 3D **28**
Rossefield Cl. LS13: Leeds ... 3D **28**
Rossefield Dr. LS13: Leeds ... 3D **28**
Rossefield Gdns. LS13: Leeds ... 3D **28**
Rossefield Gth. LS13: Leeds ... 3D **28**
Rossefield Grn. LS13: Leeds ... 3D **28**
... *(off Rossefield Dr.)*
Rossefield Gro. LS13: Leeds ... 3D **28**
Rossefield Lawn LS13: Leeds ... 3D **28**
Rossefield Pde. LS13: Leeds ... 3D **28**
... *(off Rossefield Wlk.)*
Rossefield Pl. LS13: Leeds ... 3D **28**

A-Z Leeds 97

Rossefield Ter. – St Josephs Way

Rossefield Ter. LS13: Leeds........3D **28**
Rossefield Vw. LS13: Leeds........3D **28**
Rossefield Wlk. LS13: Leeds.......3D **28**
Rossefield Way LS13: Leeds.......3D **28**
Rossett Bus. Pk. LS13: Leeds......1B **28**
Ross Gro. LS13: Leeds.................1A **28**
Rossington Gro. LS8: Leeds.........1A **32**
Rossington Pl. LS8: Leeds...........1A **32**
Rossington Rd. LS8: Leeds..........6C **22**
Rossington St.
LS2: Leeds......................3D **4** (5F **31**)
Ross Ter. LS13: Leeds.................1A **28**
Rotary Dr. LS27: Morl..................4B **50**
Rotary Vw. LS27: Morl.................4B **50**
Rothbury Gdns. LS16: Leeds.......6H **11**
ROTHWELL....................................4G 53
Rothwell Country Pk.......................1A 54
ROTHWELL HAIGH...........................3F 53
Rothwell La. LS26: Rothw............3A **54**
Rothwell Leisure Cen. 5C 54
ROUNDHAY 2C 22
Roundhay Av. LS8: Leeds...........6B **22**
Roundhay Ct. LS8: Leeds.............2C **22**
Roundhay Cres. LS8: Leeds.........6B **22**
Roundhay Gdns. LS8: Leeds........6B **22**
Roundhay Golf Course....................1E 23
Roundhay Gro. LS8: Leeds...........6B **22**
Roundhay Mt. LS8: Leeds.............6B **22**
Roundhay Pk...................................2D 22
Roundhay Pk. La. LS17: Leeds ... 4D **14**
Roundhay Pl. LS8: Leeds..............6B **22**
Roundhay Rd. LS7: Leeds.............3H **31**
Roundhay Rd. LS8: Leeds.............1C **32**
Roundhay Vw. LS8: Leeds.............6B **22**
Roundhead Fold BD10: B'ford......3A **16**
Round Hill Rd. LS28: Pud..............6E **27**
Roundhouse Bus. Pk.
LS12: Leeds....................6A **4** (6D **30**)
Roundway, The LS27: Morl 5E **49**
Roundwood Av. BD10: B'ford.......6A **16**
Roundwood Glen BD10: B'ford.....4A **16**
Roundwood Vw. BD10: B'ford......5A **16**
Row, The LS19: Raw......................5C **8**
................................*(off Apperley La.)*
Rowan Av. BD3: B'ford.................6A **26**
Rowan Av. LS16: Leeds................4A **12**
Rowan Ct. LS19: Raw.................... 4D **8**
Rowan Ct. LS26: W'frd..................3E **55**
Rowan M. WF3: Rob H..................6C **52**
Rowans, The LS13: Leeds........... 2H **27**
Rowans, The WF3: Rob H.............1C **58**
Rowan Tree Ct. WF1: Outw 6D **58**
Rowanwood Gdns.
BD10: B'ford...................................6A **16**
Rowland Pl. LS11: Leeds..............4F **41**
Rowland Rd. LS11: Leeds.............4F **41**
Rowland Ter. LS11: Leeds.............4F **41**
Rowlestone Ri. BD10: B'ford........5A **16**
Rowton Thorpe BD10: B'ford 5A **16**
Roxburgh M. LS12: Leeds............3F **29**
Roxby Cl. LS9: Leeds....................4A **32**
Roxholme Av. LS7: Leeds.............6A **22**
Roxholme Ct. LS7: Leeds.............6A **22**
Roxholme Gro. LS7: Leeds...........6A **22**
Roxholme Pl. LS7: Leeds..............6A **22**
Roxholme Rd. LS7: Leeds.............6A **22**
Roxholme Ter. LS7: Leeds.............6A **22**
Royal Armouries
Mus., The 6H 5 (1H 41)
Royal Armouries Sq.
LS10: Leeds................................ 1H **41**
..............................*(off Armouries Dr.)*
Royal Birkdale Way
LS26: Rothw...................................5A **54**
Royal Cl. LS10: Leeds...................5H **41**
Royal Ct. LS10: Leeds...................5H **41**
Royal Dr. LS10: Leeds...................5H **41**
Royal Gdns. LS10: Leeds..............5H **41**
Royal Gro. LS10: Leeds.................5H **41**
Royal Pk. Av. LS6: Leeds..............3D **30**
Royal Pk. Gro. LS6: Leeds.............2D **30**
Royal Pk. Mt. LS6: Leeds 2D **30**
Royal Pk. Rd. LS6: Leeds 3C **30**
Royal Pk. Ter. LS6: Leeds.............3D **30**
Royal Pk. Vw. LS6: Leeds..............2D **30**
Royal Pl. LS10: Leeds...................5H **41**
Royd Moor Rd. BD4: B'ford..........6B **36**
Royds Av. BD11: B'haw..................4D **46**
Royds Cl. LS12: Leeds...................3A **40**
Royds Ct. LS26: Rothw...................4H **53**
.....................................*(off Royds La.)*
Royds Farm Rd. LS12: Leeds.......5A **40**
Royds Grn. Farm LS26: Oult.........6A **54**
Royds Gro. WF1: Outw..................6E **59**
Royds Hall Rd. LS12: Leeds.........3A **40**
Royds La. LS12: Leeds...................3A **40**
..................................(not continuous)
Royds La. LS26: Oult.....................5H **53**
Royds La. LS26: Rothw...................5H **53**
Royds Pk. LS12: Leeds...................3A **40**
Roydstone Rd. BD3: B'ford...........5A **26**
Royd Vw. LS28: Pud.......................1E **37**
Royd Well BD11: B'haw..................4D **46**
Royston Cl. WF3: E Ard 5H **57**
Royston Hill WF3: E Ard 5H **57**
Ruby St. LS9: Leeds..........1H **5** (4A **32**)
Rufford Av. LS19: Yead................. 3D **8**
Rufford Bank LS19: Yead................3E **9**
Rufford Cl. LS19: Yead....................3E **9**
Rufford Cres. LS19: Yead................3E **9**
Rufford Dr. LS19: Yead....................3E **9**
Rufford Gdns. LS19: Yead............. 3D **8**
RUFFORD PK.......................................3D 8
Rufford Ridge LS19: Yead...............3E **9**
Rufford Ri. LS19: Yead.................... 3D **8**
Runswick Av. LS11: Leeds........... 2D **40**
Runswick Pl. LS11: Leeds............ 2D **40**
Runswick St. LS11: Leeds 2D **40**
Rushmoor Rd. BD4: B'ford............5A **36**
Rusholme Dr. LS28: Fars..............2E **27**
Rushton Av. BD3: B'ford................5A **26**
Rushton Rd. BD3: B'ford................5A **26**
Rushton St. LS28: Cal....................5D **16**
Rushton Ter. BD3: B'ford...............6A **26**
Rushworth Cl. WF3: Stly...............6G **59**
Ruskin Cres. LS20: Guis................. 5H **7**
Ruskin St. LS28: Stan....................4E **27**
Russell Gro. BD11: B'haw.............4D **46**
Russell Gro. LS8: Leeds.................1B **32**
Russell Sq. BD11: B'haw................4D **46**
Russell St. LS1: Leeds.......4D **4** (5F **31**)
Ruswarp Cres. BD10: B'ford 5A **16**
Ruthven Vw. LS8: Leeds................2C **32**
Rutland Cl. LS26: W'frd.................3D **54**
Rutland Ct. LS12: Leeds................4H **39**
Rutland Ct. LS28: Pud....................5G **27**
...........................*(off Richardshaw La.)*
Rutland Mt. LS3: Leeds.....3A **4** (5D **30**)
Rutland St. LS3: Leeds......3A **4** (5E **31**)
Rutland Ter. LS3: Leeds.....3A **4** (5D **30**)
Ryan Pl. LS8: Leeds........................1C **32**
Rycroft Av. LS13: Leeds.................4A **28**
Rycroft Cl. LS13: Leeds..................4B **28**
Rycroft Ct. LS13: Leeds..................4B **28**
Rycroft Dr. LS13: Leeds..................4B **28**
Rycroft Gdns. LS13: Leeds.............4A **28**
Rycroft Grn. LS13: Leeds................4B **28**
Rycroft Pl. LS13: Leeds...................4B **28**
Rycroft Towers LS13: Leeds 4A **28**
Rydal Cres. LS27: Morl...................4B **50**
Rydal Dr. LS27: Morl.......................4B **50**
Rydall Pl. LS11: Leeds.................. 2D **40**
Rydall St. LS11: Leeds................... 2D **40**
Rydall Ter. LS11: Leeds.................. 2D **40**
Ryder Gdns. LS8: Leeds.................4C **22**
Ryecroft Cl. BD4: B'ford.................5B **36**
Ryecroft Cl. WF1: Outw 6E **59**
Ryedale Av. LS12: Leeds................3H **39**
Ryedale Ct. LS14: Leeds................ 6H **23**
Ryedale Holt LS12: Leeds 2A **40**
Ryedale Way WF3: W Ard................3B **56**
Rye Pl. LS14: Leeds........................4H **33**
Ryton Dale BD10: B'ford..................5A **16**

S

Sackville App. LS7: Leeds........... 2G **31**
Sackville St. LS7: Leeds................2G **31**
Sadler Cl. LS16: Leeds 5A **12**
Sadler Copse LS16: Leeds 5A **12**
Sadler Way LS16: Leeds.................5A **12**
Sagar Pl. LS6: Leeds......................1B **30**
St Alban App. LS9: Leeds...............4E **33**
St Alban Cl. LS9: Leeds..................4E **33**
St Alban Ct. LS9: Leeds..................4E **33**
St Alban Cres. LS9: Leeds..............4E **33**
St Alban Gro. LS9: Leeds 4E **33**
St Alban Mt. LS9: Leeds..................4E **33**
St Alban Rd. LS9: Leeds..................4E **33**
St Alban's Pl. LS2: Leeds .. 2F **5** (4G **31**)
St Alban Vw. LS9: Leeds.................4E **33**
St Andrew's Av. LS27: Morl.............6E **49**
St Andrew's Cl. LS13: Leeds........ 6G **17**
St Andrew's Cl. LS19: Yead 1E **9**
St Andrews Cl. LS27: Morl 6E **49**
St Andrew's Ct. LS19: Yead 1D **8**
....*(off Haw La.)*
St Andrew's Ct. LS3: Leeds.......... 5D **30**
................................*(off St Andrew's St.)*
St Andrew's Cft. LS17: Leeds 5F **13**
St Andrew's Dr. LS17: Leeds......... 5G **13**
St Andrew's Gro. LS27: Morl.........6F **49**
St Andrew's Rd. LS19: Yead 2E **9**
St Andrew's St. LS3: Leeds........... 5D **30**
St Andrews Ter. LS27: Morl............6E **49**
St Andrew's Wlk. LS17: Leeds...... 5G **13**
St Andrews Way LS26: Rothw......5A **54**
St Annes Ct. LS5: Leeds.................1A **30**
St Anne's Dr. LS4: Leeds................1A **30**
St Annes Pl. LS5: Leeds 1H **29**
St Anne's Rd. LS6: Leeds..............6A **20**
St Anne's St. LS2: Leeds... 3D **4** (5F **31**)
St Ann's Av. LS4: Leeds 3B **30**
St Ann's Cl. LS4: Leeds 2A **30**
St Ann's Gdns. LS4: Leeds.............2A **30**
St Ann's Grn. LS4: Leeds................1A **30**
St Ann's La. LS4: Leeds 1A **30**
St Ann's Mt. LS4: Leeds..................2B **30**
St Ann's Ri. LS4: Leeds 2H **29**
St Ann's Sq. LS4: Leeds..................2A **30**
St Ann's Way LS4: Leeds 2A **30**
St Anthony's Dr. LS11: Leeds........ 5D **40**
St Anthony's Rd. LS11: Leeds........5C **40**
St Anthony's Ter. LS11: Leeds 6C **40**
St Augustines Ct. LS8: Leeds........2B **32**
...................................*(off Harehills Pl.)*
St Barnabas Rd. LS11: Leeds 1F **41**
St Bartholomews Cl.
LS12: Leeds......................................6A **30**
St Benedict M. LS14: Leeds.......... 6D **24**
St Benedicts Chase
LS13: Leeds...................................... 6D **18**
St Benedicts Dr. LS13: Leeds.........6E **19**
St Benedicts Gdns. LS13: Leeds..6E **19**
St Catherine's Bus. Complex
LS13: Leeds 1D **28**
....*(off Broad La.)*
St Catherines Cres.
LS13: Leeds 1D **28**
St Catherine's Dr. LS13: Leeds ... 1D **28**
St Catherines Grn. LS13: Leeds .. 1D **28**
St Catherine's Hill LS13: Leeds... 1D **28**
St Catherines Wlk. LS8: Leeds.....5C **22**
St Cecilia St. LS2: Leeds....4H **5** (5H **31**)
St Chad's Av. LS6: Leeds...............5A **20**
St Chad's Dr. LS6: Leeds................5A **20**
St Chad's Gro. LS6: Leeds..............5A **20**
St Chads Pde. LS16: Leeds 5B **20**
St Chad's Ri. LS6: Leeds.................5A **20**
St Chads Rd. LS16: Leeds...............5B **20**
St Chad's Vw. LS6: Leeds 6A **20**
St Christopher's Av
LS26: Rothw...................................... 4H **53**
St Clare's Av. BD2: B'ford...............3A **26**
St Clare's Ct. BD2: B'ford 3A **26**
St Clements Av. LS26: Rothw...... 4G **53**
St Clements Cl. LS26: Rothw 5F **53**
St Clements Ri. LS26: Rothw 4F **53**
St Cyprian's Gdns. LS9: Leeds.... 3D **32**
St Davids Cl. WF3: Rob H 1D **58**
St David's Ct. LS11: Leeds.............1F **41**
....*(off David St.)*
St Davids Gth. WF3: Rob H........... 1D **58**
St Davids Rd. WF3: Rob H............. 1D **58**
St Edgars Sq. LS27: Morl 6H **49**
St Edmunds Ct. LS8: Leeds...........1C **22**
St Elmo Gro. LS9: Leeds.................5C **32**
St Francis Cl. LS11: Leeds 4F **41**
St Francis Pl. LS11: Leeds 1F **41**
St Gabriel Ct. LS14: Leeds 6D **24**
St Gabriels Ct. LS18: Hors.............5B **10**
ST GEMMA'S HOSPICE....................2H 21
St George Bldg.
LS1: Leeds.......................3C **4** (4E **31**)
............................*(off Gt. George St.)*
St George's Av. LS26: Rothw........2E **53**
St George's Cres. LS26: Rothw......2E **53**
St George's Rd.
LS1: Leeds.......................2C **4** (4F **31**)
St Georges Rd. LS10: Leeds........ 4H **51**
St Helens Av. LS16: Leeds.............6B **12**
St Helens Cl. LS16: Leeds 6B **12**
..................................(not continuous)
St Helens Cft. LS16: Leeds............6A **12**
St Helens Gdns. LS16: Leeds 6A **12**
St Helens Gro. LS16: Leeds...........6A **12**
St Helens La. LS16: Leeds............ 6H **11**
St Helen's St. LS10: Leeds............ 2H **41**
St Helens Way LS16: Leeds...........6B **12**
St Hilaire Wlk. LS10: Leeds............5A **52**
..................................*(off Topliss Way)*
St Hilda's Av. LS9: Leeds................1B **42**
St Hilda's Cres. LS9: Leeds............1B **42**
St Hilda's Mt. LS9: Leeds................1B **42**
St Hilda's Pl. LS9: Leeds 1B **42**
St Hilda's Rd. LS9: Leeds................1B **42**
St Hilda's Ter. BD3: B'ford..............5A **26**
St Hilda's Way LS9: Leeds..............1B **42**
St Hughes Lodge LS12: Leeds 5A **30**
..........................*(off Armley Lodge Rd.)*
St Ives Gro. LS12: Leeds............... 5G **29**
St Ives Mt. LS12: Leeds.................. 5G **29**
St James App. LS14: Leeds 1A **34**
St James Av. LS18: Hors.................2C **18**
St James Cl. LS12: Leeds 5F **29**
St James Cres. LS28: Pud.............. 6D **26**
St James Dr. LS18: Hors 2D **18**
St James M. LS12: Leeds................5F **29**
St James M. LS15: Leeds................ 2D **34**
St James's Ct. LS9: Leeds 3A **32**
ST JAMES'S UNIVERSITY
HOSPITAL 3B 32
St James Ter. LS18: Hors.............. 2D **18**
St James Wlk. LS18: Hors.............. 2D **18**
St John's Av. LS28: Fars.................3F **27**
St John's Av. LS6: Leeds................ 3D **30**
St John's Cen.........................3E **5** (5G **31**)
St John's Church Leeds ...3E 5 (5G 31)
St John's Cl. LS6: Leeds 3D **30**
St John's Ct. LS19: Yead.................3C **8**
St John's Ct. LS7: Leeds 1H **31**
St John's Dr. LS19: Yead.................3C **8**
St John's Gro. LS6: Leeds.............. 3D **30**
St Johns Ho. LS3: Leeds ...2A **4** (4D **30**)
St John's Pk. LS29: Men...................1B **6**
St Johns Pk. LS8: Leeds..................4F **23**
St John's Pl. BD11: B'haw...............3C **46**
St John's Pl. LS5: Leeds................. 1H **29**
...................................*(off Vicarage Ter.)*
St John's Rd. LS19: Yead.................3C **8**
St John's Rd. LS3: Leeds 4D **30**
St John's St. LS26: Oult 4C **54**
St John's Ter. LS3: Leeds 3D **30**
St Johns Wlk. LS26: Swil 6H **45**
St John's Way LS19: Yead 3C **8**
St John's Yd. LS26: Oult 4C **54**
St Joseph's Ct. LS19: Raw............ 1D **16**
St Josephs Way LS28: Pud 5H **27**

98 A-Z Leeds

St Lawrence Cl. – Scott Hall Dr.

St Lawrence Cl. LS28: Pud 6F **27**
St Lawrence St. LS7: Leeds 5H **21**
St Lawrence Ter. LS28: Pud 6G **27**
St Luke's Cres. LS11: Leeds 3E **41**
St Luke's Grn. LS11: Leeds 3E **41**
St Luke's Rd. LS11: Leeds 3E **41**
St Luke's St. LS11: Leeds 3E **41**
St Lukes Va. BD4: B'ford 3A **36**
St Luke's Vw. LS11: Leeds 3E **41**
St Margaret's Av. LS18: Hors 2B **18**
St Margaret's Av. LS8: Leeds 5C **22**
St Margaret's Cl. LS18: Hors 1B **18**
St Margaret's Dr. LS18: Hors 1B **18**
St Margaret's Dr. LS8: Leeds 5C **22**
St Margaret's Gro. LS8: Leeds 5C **22**
St Margaret's Rd. LS18: Hors 1B **18**
St Margaret's Vw. LS8: Leeds 5C **22**
St Mark's Av. LS2: Leeds 3E **31**
St Mark's Ct. LS6: Leeds 2F **31**
St Mark's Ho. LS2: Leeds 2F **31**
(off St Mark's Rd.)
St Mark's Residence
LS2: Leeds 2E **31**
(off St Mark's St.)
St Mark's Rd. LS2: Leeds 3F **31**
St Mark's Rd. LS6: Leeds 2E **31**
(not continuous)
St Mark's St. LS2: Leeds 3E **31**
St Martin's Av. LS7: Leeds 6G **21**
St Martins Ct. WF3: Rob H 1D **58**
St Martin's Cres. LS7: Leeds 6H **21**
St Martin's Dr. LS7: Leeds 5G **21**
St Martins Fold WF3: Rob H 1D **58**
St Martin's Gdns. LS7: Leeds 6G **21**
St Martin's Gro. LS7: Leeds 6H **21**
St Martin's Rd. LS7: Leeds 5H **21**
St Martin's Ter. LS7: Leeds 6H **21**
St Martin's Vw. LS7: Leeds 6H **21**
St Mary's Av. LS26: Swil 6G **45**
St Mary's Cl. LS12: Leeds 1B **40**
St Mary's Cl. LS7: Leeds 6H **21**
St Mary's Cl. WF3: W Ard 4A **56**
St Mary's Ct. LS7: Leeds 6H **21**
St Mary's Hall
LS9: Leeds 3H **5** (5A **32**)
(off St Mary's La.)
ST MARY'S HOSPITAL Leeds 5F **29**
St Mary's La. LS9: Leeds 3H **5** (5A **32**)
St Mary's Pk. App. LS12: Leeds 5F **29**
St Mary's Pk. Ct. LS12: Leeds 5F **29**
St Mary's Pk. Cres. LS12: Leeds 5F **29**
St Mary's Pk. Grn. LS12: Leeds 5F **29**
St Mary's Rd. LS7: Leeds 6H **21**
St Mary's Sq. LS27: Morl 5G **49**
St Mary's St. LS9: Leeds 3H **5** (5H **31**)
St Mathew Way LS14: Leeds 6E **25**
St Matthew's St. LS11: Leeds 2E **41**
St Matthews Wlk. LS7: Leeds 3G **21**
St Matthias Ct. LS4: Leeds 3B **30**
St Matthias Gro. LS4: Leeds 3B **30**
St Matthias St. LS4: Leeds 4B **30**
(not continuous)
St Matthias Ter. LS4: Leeds 3B **30**
St Michael Ct. LS13: Leeds 2C **28**
St Michael's Ct. LS6: Leeds 6B **20**
St Michael's Cres. LS6: Leeds 1B **30**
St Michael's Gro. LS6: Leeds 1B **30**
St Michael's La. LS4: Leeds 2A **30**
St Michael's La. LS6: Leeds 1B **30**
St Michael's Rd. LS6: Leeds 1B **30**
St Michael's Ter. LS6: Leeds 1B **30**
St Michael's Vs. LS6: Leeds 1B **30**
(off St Michael's Cres.)
St Oswald's Gth. LS20: Guis 4H **7**
St Oswald's Ter. LS20: Guis 4G **7**
St Oswald's Wlk. LS20: Guis 4H **7**
St Paul's Av. BD11: B'haw 4D **46**
St Paul's Pl. LS1: Leeds 4C **4** (5F **31**)
St Paul's Rd. BD11: B'haw 4D **46**
St Paul's St. LS1: Leeds 4B **4** (5E **31**)
St Paul's St. LS27: Morl 6H **49**
St Peter's Av. LS26: Rothw 4H **53**
St Peter's Bldgs.
LS9: Leeds 4H **5** (6H **31**)
(off St Peter's Sq.)
St Peter's Ct. LS11: Leeds 3G **41**
St Peter's Ct. LS13: Leeds 2D **28**
St Peter's Cres. LS27: Morl 3G **49**
St Peter's Gdns. LS13: Leeds 2C **28**
St Peter's Mt. LS13: Leeds 3D **28**
St Peter's Pl. LS9: Leeds 4H **5** (5H **31**)
St Peter's Sq. LS9: Leeds 4H **5** (5H **31**)
St Peter's St. LS2: Leeds 4G **5** (5H **31**)
St Peters Vw. LS27: Morl 3G **49**
(off Rooms La.)
St Peter's Way LS29: Men 1B **6**
St Philip's Av. LS10: Leeds 4F **51**
St Philip's Cl. LS10: Leeds 4F **51**
St Rhodes Ter. LS12: Leeds 1C **40**
St Stephen's Ct. LS9: Leeds 5B **32**
St Stephen's Rd. LS28: Cal 4C **16**
St Stephen's Rd. LS9: Leeds 5B **32**
St Thomas Row
LS2: Leeds 2G **5** (4H **31**)
St Vincent Ct. LS28: Pud 1G **37**
(off Littlemoor Rd.)
St Vincent Rd. LS28: Pud 1G **37**
St Wilfrid's Av. LS8: Leeds 1C **32**
(not continuous)
St Wilfrid's Cir. LS8: Leeds 2D **32**
St Wilfrid's Cres. LS8: Leeds 1D **32**
St Wilfrid's Dr. LS8: Leeds 1C **32**
St Wilfrid's Gth. LS8: Leeds 2D **32**
St Wilfrid's Gro. LS8: Leeds 1C **32**
St Wilfrid's St. LS28: Cal 4D **16**
Sakura Wlk. LS14: Leeds 4A **34**
Salamanca Ct. LS10: Leeds 1H **51**
Salamanca Cres. LS10: Leeds 5A **52**
Salcombe Pl. BD4: B'ford 5A **36**
Salem Pl. LS10: Leeds 6F **5** (1G **41**)
Salisbury Av. LS12: Leeds 5A **30**
Salisbury Ct. LS18: Hors 2D **18**
Salisbury Gro. LS12: Leeds 5A **30**
Salisbury M. LS18: Hors 2D **18**
Salisbury M. WF3: Ting 2B **56**
Salisbury Pl. LS28: Cal 5C **16**
Salisbury Rd. LS12: Leeds 5A **30**
Salisbury St. LS19: Raw 5D **8**
Salisbury St. LS28: Cal 5C **16**
Salisbury Ter. LS12: Leeds 5A **30**
Salisbury Vw. LS12: Leeds 5A **30**
Salisbury Vw. LS18: Hors 2D **18**
Salmon Cres. LS18: Hors 2C **18**
Salters Gdn. LS28: Pud 6G **27**
(off Crawshaw Rd.)
Samara W. Mt.
LS2: Leeds 2A **4** (4E **31**)
(off Clarendon Rd.)
Samuel Dr. WF3: Stly 6G **59**
Sandacre Cl. BD10: B'ford 2A **26**
Sandbed Ct. LS15: Leeds 2D **34**
Sandbed La. LS15: Leeds 2D **34**
Sandbed Lawns LS15: Leeds 2D **34**
Sanderling Gth. LS10: Leeds 4H **51**
Sanderling Way LS10: Leeds 4H **51**
Sandfield Av. LS6: Leeds 5C **20**
Sandfield Gth. LS6: Leeds 5C **20**
Sandfield Ho. LS6: Leeds 5C **20**
(off Sandfield Av.)
Sandfield Vw. LS6: Leeds 5C **20**
(off Highbury Mt.)
SANDFORD 1E **29**
Sandford Pl. LS5: Leeds 1G **29**
Sandford Rd. LS5: Leeds 2H **29**
Sandgate Wlk. BD4: B'ford 5B **36**
Sandhill Ct. LS17: Leeds 6H **13**
Sandhill Cres. LS17: Leeds 5A **14**
Sandhill Dr. LS17: Leeds 5H **13**
Sandhill Gdns. LS17: Leeds 6H **13**
Sandhill Gro. LS17: Leeds 4A **14**
Sandhill La. LS17: Leeds 6H **13**
Sandhill Lawns LS17: Leeds 6H **13**
Sandhill Mt. LS17: Leeds 4A **14**
Sandhill Oval LS17: Leeds 4A **14**
Sandhurst Av. LS8: Leeds 2C **32**
Sandhurst Gro. LS8: Leeds 2C **32**
Sandhurst Mt. LS8: Leeds 1C **32**
Sandhurst Pl. LS8: Leeds 2C **32**
Sandhurst Rd. LS8: Leeds 2C **32**
Sandhurst St. LS28: Cal 4C **16**
Sandhurst Ter. LS8: Leeds 2C **32**
Sandiford Cl. LS15: Leeds 2D **34**
Sandiford Ter. LS15: Leeds 2D **34**
Sandleas Way LS15: Leeds 3F **35**
Sandlewood Cl. LS11: Leeds 2E **41**
Sandlewood Ct. LS6: Leeds 2D **20**
Sandlewood Cres. LS6: Leeds 2D **20**
Sandlewood Grn. LS11: Leeds 2F **41**
Sandmead Cl. BD4: B'ford 4A **36**
Sandmead Cl. LS27: Morl 3G **49**
Sandmead Cft. LS27: Morl 3G **49**
Sandmead Way LS27: Morl 3G **49**
Sandmoor Av. LS17: Leeds 3H **13**
Sandmoor Chase LS17: Leeds 4H **13**
Sandmoor Cl. LS17: Leeds 4H **13**
Sandmoor Ct. LS17: Leeds 4H **13**
Sandmoor Dr. LS17: Leeds 3H **13**
Sand Moor Golf Course 3G **13**
Sandmoor Grn. LS17: Leeds 3G **13**
Sandmoor La. LS17: Leeds 3H **13**
Sandmoor M. LS17: Leeds 4H **13**
Sandon Gro. LS10: Leeds 5A **42**
Sandon Mt. LS10: Leeds 5A **42**
Sandon Pl. LS10: Leeds 5A **42**
Sandon Vw. LS10: Leeds 5A **42**
Sandpiper App. LS27: Morl 6A **50**
Sandringham App. LS17: Leeds 6A **14**
Sandringham Av. LS28: Pud 1G **37**
Sandringham Cl. LS27: Morl 4A **50**
Sandringham Ct. LS17: Leeds 5H **13**
Sandringham Cres.
LS17: Leeds 6H **13**
Sandringham Dr. LS17: Leeds 6H **13**
Sandringham Dr. LS6: Leeds 1D **30**
Sandringham Dr. WF3: W Ard 4D **56**
Sandringham Fold LS27: Morl 4A **50**
Sandringham Gdns.
LS17: Leeds 6H **13**
Sandringham Grn. LS17: Leeds 5A **14**
Sandringham Ho. LS17: Leeds 4H **13**
Sandringham Mt. LS17: Leeds 6A **14**
Sandringham Way LS17: Leeds 6H **13**
Sandstone Dr. LS12: Leeds 6C **28**
Sandway LS15: Leeds 3B **34**
Sandway Gdns. LS15: Leeds 3B **34**
Sandway Gro. LS15: Leeds 3B **34**
Sandyacres LS26: Rothw 3H **53**
Sandyacres Cres. LS26: Rothw 3H **53**
Sandyacres Dr. LS26: Rothw 3H **53**
Sandy Bank Av. LS26: Rothw 3H **53**
Sandygate Ter. BD4: B'ford 2A **36**
Sandy Gro. LS26: Rothw 3H **53**
Sandy Way LS19: Yead 2D **8**
Sandywood Ct. LS18: Hors 4C **18**
Santorini LS12: Leeds 5A **4** (6E **31**)
Sarah St. WF3: E Ard 3H **57**
Sardinia St. LS10: Leeds 2H **41**
Sark Ct. LS14: Leeds 2C **24**
Savannah Way LS10: Leeds 1C **52**
Savile Av. LS7: Leeds 2H **31**
Savile Dr. LS7: Leeds 1H **31**
Savile Mt. LS7: Leeds 2H **31**
Savile Pk. Rd. BD19: Hun 6A **46**
Savile Pl. LS7: Leeds 2H **31**
Savile Rd. LS7: Leeds 2H **31**
Saville Cl. WF3: Loft 2E **59**
Saville Grn. LS9: Leeds 5B **32**
Saville's Sq. LS27: Morl 5G **49**
(off Queen St.)
Savins Mill Way LS5: Leeds 1G **29**
Savoy Ct. LS28: Stan 4F **27**
Saw Mill St. LS11: Leeds 1F **41**
Saw Mill Yd. LS11: Leeds 1F **41**
Saxon Ct. LS17: Leeds 6F **13**
Saxon Ga. LS17: Leeds 1F **21**
Saxon Grn. LS17: Leeds 1E **21**
Saxon Gro. LS17: Leeds 6E **13**
Saxon Mt. LS17: Leeds 6F **13**
Saxon Rd. LS17: Leeds 1E **21**
Saxstead Ri. LS12: Leeds 1A **40**
Saxton LS9: Leeds 6A **32**
Saxton Gdns. LS9: Leeds 6A **32**
(off The Avenue)
Saxton Ho. LS19: Yead 3D **8**
Saxton La. LS27: Morl 4A **50**
Saxton La. LS9: Leeds 5H **5** (6A **32**)
Saxton Pl. BD4: B'ford 3A **36**
Sayers Cl. LS5: Leeds 1H **29**
Sayner La. LS10: Leeds 1H **41**
Sayner Rd. LS10: Leeds 1H **41**
Scala Ct. LS10: Leeds 2H **41**
Scampston Dr. WF3: E Ard 2H **57**
Scarborough Junc.
LS13: Leeds 4C **28**
Scarborough La. WF3: Ting 3B **56**
Scarborough St. WF3: Ting 2B **56**
Scarcroft Vw. LS17: Leeds 3H **15**
Scargill Bldgs. LS27: Morl 5B **50**
Scargill Cl. LS9: Leeds 4B **32**
Scargill Grange LS9: Leeds 5B **32**
Scarth Av. LS9: Leeds 3C **32**
Scatcherd Ct. LS27: Morl 4B **50**
Scatcherd Dr. LS27: Morl 4B **50**
Scatcherd Gth. LS27: Morl 4B **50**
Scatcherd Gro. LS27: Morl 5F **49**
Scatcherd La. LS27: Morl 6F **49**
Scatcherd M. LS27: Morl 4B **50**
Scatcherd Pk. Av. LS27: Morl 4G **49**
Scatcherd's Bldgs. LS27: Morl 3G **49**
Schofield Ct. LS27: Morl 5G **49**
(off Queenscourt)
Scholars Way LS15: Leeds 1E **45**
Scholebroke La. LS28: Pud 3E **37**
SCHOLEBROOK 4E **37**
Scholebrook Ct. BD4: B'ford 6A **36**
(off Broadfield Cl.)
Scholebrook La. BD4: B'ford 4E **37**
SCHOLES 5F **25**
Scholes La. LS15: Leeds 3E **25**
Scholes Lodge La. LS15: Scho 6G **25**
School Cl. LS12: N Far 4D **38**
School Cft. LS26: Rothw 3G **53**
School La. LS15: Leeds
Colton Rd. E. 1E **45**
School La. LS15: Leeds
Pinfold Gro. 5A **34**
School La. LS17: Wike 1D **14**
School La. LS6: Leeds 5C **20**
School La. LS7: Leeds 4G **21**
School M. LS12: Leeds 6A **30**
School St. LS27: Chur 1A **50**
School St. LS27: Morl 5H **49**
School St. LS28: Fars 2F **27**
School St. LS28: Pud 1F **37**
School St. WF3: W Ard 6B **56**
School Vw. LS6: Leeds 2C **30**
Scotch Pk. Trad. Est.
LS12: Leeds 5B **30**
SCOTLAND 4B **10**
Scotland Cl. LS18: Hors 6B **10**
Scotland La. LS18: Hors 1A **10**
Scotland Mill La. LS17: Leeds 1D **20**
Scotland Mill La. LS6: Leeds 1D **20**
Scotland Way LS18: Hors 5A **10**
Scotland Wood Rd.
LS17: Leeds 1D **20**
Scott Cl. LS26: Swil 6G **45**
SCOTT GREEN 2B **48**
Scott Grn. LS27: Gil 1B **48**
Scott Grn. Cres. LS27: Gil 1B **48**
Scott Grn. Dr. LS27: Gil 1B **48**
Scott Grn. Gro. LS27: Gil 1C **48**
Scott Grn. Mt. LS27: Gil 1B **48**
Scott Grn. Vw. LS27: Gil 1C **48**
SCOTT HALL 6G **21**
Scott Hall Av. LS7: Leeds 6G **21**
Scott Hall Cres. LS7: Leeds 5F **21**
Scott Hall Dr. LS7: Leeds 1G **31**

A-Z Leeds 99

Sledmere La. – Springs Rd.

Sledmere La. LS14: Leeds 5C **24**
.... (not continuous)
Sledmere Pl. LS14: Leeds 5C **24**
Sledmere Sq. LS14: Leeds 5C **24**
.... *(off Sledmere Pl.)*
Slingsby Cl. BD10: B'ford 3A **16**
Smalewell Cl. LS28: Pud 1F **37**
Smalewell Dr. LS28: Pud 1E **37**
Smalewell Gdns. LS28: Pud 1E **37**
Smalewell Grn. LS28: Pud 1F **37**
Smalewell Rd.
LS28: Pud Smalewell Dr. 1E **37**
Smalewell Rd.
LS28: Pud Tyersal La. 1D **36**
Smeaton App. LS15: Leeds 2E **35**
Smeaton Ct. LS18: Hors 3E **19**
Smeaton Gro. LS26: Swil 5G **45**
Smiths Cotts. LS6: Leeds 5B **20**
.... *(off Weetwood La.)*
Smithson St. LS26: Rothw 5H **53**
Smithy La. LS16: Leeds 3E **11**
Smithy La. WF3: Ting 3D **56**
Smithy Mills La. LS16: Leeds 1B **20**
Smools La. LS27: Chur 2H **49**
Smools La. LS27: Morl 2H **49**
Snaith Wood Dr. LS19: Raw 2E **17**
Snaith Wood M. LS19: Raw 2E **17**
Snake La. LS9: Leeds 1C **42**
Snowden App. LS13: Leeds 2E **29**
Snowden Cl. LS13: Leeds 3D **28**
Snowden Cres. LS13: Leeds 3D **28**
Snowden Fold LS13: Leeds 3D **28**
Snowden Gdns. LS13: Leeds 3E **29**
Snowden Grn. LS13: Leeds 3D **28**
.... *(off Snowden Cl.)*
Snowden Gro. LS13: Leeds 3D **28**
Snowden Lawn LS13: Leeds 3D **28**
Snowden Royd LS13: Leeds 2D **28**
Snowden Va. LS13: Leeds 3D **28**
Snowden Wlk. LS13: Leeds 3D **28**
Snowden Way LS13: Leeds 2D **28**
Sofia Cl. LS9: Leeds 3D **32**
Sofia Ct. LS13: Leeds 1D **28**
.... *(off Wellington Gth.)*
Solar Av. LS9: Leeds 1A **42**
Somerdale Cl. LS13: Leeds 4D **28**
Somerdale Gdns. LS13: Leeds 4D **28**
Somerdale Gro. LS13: Leeds 4D **28**
Somerdale M. LS13: Leeds 4D **28**
Somerdale Wlk. LS13: Leeds 4D **28**
Somerset Rd. LS28: Pud 5G **27**
Somers Pl. LS1: Leeds 4C **4** (5F **31**)
.... *(off Somers St.)*
Somers St. LS1: Leeds 4B **4** (5F **31**)
Somerton Dr. BD4: B'ford 5A **36**
Somerville Av. LS14: Leeds 3H **33**
Somerville Dr. LS14: Leeds 3H **33**
Somerville Grn. LS14: Leeds 3H **33**
Somerville Gro. LS14: Leeds 2H **33**
Somerville Mt. LS14: Leeds 3H **33**
Somerville Vw. LS14: Leeds 3H **33**
Sommerville M. LS28: Stan 4E **27**
Soureby Cross Way BD4: E Bier ...2B **46**
Sth. Accommodation Rd.
LS10: Leeds 2H **41**
Sth. Accommodation Rd.
LS9: Leeds 2A **42**
South Cl. LS20: Guis 5D **6**
Southcote St. LS28: Fars 3F **27**
.... *(off Northcote St.)*
South Cft. Av. BD11: B'haw 3C **46**
Southcroft Dr. BD11: B'haw 2C **46**
Southcroft Ga. BD11: B'haw 3C **46**
South Dr. LS20: Guis 5D **6**
South Dr. LS28: Fars 2F **27**
Sth. End Av. LS13: Leeds 4E **29**
Sth. End Ct. LS13: Leeds 3E **29**
Sth. End Gro. LS13: Leeds 4E **29**
Sth. End Mt. LS13: Leeds 4E **29**
Sth. End Ter. LS13: Leeds 4E **29**
Sth. Farm Cres. LS9: Leeds 3E **33**
Sth. Farm Rd. LS9: Leeds 3E **33**
Southfield Av. LS17: Leeds 1A **22**
Southfield Dr. LS17: Leeds 1A **22**
Southfield Mt. LS10: Leeds 6A **42**
.... *(off Woodville Mt.)*
Southfield Mt. LS12: Leeds 6A **30**
Southfield St. LS12: Leeds 6A **30**
Southfield Ter. BD11: B'haw 3C **46**
Southfield Ter. LS12: Leeds 6A **30**
.... *(off Southfield Mt.)*
Southgate LS20: Guis 6D **6**
Southgate LS26: Oult 3C **54**
Sth. Hill Cl. LS10: Leeds 2B **52**
Sth. Hill Cft. LS10: Leeds 2B **52**
Sth. Hill Gdns. LS10: Leeds 2B **52**
Sth. Hill Gro. LS10: Leeds 2B **52**
Sth. Hill Ri. LS10: Leeds 2B **52**
Sth. Hill Way LS10: Leeds 2B **52**
Southlands LS18: Hors 2B **18**
Southlands Av. LS17: Leeds 3G **21**
Southlands Av. LS19: Raw 1F **17**
Southlands Cl. LS17: Leeds 2G **21**
Southlands Cres. LS17: Leeds 3G **21**
Southlands Dr. LS17: Leeds 3G **21**
Sth. Lea WF3: Ting 2D **56**
Sth. Lee LS18: Hors 2B **18**
Sth. Leeds Bus. Cen.
LS11: Leeds 2G **41**
South Leeds Family
Learning Cen. 5H **51**
South Leeds Golf Course 3E **51**
South Leeds Stadium 1G **51**
Southleigh Av. LS11: Leeds 1E **51**
Southleigh Cres. LS11: Leeds 1E **51**
Southleigh Cft. LS11: Leeds 1F **51**
Southleigh Dr. LS11: Leeds 1E **51**
Southleigh Gdns. LS11: Leeds 1E **51**
Southleigh Gth. LS11: Leeds 1F **51**
Southleigh Grange LS11: Leeds ...1F **51**
Southleigh Gro. LS11: Leeds 1E **51**
Southleigh Rd. LS11: Leeds 1E **51**
Southleigh Vw. LS11: Leeds 1E **51**
Sth. Nelson St. LS27: Morl 4G **49**
Southolme Cl. LS5: Leeds 5F **19**
South Pde. LS1: Leeds 4D **4** (5F **31**)
South Pde. LS27: Morl 5H **49**
South Pde. LS28: Pud 1F **37**
South Pde. LS6: Leeds 6B **20**
South Pde. Cl. LS28: Pud 1G **37**
South Pk. Ter. LS28: Pud 3H **37**
Sth. Parkway LS14: Leeds 2G **33**
.... (not continuous)
Sth. Parkway App. LS14: Leeds .. 2G **33**
South Pl. LS27: Morl 5H **49**
.... *(off South St.)*
Sth. Queen St. LS27: Morl 6H **49**
Sth. Row LS18: Hors 2C **18**
Southroyd Gdns. LS28: Pud 2H **37**
Southroyd Pde. LS28: Pud 2G **37**
.... *(off Fartown)*
Southroyd Pk. LS28: Pud 2G **37**
.... (not continuous)
Southroyd Ri. LS28: Pud 2G **37**
Southroyd Vs. LS28: Pud 2G **37**
Sth. Side Ridge LS28: Leeds 6B **28**
South St. LS19: Raw 5D **8**
South St. LS27: Morl 5H **49**
South Vw. BD10: B'ford 4A **16**
South Vw. LS15: Leeds 3C **34**
.... *(off Church La.)*
South Vw. LS18: Hors 4C **18**
South Vw. LS19: Yead 6H **7**
South Vw. LS20: Guis 4G **7**
South Vw. LS26: Rothw 3G **53**
South Vw. LS27: Chur 2H **49**
South Vw. LS28: Pud 6H **27**
South Vw. LS28: Stan 4E **27**
South Vw. LS29: Men 2C **6**
South Vw. WF3: W Ard 6B **56**
Southview Bus. Pk. LS20: Guis 6G **7**
South Vw. Cl. BD4: E Bier 2A **46**
South Vw. Cl. LS19: Yead 6H **7**
South Vw. Cotts. LS17: Shad 6H **15**
South Vw. Cres. LS19: Yead 6H **7**
South Vw. Dr. BD4: E Bier 2B **46**
South Vw. Rd. BD4: E Bier 2B **46**
South Vw. Rd. LS19: Yead 2D **8**
South Vw. Ter. LS19: Yead 3E **9**
Southwaite Cl. LS14: Leeds 1H **33**
Southwaite Gth. LS14: Leeds 1H **33**
Southwaite La. LS14: Leeds 1H **33**
Southwaite Lawn LS14: Leeds ... 1H **33**
Southwaite Pl. LS14: Leeds 1H **33**
Southway LS18: Hors 6A **10**
Southway LS20: Guis 5C **6**
Sth. Way BD4: E Bier 2A **46**
Southwood Cl. LS14: Leeds 1C **34**
Southwood Cres. LS14: Leeds 1C **34**
Southwood Ga. LS14: Leeds 1C **34**
Southwood Rd. LS14: Leeds 1C **34**
Sovereign Bus. Pk.
LS10: Leeds 1H **41**
Sovereign Ct. LS17: Leeds 3A **14**
Sovereign Mill LS27: Morl 6H **49**
.... *(off Sth. Queen St.)*
Sovereign Pl. LS1: Leeds .. 6D **4** (6F **31**)
Sovereign Quay
LS1: Leeds 6E **5** (6G **31**)
.... *(off Bridge End)*
Sovereign Sq.
LS1: Leeds 6E **5** (6G **31**)
Sovereign St.
LS1: Leeds 6D **4** (6F **31**)
Sowood St. LS4: Leeds 3A **30**
Spa Ind. Est. LS7: Leeds 1G **31**
Spalding Towers LS9: Leeds 4A **32**
.... *(off Lindsey Gdns.)*
Speedwell Mt. LS6: Leeds 2F **31**
Speedwell St. LS6: Leeds 2F **31**
Spen App. LS16: Leeds 4F **19**
Spen Bank LS16: Leeds 4F **19**
Spence La. LS12: Leeds 1D **40**
Spenceley St. LS2: Leeds 2E **31**
.... (not continuous)
Spencer Mt. LS8: Leeds 2A **32**
Spencer Pl. LS7: Leeds 2A **32**
Spen Cres. LS16: Leeds 4F **19**
Spen Dr. LS16: Leeds 3G **19**
Spenfield Ct. LS16: Leeds 3H **19**
Spen Gdns. LS16: Leeds 3H **19**
Spen Grn. LS16: Leeds 4F **19**
Spen La. LS16: Leeds 2G **19**
.... (not continuous)
Spen La. LS5: Leeds 6G **19**
Spen La. LS6: Leeds 5G **19**
Spen Lawn LS16: Leeds 4F **19**
Spen M. LS16: Leeds 4G **19**
Spennithorne Av. LS16: Leeds ... 1G **19**
Spennithorne Dr. LS16: Leeds 2G **19**
Spen Rd. LS16: Leeds 3G **19**
Spenser Ri. LS20: Guis 5H **7**
Spenser Rd. LS20: Guis 5H **7**
Spens Ho. LS2: Leeds 1D **4** (3G **31**)
.... *(off Carlton Hill)*
Spen Wlk. LS16: Leeds 4F **19**
Spen Way LS16: Leeds 5G **19**
Spibey Cres. LS26: Rothw 2F **53**
Spibey La. LS26: Rothw 2F **53**
Spindle Cl. BD4: B'ford 1A **36**
Spindle Ho. LS9: Leeds 6H **5** (6A **32**)
.... *(off East St.)*
Spindles, The LS10: Leeds 1H **51**
Spinks Gdns. LS14: Leeds 1B **34**
Spink Well La. WF3: Ting 2D **56**
Spinners Chase LS28: Pud 6G **27**
Spinners Fold LS18: Hors 3F **17**
Spinners Ga. BD4: B'ford 1A **36**
Spinney, The LS17: Leeds 1A **22**
Spinney, The LS19: Raw 1C **16**
Spinney, The LS9: Leeds 6A **32**
Spinneyfield Ct. LS9: Leeds 6A **32**
Spinney Ri. BD4: B'ford 6B **36**
Spinning Acres La. LS6: Leeds 5B **20**
Spring Av. LS27: Gil 2C **48**
Spring Bank LS5: Leeds 1G **29**
Springbank LS19: Raw 6C **8**
Springbank Av. LS27: Gil 2C **48**
Springbank Av. LS28: Fars 2G **27**
Springbank Cl. LS28: Fars 2F **27**
Spring Bank Cres. LS6: Leeds 1C **30**
Springbank Cres. LS27: Gil 1C **48**
Springbank Dr. LS28: Fars 2G **27**
Springbank Gro. LS28: Fars 2G **27**
Spring Bank Ho. LS6: Leeds 1C **30**
Springbank M. WF3: Loft 4B **58**
Springbank Ri. LS28: Fars 2G **27**
Springbank Rd. LS27: Gil 1C **48**
Springbank Rd. LS28: Fars 2F **27**
Spring Bank Ter. LS20: Guis 4G **7**
Spring Cl. Av. LS9: Leeds 1B **42**
Spring Cl. Gdns. LS9: Leeds 1A **42**
Spring Cl. St. LS9: Leeds 1A **42**
Spring Cl. Wlk. LS9: Leeds 1B **42**
Springfield Av. LS27: Morl 3F **49**
Springfield Av. WF3: Loft 4E **59**
Springfield Cl. LS18: Hors 2E **19**
Springfield Cl. WF3: Loft 4E **59**
Springfield Commercial Cen.
LS28: Fars 1G **27**
Springfield Ct. LS17: Leeds 5C **14**
Springfield Ct. LS19: Yead 1C **8**
Springfield Ct. LS20: Guis 4G **7**
.... *(off West St.)*
Springfield Ct. WF3: Loft 4E **59**
Springfield Cres. LS27: Morl 3G **49**
Springfield Cres. WF3: Loft 4F **59**
Springfield Dr. WF3: Loft 4F **59**
Springfield Gdns. LS18: Hors 2D **18**
Springfield Gdns. LS28: Pud 1H **37**
Springfield Grange LS28: Fars 1G **27**
Springfield Grn. LS10: Leeds 5A **42**
Springfield La. BD4: B'ford 5G **37**
Springfield La. LS27: Morl 3G **49**
Springfield M. LS27: Morl 3G **49**
Springfield M. WF3: Loft 4E **59**
.... *(off Park Dr.)*
Springfield Mt. LS12: Leeds 5G **29**
Springfield Mt. LS18: Hors 2D **18**
Springfield Mt.
LS2: Leeds 1A **4** (4E **31**)
Springfield Pl. LS10: Leeds
Leasowe Rd. 5A **42**
Springfield Pl. LS10: Leeds
Pontefract Rd. 5C **42**
Springfield Pl. LS20: Guis 4G **7**
Springfield Ri. LS18: Hors 2D **18**
Springfield Ri. LS26: Rothw 5H **53**
Springfield Ri. WF3: Loft 4E **59**
Springfield Rd. LS20: Guis 5G **7**
Springfield Rd. LS27: Morl 3F **49**
Springfield Rd. WF3: Loft 4E **59**
Springfield St. LS26: Rothw 5H **53**
Springfield Ter. LS17: Leeds 5C **14**
.... *(off Springfield Ct.)*
Springfield Ter. LS20: Guis 5G **7**
Springfield Ter. LS28: Stan 4F **27**
Springfield Vs. LS27: Gil 1B **48**
Springfield Wlk. LS18: Hors 2D **18**
Spring Gdns. BD11: Drig 3H **47**
Spring Gdns. LS27: Chur 2A **50**
Spring Gro. Av. LS6: Leeds 3C **30**
Spring Gro. Vw. LS6: Leeds 3C **30**
Spring Gro. Wlk. LS6: Leeds 3C **30**
Springhead Rd. LS26: Rothw 3A **54**
Spring Hill LS16: Leeds 5C **12**
Spring Hill LS7: Leeds 1G **31**
Springhill Cl. WF1: Outw 6C **58**
Spring Hill Cotts. LS6: Leeds 5C **20**
.... *(off Monk Bri. Rd.)*
Springhills WF1: Outw 6C **58**
Spring Hill Ter. LS6: Leeds 5C **20**
.... *(off Monk Bri. Rd.)*
Spring Ram Retail Pk. 5B **48**
Spring Rd. LS6: Leeds 1C **30**
Springrove Ter. LS6: Leeds 3C **30**
Springs, The 5F **35**
Springs Rd. LS19: Yead 3A **8**

A-Z Leeds 101

Stubley Farm M. – Temple Newsam Home Farm (Rare Breeds)

Stubley Farm M. LS27: Morl 4G **49**
Studfold Vw. LS14: Leeds 2A **34**
Studio Rd. LS3: Leeds 4C **30**
Studley Ter. LS28: Pud 5G **27**
Styebank La. LS26: Rothw 3H **53**
SUE RYDER WHEATFIELDS HOSPICE 6C **20**
Suffield Cl. LS27: Gil 1B **48**
Suffield Cres. LS27: Gil 1B **48**
Suffield Dr. LS27: Gil 1B **48**
Suffield Rd. LS27: Gil 1B **48**
Suffolk Ct. LS19: Yead 2D **8**
Sugar Hill Cl. LS26: Oult 6C **54**
Sugar Well App. LS7: Leeds 6E **21**
Sugar Well Ct. LS7: Leeds 1F **31**
Sugar Well Mt. LS7: Leeds 6E **21**
Sugar Well Rd. LS7: Leeds 6E **21**
Sulby Gro. BD10: B'ford 4A **16**
Summerbank Cl. BD11: Drig 2H **47**
Summerbridge Dr. BD10: B'ford 6A **16**
Summerfield Av. LS13: Leeds 2A **28**
Summerfield Dr. LS13: Leeds 2A **28**
Summerfield Gdns. LS13: Leeds 2A **28**
Summerfield Grn. LS13: Leeds 2A **28**
Summerfield Gro. LS13: Leeds 2A **28**
Summerfield Pl. LS13: Leeds 2A **28**
Summerfield Rd. LS13: Leeds 2A **28**
Summerfield Wlk. LS13: Leeds 2A **28**
Summerhill Gdns. LS8: Leeds 1D **22**
Summerhill Pl. LS8: Leeds 1D **22**
Summerseat LS19: Raw 6F **9**
Summersgill Sq. LS18: Hors 3B **18**
Summerville Rd. LS28: Stan 4E **27**
Sunbeam Av. LS11: Leeds 4F **41**
Sunbeam Gro. LS11: Leeds 4F **41**
Sunbeam Pl. LS11: Leeds 4F **41**
Sunbeam Ter. LS11: Leeds 4F **41**
Sunbeam Ter. WF3: Ting 2C **56**
Sun Fld. LS28: Stan 4F **27**
Sunfield Cl. LS28: Stan 3F **27**
Sunfield Dr. LS28: Stan 3F **27**
Sunfield Gdns. LS28: Stan 3F **27**
Sunfield M. LS28: Stan 4F **27**
Sunfield Pl. LS28: Stan 4F **27**
Sungleam Hill LS16: Leeds 1B **20**
Sunningdale Av. LS17: Leeds 5E **13**
Sunningdale Cl. LS17: Leeds 5E **13**
Sunningdale Dr. LS17: Leeds 5E **13**
Sunningdale Grn. LS17: Leeds 5E **13**
Sunningdale Pl. LS26: Rothw 5A **54**
Sunningdale Wlk. LS17: Leeds 5E **13**
Sunningdale Way LS17: Leeds 5E **13**
Sunny Bank LS27: Chur 1A **50**
(off Sunny Gro.)
Sunny Bank LS8: Leeds 6B **22**
Sunnybank Av. BD3: B'ford 4B **26**
Sunnybank Av. LS18: Hors 4B **18**
Sunnybank Ct. LS19: Yead 2F **9**
Sunnybank Cres. LS19: Yead 2F **9**
Sunny Bank Gro. LS8: Leeds 6B **22**
Sunnybank Gro. BD3: B'ford 4B **26**
Sunny Bank Ho. LS28: Fars 2F **27**
Sunnybank La. BD3: B'ford 4B **26**
Sunny Bank Mills LS28: Fars 2F **27**
Sunnybank Rd. LS18: Hors 4B **18**
Sunnybank St. LS18: Hors 4B **18**
Sunnybank Ter. LS18: Hors 4B **18**
Sunny Bank Vw. LS8: Leeds 6B **22**
Sunnydene LS14: Leeds 4H **33**
Sunnyfield WF3: E Ard 4G **57**
Sunny Gro. LS27: Chur 1A **50**
Sunnyridge Av. LS28: Pud 5D **26**
Sunnyside WF3: Ting 3B **56**
(off Dewsbury Rd.)
Sunnyside Av. WF3: Ting 3B **56**
Sunnyside Rd. LS13: Leeds 4B **28**
Sunnyview WF3: E Ard 4G **57**
Sunnyview Av. LS11: Leeds 4D **40**
Sunnyview Gdns. LS11: Leeds 4D **40**
Sunnyview Ho. LS11: Leeds 4D **40**
(off Manorfield)
Sunnyview Ter. LS11: Leeds 4D **40**
Sunrise Ct. LS27: Gil 2C **48**
Sunset Av. LS6: Leeds 3C **20**
Sunset Dr. LS6: Leeds 4C **20**
Sunset Hill Top LS6: Leeds 3C **20**
Sunset Mt. LS6: Leeds 4C **20**
Sunset Ri. LS6: Leeds 3C **20**
Sunset Rd. LS6: Leeds 3C **20**
Sunset Vw. LS6: Leeds 3C **20**
Sunshine Mills LS12: Leeds 6G **29**
Sun St. LS19: Yead 2E **9**
Sun St. LS28: Stan 4G **27**
Surrey Gro. LS28: Pud 5G **27**
Surrey Rd. LS28: Pud 5G **27**
Sussex App. LS10: Leeds 4B **42**
Sussex Av. LS10: Leeds 4B **42**
Sussex Av. LS18: Hors 6C **10**
Sussex Gdns. LS10: Leeds 4B **42**
Sussex Grn. LS10: Leeds 4B **42**
Sussex Pl. LS10: Leeds 4B **42**
Sussex St. LS9: Leeds 6A **32**
(not continuous)
Sutherland Av. LS8: Leeds 2C **22**
Sutherland Cres. LS8: Leeds 1C **22**
Sutherland Mt. LS9: Leeds 3C **32**
Sutherland Rd. LS9: Leeds 3C **32**
Sutherland St. LS12: Leeds 1C **40**
Sutherland Ter. LS9: Leeds 3C **32**
Sutton App. LS14: Leeds 4G **33**
Sutton Cres. BD4: B'ford 3A **36**
Sutton Cres. LS14: Leeds 4G **33**
Sutton Gro. BD4: B'ford 2A **36**
Sutton Gro. LS27: Morl 6G **49**
Sutton Ho. BD4: B'ford 1A **36**
Sutton Rd. BD4: B'ford 2A **36**
Sutton Row LS14: Leeds 4H **33**
Sutton St. LS12: Leeds 1D **40**
Swaine Hill Cres. LS19: Yead 2C **8**
Swaine Hill St. LS19: Yead 2C **8**
Swaine Hill Ter. LS19: Yead 2C **8**
Swallow Av. LS12: Leeds 1G **39**
Swallow Cl. LS12: Leeds 5F **29**
Swallow Cl. LS17: Leeds 5B **14**
Swallow Cres. LS12: Leeds 1F **39**
Swallow Dr. LS17: Leeds 5B **14**
SWALLOW HILL 6F **29**
Swallow Mt. LS12: Leeds 1G **39**
Swallow Va. LS27: Morl 5B **50**
Swallow Vw. LS12: Leeds 5F **29**
Swan Apts. LS1: Leeds 4E **5** (5G **31**)
(off Swan St.)
Swan Ct. LS20: Guis 3F **7**
Swan St. LS1: Leeds 4E **5** (5G **31**)
(off Thornton's Arc.)
SWARCLIFFE 1C **34**
Swarcliffe App. LS14: Leeds 1C **34**
Swarcliffe Av. LS14: Leeds 1C **34**
Swarcliffe Bank LS14: Leeds 6C **24**
Swarcliffe Dr. LS14: Leeds 6C **24**
Swarcliffe Dr. E. LS14: Leeds 1D **34**
Swarcliffe Grn. LS14: Leeds 1D **34**
Swarcliffe Pde. LS14: Leeds 1C **34**
Swarcliffe Rd. LS14: Leeds 6C **24**
Swardale Grn. LS14: Leeds 1C **34**
Swardale Rd. LS14: Leeds 1C **34**
Sweet St. LS11: Leeds 1F **41**
Sweet St. W. LS11: Leeds 1E **41**
(not continuous)
SWILLINGTON 6G **45**
SWILLINGTON COMMON 1G **45**
Swillington La. LS15: Swil C 2G **45**
Swillington La. LS26: Swil 6F **45**
Swincar Av. LS19: Yead 2C **8**
SWINCLIFFE 5C **46**
Swincliffe Cl. BD19: Gom 5C **46**
Swincliffe Cres. BD19: Gom 6C **46**
Swincliffe Gdns. BD19: Gom 6C **46**
Swinegate LS1: Leeds 6E **5** (6G **31**)
SWINNOW 3A **28**
Swinnow Av. LS13: Leeds 4A **28**
Swinnow Cl. LS13: Leeds 4A **28**
Swinnow Cres. LS28: Stan 3A **28**
Swinnow Dr. LS13: Leeds 4A **28**
Swinnow Gdns. LS13: Leeds 4A **28**
Swinnow Gth. LS13: Leeds 4A **28**
Swinnow Grn. LS28: Pud 4H **27**
Swinnow Gro. LS13: Leeds 4A **28**
Swinnow La. LS13: Leeds 3A **28**
Swinnow La. LS28: Stan 3A **28**
SWINNOW MOOR 5B **28**
Swinnow Rd. LS13: Leeds 5A **28**
Swinnow Rd. LS28: Leeds 5H **27**
Swinnow Rd. LS28: Pud 5H **27**
Swinnow Shop. Cen. 5A **28**
Swinnow Vw. LS13: Leeds 4A **28**
Swinnow Wlk. LS13: Leeds 4A **28**
Swinroyd Cl. BD11: B'haw 4D **46**
Swithen's Ct. LS26: Rothw 5H **53**
Swithen's Dr. LS26: Rothw 5G **53**
Swithen's Farm 6H **53**
Swithen's Gro. LS26: Rothw 5G **53**
Swithen's La. LS26: Rothw 5H **53**
Swithen's St. LS26: Rothw 5H **53**
Sycamore Av. LS14: Leeds 4C **24**
Sycamore Av. LS15: Leeds 5A **34**
Sycamore Av. LS8: Leeds 6B **22**
Sycamore Chase LS28: Pud 6H **27**
Sycamore Cl. LS15: Leeds 5G **33**
Sycamore Cl. LS6: Leeds 1E **31**
Sycamore Cl. LS7: Leeds 4D **20**
Sycamore Ct. LS8: Leeds 5E **23**
Sycamore Cft. LS11: Leeds 4F **41**
Sycamore Fold LS11: Leeds 4F **41**
Sycamore Gdns. LS14: Leeds 1C **34**
Sycamore Row LS13: Leeds 1A **28**
Sycamores, The LS20: Guis 3G **7**
Sycamore Wlk. LS28: Fars 3F **27**
Sydenham Rd. LS11: Leeds 1D **40**
Sydenham St. LS11: Leeds 1D **40**
Sydney St. LS26: W'frd 3D **54**
Sydney St. LS28: Fars 3F **27**
Syke Av. WF3: W Ard 4B **56**
Syke Cl. WF3: W Ard 4A **56**
Syke Gdns. WF3: W Ard 4B **56**
Syke La. LS14: S'cft 1H **15**
Syke Pde. WF3: W Ard 3A **56**
Syke Rd. WF3: W Ard 4B **56**
Syke Ter. WF3: W Ard 4A **56**
Sylvan Vw. LS18: Hors 2C **18**

T

Tagore Ct. BD3: B'ford 1A **36**
Tagore Ho. LS6: Leeds 2C **30**
(off Brudenell Rd.)
Talbot Av. LS17: Leeds 1A **22**
Talbot Av. LS4: Leeds 2A **30**
Talbot Av. LS8: Leeds 1B **22**
Talbot Ct. LS8: Leeds 2B **22**
Talbot Cres. LS8: Leeds 1B **22**
Talbot Fold LS8: Leeds 2B **22**
Talbot Gdns. LS8: Leeds 1B **22**
Talbot Gro. LS8: Leeds 1B **22**
Talbot Mt. LS4: Leeds 2A **30**
Talbot Ri. LS17: Leeds 1B **22**
Talbot Rd. LS8: Leeds 1B **22**
Talbot Ter. LS26: Rothw 5G **53**
Talbot Ter. LS4: Leeds 2A **30**
Talbot Vw. LS4: Leeds 2A **30**
Tall Trees LS17: Leeds 6G **13**
TallL Trees Cl. LS16: Leeds 4E **11**
Tamworth St. BD4: B'ford 1A **36**
Tandy Trad. Est., The LS12: Leeds 4B **30**
Tanglewood LS11: Leeds 2E **51**
Tanhouse Hill LS18: Hors 3E **19**
Tan Ho. Yd. LS27: Chur 6A **40**
Tannery, The LS3: Leeds 5D **30**
(off Cavendish St.)
Tannery Ct. BD10: B'ford 3A **16**
Tannery Ct. LS28: Pud 5G **27**
Tannery Sq. LS6: Leeds 4C **20**
Tannery Yd. LS28: Pud 6H **27**
Tarn La. LS17: Leeds 3E **15**
Tarn La. LS17: S'cft 3E **15**
Tarnside Dr. LS14: Leeds 2H **33**
Tarn Vw. Rd. LS19: Yead 2F **9**
Tarran Way WF3: Rob H 5C **52**
Tate Ho. LS2: Leeds 3G **5** (5H **31**)
(off New York Rd.)
Tatham Way LS8: Leeds 5E **23**
Tatton La. WF3: Thpe H 1B **58**
Taverngate LS20: Hawk 5A **6**
Tavistock Cl. LS12: Leeds 1B **40**
Tavistock M. LS12: Leeds 1B **40**
Tavistock Pk. LS12: Leeds 1B **40**
Tavistock Way LS12: Leeds 1B **40**
Tawny Beck LS13: Leeds 5C **28**
Tawny Cl. BD4: B'ford 6A **36**
Tawny Cl. LS27: Morl 5B **50**
Taylor La. LS15: B Elm 5H **25**
Taylors Cl. LS14: Leeds 1B **34**
Tealby Cl. LS16: Leeds 1E **19**
Teal Dr. LS27: Morl 5B **50**
Teale Ct. LS7: Leeds 6A **22**
Teale Dr. LS7: Leeds 6A **22**
Teal M. LS10: Leeds 4H **51**
Team Sport Indoor Karting Leeds 2H **41**
Teasel Bank LS28: Pud 6D **26**
Teasel Row LS12: Leeds 5A **30**
(off Eyres Mill Side)
Teasel Vw. LS28: Pud 6D **26**
(off Bradley La.)
Techno Cen. LS18: Hors 1C **18**
Telephone Pl. LS7: Leeds 1H **5** (4H **31**)
Telford Cl. LS10: Leeds 5A **42**
Telford Gdns. LS10: Leeds 5A **42**
Telford Pl. LS10: Leeds 5A **42**
Telford St. LS10: Leeds 5A **42**
Telford Ter. LS10: Leeds 5A **42**
Telford Wlk. LS10: Leeds 5A **42**
Telford Way WF2: Carr G 6A **58**
Telscombe Dr. BD4: B'ford 5A **36**
Temperance Ct. LS18: Hors 3B **18**
Temperance Ho. LS12: Leeds 6A **30**
(off Wesley Rd.)
Temperance St. LS28: Stan 4G **27**
Tempest Pl. LS11: Leeds 4E **41**
Tempest Rd. LS11: Leeds 4E **41**
Tempest Sq. BD4: B'ford 2A **36**
Templar La. LS15: Leeds 1D **34**
Templar La. LS2: Leeds 3G **5** (5H **31**)
Templar Pl. LS2: Leeds 3G **5** (5H **31**)
Templar St. LS2: Leeds 3F **5** (5G **31**)
Templar Ter. LS27: Morl 6H **49**
Temple Av. LS15: Leeds 1A **44**
Temple Av. LS26: Rothw 2H **53**
Temple Cl. LS15: Leeds 1A **44**
Temple Ct. LS15: Leeds 6H **33**
Temple Ct. LS26: Rothw 2H **53**
Temple Cres. LS11: Leeds 4E **41**
Temple Gth. LS11: Leeds 2E **41**
Temple Ga. LS15: Leeds 6B **34**
Templegate Av. LS15: Leeds 1A **44**
Templegate Cl. LS15: Leeds 6B **34**
Templegate Cres. LS15: Leeds 1B **44**
Templegate Dr. LS15: Leeds 6A **34**
Templegate Grn. LS15: Leeds 6B **34**
Templegate Ri. LS15: Leeds 1A **44**
Templegate Rd. LS15: Leeds 1A **44**
Templegate Vw. LS15: Leeds 1A **44**
Templegate Wlk. LS15: Leeds 6B **34**
Templegate Way LS15: Leeds 1B **44**
Temple Grn. LS26: Rothw 2A **54**
Temple Green Park & Ride 4G **43**
Temple Gro. LS15: Leeds 6A **34**
Temple La. LS15: Leeds 6B **34**
Temple Lawn LS26: Rothw 2A **54**
Temple Lea LS15: Leeds 6A **34**
Temple M. LS15: Leeds 6A **34**
(off Selby Rd.)
Temple Newsam Golf Course 1H **43**
Temple Newsam Home Farm (Rare Breeds) 2B **44**

A-Z Leeds 103

W

Winthorpe Cres. – Wormald Lea

Winthorpe Cres. WF3: Thpe H 1H 57
Winthorpe St. LS6: Leeds 5D 20
Winthorpe Vw. WF3: Thpe H 1A 58
Wintoun St. LS7: Leeds 1G 5 (4H 31)
Wira Ho. LS16: Leeds 2F 19
WIRING FIELD 6A 30
Withens Rd. WF17: Birs 6G 47
Wolley Av. LS12: N Far 4D 38
Wolley Ct. LS12: N Far 4D 38
Wolley Dr. LS12: N Far 4D 38
Wolley Gdns. LS12: N Far 4D 38
Wolseley Rd. LS4: Leeds 4B 30
(not continuous)
Wolston Cl. BD4: B'ford 5A 36
Womersley Ct. LS28: Pud 1F 37
(off Womersley Pl.)
Womersley Pl. LS28: Pud 1F 37
Womersley Pl. LS28: Stan 4D 26
Woodbine Ter. LS13: Leeds 2C 28
Woodbine Ter. LS18: Hors 4C 18
(off Wood La.)
Woodbine Ter. LS6: Leeds 5C 20
Wood Bottom LS19: Raw 3F 17
WOODBOTTOM 3F 17
Wood Bottom Gdns. LS18: Hors 3G 17
Wood Bottom La. LS18: Hors 3G 17
Wood Bottom Vw. LS18: Hors 3G 17
Wood Bottom Wlk. LS18: Hors 3G 17
Woodbourne LS8: Leeds 4E 23
Woodbourne Av. LS17: Leeds 2G 21
Woodbridge Cl. LS6: Leeds 6G 19
Woodbridge Cres. LS6: Leeds 5G 19
Woodbridge Fold LS6: Leeds 6G 19
Woodbridge Gdns. LS6: Leeds 6G 19
Woodbridge Gth. LS6: Leeds 6H 19
Woodbridge Grn. LS6: Leeds 6H 19
Woodbridge Lawn LS6: Leeds 6G 19
Woodbridge Pl. LS6: Leeds 6G 19
Woodbridge Rd. LS6: Leeds 6G 19
Woodbridge Va. LS6: Leeds 6G 19
Wood Cl. LS26: Rothw 3F 53
Wood Cl. LS7: Leeds 4G 21
Wood Cres. LS26: Rothw 3F 53
Woodcross LS27: Morl 3G 49
Woodcross End LS27: Morl 2G 49
Woodcross Fold LS27: Morl 3G 49
Woodcross Gdns. LS27: Morl 3G 49
Woodcross Gth. LS27: Morl 2G 49
Wood Dr. LS26: Rothw 3E 53
Woodeson Ct. LS13: Leeds 6H 17
Woodeson Lea LS13: Leeds 6H 17
Woodfield Ct. LS8: Leeds 1F 33
Woodfield Ter. LS28: Pud 1H 37
Woodgarth Gdns. BD4: B'ford 4B 36
Wood Gro. LS12: Leeds 6D 28
WOODHALL 3C 26
Woodhall Av. BD3: B'ford 4A 26
Woodhall Av. LS5: Leeds 5E 19
Woodhall Cl. LS28: Stan 3C 26
Woodhall Ct. LS15: Leeds 1D 44
Woodhall Ct. LS28: Cal 6C 16
Woodhall Cft. LS28: Stan 3C 26
Woodhall Dr. LS5: Leeds 5E 19
Woodhall Hills LS28: Cal 2B 26
WOODHALL HILLS 2C 26
Woodhall Hills Golf Course 1B 26
Woodhall La. LS28: Cal 2C 26
Woodhall La. LS28: Stan 2C 26
WOODHALL PK. 3D 26
Woodhall Pk. Av. LS28: Stan 3C 26
Woodhall Pk. Cres. E. LS28: Stan 4D 26
Woodhall Pk. Cres. W. LS28: Stan 4C 26
Woodhall Pk. Dr. LS28: Stan 4C 26
Woodhall Pk. Gdns. LS28: Stan 4D 26
Woodhall Pk. Gro. LS28: Stan 4C 26
Woodhall Pk. Mt. LS28: Stan 3C 26
Woodhall Pl. BD3: B'ford 4A 26
Woodhall Retail Pk. 4A 26
Woodhall Rd. BD3: B'ford 5A 26
Woodhall Rd. LS28: Cal 2A 26
Woodhall Ter. BD3: B'ford 4A 26
Woodhall Vw. BD3: B'ford 4B 26
Woodhead La. LS27: Gil 2C 48
Woodhead Rd. WF17: Birs 6B 48
Wood Hill LS26: Rothw 3F 53
Wood Hill Ct. LS16: Leeds 5D 10
Wood Hill Cres. LS16: Leeds 6C 10
Wood Hill Gdns. LS16: Leeds 5D 10
Wood Hill Gth. LS16: Leeds 5D 10
Wood Hill Gro. LS16: Leeds 6C 10
Wood Hill Ri. LS16: Leeds 5D 10
Woodhill Ri. BD10: B'ford 3A 16
Wood Hill Rd. LS16: Leeds 6D 10
WOODHOUSE 3F 31
WOODHOUSE CARR 2F 31
Woodhouse Cliff LS6: Leeds 1E 31
WOODHOUSE CLIFF 1E 31
Woodhouse Cl. WF3: E Ard 5F 57
Woodhouse Flats LS2: Leeds 2E 31
(off St Mark's St.)
WOODHOUSE HILL 5A 42
Woodhouse Hill Av. LS10: Leeds 5A 42
Woodhouse Hill Dr. LS10: Leeds 5B 42
Woodhouse Hill Gro. LS10: Leeds 5A 42
Woodhouse Hill Pl. LS10: Leeds 5A 42
Woodhouse Hill Rd. LS10: Leeds 5A 42
Woodhouse La. LS1: Leeds 1D 4 (4F 31)
Woodhouse La. LS2: Leeds 2E 31
Woodhouse Sq. LS3: Leeds 2B 4 (5E 31)
Woodhouse St. LS6: Leeds 2E 31
WOODKIRK 4B 56
Woodkirk Av. WF3: Ting 3A 56
Woodkirk Gdns. WF12: Dew 5A 56
Woodkirk Gro. WF3: Ting 3B 56
Woodland Av. LS26: Swil 6F 45
Woodland Chase LS14: Leeds 3A 24
Woodland Cl. LS15: Leeds 5C 34
Woodland Ct. LS8: Leeds 6B 22
Woodland Cres. LS26: Rothw 3F 53
Woodland Cres. LS26: Swil 6G 45
Woodland Cft. LS18: Hors 1C 18
Woodland Dr. LS10: Leeds 5B 52
Woodland Dr. LS26: Swil 6F 45
Woodland Dr. LS7: Leeds 4H 21
Woodland Gth. LS26: Rothw 3F 53
Woodland Gro. LS26: Swil 6G 45
Woodland Gro. LS7: Leeds 1A 32
Woodland Hill LS15: Leeds 5B 34
Woodland La. LS7: Leeds 4G 21
Woodland Mt. LS7: Leeds 1A 32
Woodland Pk. LS26: Oult 4C 54
Woodland Pk. Rd. LS6: Leeds 6C 20
Woodland Ri. LS15: Leeds 5C 34
Woodland Rd. LS15: Leeds 5B 34
Woodlands, The LS26: Oult 4C 54
(off Farrer La.)
Woodlands LS17: Leeds 1A 22
Woodlands WF3: E Ard 4G 57
Woodlands Av. LS28: Stan 4E 27
Woodlands Cl. BD10: B'ford 2B 16
Woodlands Cl. WF3: E Ard 4G 57
Woodlands Ct. LS16: Leeds 2H 19
Woodlands Ct. LS28: Pud 2F 37
Woodlands Dr. BD10: B'ford 2B 16
Woodlands Dr. LS16: Leeds 6H 11
Woodlands Dr. LS19: Raw 1C 16
Woodlands Dr. LS27: Morl 3F 49
Woodlands Dr. WF3: E Ard 4F 57
Woodlands Fold BD11: B'haw 4D 46
Woodlands Gro. LS16: Leeds 6H 11
Woodlands Gro. LS28: Stan 4E 27
Woodlands La. LS16: Leeds 6A 12
Woodlands Pk. Gro. LS28: Pud 2F 37
Woodlands Pk. Rd. LS28: Pud 2F 37
Woodland Sq. LS12: Leeds 5F 29
Woodlands Ter. LS28: Stan 4E 27
Woodlands Way LS14: Leeds 4C 24
Woodland Ter. LS7: Leeds 4E 21
Woodland Vw. LS28: Cal 4C 16
Woodland Vw. LS7: Leeds 4H 21
Woodland Vw. WF3: W Ard 6B 56
Woodland Vs. LS14: Leeds 1D 34
Wood La. LS13: Leeds Bellmount Pl. 1C 28
Wood La. LS13: Leeds Ring Rd. Farnley 5D 28
Wood La. LS12: Leeds 5D 28
Wood La. LS12: N Far 5D 38
Wood La. LS15: Leeds 6E 25
Wood La. LS15: Scho 6E 25
Wood La. LS18: Hors 4C 18
Wood La. LS26: Rothw 2D 52
Wood La. LS28: Cal 4D 16
Wood La. LS6: Leeds 6B 20
Wood La. LS7: Leeds 4G 21
(not continuous)
Wood La. Ct. LS12: N Far 3G 39
Wood La. Ct. LS6: Leeds 6C 20
Wood La. M. LS12: N Far 3G 39
Woodlea App. LS19: Yead 3B 8
Woodlea App. LS6: Leeds 2D 20
Woodlea Av. LS6: Leeds 2D 20
Woodlea Chase LS6: Leeds 3D 20
Woodlea Cl. LS19: Yead 4B 8
Woodlea Ct. LS17: Leeds 5D 14
Woodlea Ct. LS6: Leeds 3D 20
Woodlea Cft. LS6: Leeds 2D 20
Woodlea Dr. LS19: Yead 4B 8
Woodlea Dr. LS6: Leeds 2D 20
Woodlea Fold LS6: Leeds 2D 20
Woodlea Gdns. LS6: Leeds 2D 20
Woodlea Gth. LS6: Leeds 2D 20
Woodlea Ga. LS6: Leeds 3D 20
Woodlea Grn. LS6: Leeds 2D 20
Woodlea Gro. LS11: Leeds 4D 40
(off Woodlea Mt.)
Woodlea Gro. LS19: Yead 3B 8
Woodlea Gro. LS6: Leeds 3D 20
Woodlea Hall LS6: Leeds 2D 20
Woodlea Holt LS6: Leeds 2D 20
Woodlea La. LS6: Leeds 2D 20
Woodlea Lawn LS6: Leeds 2D 20
Woodlea Mt. LS11: Leeds 4D 40
Woodlea Mt. LS19: Yead 3B 8
Woodlea Pk. LS6: Leeds 3D 20
Woodlea Pl. LS11: Leeds 4D 40
Woodlea Pl. LS6: Leeds 2D 20
Woodlea Rd. LS19: Yead 3B 8
Woodlea Sq. LS6: Leeds 3D 20
Woodlea St. LS11: Leeds 4D 40
Woodlea Vw. LS19: Yead 4B 8
Woodlea Vw. LS6: Leeds 3D 20
Woodleigh Hall M. LS19: Raw 2F 17
Woodleigh Hall Vw. LS19: Raw 2G 17
WOODLESFORD 2C 54
Woodlesford Station (Rail) 2D 54
Woodliffe Ct. LS7: Leeds 4G 21
Woodliffe Cres. LS7: Leeds 4G 21
Woodliffe Dr. LS7: Leeds 4G 21
Woodman St. LS15: Leeds 5A 34
Woodman Yd. LS16: Leeds 5B 20
(off Otley Rd.)
Wood Moor Ct. LS17: Leeds 3A 14
Wood Mt. LS26: Rothw 3E 53
Woodnook Cl. LS16: Leeds 1D 18
Woodnook Dr. LS16: Leeds 1D 18
Woodnook Gth. LS16: Leeds 1D 18
Woodnook Rd. LS16: Leeds 6D 10
Wood Nook Ter. LS28: Stan 4E 27
Wood Row LS26: Meth 6H 55
WOOD ROW 6H 55
Woodrow Cres. LS26: Meth 6G 55
Woodside LS26: Meth 6G 55
Woodside Av. LS4: Leeds 3A 30
Woodside Av. LS7: Leeds 4D 20
Woodside Cl. LS27: Morl 3G 49
Woodside Ct. LS18: Hors Tanhouse Hill 3E 19
Woodside Ct. LS10: Leeds 5A 52
Woodside Ct. LS16: Leeds 2F 19
Woodside Ct. LS18: Hors 3E 19
(off Broadgate La.)
Woodside Dr. LS27: Morl 2G 49
Woodside Gdns. LS27: Morl 2G 49
Woodside Hill Cl. LS18: Hors 3D 18
Woodside La. LS27: Morl 2G 49
Woodside Lawn LS12: Leeds 6D 28
Woodside M. LS7: Leeds 4D 20
Woodside Pk. Av. LS18: Hors 3D 18
Woodside Pk. Dr. LS18: Hors 3D 18
Woodside Pl. LS4: Leeds 3A 30
Woodside Ter. LS4: Leeds 3A 30
Woodside Vw. LS10: Leeds 5A 52
Woodside Vw. LS4: Leeds 2A 30
Woodside Vw. WF3: Loft 3D 58
Woodsley Community Cen. 3D 30
Woodsley Dr. LS16: Leeds 1H 19
Woodsley Grn. LS6: Leeds 3D 30
Woodsley Rd. LS2: Leeds 3D 30
Woodsley Rd. LS3: Leeds 4C 30
Woodsley Rd. LS6: Leeds 3D 30
Woodsley Ter. LS2: Leeds 1A 4 (4E 31)
Woodsley Vw. LS16: Leeds 1A 20
Woods Row LS28: Stan 4G 27
Woodstock Cl. LS16: Leeds 6B 12
Wood St. LS18: Hors 1C 18
Wood St. LS27: Morl 4F 49
Wood St. WF3: E Ard 3H 57
Woodthorne Cft. LS17: Leeds 5C 14
Woodvale Cl. BD4: B'ford 2A 36
Woodvale Ter. LS18: Hors 4D 18
Wood Vw. LS27: Chur 1B 50
Woodview BD11: Drig 2F 47
Woodview Cl. LS18: Hors 1C 18
Woodview Ct. LS14: Leeds 1D 34
Woodview Gro. LS11: Leeds 5F 41
Woodview M. LS14: Leeds 6D 24
Woodview Mt. LS11: Leeds 5F 41
Woodview Pl. LS11: Leeds 5F 41
Woodview Rd. LS11: Leeds 5F 41
Woodview St. LS11: Leeds 5F 41
Wood Vw. Ter. LS27: Chur 1B 50
Woodview Ter. LS11: Leeds 5F 41
Woodville Av. LS18: Hors 3D 18
Woodville Cl. LS14: Leeds 5B 24
Woodville Ct. LS8: Leeds 2D 22
Woodville Cres. LS18: Hors 2E 19
Woodville Gro. LS10: Leeds 6A 42
Woodville Gro. LS18: Hors 3D 18
Woodville Mt. LS10: Leeds 6A 42
Woodville Pl. LS18: Hors 2E 19
Woodville Sq. LS10: Leeds 6A 42
Woodville St. LS18: Hors 3E 19
Woodville Ter. LS18: Hors 2D 18
Wood Vine St. LS28: Stan 4E 27
Woodway LS18: Hors 4C 18
Woodway Dr. LS18: Hors 4C 18
Woolcombers Way BD4: B'ford 2A 36
Wooler Av. LS11: Leeds 5E 41
Wooler Dr. LS11: Leeds 5E 41
Wooler Gro. LS11: Leeds 5E 41
Wooler Rd. LS11: Leeds 5D 40
Wooler St. LS11: Leeds 5D 40
Woolford Way WF3: Loft 5F 59
Woollin Av. WF3: W Ard 6C 56
Woollin Cres. WF3: W Ard 5C 56
Worcester Av. LS10: Leeds 5B 52
Worcester Cl. WF3: E Ard 2G 57
Worcester Dr. LS10: Leeds 5B 52
Wordsworth Ct. LS26: Oult 6C 54
Wordsworth Dr. LS26: Oult 6C 54
Wordsworth Gro. WF3: Stly 6G 59
Works Skatepark, The 2H 41
World's End LS19: Yead 2E 9
Wormald Lea BD4: B'ford 4A 36
(off Kirkwall Dr.)

A-Z Leeds 109

Published by Geographers' A-Z Map Company Limited
An imprint of HarperCollins Publishers
Westerhill Road
Bishopbriggs
Glasgow
G64 2QT

www.az.co.uk
a-z.maps@harpercollins.co.uk

6th edition 2020

© Collins Bartholomew Ltd 2020

This product uses map data licenced from Ordnance Survey
© Crown copyright and database rights 2020 OS 100018598

AZ, A-Z and AtoZ are registered trademarks of Geographers' A-Z Map Company Limited

Every care has been taken in the preparation of this atlas. However, the Publisher accepts no responsibility whatsover for any loss, damage, injury or inconvenience sustained or caused as a result of using this atlas. The representation of a road, track or footpath is no evidence of a right of way.

A catalogue record for this book is available from the British Library.

ISBN 978-0-00-843670-4

10 9 8 7 6 5 4 3 2 1

Printed and bound by CPI Group (UK) Ltd, Croydon, CR0 4YY